Hired Hands and Plowboys

Hired Hands
and Plowboys

FARM LABOR IN
THE MIDWEST, 1815-60

DAVID E. SCHOB

UNIVERSITY OF ILLINOIS PRESS
Urbana Chicago London

Publication of this work has been supported by a grant from
the Oliver M. Dickerson Fund. The Fund was established by
Mr. Dickerson (Ph.D., Illinois, 1906) to enable the University
of Illinois Press to publish selected works in American history,
designated by the executive committee of the Department of History.

LIBRARY OF CONGRESS CATALOGING IN PUBLICATION DATA

Schob, David E.   1941–
  Hired hands and plowboys.

  Bibliography: p.
  Includes index.
  1. Agricultural laborers—Middle west—History.
I. Title.
HD1527.A14S3   331.7′63′0977   75–12897
ISBN 0–252–00509–0

To my father and mother,

ALBERT W. AND MARTHA L. SCHOB

Acknowledgments

MY INTEREST in the topic of farm labor had its beginnings in Clark C. Spence's graduate course in American economic history at the University of Illinois. He encouraged me to probe deeply in pursuit of that elusive, obscure breed of individuals known simply as hired hands, and the results were expanded into a doctoral dissertation under his patient and skillful direction. The Kendric C. Babcock Fellowship, awarded by the department of history, permitted extensive research at archives and historical societies throughout the Midwest during 1968–69. I am also indebted to Robert M. Sutton, director of the Illinois Historical Survey, for placing its facilities at my disposal and acquiring materials pertinent to my research.

The primary sources, in the form of manuscript letters, diaries, farm ledgers, and accountbooks, were drawn from midwestern archives and historical repositories, and I am indebted to the staffs of the Minnesota Historical Society at St. Paul, the State Historical Society of Wisconsin at Madison, the Michigan Historical Collections and the William L. Clements Library at Ann Arbor, the Ohio Historical Society at Columbus, the Cincinnati Historical Society, the Indiana State Library and the Indiana State Historical Society at Indianapolis, the Chicago Historical Society, the Illinois State Historical Library at Springfield, the Illinois Historical Survey and the University of Illinois Archives at Urbana. Numerous books, pamphlets, and printed documents were obtained from diverse sources, and I am grateful to the interlibrary loan staffs at the University of Illinois and at Texas A & M University. The Center for Research Libraries at Chicago also rendered valuable assistance in obtaining newspapers and microfilms.

The manuscript benefited from critical advice and comments at various stages. One of my colleagues, Henry Dethloff, supplied helpful insight to the first four chapters. The entire manuscript was read by Paul Gates and Clark Spence, to whom I am especially grateful. I assume total responsibility for the final version and its contents. Portions of the chapter dealing with prairie breaking were published earlier in *Agricultural History*, XLVII (1973), and I thank its editor and the University of California Press for permission to use this material. The map of midwestern prairie grasslands was adapted from Edgar N. Transeau's map that appeared originally in *Ecology*, XVI (1935). I am grateful to the executive council of the department of history at the University of Illinois for providing financial support which facilitated publication through the Oliver M. Dickerson Fund. Texas A & M University also lent helpful support from its research fund to facilitate the final typing of the manuscript.

College Station, Texas
May, 1975

Contents

Introduction

Twas said that o'er the hills, and far away
Towards the setting sun, a land there lay,
Whose unexhausted energies of soil
Nobly repaid the hardy lab'rer's toil;
Where men were worth full twice their weight in gold,
And goodly farms were for almost nought sold;
Prairies of flowers, and grassy meads abound,
And rivers everywhere meander round.[1]

BEFORE the Civil War, the livelihood of most Americans was involved in one way or another with farming. The agricultural labor force in the Deep South consisted primarily of the Negro slave, whose servitude seemed reasonable from an economic viewpoint, given the warm climate, long growing season, and plantation type of production. In contrast, northern farmers relied on the seasonal laborer or hired hand whose employment lasted from spring to autumn. Once an integral though lowly member of rural society, the farm wage laborer gradually disappeared from sight yet retained a nostalgic place in tradition and American folklore. The years 1815–60 form an appropriate period for a study of farm labor, coinciding with western territorial expansion in the region north of the Ohio River and east of the Mississippi River—the old Northwest Territory.[2]

The growth of the Midwest, including the states of Ohio, Indiana, Illinois, Michigan, Wisconsin, and Minnesota, reflected the transition from a frontier subsistence economy in 1815 to more sophisticated, large-scale farming by 1860, a development accompanied by a general westward movement of population. In the beginning of the nineteenth century, a thin line of settlements had been established in the forested areas of eastern Ohio, extending from Lake Erie down to the

1. J[ames] K[irke] Paulding, *The Backwoodsman. A Poem* (Philadelphia, 1818), p. 19.
2. For examples which use 1815–60 as a framework, see Paul W. Gates, *Farmer's Age: Agriculture, 1815–1860* (New York, 1960); George Rogers Taylor, *The Transportation Revolution: Industry, 1815–1860* (New York, 1949).

Ohio River. Settlement moved westward along the Ohio River into neighboring Indiana and Illinois, simultaneously advancing northward along the river valleys into the central portions. Primarily of southern background, this first wave of settlers remained close to the timbered lands and rarely ventured on the open prairies until the mid-1820's. As late as 1830, the density of population extended from east to west in a crescent arch through the lower Midwest.

Occasional pockets of settlement developed at northern ports along the Great Lakes, such as Cleveland and Detroit. They became the points of departure for westward-bound settlers who took up timber and prairie land in lower Michigan; this early stream of pioneers turned into a flood of Easterners, occupying central Michigan and extending beyond to the prairies of Illinois and Wisconsin. The principal route of migration was the Erie Canal that connected with the port of Buffalo on Lake Erie, whence sailing vessels and lake steamers conveyed settlers to points westward. During the 1840's and 1850's, the upper Midwest absorbed additional waves of newcomers from the East, inhabitants from older parts of the lower Midwest, and thousands of emigrants from Europe in search of new homes in America. And in the decade just prior to the Civil War, this expansion spilled over into the prairie and timber tracts of southeastern Minnesota. Testimony of this swift growth is perceived in the population figures for the individual states.

TABLE 1. MIDWESTERN POPULATION, 1820–60

	1820	1830	1840	1850	1860
Ohio	581,434	937,903	1,519,467	1,980,329	2,339,511
Indiana	147,178	343,031	685,866	988,416	1,350,428
Illinois	55,211	157,445	476,183	851,470	1,711,951
Michigan	8,896	31,639	212,267	397,654	749,113
Wisconsin	—	—	30,945	305,391	775,881
Minnesota	—	—	—	6,077	172,123

Sources: *Statistical View of the United States* (Washington, 1854), p. 40; *Preliminary Report on the Eighth Census* (Washington, 1862), p. 131.

Because of its rapid growth, this region is an ideal geographical unit for a study of labor and its adaptation to various stages of agricultural development. Corn was the main crop for most farmers during the pioneer log cabin era, when farms were usually established in timbered areas. The tenacious corn thrived in most situations and required minimal attention. When ground into meal, it served as the dietary staple for the early pioneer family. As markets and new lines of transportation developed, farming became more diversified to the extent that small grains and hay were assuming importance, coinciding with the settlement of prairie lands. Ohio had been the leading wheat producer for some time, but the center of wheat production shifted steadily westward with the opening of new, rich prairie soil so conducive to large-scale farming operations. The prairie state of Illinois emerged by 1860 as the leading wheat producer, while Wisconsin and Indiana were in second and third places of importance respectively.[3] Unable to compete with Illinois and Wisconsin wheat, farmers in the older Midwest expanded along new lines, including cattle breeding, dairy farming, and cultivation of fruit-vegetable truck produce to meet increased urban food requirements.

Westward expansion, establishment of new farms, gradual diversification, and the emergence of large-scale farming explain why farm labor became a crucial aspect of the economy, especially in the decades before the Civil War. Since agricultural laborers were usually scarce and expensive even when available, and because of greater crop yields, a partial solution was greater use of labor-saving or mechanical devices. Indeed, the federal government concluded in 1860 that "the high price of labor has stimulated mechanical inventions."[4] The inefficient wrought-iron plow of colonial times was modified and improved during the first half of the nineteenth century, the most important innovation being the steel plowshare for cutting open tough prairie sod. The mechanical reaper replaced the sickle, scythe, and cradle in harvesting grains and hay; the mechanical thresher supplanted the manual flailing and winnowing of grain; and numerous patents were issued for improved designs of seed drills, mechanical sowers, harrows, cultivators, and rakes, to name only a few. Although statistical data are imperfect, the thrust of this mechanical and economic expansion in agriculture is apparent from the federal census reports in 1850 and 1860.

Farming was a seasonal occupation which provided employment primarily from spring to autumn. Hired hands earned good wages in season but invariably faced unemployment in the slack winter months. The off-seasonal employments included land clearing, cording fuel

3. *Statistical View of the United States,* p. 171. *Preliminary Report on the Eighth Census,* p. 200. For a general discussion of the shift in wheat production to the western states, see *Agriculture of the United States in 1860* (Washington, 1864), introduction, xxix–xxxi; Hugh Seymour Tremenheere, *Notes on Public Subjects, Made during a Tour in the United States and in Canada* (London, 1852), pp. 70–72.

4. *Agriculture of the United States in 1860,* introduction, xi–xii.

TABLE 2. LANDS IMPROVED (ACRES), VALUE OF FARMS, VALUE OF FARM-
ING IMPLEMENTS AND MACHINERY, 1850–60

	Lands Improved (Acres)		Value of Farms	
	1850	1860	1850	1860
Ohio	9,851,493	12,665,587	$358,758,603	$666,564,171
Indiana	5,046,543	8,161,717	136,385,173	344,902,776
Illinois	5,039,545	13,251,473	96,133,290	432,531,072
Michigan	1,929,110	3,419,861	51,872,446	163,279,087
Wisconsin	1,045,499	3,746,036	28,528,563	131,117,082
Minnesota	5,035	554,397	161,948	19,070,737

Value of Farming Implements and Machinery		
	1850	1860
Ohio	$12,750,585	$16,790,226
Indiana	6,704,444	10,420,826
Illinois	6,405,561	18,276,160
Michigan	2,891,371	5,855,642
Wisconsin	1,641,568	5,758,847
Minnesota	15,981	1,044,009

Source: *Preliminary Report on the Eighth Census*, pp. 196–97.

wood, and pork packing. Basically itinerants in a free labor market, farm hands were in many instances highly trained and versatile individuals whose skills were adaptable to such specialized work as prairie breaking, harvesting, horticulture, short-haul teamstering, drainage ditching, and well digging. These tasks clearly indicate that farming was not always a simple endeavor, but a complicated operation requiring specialized laborers. Furthermore, no discussion of farm labor is complete without mention of chore boys and hired girls, whose services were equally important to industrious farmers. And a previously ignored aspect is the role of free black farm hands, who augmented the white labor force in the harvest fields and the hazardous work of well digging. Farm labor in its diverse forms was a vital occupation for thousands of people, and essential to the economic development of the Midwest prior to the Civil War.

Set-up Labor

> They rightly belong to the first class of pioneers. These men
> chopped and hewed, grubbed and rolled, plowed and hoed, with
> their own hands. If a stranger had walked into a clearing or
> a corn field, in that day, he could not have told, from anything
> he saw, which was the employer and which was the employed.
> All were dressed alike in homespun clothes; all alike sweaty and
> sooty.[1]

PRELIMINARY STEPS for establishing a farm in forested areas included chopping timber, preparing the cleared land for the first crop, and constructing a temporary dwelling. When obtainable, hired help was employed to assist settlers with these backbreaking tasks. Some were regular hired hands working at the usual variety of farm chores, while others were hired specifically as choppers to clear and ready the land for its owner and his family. Common laborers and choppers who performed this essential task of carving farms out of the wilderness are referred to as set-up hands in this study.

Clearing work was an integral part of frontier settlement in the lower half of the Midwest, and also in the northern areas, where stands of timber interspersed the prairies. Ohio as well as the southern sections of Indiana and Illinois absorbed the initial waves of settlers, who tended to avoid the prairies and open spaces until the late 1820's.[2] During these early years, tracts of timber land acted as a magnet drawing both capital and labor away from towns—much to the fear of their early inhabitants. In 1815 Daniel Drake worried about the future of manufacturing at Cincinnati, where a labor shortage occurred because men chose rather to pursue employment in setting

1. Logan Esarey, "The Pioneers of Morgan County: Memoirs of Noah J. Major," *Indiana Historical Society Publications*, V (1915), 278–79.
2. Percy Bidwell and John I. Falconer, *History of Agriculture in the Northern United States, 1620–1860* (New York, 1941), pp. 149–51, esp. population density maps, figs. 6–8.

up farms: "As this town is older than the surrounding country, it has at no time had a surplus of laboring population or of capital. The former have been required to assist in clearing and improving the wilderness, the latter has been invested in lands, which from their low price and certain rise, have held out to capitalists a powerful inducement."[3]

Clearing work or set-up labor consisted of chopping, rolling of logs, grubbing, lopping off small trees, slashing, cutting out brush and weeds, and piling refuse material in heaps for burning. This process was nicknamed "smacking smooth" or "smacking clear" by the early settlers.[4] But in the opinion of a German visitor to the Wabash River bottoms in southeastern Illinois, it was the hardest work on a farm because new brush grew up in the cleared spaces within a short time: "Grubbing means pulling out all plants, bushes, and small trees by the roots in order to clear the ground. For this work one uses a particular kind of axe, shaped like a scythe and fastened to a long stick. This brush prefers to grow over fences, and in a few years it looks like a small forest."[5]

The basic tool for land clearing was the ax. Its price averaged $1.75 to $2, and an early Illinois guidebook recommended Yankee axes cast from steel.[6] Men made the acquisition of an ax the first priority. An eighteen-year-old who came out to the Western Reserve of Ohio in 1812 worked at chopping to pay for an ax, afterwards obtaining clearing jobs on farm tracts.[7] Similarly, two brothers from New York trekked out to the Michigan Territory in 1824. Their first employment in Oakland County was four days of labor for an ax, after which the pair secured another job at clearing and fencing twelve acres of land.[8]

3. Issac Lippincott, *A History of Manufactures in the Ohio Valley to the Year 1860* (New York, 1914), pp. 71–72; see Daniel Drake's letter in *Niles' Register*, IX (September 15, 1815), 35.

4. *History of Rush County, Indiana* (Chicago, 1888), pp. 326–27.

5. Fred Gustorf, "Frontier Perils Told by an Early Illinois Visitor," *Journal of the Illinois State Historical Society*, LV (1962), 142–43. Hereafter cited as *Illinois Historical Journal*.

6. William Oliver, *Eight Months in Illinois; with Information to Emigrants* (Newcastle upon Tyne, 1843), pp. 38, 136. According to a guidebook in 1852, an ax cost $1 to $1.50 while log chains sold at the rate of 10 to 12 cents per pound. Josiah Marshall, *The Farmer's and Emigrant's Handbook* (Boston, 1852), pp. 16, 24.

7. *History of Geauga and Lake Counties, Ohio* (Philadelphia, 1878), p. 257.

8. *History of Livingston County, Michigan* (Philadelphia, 1880), p. 232. Farmers sometimes supplied axes and other equipment, as was the case with Nathan Pierce, who employed two local men to clear brush and small timber from a lot on his farm at Calhoun County, Michigan, in 1855. Nathan Pierce Accountbook 1848–60, p. 158, entry of August 23, 1855.

With the value of an ax at two dollars, the men were working for about fifty cents a day, approximating the prevailing wage standard for unskilled labor.

Chopping was arduous labor, a fact soon realized by a Vermont man working out in northeastern Ohio in the 1820's: Plin Smith paid seven dollars for an ax, doubtless of first-rate quality, and worked this sum off by piling brush and clearing land. Afterwards he was hired to chop one hundred acres, a task which left him severely incapacitated.[9] A man had to be not only skilled, but also accustomed to chopping and clearing work. An Indiana pioneer who cleared bottomland in the winter of 1836–37 reached the point where ". . . with my hands covered with blisters from hard and incessant chopping (a kind of labor I was not accustomed to)—this, I say, provoked me almost beyond endurance. . . ."[10]

Who were set-up men, and what was their role as laborers in the frontier economy? Basically common laborers wandering from place to place in pursuit of temporary employment, they were described negatively by one authority as "Workmen of the Road."[11] While this was true in some situations, it should not be a total indictment of all who happened to engage in this line of work and for whatever personal reasons. In fact, some men who worked at this employment regarded themselves as professionals or experts in the fine art of slashing open a tract of timber, and they claimed the ability to chop an acre within three to seven days.[12] Others were local inhabitants who chopped and cleared on a part-time basis for their more affluent neighbors. They were actually respectable farm hands and citizens in the neighborhood, rather than menial itinerants passing through a locale.

Itinerants who worked at clearing farm and timber lands occasionally accompanied migrating farmers from the East. They were hired primarily to assist their employers and families along the trek and establish the farm site. Hired hands welcomed the opportunity to use their employment as a means of getting to the West, where they might secure a fresh start. As Caleb Atwater boasted of Ohio in the 1830's,

9. *History of Ashtabula County, Ohio* (Philadelphia, 1878), p. 168.
10. S. W. Widney, "Pioneer Sketches of De Kalb County," *Indiana Magazine of History,* XXV (1929), 139. Hereafter cited as *Indiana History.*
11. Richardson Wright, *Hawkers and Walkers in Early America* (New York, 1965), pp. 108–9.
12. For examples, see F. E. Weeks, *Pioneer History of Clarksfield* (Clarksfield, Ohio, 1908), p. 13; *Biographical and Historical Record of Jay and Blackford Counties, Indiana* (Chicago, 1887), p. 665.

for example, a young man could come to the state, obtain employment, buy a farm, and become a responsible citizen.[13] Similarly, the
ambitious farmer who desired to get his land established for cultivation wisely brought a hired hand.[14]

When money was available, the set-up man was retained as a regular hired hand, especially if labor was scarce. Early settlers at Indianapolis, such as Matthias Nowland, influenced many to come north
from neighboring states: ". . . he returned to Kentucky and induced
several families to emigrate and help swell the population. In the
meantime the two young men he had brought here were busy in
clearing the common field, and preparing for a crop the coming season."[15] A pioneer family in southern Indiana moved to Morgan County, in the central part of the state, in 1820. The hired hand made the
trek with them and remained at the new farm site to help clear ten
acres and plant a crop.[16] A farmer at Ann Arbor, Michigan, moved
northward to Clinton County in 1833; his hired hand not only helped
move the family, belongings, and livestock, but also stayed with them
during the following year.[17] Indeed lucky was the farmer who could
depend on his hands to remain with him on a new farm in case misfortune occurred: a Michigan farmer moved to a new farm site with
the assistance of two young men. Their services were invaluable after
the farmer became ill and was laid up during part of the time.[18] Lack
of help on a new farm created hardships when sickness or mishap

13. Caleb Atwater, *A History of the State of Ohio, Natural and Civil* (Cincinnati, 1838), pp. 316–17.

14. For examples, see H. W. Beckwith, *History of Fountain County, Together
with Historic Notes on the Wabash Valley* (Chicago, 1881), "History of
Montgomery County" section, pp. 178–79; *Biographical and Genealogical
Record of La Salle County, Illinois* (Chicago, 1900), II, p. 551; *Portrait and
Biographical Album of Peoria County, Illinois* (Chicago, 1890), p. 710; *History
of Sangamon County, Illinois* (Chicago, 1881), pp. 432, 444, 784; *History of
Jo Daviess County, Illinois* (Chicago, 1878), p. 583; Kable Brothers, *Mount
Morris: Past and Present* (Mt. Morris, Ill., 1900), p. 15; *Historical Collections:
Collections and Researches Made by the Michigan Pioneer and Historical
Society* (Lansing), XIII, p. 591; XXVIII, pp. 137, 139; XXIX, p. 377, hereafter
cited as *Michigan Pioneer Collections*; James B. Finley, *History of the Wyandott
Mission, at Upper Sandusky, Ohio* (Cincinnati, 1840), pp. 115–17.

15. John H. B. Nowland, *Early Reminiscences of Indianapolis* (Indianapolis,
1870), pp. 52–53.

16. Charles Blanchard, ed., *Counties of Morgan, Monroe and Brown, Indiana*
(Chicago, 1884), pp. 273–74. For a similar case, in which an Ohio farm hand
worked on his employer's new farm site in Indiana, see H. S. Knapp, *A
History of the Pioneer and Modern Times of Ashland County* (Philadelphia,
1863), pp. 320–21.

17. *Michigan Pioneer Collections*, XVII, pp. 410–11.

18. *Ibid.*, XXXVIII, p. 367.

struck. As a farmer's wife at Ann Arbor in the 1820's recalled, when her husband injured himself, the only alternative was to request a nephew to come out from New York to help with the work.[19]

The flow of laboring men back and forth between Ohio and Indiana during the early decades was also common in harvest season, when extra hands were required in Ohio. This was true when there was an expanding frontier to the immediate west of an older and more established section. While new lands in Indiana were being developed for cultivation and as yet remote from markets, settlers found it profitable to divide their time between improving their farms and returning to Ohio to work out for wages. During the winter of 1836–38, an Ohio youth went over to Randolph County, Indiana, to clear land on the new farm, taking the family hired hand with him to assist with the work. Yet, after the family finally moved to their new Indiana home, the son continued to go back to Ohio to work out for eight to ten dollars per month.[20]

The movement of labor across the Ohio-Indiana state line in the 1830's was also prompted by the construction of the Wabash and Erie Canal, which passed through the Fort Wayne area. As new farms were developed on the Indiana frontier, men still sought wage employment back in Ohio. For example, John Zeimmer came over from Ohio into Indiana during 1836 on a land prospecting trip and entered 160 acres; yet it was necessary to return to Ohio and hire out by the month to raise money for his new Indiana home.[21] Others found job situations which enabled them to remain and work in Indiana: sufficient work was available from newly arriving settlers who desired to open up farms. In the fall of 1833 Samuel Wasson left Fort Wayne for the northeastern section of the state in company with six or seven families, and he hired out to new settlers for several years until he obtained his own land.[22] Help for clearing land remained critical, even as late as the 1850's, according to one Indiana farmer: "I went there [Indianapolis] to get laborers, only two for a few months, but could not find any, so scarce is labor here. Up to now I have been compelled to pay 75 cents a day and meals, and can't even get any. If I did not have a family or workers, I'd be in a bad way. . . . A few

19. Elizabeth F. Ellet, *Pioneer Women of the West* (New York, 1852), p. 395.
20. *A Portrait and Biographical Record of Delaware and Randolph Counties, Ind.* (Chicago, 1894), p. 1438.
21. *Valley of the Upper Maumee River with Historical Account of Allen County and the City of Fort Wayne, Indiana* (Madison, 1889), I, pp. 362–63.
22. *History of De Kalb County, Indiana* (Chicago, 1885), pp. 548–49.

days ago I contracted to have four acres cleared at $5 per acre plus board."[23]

Opportunities for employment were also available from large land operators and developers of townships. A prominent landholder at Trumbull County in northern Ohio, Ephraim Brown started improvement of his various tracts in 1817. Both hired and tenant laborers were employed for this project. Enos Mann, a regular hand and probably a tenant of Brown, cleared timber from Brown's land. In October, 1817, his account was credited with $100.14 for chopping, clearing, and fencing slightly more than ten acres of land. This rather high rate per acre demanded a superior job, and the fact that the cleared tract was also to be fenced explains the high cost, averaging about ten dollars per acre. Another hand at this same time cleared land at an even higher rate of twenty dollars per acre.[24]

Individuals who established large tracts were successful in recruiting men from urban areas. The first settlement at St. Clair County, north of Detroit, was developed by a partnership of two men who needed a crew of men to clear timber for a town site with adjacent farms. Barzillai Wheeler had been a soldier stationed at Detroit during the War of 1812; he was discharged in 1817. In May, 1818, he was employed to go up to St. Clair County as one of an eighteen-man task force whose purpose involved clearing lands, erecting buildings, planting corn and trees; the men were subsequently used in the autumn to harvest crops.[25] A farmer in Oakland County also recalled using discharged soldiers from Detroit for barn construction and farm work during these early years.[26]

In western areas, large land operators brought in laborers to develop their estates. In 1846 William Johnson recruited a number of men from West Virginia to work on his 1,260 acres, located at McLean County in central Illinois.[27] Similarly, Michael Sullivant, whose father and brothers had assembled a cattle and farm empire back in Ohio,

23. John C. Andressohn, "The Kothe Letters," *Indiana History,* XLIII (1947), 174–75.
24. Ephraim Brown Ledger-Daybook, 1817–29, p. 2, entry of March 27, 1817; p. 17, entry of October 19, 1817. Brown allowed Mann to keep the logs, providing that he cleared them from the land by the following autumn; see p. 22, entry of November 8, 1817. Density of timber also determined the rate per acre: for example, Levi Mills cleared 11½ acres, but at a lower rate of $7 per acre; p. 15, entry of October 12, 1817.
25. *History of St. Clair County, Michigan* (Chicago, 1883), p. 262.
26. *Michigan Pioneer Collections,* IX, p. 172. For other examples of large-scale operators in Michigan, see *ibid.,* I, pp. 157–58; Franklin Everett, *Memorials of the Grand River Valley* (Chicago, 1878), pp. 176–77, 183–84.
27. *History of McLean County, Illinois* (Chicago, 1879), pp. 1029–30.

arranged the interstate movement of not one but several task forces of laborers to his Champaign County tracts in east central Illinois.[28] "Long John" Wentworth, editor of the *Chicago Democrat*, established his farm a short distance from the city; it was expanded to include 1,500 acres by 1855. In the initial operations, Wentworth hired men who cut drainage ditches, fenced pastures, and performed other tasks associated with the opening of a new farm.[29]

Skilled laborers, especially those of the building and carpenter trades, filled an important niche in frontier agricultural areas in terms of set-up and establishment of farms. These skilled artisans found ready employment, both in their trades and at common labor.[30] One such individual, Abijah Crosby, at the Western Reserve in northern Ohio, made chairs and fashioned rakes, flails, and other agricultural implements, in addition to plowing land, building fences, laying barn floors, and even rolling logs for seventy-five cents per day during the years following 1815.[31] At Lawrence County in southern Ohio, a settler wrote back to Massachusetts requesting help to be sent out for clearing timber from the land and building a sawmill. His terms were generous: he offered $150–160 per year for anyone who would come out to Ohio, and ten days of free time were provided for the hands to scout about in search of land for themselves.[32]

Part of the task in clearing and setting up a new farm site was the construction of a log cabin. Settlers sometimes contracted in advance to have a home completed by the time of their arrival. Desirable and expedient as this seemed, it was an inconvenience if the set-up man failed to fulfill his bargain. In 1825 a Kentuckian hired several men to build a cabin on his land in Indiana for thirty dollars, but he arrived to find it only partially completed. In addition to finishing the

28. *Ohio Statesman*, February 20, 1855, as cited in Newton Bateman and Paul Selby, eds., *Historical Encyclopedia of Illinois and History of Champaign County* (Chicago, 1905), II, pp. 802–3. Ohio had a labor shortage at this time, and such migration was deplored by the *Ohio Cultivator*, XI (March 1, 1855), 68.

29. Don E. Fehrenbacher, *Chicago Giant: A Biography of "Long John" Wentworth* (Madison, 1957), pp. 114, 116, 210, 233. See also Paul W. Gates's discussion of the importance of these large-scale operations, in "Large-Scale Farming in Illinois, 1850 to 1870," *Agricultural History*, VI (1932), 14–25.

30. There was a critical need for such laborers in the early Midwest: "There is hardly any part of the western country that does not abound with employment for mechanics and laborers. Among the parts peculiarly favorable for persons seeking it, we may mention the southern side of lake Erie—a wilderness at the close of the war [of 1812], but now rapidly settling with an industrious people." *Niles' Register*, XI (August 31, 1816), 13.

31. Abijah Crosby Accountbook, 1796–1832.

32. Benjamin Thurston to Dr. David Plummer (Lawrence County, Ohio, August 16, 1817, and April, 1819), Benjamin Thurston Letters.

cabin himself, he had to do his own clearing and plowing.[33] This charge for building a log cabin approximates a bill submitted to an early Danville, Illinois, merchant who had a man construct a log house in the fall of 1835: two dollars and twenty-five cents for three days of chopping, sixteen dollars for eight days of hauling, four dollars for hewing puncheons, one dollar for raising, three dollars for chinking and daubing, and one dollar for clapboards. This early business record proves that not all cabin raisings were done by community cooperative effort, but rather by hired labor.[34]

Arrangement of set-up work in a far-off frontier, such as Wisconsin, provides information on the migration of laborers and what prompted them to go west. In 1836 the Reverend Alfred Brunson established a mission at Prairie du Chien. His hired hands were skilled carpenters whose work required dexterity with an ax for the construction of log buildings as well as clearing timber: "Owing to the scarcity of men to hire in the country, and the high wages, I employed two young men for a year to accompany me; and two more—one a carpenter and joiner —worked their passage [from St. Louis]. With the carpenter and two hands we put up my house, and also prepared for Winter wood, hay, etc." A few years later Brunson complained about a lack of help, lamenting that as a result "I must chop, plow, hoe, roll logs, voyage, wade in the water, hunt some food, get up and drive cattle, all of which calls me through the brush, and tears and wears out my clothes. . . ." Pitiful as it was for the circuit rider on the frontier, this serves as a realistic picture of what the hired hand must have endured, too.[35]

Some settlers attempted to have farm sites developed during their absence. A shoemaker from the East took up a land claim near Milwaukee during the late 1830's. He hired a set-up hand to make im-

33. Charles Blanchard, ed., *Counties of Clay and Owen, Indiana* (Chicago, 1884), p. 795.

34. Amos Williams, *Scrap Book: Amos Williams and Early Danville, Illinois* (Danville, Ill., 1935), p. 111. More elaborate structures with detailed lists of costs for materials are described in Oliver, *Eight Months in Illinois*, pp. 133–34; Henry William Ellsworth, *Valley of the Upper Wabash, Indiana* (New York, 1838), pp. 52–56; James Caird, *Prairie Farming in America* (London, 1859), p. 50. Helpful also are Donald A. Hutslar, "The Log Architecture of Ohio," *Ohio History*, LXXX (1971), 171–271, esp. 208–41, and Martin L. Primack, "Farm Construction as a Use of Farm Labor in the United States, 1850–1910," *Journal of Economic History*, XXV (1965), 118.

35. Alfred Brunson, *A Western Pioneer* (Cincinnati, 1880), II, pp. 62–63, 132. For other examples of cabins constructed in advance on the Wisconsin frontier, see *History of Green County, Wisconsin* (Springfield, 1884), pp. 662, 825.

provements on the farm and cultivate it according to the rules of the local settlers' association. To minimize absentee land ownership in the area, the association stipulated that each claimant was to have three acres plowed and under cultivation in six months and erect a cabin by the end of the year. The shoemaker discovered, however, that he had run afoul of the association because the set-up hand had not completed the prescribed work. As a result, another hand was hired to finish the task. Whatever virtue these associations enjoyed, they influenced landholders, especially absentee owners, to improve their property; if the latter could not do so themselves, recourse to hired or tenant labor was the solution.[36]

Men who secured their first employment in an area as set-up hands often settled there. Although farmers or small landowners themselves, they continued to chop and clear land to make extra money. For example, a Pennsylvania man came out to Ohio in 1823 and purchased eighty acres of wilderness land. He had the foresight to bring a hired hand along with him; the two men commenced living on uncleared land in a four-by-six-foot pole shanty. After lopping ten acres of his own, Frederick Udell hired himself out to a neighbor for ten dollars per month and continued this sort of work throughout the 1820's.[37] Given the uncertain times and the undeveloped nature of the land, men found it wiser and more profitable to hire out at clearing tracts for eight to ten dollars per month or for fifty cents per day. One ambitious New Yorker came out to Clinton County, Michigan, in 1853 with two hundred dollars which he used for the purchase of a tract of unimproved land. Yet he felt it was necessary to work out at clearing neighbors' lands during the day while he cleared his own first fifty acres at night, working sometimes until 2:00 A.M.[38]

36. Mary D. Bradford, "Memoirs of Mary D. Bradford: Chapter I: A Pioneer Family at Paris, Kenosha County," *Wisconsin History Magazine*, XIV (1930), 4–7. Hereafter cited as *Wisconsin History*. At Lake County, Indiana, during the 1830's, the nonresident had to occupy the land claim within thirty days by his family or a substitute, in addition to building a cabin or plowing four acres. Weston A. Goodspeed and Charles Blanchard, eds., *Counties of Porter and Lake, Indiana* (Chicago, 1882), pp. 407–9. Frontier settlers' associations and their role are discussed by Allan G. Bogue, "The Iowa Claim Clubs: Symbol and Substance," *Mississippi Valley Historical Review*, XLV (1958), 231–58.

37. *Condensed History of Jefferson, Ashtabula County, Ohio* (Jefferson, 1878), pp. 48–50. This individual also hired himself out in the 1820's for chopping and clearing of roads. Indiana farmers, too, employed hands to cut roads into farm sites: see Nowland, *Reminiscences of Indianapolis*, p. 56.

38. *Michigan Pioneer Collections*, XXVII, pp. 64–65. For examples of men who worked nights clearing timber by the light of burning piles, see D. Griffiths, Jr., *Two Years' Residence in the New Settlements of Ohio* (London,

Once a region was settled and brought under active cultivation, the demand for set-up work diminished. In Indiana during the 1820's many young men obtained a start through such employment. By the 1840's, however, as the state became populated and the lands settled, Indiana underwent a transition whereby the remaining clearing work was handled by the farmer himself or simply done on a smaller scale. While large operators (like Calvin Fletcher near Indianapolis) were still clearing tracts as late as the 1850's, there was clearly less demand for set-up men than there had been in the 1820's and 1830's: "It is during these years [1830's] that we find that the young men of the county, who had grown up beside the hardships of the country, were going out and making entries of land in their own names, with money earned with the grubbing-hoe, the axe and the maul. From 1840 to 1850, the population and wealth continued on the increase, but not at so great as during the former period."[39]

Clearing work tended to follow a seasonal pattern, although variations of all sorts occurred. Spring had its advantages, particularly if the set-up man was retained through the summer as a regular hand; but generally fall and winter were the months devoted to chopping and clearing work, for the lack of anything better to do. Individual situations also determined the season when a man worked, as in the case of a twenty-two-year-old who left Ohio and trekked out to Indiana, spending the summer of 1841 chopping timber. During the following autumn he worked for another man in the area, although this chopping was involved with a sawmill.[40] Since schoolteachers were employed to teach mainly during the winter months, they had to seek work elsewhere during the remainder of the year. Often they worked about the neighborhood on farms in spring, summer, and at harvesting in autumn, while picking up random jobs at chopping and clearing.[41]

Sometimes the arrangement was casual when the work of clearing was limited. Andrew Tenbrook recalled his early Indiana days: "In about 1827 after the corn was planted we had a potato patch to clear.

1835), p. 33; *History of Genesee County, Michigan* (Philadelphia, 1879), p. 262; *Biographical and Historical Record of Kosciusko County, Indiana* (Chicago, 1887), pp. 583–84.

39. D. D. Banta, *A Historical Sketch of Johnson County, Indiana* (Chicago, 1881), p. 77; see also *History of Rush County, Indiana*, pp. 326–27. During the 1850's, Fletcher switched over to cattle and cleared land for pasturage; see Calvin Fletcher Diary, entry of April 30, 1850.

40. John S. Morris, "Ancestor statement filed with Society of Indiana Pioneers."
41. *Firelands Pioneer*, n.s. IV (January, 1888), 120–21.

Near the first of June two men came from Sandcreek with axes on their shoulders and wanted to work for potatoes. We set in five hands in deadning [*sic*] of as good land as we had."[42] Yet autumn and winter represented a more practical and realistic time for this work, because harvesting was over and hands were available for clearing work during the dead months of the year. A Pulaski County farmer in northwestern Indiana used his hired man during the winter to get out timber which was not used until later at a raising.[43]

In time Midwesterners realized that there were better ways than the old traditional approach of pioneers who chopped in winter, cleared land in spring, and spent sleepless summer nights staying up to burn off green timber. According to more knowledgeable sources, the best time to chop timber was during June through August. The logs could then be allowed to dry thoroughly; early burning only seared the green wood and inhibited the subsequent rotting process. Timber and brush were to be piled into windrows running on a north-south line and spaced seven to eight rods apart. After the windrows had dried sufficiently, they were easily fired during a convenient dry spell.[44]

In 1854 a Michigan farmer recounted his own personal experiences in clearing timber lands during 1836; his sensible advice showed how hired labor could be utilized. Initially he had opened up part of his farm by chopping off the timber. This process proved slow and expensive, costing ultimately about fifteen dollars per acre with the fencing. He decided a change was in order as a result of this experience. In June he measured off an eight-acre lot and hired a hand by

42. Donald F. Carmony, "From Lycoming County, Pennsylvania to Parke County, Indiana: Recollections of Andrew Tenbrook, 1786–1823," *Indiana History*, LXI (1965), 29.

43. *Counties of White and Pulaski, Indiana* (Chicago, 1883), p. 604. Pioneers did not receive help in the chopping of logs and timber for a cabin, but only for the raising of it. Oliver makes this point clear to settlers in 1843: "I ought to mention, that it is only at the *raising* of the house that the stranger will receive assistance. . . . He must, either himself or with hired assistance, cut down the timber, log it off at the proper lengths, and score or hew it down on two opposite sides to the proper thickness (about nine inches); he must also cut timber, and split it for clapboards and shingles, for roofing and weather-boarding; then he must prepare joists and spars, which are laid lengthwise between the gables instead of couples; and lastly, must have all hauled to the spot. At this stage the assistance of his neighbors is requested. . . ." *Eight Months in Illinois*, p. 129.

44. *Michigan Farmer*, VIII (January, 1850), 11; (December, 1850), 374; *Alton Telegraph and Democratic Review*, January 8, 1847; *Report of the Commissioner of Patents for the Year 1849: Part II. Agriculture* (Washington, 1850), 367–68. Hereafter cited as *U.S. Pat. Office Report*, according to year.

the month who cut and piled the underbrush. Timber suitable for rails was chopped, while all trees over four inches in diameter were girdled. Later in August another hand was obtained to help finish the clearing and fencing; the expense, including the hired man's board, averaged out to $4.38 per acre. The area was then used for pasturage and as a source of dry wood for fuel during the next four years, after which the dead trees were easily felled. He paid a man fifteen dollars to complete the last of this clearing, assisted by a nine-year-old boy and a yoke of oxen. A different approach, however, was followed with a separate ten-acre tract. A man was employed to girdle ten acres of trees for five dollars, and the farmer then used his leisure time in cutting away the underwood. Within two years it was fenced and ready for grass seed. The clearing was easily accomplished by a chopper, who removed the dead trees at the rate of two dollars per acre.[45]

The cost of clearing averaged between five and twenty dollars per acre; the determining factor was, of course, the number of trees or timber density per acre.[46] Admittedly, clearing was an expensive item in any settler's budget, and fair warning was issued to all, as was apparent in a conversation between Alexis de Tocqueville and an innkeeper at Pontiac, Michigan, in 1831: "The greatest expense is the clearing. If the pioneer comes into the wilds with a family able to help in the first work, his task is fairly easy. But that is generally not so. Usually the emigrant is young, and if he already has children, they are in infancy. Then he must either see to all the first needs of his family himself, or hire the services of his neighbours. It will cost 4–5 dollars to clear one acre."[47]

Individual arrangements were subject to negotiation and executed on the basis of a formal or informal contract. Men who pursued this type of work generally labored according to a rate per acre, although it was not uncommon to hire a man by the month.[48] Charles Kane, a New Yorker, came out to Hillsdale County, Michigan, in 1844. After working by the month, he decided that it was advantageous to chop and clear land by the job or on an acre rate; he followed this line of work successfully for six years, while clearing his own forty acres at

45. *Michigan Farmer*, XII (October, 1854), 297.
46. Clarence H. Danhof, "Farm-Making Costs of the 'Safety Valve': 1850–1860," *Journal of Political Economy*, XLIX (1941), 339–41; see also Danhof's *Change in Agriculture: The Northern United States, 1820–1870* (Cambridge, 1969), pp. 114–21.
47. Alexis de Tocqueville, *Journey to America* (New Haven, 1960), p. 343; see also p. 209.
48. *Michigan Farmer*, XII (October, 1854), 297.

intervals between jobs.[49] Using this approach to clearing work enabled the set-up man to be flexible in his contracts with farmers, but there were specific understandings in these agreements. For example, in the 1850's at Jefferson County, Wisconsin, an Irishman from the village was hired to grub out several acres, using an ax, pick, and shovel to remove the brush and roots. His remuneration was the right to have all firewood taken from the tract and to grow crops on the land for several years.[50]

Farmers recognized the value of timber as fence rails or fuel and sometimes retained control over its disposal. This arrangement was made perfectly clear in a contract negotiated by Lucius Lyon, a large Michigan land developer, in the 1830's. In July, 1836, Lyon hired Calvin Ray to cut and clear a ten-acre tract in Kent County near the Grand River Rapids. Ray agreed to remove all underbrush less than three inches in diameter down to the surface of the ground, except for mulberry, cherry, and other trees of ornamental value. Timber of suitable size was to be cut into rails ten feet long for fencing. As part of the contract, an eight-rail fence six feet high was to be erected, while timber not suitable for rails was to be cut into cord wood four feet long and piled. Any fallen timber that could serve as fuel was also to be corded and stacked. Trees and bushes unsuited for either rails or fuel were to be piled and burnt off. According to the agreement, the ground was ready and clean by mid-October. This set-up man was paid for his clearing work at the rate of five dollars per acre. Additionally, a provision in the contract stipulated that he was to be paid forty-four cents per cord for all fuel wood and thirty-seven cents per rod for the fence.[51]

49. *History of Hillsdale County, Michigan* (Philadelphia, 1879), p. 326; see also *History of Livingston County, Michigan*, p. 253; Alan Conway, ed., *The Welsh in America: Letters from the Immigrants* (Minneapolis, 1961), p. 83.

50. "An Autobiography of Alexis Crane Hart covering the period of his childhood spent in Jefferson and Trempealeau counties up to the year 1863," p. 23. It was reported that woodlands in Wisconsin were cleared at the rate of ten dollars per acre, and the chopper had the right to dispose of the wood that was worth sometimes five to six dollars per acre. Oak rails, for example, fetched a price of ten dollars per thousand, according to Charles Lindsey, *The Prairies of the Western States: Their Advantages and Their Drawbacks* (Toronto, 1860), p. 33. Wood had value also as fuel when corded, and it was estimated that an acre yielded roughly thirty cords. *Wisconsin Farmer*, VIII (January, 1856), 29–30.

51. Contract between Lucius Lyon and Calvin Ray (Grand Rapids, Mich., July 25, 1836), Lucius Lyon Papers. Twenty rails were needed for each rod (16.5 feet) of fence: "this makes a 'Virginia' or 'worm fence,' eight rails high. The eighth rail, called a rider, is elevated twelve or eighteen inches from the seventh rail, and rests on crotches eight feet long, crossing at each corner of the

A winter contract, negotiated between an Ohio farmer and a chopper in 1846, documents the value of rails and wood. While the wage rate was not entirely clear, its payment was stipulated in a combination of rails and cord wood which the hired hand probably sold at a later date:

> This witnesseth: That Charles Turner is to chop for Wm C. Holgate one hundred cords of wood and two thousand rails. He is to commence said work right away and continue it as same 'till it is finished. He is first to chop all timber into wood & rails—above Philips Hiram on said Holgates 40 acre lot adjacent town and to make up balance is to chop at such place as said Holgate is to direct within a mile and a half of town. Said Holgate is to pay ⅓ and ⅔ as trade at the rate of 3½ a cord for wood and 5/a hundred for rails. He is to pile the brush as he sees fit for burning.[52]

This contract was doubtless written for the benefit of a local man who was not obligated to go a great distance to reach the clearing locations, unlike many set-up men who trekked over considerable distances to the job sites.

Specific cost data on clearing jobs were obtained from the *Michigan Farmer* in 1851. Several methods of clearing land were recommended with a breakdown for each phase, stressing the advantages and disadvantages in terms of speed, cost, and quality of the job. The quickest but least desirable method was to cut trees and brush in spring, despite the fact that greenness of wood made firing a difficult and exhausting task. Moreover, green stumps were difficult to dig out, while repeated grubbings damaged the ground. The cost of clearing per acre approximated:

For chopping an acre,	$5.00
" burning the brush, between 1 and 2 days' work,	1.00
" logging 1½ days' work of 3 men and a team, at 5s. per day,	3.75
" burning log heaps, 2 days' work,	1.25
" drawing, splitting, and laying up 300 rails, (a fair proportion per acre,)	3.00
	$14.00

'worm.' Rails of ordinary size, laid in this manner, make a durable and light fence, over and through which no cattle or stock can pass." Ellsworth, *Valley of the Upper Wabash, Indiana*, p. 50. It was estimated that ". . . any man of ordinary physical powers can put up 200 yards of rail fence in a day, or fence about 30 acres in a week. . . ." Oliver, *Eight Months in Illinois*, p. 131.

52. William Holgate Accountbook, 1846–70, p. 29, entry for Charles Turner during 1846.

A preferred method was to chop timber in the summer months. Trunks of trees were cut into fifteen- to eighteen-foot lengths and placed in windrows along with refuse brush. When the farmer later fired the windrows, their dryness assured rapid and even burning. The ground was then cleared and sown with wheat, while stumps were allowed to rot out over the next five to ten years:

Chopping, per acre,	$5.00
Burning brush, ½ day's work,	.31
1¼ days, 3 hands and a team, at 5s. per day, logging,	3.13
Burning log heaps, 2 days' work,	1.25
Fencing, about	3.00
Cost per acre, in this way,	$12.69

Another method was to complete underbrushing in August and chop timber during winter, allowing wood to dry out until harvest of the following year:

Chopping,	$5.00
Burning the brush does not take any time worth mentioning	—.—
1 day's work of 3 hands and a team, logging,	2.50
2 days at burning log heaps,	1.25
Fencing, say	3.00
Cost per acre, in this way,	$11.75[53]

A popular and simple approach was to cut underbrush and fell timber, letting the timber dry for two years. The farmer could then chop out rail timber, clear and burn logs at his convenience. The total cost by this method amounted to only ten dollars per acre. Girdling was recommended as the best method, but it required time. Trunks of trees were girdled five feet above the ground, cutting into the trunk for a depth of one to two inches. The object was to leave five feet of trunk below the girdle strips, in order to retain the natural water in the trunk cavity which later helped rot out the tree base. Trees were then felled when dead, while the roots and base enriched the soil and facilitated removal. The stump of a girdled tree decayed more rapidly than the stump of a felled green tree. No precise estimate was given, but the cost averaged considerably less than the above methods. However, if timber was felled, it was essential to construct windrows which were not simply piles of brush and logs, but an orderly arrangement of the timber materials so as to facilitate drying and later firing. They were to run on a north-south line in order

53. *Michigan Farmer,* IX (March, 1851), 70–71.

not to be blown apart. The material was not to be criss-crossed but laid in the same direction and packed tightly together, so that the windrow structure remained compact and thus assured even and complete firing.[54]

Such employment was grim, back-breaking toil, and graphic was the description by an Indiana pioneer of the 1830's whose financial plight was taken advantage of by a dishonest farmer:

> The job was on the river bottoms, where the timber was very heavy. Huge oaks and elms, with enormous tops, being rather plenty to get along fast; as I had to take down all timber, and cut it up ready for logging. I only got four or five dollars (I do not now remember distinctly the wages) and was to take my pay in potatoes, pork, beans, &c. . . . The price of chopping was low and that of the articles of pay high—yet I could not do better, as provisions must be had. While I kept busy on my job, I could just about get provisions enough to keep up in the bare necessaries of life, so far as eating was concerned; but I had no time to be sick and no rest but the Sabbath. . . . The worst part of the tale is, that Lytle [the landowner] was not satisfied with my doing the job so cheap, and taking the pay in high priced trade; but he actually moved the stakes first set, so that the lines might take in several large elms that were just outside the job; and besides, he wanted me to chop up to a curving brush fence, which ran from stake to stake on one side of my square job, including about a quarter of an acre more than the straight line agreed upon.[55]

Set-up work was itinerant labor performed at all times of the year, but especially during the fall and winter months. Choppers also worked as farm hands, and in fact both occupations were considered one and the same by many common laborers. Clearing land was a poor man's employment, but it was generally available even when other jobs were scarce.

54. *Ibid.*; see also VIII (January, 1850), 11; XIV (March, 1856), 68–69. A farmer in central Indiana advised that trees girdled in summer required four to six years to deaden; however, corn and wheat could be raised on the cleared land between the trees during this period. *U.S. Pat. Office Report, 1852* (Washington, 1853), 293–94.

55. Widney, "Pioneer Sketches of De Kalb County," 139. The farmer and set-up man who wished to avoid any misunderstanding measured the tract carefully. A Michigan farmer hired a man to chop and clear five acres at the rate of five dollars per acre. His diary recorded that his son helped measure off the five acres of land for the hand. Philip Cumings Diary, 1840–47, entries of October 9, 29, 1845. Proper measuring and laying out the tract eliminated the irregular patches of clearings. *Michigan Farmer*, XIV (March, 1856), 68–69.

Prairie Breaking

The glittering plow-share cleaves the ground
With many a slow, decreasing round.
With lifted whip and gee-whoa-haw,
He guides his oxen as they draw.[1]

BY THE 1820's westward-bound settlers became attracted
to the vast prairies, whose broad expanses opened up a new way of
life but required considerable labor for farm-making. In contrast to
set-up work in heavily forested sections of lower Ohio, Indiana, and
Illinois, the prairies of the upper Midwest posed a problem necessitating specialized labor known as prairie breaking or sodbusting.
Men drove teams of oxen hitched to heavy plows which made the
initial cut in the thick sod, a task of immense struggle with a virgin
land unviolated by the sharp edge of the plowshare. According to a
popular phrase of the time, it was necessary "to tickle it with a plow
so it would laugh with a crop." Yet cutting prairie sod was no laugh-
ing matter, but grim and toilsome work; a less cheerful and more
realistic adage termed prairie breaking as the art of "deviling."[2]

The stubborn quality of prairie sod prompted the refinement of
plowing equipment, and it encouraged the appearance of men who
specialized in the skillful techniques required for the task.[3] This
specialized laborer occupied a position parallel to that of the set-
up hand, whose work also involved the establishment of a new farm
—but with some difference. Whereas the set-up hand found employment mainly in forested or timbered tracts, the prairie breaker
operated in new settlements on sparsely timbered areas and open expanses of tall grass.

1. *Michigan Pioneer Collections*, V, p. 300.
2. *History of Lee County* (Chicago, 1881), p. 282.
3. Specialized plowing is briefly treated in Gates, *Farmer's Age*, p. 181,
and Allan G. Bogue, *From Prairie to Corn Belt* (Chicago, 1963), pp. 70–73.

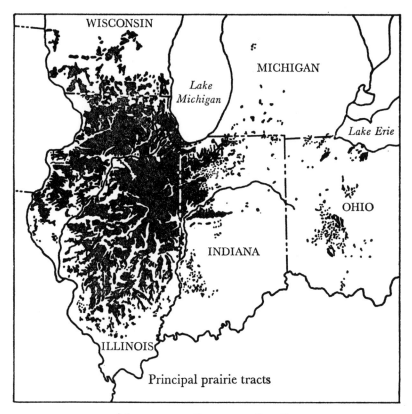

MIDWESTERN PRAIRIES, 1820–60

Source: Adapted from Edgar N. Transeau, "The Prairie Peninsula," *Ecology*, XVI (1935), 423–37, fig. 1.

Diversity and beauty best describe the midwestern prairies. Some regions, like Michigan, had both open expanses and smaller compact breaks or "oak openings" in the timbered stretches, especially in the south central area.[4] Wisconsin's prairie lands, occupying a latitude analogous to Michigan's, also reflected a varied topography where grasslands combined with timber and running rivers.[5] Northern Indi-

4. *History of Kalamazoo County, Michigan* (Philadelphia, 1880), p. 58; see also Albert F. Butler, "Rediscovering Michigan's Prairies," *Michigan History*, XXXI (1947), 267–86; XXXII (1948), 15–36; XXXIII (1949), 117–30, 220–31.
5. "The prairies of Wisconsin are not as extensive as those of Illinois, Iowa or Minnesota, but, as they are skirted and belted by timber, are adapted to immediate and profitable occupation. The soil of the prairies is a rich, dark vegetable mould, varying from two to eight feet in depth, capable of producing,

ana's prairie region often became a morass of seasonal swamps and
sloughs during the wet months, while in neighboring Illinois such
conditions were also found, but in smaller proportion to the wide-
open grasslands that were dotted with meadows of flowers and small
bushes. An early midwestern traveler described a prairie tract extending deep into southern Illinois:

> The prairies in this state are charming—great stretches of flat land,
> covered with wild meadows which are hemmed by thin forests. The
> prairies are covered all summer long with flowers that change color
> every month—yellow, blue, then red. By wandering from one meadow
> to another, one encounters a series of surprises. Huge green surfaces
> of unbelievably high grass which waves in the wind like the sea
> against the wooded background, more beautiful than the English
> parks. . . .[6]

Despite their beauty, the prairie regions loomed foreign in the eyes
of the upland, forest-oriented Southerners who constituted the bulk
of the population streaming across the Ohio River into Illinois and
Indiana prior to 1830: "A prejudice at one time prevailed against the
prairies, as not being for cultivation; but this was found to be er-
roneous, and they are more in request, as it is a most important object
to save the labour of clearing wood."[7]

Prairie breaking was a spring and summer employment. In many
parts of the Midwest the soil was ready for plowing by spring. While
contemporary accounts note that prairie breaking was done throughout the entire summer, the recommended time was primarily in the
months of May and June but no later than July. The sod matting of
roots, often several inches thick, had to be cut and turned over. If the
sod was broken too early in the season, the overturned roots might
have a chance to take root again before autumn. Equally important,

---

in greatest profusion, anything which will grow in these latitudes. . . ." James
S. Ritchie, *Wisconsin and Its Resources* (Philadelphia, 1857), p. 37. For a list
of the types of prairie grass, see *Transactions of the Wisconsin State Agricultural
Society*, III (Madison, 1853), 397–488. Hereafter cited as *Wisconsin Agricultural
Transactions*.

6. Gustorf, "Frontier Perils Told by an Early Illinois Visitor," 146. For a
list of early Illinois prairies, drawn from John Mason Peck's *A Gazetteer of Illinois*
(1834), see Douglas R. McManis, *The Initial Evaluation and Utilization of
the Illinois Prairies, 1815–1840* (Chicago, 1964), pp. 83–85.

7. S. Augustus Mitchell, *Illinois in 1837: A Sketch Descriptive of the Situation*
(Philadelphia, 1837), p. 11. This issue of whether or not early pioneers avoided
the prairies is examined by Terry G. Jordan, "Between the Forest and the
Prairie," *Agricultural History*, XXXVIII (1964), 205–16.

prairie breaking had to be completed in season for the overturned sward to rot sufficiently in the ground. Plowing late in the fall impeded the rotting process, and as the frost left the soil the following spring, the sod roots tended to grow back in.[8]

Despite recommendations for suitable plowing times, prairie breakers worked throughout the summer whenever the opportunity presented itself. As a seasonal employment, prairie breaking was performed during the hot summer months; the teamster with a string of breaking oxen had to make his money in a short time. Travel from one job location to the next depended on slow-moving oxen to haul the heavy equipment. Moreover, settlers arrived at new farms at various times and probably considered themselves lucky to obtain the services of a prairie breaker regardless of the month in the summer season. As a rule, most breakers worked an average of three months; this provided sufficient remuneration for their time and effort, based on the average of two acres per day and paid at the rate of $2.50 to $3 an acre. An even moderately good breaker charging less per acre —$1.50 to $2—could easily make several hundred dollars in one season without working every day. When sodbusting work was unavailable, especially during the cold months, these men sought other employment such as itinerant labor and part-time teamstering.[9]

Although oxen usually fulfilled the power requirement for a breaker's plow, some debate existed as to whether horses were more suitable for the task. For example, Matthias Dunlap, editor of the *Illinois Farmer*, voiced a preference for horses primarily on the grounds of versatility and speed: "We will commence by saying that prairie

8. In Illinois the May 1–15 period was recommended by Fred Gerhard, *Illinois as It is* (Chicago and Philadelphia, 1857), p. 311. A farmer at Janesville, Wisconsin, advised May 20–June 20; *Wisconsin Agricultural Transactions*, I (1851), 245. According to a farmer at Cass County, Michigan, May 10 through July 20 was the best time. Sod overturned earlier, for example in April, resulted in fields of grubs that sprouted up later in season; however, sheep and livestock could check this spurious growth by feeding on the overturned ground. *Michigan Farmer*, VIII (September, 1850), 265.

9. For examples, see *Counties of White and Pulaski, Indiana*, pp. 695–96; *Counties of Warren, Benton, Jasper and Newton, Indiana* (Chicago, 1883), p. 573; *County of Douglas, Illinois* (Chicago, 1884), pp. 479–80; *Biographical Review of Hancock County, Illinois* (Chicago, 1907), pp. 408–9; *History of McDonough County, Illinois* (Springfield, 1885), p. 917; *Biographical Record of Ogle County, Illinois* (Chicago, 1899), p. 449; Portrait and Biographical *Album of Henry County, Illinois* (Chicago, 1885), pp. 240–41. That these men were constantly on the move aroused suspicion in the minds of some settlers; see *Commemorative Biographical and Historical Record of Kane County, Illinois* (Chicago, 1888), pp. 860–61.

breaking can be chiefly done with a single span of horses, and as effectually as with a half dozen yoke of oxen. Three horses make an admirable team, cutting a furrow sixteen inches wide, while two horses will cut a foot; plowing one and a fourth to one and a half acres per day. Six yoke of oxen are generally used to cut two feet, breaking one and a half to two acres per day."[10] Others recommended horses for established and improved farms but oxen for new, undeveloped farms.[11] Yet in practice, well-matched oxen excelled as the primary power source for sodbusting; and the advice of Timothy Dwight, with reference earlier to New England, applied equally well in the West: "The advantages of employing oxen are, that they will endure more fatigue, draw more steadily and surely; are purchased for a smaller price; are kept at less expense; are free from disease; suffer less from laboring on rough grounds; and perform the labour better; and, when by age or accident they become unfit for labour, they are converted into beef. The only advantage of employing horses instead of oxen, is derived from their speed."[12]

It was estimated in 1819 that in southern Indiana a "stout horse for drawing" cost $60 and "upwards," while at the same time in Illinois two horses, harness, and plow came to $100.[13] By the 1830's guidebooks for Illinois settlers advised that good farm horses were obtainable at $50 each,[14] although one settler in 1837 reported the price had risen 25 percent in the previous two years.[15] This information matches the figures provided by Oliver, who listed the cost of a horse at $55 in 1830 but rising in 1837 to in excess of $100.[16] In the early 1840's an

10. Matthias Dunlap Clippings Book, September, 1853–September, 1858, article written from West Urbana, Illinois, June 8, 1857. Mitchell similarly claimed that horses were used extensively in plowing. *Illinois in 1837*, p. 42. Horses were preferable because they plowed two acres a day in contrast to one and a half acres with oxen, according to Gerhard, *Illinois as It is*, p. 317.

11. *Farmer's Companion and Horticultural Gazette*, I (May 1, 1853), 89.

12. As cited in Louis B. Schmidt and Earle D. Ross, *Readings in the Economic History of American Agriculture* (New York, 1925), p. 184. Danhof suggests that horses were increasingly used in preference to oxen with the improvement of plowing equipment. *Change in Agriculture*, p. 143.

13. D. B. Warden, *A Statistical, Political, and Historical Account of the United States of North America* (Edinburgh, 1819), II, p. 308; III, p. 61; William Kingdom, *America and the British Colonies* (London, 1820), p. 71.

14. John Mason Peck, *A New Guide for Emigrants to the West* (Boston, 1836), p. 281; Mitchell, *Illinois in 1837*, p. 42.

15. "Farming in Illinois in 1837," *Illinois Historical Journal*, XXVII (1934), 235–37.

16. Oliver, *Eight Months in Illinois*, p. 136; see also C. D. Arfwedson, *The United States and Canada, in 1832, 1833, and 1834* (London, 1834), I, p. 204.

Ohio settler reported ordinary horses costing $35–45 each and good horses $60–$100 each.[17] By the 1850's in Illinois, a horse commanded from $100 to $200.[18]

In 1830 a pair of work oxen could be obtained for $45, but this figure rose to $70 in 1837, leveling off to $55 by 1841, a reflection of speculation and inflation in the 1830's.[19] A Michigan farm couple wrote in 1839 that, despite high taxes and a scarcity of money, they were finally able to purchase a yoke of oxen for $100.[20] A Wisconsin pioneer in the 1840's observed: "I have not bought a team yet and can not unless I have a 'windfall' from somewhere. If I had about 25 or $30 more than I now have I could buy me a yoke of cattle. I can get 4 yr old steers for about 40 or $50. After buying my land and paying $18 for breaking 8 acres I had $16 left."[21] By the 1850's oxen had risen in value to $100–200 per yoke.[22]

Whether horses or oxen were used, experienced animals and skilled drivers counted as equally important factors, but few newly arrived settlers on the prairies owned trained teams. Josiah Marshall's handbook for western settlers emphasized that a decent job could not be accomplished with less than three yoke of oxen, while four yoke were definitely more advantageous.[23] The Reverend Gustaf Unonius, who came to the southeastern part of Wisconsin during the early 1840's, lent his note of caution, advising pioneers that breaking work was difficult and required experience. Pioneers on the prairies cooperated by pooling their draft animals to form breaking teams, but Unonius expressed doubt regarding this approach. His advice coincided with that of Marshall, who urged the employment of an experienced prairie breaker.[24]

In general, breakers ran teams consisting of three to seven yoke of oxen, the larger operator usually commanding more than the local person who engaged in the business as a sideline. Three were the

17. Conway, ed., *The Welsh in America*, p. 86.
18. Samuel Templeton to O. Gross (Freeporte [sic], Stephenson County, Ill., February 20, 1856), Templeton Letters.
19. Oliver, *Eight Months in Illinois*, p. 137.
20. John Abbey, L. Hart, and Emaline Hart to Lyman Abbey (Sanilac County, Mich., February 10, 1839), Lovira Hart Correspondence.
21. Ruth Seymour Burmester, "Silas Seymour Letters," *Wisconsin History*, XXXII (1948), 195.
22. Samuel Templeton to O. Gross (Freeporte [sic], Stephenson County, Ill., February 20, 1856), Templeton Letters.
23. Marshall, *Farmer's and Emigrant's Handbook*, p. 29.
24. *A Pioneer in Northwest America 1841–1858. The Memoirs of Gustaf Unonius* (Minneapolis, 1960), I, pp. 261–64. Hereafter cited as Unonius, *Memoirs*.

minimum, but they had to be well trained. Young men often engaged in the task of training animals for prairie breaking as well as other teamstering jobs.[25] In 1850 a letter appeared in the *Michigan Farmer* describing the process of training oxen. When first teamed together, they were likely to bolt and were allowed to run free until they stopped at a fence. This was repeated several times until the oxen tired of breaking off into a run. At this point they were ready to be trained to voice commands and introduced to hauling, generally light loads at first. In addition, they learned to step backwards for a step or two before responding to a fast charging thrust, the type of ramming necessary for the plow blade to cut and snap through the tough prairie roots. Another technique of training used by breakers, especially applicable with several yoke of oxen, was to match two yoke of well-broken animals with inexperienced ones.[26]

Breaking tough prairie sod required skillful direction of teams. Handling of animals could be a tricky business, wrote a new farmer in Illinois in 1843: "Yesterday I drove four yoke of oxen between two stumps four rods apart without touching which is better than I could do at first."[27] Animals were temperamental and easily recognized inexperience and lack of forcefulness in strange hands.[28] Needless to say, not all men liked such work or continued in it. In the 1830's one young man followed prairie breaking as well as hauling and general farm labor until the severity of it displeased him so much that an opening in the general store business quickly enticed him away from farming.[29] For some men, employment at prairie breaking lasted only one season, as was the case with an Irish immigrant who was employed as a farm hand in Pennsylvania during 1849–54 and then came

25. Asher Edgerton to Elisha Edgerton (Quincy, Ill., May 28, 1832). The number of yoke per breaking rig varied with an average of four to six but occasionally reaching as many as twelve yoke, according to Leo Rogin, *The Introduction of Farm Machinery* (Berkeley, 1931), p. 45n. For an example of a nineteen-year-old who trained cattle for sodbusting and also drove a team to St. Louis, see *Biographical Record of Logan County, Illinois* (Chicago, 1901), pp. 444–47.

26. *Michigan Farmer*, VIII (December, 1850), 362–63; see also *History of McDonough County, Illinois*, p. 1045.

27. Jennie M. Patten in collaboration with Andrew Graham, *History of the Somonauk United Presbyterian Church near Sandwich, De Kalb County, Illinois* (Chicago, 1928), p. 278.

28. For a humorous example of a green-horn amateur attempting to drive a prairie-breaking rig in Illinois, see Seraphina Gardner Smith, *Recollections of the Pioneers of Lee County* (Dixon, Ill., 1893), pp. 452–53.

29. *Portrait and Biographical Record of Adams County, Illinois* (Chicago, 1892), pp. 527–28.

west to Illinois, working as a farm hand and at sodbusting. The latter
occupation he followed only three months.[30]

The basic equipment for the prairie breaker was the plow.[31] In the
Midwest a specific design of plowing equipment proved most suitable for the tough prairie sod. The wooden beam breaker plow found
wide application up to the 1840's, when it was further improved by
the substitution of lighter but stronger steel frames. Basically it was
a wooden beam, usually fourteen feet long, with the front end riding
on a wheel carriage which supported the weight of the beam and also
guided it. The plowshare itself was a cumbersome item, weighing
from 60 to 125 pounds, cutting a furrow sixteen to thirty inches wide
and two to six inches deep. The first cutting of the prairie sod did not
require a deep furrow; in fact, a shallow cut was recommended to
assure adequate decomposition.[32]

This heavy gear demanded both skill and knowledge in handling
and hooking up. The Reverend Unonius, who had reservations about
inexperienced men doing their own breaking, considered the most
difficult portion of the job to be adjusting the plow and getting proper
length of chain to which the oxen were hooked. If properly arranged,
the plow could easily be driven by even a half-grown boy, and
Unonius claimed that he once saw a perfectly adjusted plow cut long
furrows with a minimum of control.[33] In addition, adjustment and
setting were required for the plowshare and coulter, the latter being
a sharp wheel which rolled in advance of the plowshare cutting open
the surface of the sod. As a youth on the Wisconsin prairie frontier,
John Muir learned the importance of a well-adjusted plow that
turned a true, straight furrow:

> . . . with the share and coulter sharp and nicely adjusted, the plough,
> instead of shying at every grub and jumping out, ran straight ahead
> without need of steering or holding, and gripped the ground so firmly

30. Bateman and Selby, eds., *Historical Encyclopedia of Illinois and History
of Henderson County* (Chicago, 1911), II, p. 771.

31. For a general discussion and history of plows, see Rogin, *Introduction
of Farm Machinery*, pp. 21–52; Danhof, *Change in Agriculture*, pp. 181–99.

32. According to a Wisconsin farmer in 1851, whereas two men were required
previously to handle the old wooden beam plow, the new steel frame plow
could be run by one man; the cost for plowing prairie sod could be easily
reduced by one-third to one-half of the former cost per acre. *Wisconsin Agricultural Transactions*, I (1851), 244. Experience proved that better results were
achieved by plowing two-and-one-half to three inches deep, which was sufficient
to sever the roots from the overhead grass. *Peoria Register and North-Western
Gazetteer*, November 11, 1842.

33. Unonius, *Memoirs*, I, pp. 261–64.

that it could hardly be thrown out at the end of the furrow. Our breaker turned a furrow two feet wide, and on our best land, where the sod was toughest, held so firm a grip that at the end of the field my brother, who was driving the oxen, had to come to my assistance in throwing it over on its side to be drawn around the end of the land; and it was all I could do to set it up again. But I learned to keep that plough in such trim that after I got started on a new furrow I used to ride on the crossbar between the handles with my feet resting comfortably on the beam, without having to steady or steer it in any way on the whole length of the field, unless we had to go round a stump, for it sawed through the biggest grubs without flinching.[34]

When properly adjusted, the sharp plowshare was capable of severing grubs and roots two inches in diameter with barely a perceptible shock to the plow. If a jam occurred, with the plow unable to cut through a grub or root, the breaker used an ax to chop out the obtrusive root.[35] Sometimes use of an ax was impractical, and one Illinois farmer provided a description of the alternative: "Often the plow would stick so tight in the red roots and 'devil's shoestrings,' that he had to take two yoke of oxen and hitch to the back of the plow to haul it out. The prairie grass, knee-deep and wet with dew until about eleven o'clock each day, did not make the work a pleasant one."[36] The tedious process of cutting, chopping, and back-hauling across a field of tough prairie sod in midsummer indicates the grimness of sodbusting and explains why specialists demanded and received higher rates than the average farm hand.

Lead teams were very important, and the largest oxen were placed at the head.[37] On the Koshkonong Prairie in lower Wisconsin the head team was called "Snatch," for it was brought around to the rear for pulling back or snatching out the entrapped plow from roots and grubs.[38] The breaker stayed at the rear of the plow, guiding it down the field but also moving to other positions as the situation required. In addition to managing the teams, he watched the coulter to make

34. John Muir, *The Story of My Boyhood and Youth* (New York and Boston, 1925), pp. 228–29.

35. Bateman and Selby, eds., *Historical Encyclopedia of Illinois and History of Kane County* (Chicago, 1904), p. 646; *Michigan Pioneer Collections*, XXXII, p. 242.

36. Bateman and Selby, eds., *Historical Encyclopedia of Illinois and History of Ogle County* (Chicago, 1909), II, p. 974.

37. David F. Sayre, "Early Life in Southern Wisconsin," *Wisconsin History*, III (1920), 422.

38. Angie Kumlien Main, "Thures Kumlien, Koshkonog Naturalist," *ibid.*, XXVII (1943), 209.

certain that leaves, sticks, and rocks did not gather up, and he moved along the teams of oxen, keeping them in line while goading the laggards.[39]

One aspect of the process which impeded the rate of plowing—and usually most breakers sought to open up one and a half to two acres per day—was the constant need to resharpen the plowshare and coulter wheel. These two parts were removable but had to be sharpened by a blacksmith. Out on the prairie and far removed from settlements, sharpening time meant an extended break unless an extra plowshare was brought along. If not, long treks had to be made. An early Michigan sodbuster at Ann Arbor worked westward to Calhoun County during the 1830's. Whenever the plowshare was removed from the plow, it was carried in a bag slung over the back of a horse, and on one occasion carried seventy miles back to Ann Arbor for sharpening.[40] Similarly, instances occurred in Wisconsin during the 1830's when men rode forty miles from Elkhorn to Racine, and it was not unusual to travel ten or fifteen miles on foot with a plowshare on one's back.[41]

The normal breaking operation required the labor of two men, although the prairie breaker could handle the task alone. An early source on Michigan sodbusters mentioned one factor which eliminated the need for an additional hand or boy. The turf on the open prairies and plains was tough and usually heavily matted with thick, deep roots, making the breaking work more difficult, while the smaller prairies in Michigan—the "oak openings"—located in close proximity to timber groves, were of soft soil and less difficult to break. As a general rule, heavier timber meant softer turf.[42]

From a point of convenience and sometimes necessity the average breaker had the assistance of a hand, although some operators eliminated this need by going into partnership with another man with whom they could share expenses as well as labor. Commencement in the sodbusting business required money for equipment: the plow,

39. *Michigan Pioneer Collections*, V, p. 300.
40. *Ibid.*, p. 256.
41. Charles M. Baker, "Pioneer History of Walworth County," *Report and Collections of the State Historical Society of Wisconsin*, VI (1872), 469. Near Jacksonville in central Illinois, William Sewall recorded in his diary that he and his son broke sod during June 3–11, 1835. As an indication of the frequency of plowshare sharpenings, two visits were made to the blacksmith in one week. *Diary of William Sewall, 1797–1846* (Lincoln, Ill., 1930), p. 164. Hereafter cited as Sewall, *Diary.*
42. *Michigan Pioneer Collections*, V, p. 299.

additional yokes of oxen, and a wagon if possible.[43] John Darius Scofield, who teamstered on the Minnesota frontier during the 1850's, began his initial enterprise with a purchase of one-half interest in two
yoke of oxen, and for the first year he and his partner contracted to
break land around the St. Paul area.[44] Others used a partnership in
the beginning solely to get a start and then went off on their own.
William L. Fearer formed a partnership with a friend, setting up a
yoke of breaking oxen. Eventually they acquired five yoke and the
necessary plows, breaking about three acres per day and hiring an
extra hand. They charged a basic rate of two dollars per acre, plus
board for themselves, their hired hands, and teams. At harvest time
they worked with their teams in the field or hired the animals out to
farmers. After one year of the partnership Fearer was able to operate
independently.[45]

A source of extra labor for the breaker was a teenage boy. Because
the work was of short duration, it was difficult to attract farm and
harvest hands who earned better wages, especially during the key
haying and harvesting weeks. As a result farm boys were tapped on
frequent occasions. The youth's duties varied, and he was required to
be handy at a little of everything on the job. Breakers sought out boys
who had a knack or feeling for handling teams, as well as being able
to drive a wagon.[46] The professional sodbuster could use his youthful
assistant to ride or drive to a nearby town or settlement for blacksmith repairs on a plowshare or for additional supplies.[47]

43. Information on equipment prices is rather vague, depending on the
type of plow and period of time. The Jethro Wood model with interchangeable
parts might cost as little as seven or eight dollars; however, the heavier prairie
plow usually ranged from twelve to twenty dollars. Solon J. Buck, "Pioneer
Letters of Gershom Flagg," *Transactions of the Illinois Historical Society for the
Year 1910* (Springfield, 1910), 145; R. C. Buley, *The Old Northwest: Pioneer
Period, 1815–1840* (Indianapolis, 1950), I, pp. 170–71; Danhof, *Change in Agriculture*, p. 97. It seems wise to rely on William Oliver's estimate in the 1840's
of a wagon, plow, and gear for oxen totaling $100. *Eight Months in Illinois*,
p. 136.
44. "The Biography of John Darius Scofield, By Himself."
45. Bateman and Selby, eds., *Historical Encyclopedia of Illinois and History
of Ogle County*, III, pp. 892–93.
46. For examples, see Bateman and Selby, eds., *Historical Encyclopedia of
Illinois and History of McDonough County* (Chicago, 1907), p. 887; *Biographical Record of Logan County, Illinois*, pp. 444–47.
47. An Illinois sodbuster in the 1830's employed his teenage sons to drive the
wagon teams from one site to the next, which was also the case with many
youthful assistants working with sodbreakers. E. W. Hicks, *History of Kendall
County, Illinois* (Aurora, 1877), pp. 62–63.

One task, particularly distasteful, was searching for the oxen in the dew-laden early morning hours. Teams were generally turned loose for the night to feed, and frequently they slipped into bushes and brush to hide. The boy had to be up at the crack of dawn, setting off into the prairie grass to find the teams: "He was wet to the waist with the cold night dew, and the saw-edged wire grass cut his feet painfully, but the cattle must be in and yoked before breakfast at sunrise." [48]

Aside from these secondary duties and errands, the bulk of the day's operation found the boy acting as a driver for the oxen; in most instances this was the primary task, though much depended on the wishes of the breaker and his operational techniques. The driver-boy on a prairie-breaking rig generally walked barefoot alongside the teams, carrying a handmade whip which was an essential piece of equipment as well as a weapon of sorts. Walking near the center of the oxen teams, he could effectively direct and drive them on with a flick of the whip. Plowing work for a barefoot boy inculcated a sense of awareness for what lay at his feet. Small rattlesnakes were prevalent in plowing operations, especially in unbroken prairie grass. As the plow advanced, narrowing the remaining unplowed strips, reptiles and other wildlife glided and scurried across the newly overturned sod. With an expert crack of a well-aimed whip, snakes and small gophers were rapidly dispatched by the boy as he walked alongside the oxen. [49]

Some information is available on the circumstances of employment and wages of these farm boys who worked with sodbusters. Economic necessity was a major factor in most cases. A fairly representative description of conditions and wages in the 1820's was provided by Daniel Brush, who hired out at age twelve to an Illinois sodbuster:

48. Bateman and Selby, eds., *Historical Encyclopedia of Illinois and History of Kane County*, p. 647; see also *History of McDonough County, Illinois*, p. 1045. A Wisconsin prairie breaker complained about the rounding up of oxen in the morning, often having to walk long distances before breakfast to find them. His letter indicated that if he were on horseback, the oxen could be found more easily and rapidly. Luke Cheseboro to Cyrus Williams (Janesville, Wis., April 10, 1846), Wisconsin Territorial Letter Collection.

49. Bateman and Selby, eds., *Historical Encyclopedia of Illinois and History of Kane County*, p. 646. The presence of snakes in the prairie grass was annoying to settlers; equally unpleasant were flies that bred in the low, marshy places known as sloughs. The attack of bilious fevers was also a common complaint of prairie pioneers. *Alton Telegraph and Democratic Review*, June 22, 1849; Buck, "Pioneer Letters of Gershom Flagg," 158; Oliver, *Eight Months in Illinois*, pp. 99–100; William Blane, *An Excursion through the United States and Canada during the Years 1822–23* (London, 1824), p. 185.

"... I engaged with a man named Crossin, who owned some land near my home, to drive team for him to break prairie. The team consisted of three yokes of oxen attached to a large plow for turning over the sod. I was to have twenty-five cents per day and board at home. I worked twelve days and received three dollars therefor in silver, quite a pile as it appeared to me, being my first cash earnings."[50] Youth posed no barrier in prairie-breaking employment, and many were hardly twelve years old when they hired out. As a general rule, four to ten dollars a month was about what a boy received, while day rates ranged between twenty-five and fifty cents.[51]

Given the amount of prairie land and its rapid settlement, sodbusting was an important line of work, but the demand sometimes exceeded the available number of men and teams. How many entered and left this occupation is unknown, but the need for their services was well publicized. For example, the *Chicago Daily Democrat* in July, 1849, appealed to men with teams to contact the newspaper office, for a number of Chicagoans owned prairie tracts adjacent to the city and wanted them plowed.[52] Subsequent notices and requests appeared, regardless of the season: "To Teamsters" read an advertisement in December, 1851, calling for men with teams who could plow, haul, and ditch, large or small jobs with ready pay.[53]

Prairie breaking was both a local and regional employment, yet it is difficult to determine precisely how men picked up breaking jobs or how individual farmers in need of such services contacted the breakers. Word of mouth was certainly one method of advertisement, especially on the local level, where sodbusters confined their work to the immediate neighborhood and followed breaking only as the land in the area required working.[54] This type of work was often done by

50. Daniel Harmon Brush, *Growing Up with Southern Illinois 1820 to 1861* (Chicago, 1944), p. 41.

51. For examples, see *Portrait and Biographical Album of Rock Island County, Illinois* (Chicago, 1885), pp. 634–37; Bateman and Selby, eds., *Historical Encyclopedia of Illinois and History of Grundy County* (Chicago, 1914), II, p. 813; *Portrait and Biographical Album of Fulton County, Illinois* (Chicago, 1890), p. 848; *Portrait and Biographical Record of Winnebago and Boone Counties, Illinois* (Chicago, 1892), p. 1023.

52. *Chicago Daily Democrat*, July 21, 1849.

53. *Ibid.*, December 1, 1851.

54. An Illinois pioneer woman in the 1830's recalled their need to have a field plowed: "Our inability to raise a team and sow our wheat, was a source of very great anxiety. The hoeing system had answered so indifferently that we felt determined, if possible to have it ploughed. We knew a Mr. Knowles who ploughed for hire; his house was about two miles from ours." Rebecca Burland, *A True Picture of Emigration*, as cited in David Greenberg, ed., *Land That Our Fathers Plowed* (Norman, 1969), p. 80.

an early settler who had been established longer than others and who had more time for such employment. One early Illinois sodbuster whose letters constitute much information on the state's social and economic conditions during the 1820's revealed his preference for breaking work:

> I now own 270 acres of land which I have paid for. On one quarter section I have two log houses near each other and 65 acres well fenced in three fields 26 acres of which is under good cultivation as a plough field and the remainder occupied as a pasture it being in the Prairie. I have three yoke of good oxen and a good plough. I have ploughed considerable for people lately and have now contracted to brake [sic] up 90 acres more of New Prairie next spring. I get about $4 an acre for ploughing. I have rented my place this year for my board and live with the family who rent it. . . .[55]

The availability of breaking work, along with other agricultural employment, surprised one early pioneer family on the prairies near Galesburg in western Illinois. The Farnham family came to Illinois in 1837 with apparently little money, and Mr. Farnham took whatever employment he could get. His wife's diary in the summer of 1837 revealed the diversity of work he performed, including prairie breaking and teamstering: "This morning Eli started off with one of our neighbors, Mr. Avery, to Oquawka (Yellow Banks), 30 miles, for a load of salt for our merchant. Expect him here tomorrow, Eli does most anything that comes to hand, sometimes he breaks prairie, sometimes harvests grain or mows, or digs stone, or digs wells or cellars. He stands to work out better than we expected."[56]

For most newly arriving settlers who required local help in set-up and plowing, the services of a sodbuster were rendered in a competent and honest manner. However, unsuspecting pioneers occasionally encountered a prairie breaker who took unwarranted advantage of the situation. In the early spring of 1855 a pioneer came out to the prairie frontier of Sauk County in central Wisconsin with admittedly no skills or knowledge of farm-making. Fortunately a house-

---

55. Buck, "Pioneer Letters of Gershom Flagg," 171. Flagg had also sodbusted during the previous year (1820), for which he hired a hand to help break one hundred acres; see p. 167 of his letters. For additional examples of men who owned land but sodbusted for others, see *History of Green County, Wisconsin*, pp. 700–701; Hicks, *History of Kendall County, Illinois*, pp. 50, 116. An early Illinois newspaper mentioned that sodbusting was an important occupation at the local level, and the breaker furnished all the equipment needed for the job. *Peoria Register and North-Western Gazetteer*, April 29, 1842.

56. Earnest Elmo Calkins, ed., *Log City Days* (Galesburg, Ill., 1937), p. 45.

raising bee provided him with temporary housing, but after that everything began to cost money. His comments regarding a neighbor who over-charged for the first plowing and planting at the farm site tend to tarnish the traditional image of frontier honesty.[57]

Sodbusting did not always provide a solid basis of economic support, since it was only a seasonal occupation. It is difficult to believe that even a few men could make this a permanent employment without something else to fall back upon. This problem is revealed in the career of an Illinois sodbuster in the 1850's. In 1847 James Short started working out at age eighteen on farms in Sangamon County. He earned six to nine dollars per month, supplementing his income with rail splitting at forty cents per hundred and wood chopping at forty cents per cord. By 1850 Short had amassed sufficient money to buy and rig out two teams of oxen; at the same time he bought plows and began sodbusting. His field of operation extended over the counties of Sangamon, Cass, and Morgan. Certain other information can be extracted from this case: Short rented land for two of the five years in which he engaged in breaking, lending proof to the contention that breakers had to have alternate forms of employment upon which to rely. He married in 1854, which as much as any factor brought a halt to his roaming breaking operations; in the next year he purchased his own tract of land and settled down.[58] This case also demonstrates a common route up the agricultural ladder of success for aspiring farmers: starting out as a mere farm hand, advancing upwards with a team used in sodbusting, and finally amassing the necessary money to buy a farm. As economic self-reliance and farm ownership were attained, many of these individuals happily chose to end their single status and marry.

In a different combination which involved both teamstering and prairie breaking, an Ohio youth raised during the 1840's acquired expertise as a farm hand in handling draft animals for teamstering and plowing applications. At age twenty-three, with apparently no connections to hold him back, he emigrated westward to Iowa via river steamboat, working at prairie breaking and fence building. He made a reasonable success in this work; however, in 1857, after two years, he came back across the Mississippi River and east to Clay County,

57. Reminiscences of Philip Creek in pamphlet, "Eighth Annual Re-Union of the Old Settlers' Association of Sauk County, at North Freedom, June 18 and 19, 1879," 2–3, in William H. Canfield, *Outline Sketches of Sauk County* (Baraboo, 1861) [1890].

58. *History of Greene and Jersey Counties, Illinois* (Springfield, Ill., 1885), p. 1129.

Indiana. In possession of his own prairie-breaking team, he worked out by the month and teamstered in Indiana.[59]

From this individual account come several conclusions. First, prairie breaking was an occupation suited to young, unmarried men with few ties or responsibilities. Second, travel in pursuit of work posed no problem for a young man willing to go long distances. A third point emphasizes the duration of employment in this business—for the above individuals it amounted to several years, a fairly common and not unreasonable length of time, although other men followed the business for greater periods. Finally, it was a stepping-stone for making money in order to settle down on a farm, although many continued in the teamstering line, using skills and the same kind of animals employed in sodbusting.[60]

Sodbusting on the prairies was as much a process of farm-making as set-up or clearing labor in timbered areas. In sections of Wisconsin, Illinois, Michigan, and Indiana, the set-up hand also performed duties which included prairie breaking; in fact, it is difficult in many instances to separate set-up labor, normally associated with timbered areas, from prairie breaking. Men often hired themselves out to perform these double combinations, and some were hired back east and elsewhere to accompany their employers to the new farm sites. By the 1830's, as settlement pushed into the upper Midwest, prairie land topography often predominated; yet sufficient diversity existed in which forest and timber tracts interlaced these regions.

Both clearing of timberland and breaking sod by a hired hand were not uncommon on midwestern farm sites. Cass County in southwestern Michigan was a relatively remote prairie land in 1826, and Ussiel Putnam wisely hired a hand in advance to help establish his farm. In mid-March the young hired man from Ohio arrived at the farm site. In early April they started making rails, and within one month forty acres were fenced, indicating that timber abounded in the area. At the same time a breaking plow was set in motion, with the task completed by mid-May, when furrow corn was dropped. With the help of this hand, who worked at set-up and assisted with prairie-breaking, a forty-acre farm was established within a three-month

59. William Travis, A History of Clay County, Indiana (New York and Chicago, 1909), II, pp. 357–58.

60. For examples, see Bateman and Selby, eds., Historical Encyclopedia of Illinois Including Genealogy, Family Records and Biography of McHenry County Citizens (Chicago, 1903), II, pp. 646–47; History of Macoupin County, Illinois (Philadelphia, 1879), 193–94.

period.[61] Another example was Tobias Byer, who worked out by the month at clearing and breaking land in western Michigan. Work along these occupational lines from 1835 to 1850 was obtained, though apparently he was hardly a plodding common laborer at agricultural jobs; rather, his knowledge of the area enabled him to employ himself at land searching and location of new farm sites for recently arrived settlers.[62]

Large land developers took special interest in prairie-breaking operations, even to the extent of bringing along an outside labor force. As a result of an exploration trip by Samuel Hitt and Nathaniel Swingley of Maryland in the summer of 1836, a tract of prairie land was acquired at Ogle County in western Illinois. Back in Maryland they engaged a number of men to accompany them to the new settlement, agreeing to pay a dollar per day for work rendered in both set-up and prairie breaking jobs, as well as building houses, making fences, splitting rails, and harvesting crops. Eleven men constituted the group, and some brought their wives. They came via the Ohio and Mississippi Rivers to the Midwest and then up the Illinois River to Peru, where the remainder of the trip was made in wagons.[63] This arrangement suggests a variation to the customary practice of hiring professional or semi-professional breakers who were already in the area. Inexperienced men could and did break land, and no doubt hundreds of small scale farmers who trekked west to Illinois, Michigan, and Wisconsin similarly broke their own prairie sod, despite the inefficiency and lack of proper equipment connected with such an undertaking. The huge expanse of the prairie region and occasional lack of professional sodbusters simply forced many new farmers to do their own breaking.

Data for prairie-breaking costs are readily available in a variety of primary sources. The rate averaged about $1.50 to $3 per acre, although there were instances where as much as $5 per acre was

61. Howard S. Rogers, *History of Cass County, from 1825 to 1875* (Cassopolis, Mich., 1875), p. 292.

62. *History of Berrien and Van Buren Counties, Michigan* (Philadelphia, 1880), p. 477. For other examples of men who worked at sodbusting and set-up, see *Biographical Record of Henry County, Illinois* (Chicago, 1901), pp. 98–99; *History of Green County, Wisconsin*, p. 825; Bateman and Selby, eds., *Illinois Historical. Crawford County Biographical* (Chicago, 1909), p. 719; John S. Schenck, *History of Ionia and Montcalm Counties, Michigan* (Philadelphia, 1881), p. 266.

63. H. G. Kable, *Mount Morris: Past and Present. Revised Edition* (Mt. Morris, Ill., 1938), pp. 15–18.

charged.[64] Breaking of sod could in fact be rather expensive in some areas. John Blois's popular *Gazetteer of Michigan* (1838) advised newcomers to the state that they had the choice of timbered oak land or prairie, and unless a man had sufficient money, he was advised to settle in timbered areas.[65] A land agent and speculator gave his opinion to a client in 1837 regarding the cost factor of Illinois prairie land near Peoria: "Were I in yr place I would not cultivate my Ill. lands— you could not get a man [to] make fence, break the ground &c without paying a high price—and it would not be an object for you to cultivate the land; as it can be sold as it is."[66] Another factor was the remoteness of an area: the charge for breaking in older, established settlements ranged from $1.50 to $2 per acre, while in newer and more isolated sections it was as much as $5 per acre.[67]

The breaker was not always paid in cash. The determining factor was whether a breaker lived in the area and could accept other reasonable forms of payment. In the 1830's an Illinois pioneer hired a sodbuster to break eight acres of prairie for him, paying him in return with carpenter work.[68] During this same decade in Macon County, Hartwell Robinson wrote back east that a wagon was sold for the sum of forty-five dollars, with payment rendered in the form of breaking fifteen acres of sod and splitting rails.[69] At Du Page County, Amos Miner, one of the first settlers in the area in 1836, hired his prairie sod to be broken during the following year. Because he had no money, he worked out an arrangement based on a rather steep rate of $5 per acre, by which he split 2,500 rails and was under obligation to assist in driving the team.[70]

Some breakers could not be so particular about the remuneration and accepted any reasonable substitute. An example was fifteen-year-old John Wolven, who came west in 1845 to Racine County, Wisconsin, with his widowed mother. He worked on farms during the 1840's in summer seasons while finishing school in winters. Saving

64. Danhof, "Farm-Making Costs and the 'Safety Valve': 1850–1860," 317–59; Gates, *Farmer's Age*, p. 181.

65. John T. Blois, *Gazetteer of the State of Michigan* (Detroit, 1838), pp. 27–28.

66. Aaron Russell to John Wheelwright (Peoria, Ill., April 11, 1837).

67. William J. A. Bradford, *Notes on the Northwest, or Valley of the Upper Mississippi* (New York, 1846), pp. 146–47.

68. E. Duis, *The Good Old Times in McLean County, Illinois* (Bloomington, 1874), p. 800.

69. Mabel E. Richmond, comp., *Centennial History of Decatur and Macon County* (Decatur, 1930), p. 49n.

70. *The Past and Present of Kane County, Illinois* (Chicago, 1878), pp. 422–24.

his money for the purchase of oxen, he entered into a partnership in 1850 with another man in the prairie-breaking line. Apparently this work was sufficiently rewarding to enable him to make a land purchase the following year while he continued to hire out at sodbusting. His operations ranged over an extensive territory, covering southern Wisconsin and northern Illinois; in the latter state he went as far west as Freeport, where in one instance he accepted payment in the form of a store order; on another occasion he agreed to take an old cow. Between 1850 and 1855 he followed this occupation but also switched over to work as a farm hand on a mechanical reaper, pitching grain at $1.50 per day.[71]

Larger landowners sometimes recorded in their ledgers the agreement or contract made with men who performed breaking jobs. Here, evidence indicates that cash was paid for large jobs and that breakers themselves were probably professional or semi-professional. Excellent examples of breaking contracts are found in the Nathan Pierce Accounts of Michigan and the Matthew T. Scott Papers of Illinois, revealing the format and style of pre–Civil War contracts for this form of specialized agricultural labor. Nathan Pierce negotiated an agreement in 1851 with Chester Lewis to plow at the rate of one dollar per acre: "Thursday May the 1st 1851 Chester Lewis of Lima Washtenaw County came this day and commenced Ploughing for me with Plow[,] three horses and harness and is to plough until the first of July if he wishes to plough so long at one dollar per acre and I am to board him and keep his team and he is to plough and do his work well and I am to pay him cash one dollar per acres for all acres that he Ploughs." During July, August, and September Lewis performed other labor on the farm, including hoeing, raking, and harvesting. An important point here is the evidence that teamsters and breakers engaged in seasonal farm labor, especially in the peak harvest time.[72]

Matthew T. Scott, a large Illinois landholder and tenant landlord,

71. *Portrait and Biographical Record of Winnebago and Boone Counties, Illinois*, pp. 271–72. This arrangement was fairly common; for example, a Minnesota pioneer in 1855 sold a cow and calf to a man who broke prairie in return for them. Irvin Rollin Notes and Memorandum, III, p. 42, entry of September 14, 1855.

72. Nathan Pierce Accountbook, 1848–60, p. 67, entry of May 1, 1851; p. 80, entries during July–September, 1851. In an earlier contract with a man for plowing, Pierce agreed to board and feed the man and his team, in addition to paying for any damage done to the points of the plow which might wear out during the work. See p. 5, contract with Franklin Farnum, May–June, 1849. Farnum completed the job on June 13 and was paid $15 at that time; the remaining $14.25 of the bill came on October 4, 1849. In effect, Pierce spread the payments over a period of several months.

operated farms in Piatt and McLean Counties, located 140 miles
south of Chicago in the central part of the state. In 1852 Scott began
to develop his tracts for future tenant farmers, and his records reveal
the type of contract which landowners and breakers were accustomed
to negotiate. Similar to the clause in the Pierce contract in Michigan,
the breakers hired by Scott were allowed "to break all they can" by
a specified date. This contract is additionally valuable, for it includes
information about subsidiary labor in terms of what was to be done
with the land when broken and who was to supply the seed and labor
for planting on the overturned sod. The agreement was made well in
advance of the actual time of breaking. Scott negotiated it on October
4, 1852, but its execution was set for the following year:

> Today I entered into agreement with a couple of Burnes for the break-
> ing of two hundred acres of land in corn planting time. I must have
> boys to drop for them. They have privilege to break all they can by
> 15th June after that with 3 teams till 10th July. I must furnish seed-
> corn. am to pay them 1st of March through hands of Wm. H. Pyatt of
> Monticello two hundred dollars in order to help them to team. Mr.
> Pyatt is security for the work to amt of 200$ I agree to pay their board
> & what their work comes to by the 15th June, 200$ [$2.00] per acre.

Basically a cautious employer, Scott had his farm hands sign his account or memorandum books as a receipt for payment. On May 30,
1855, for example, he wrote into his notebook: "Received of M. T.
Scott on account of breaking prairie twenty-five dollars" which was
signed by the man who performed the work.[73]

In settled areas where the owner of the land was present, the
breaker considered board for himself and facilities for his teams as
part of the bill. For example, in east central Illinois during the 1830's,
a Norwegian informed his countrymen of the costs and conditions of
prairie breaking at Beaver Creek settlement, seventy miles south
Chicago: "At Beaver Creek we now can get men to break prairie for
us at two dollars an acre, provided that we furnish board."[74] A school
teacher in Knox County, Illinois, commented in similar effect: "We
have had two Prairie teams here breaking this spring and we have
had to pay two dollars and a half per acre and board the men while
they were breaking."[75] In 1844 a Wisconsin pioneer at Racine County

73. Matthew T. Scott Notebook, 1852–53, p. 92, entry of October 4, 1852;
Notebook and 3 Papers from Pocket 1855–56, p. 14, entry of May 30, 1855.
74. Theodore C. Blegen, "Ole Rynning's True Account of America," *Minnesota History*, II (1917), 254–55.
75. Paul Angle, "Story of an Ordinary Man," *Illinois Historical Journal*,
XXXIII (1940), 220.

assigned a cash value of fifty cents for boarding the sodbusters: Edwin Bottomly mentioned his plans to have ten acres of land broken at $3.50 per acre, although $3 was the actual labor rate per acre while 50 cents covered the board for the breaker and feed for his teams.[76] Another Wisconsin farmer similarly complained: "The charge is $2.00 per acre and we keep the men and cattle night and day the while. I felt I could not afford that price. . . ." As a result he had a plow built during the winter and plowed the ground himself the following spring.[77]

Finally, while many breakers expected to be boarded and some-times lodged on the job site, they also roamed over unpopulated areas. There were not always houses or cabins on the virgin prairie, especially when settlers had not yet moved onto the farm sites. In the 1830's two brothers operated in LaPorte County, Indiana. Jobs came from all directions, and their movement about the land was described as being like "Abraham of Old"; they lived in tents and followed the business wherever prairie was to be broken.[78]

A wagon was essential as a "home-on-wheels," enabling the breaker to haul the plow, extra plow share, and other gear. The case of a northern Illinois sodbuster in the 1840's shows the value of this piece of equipment. Population was sparse in those areas where Oliver Dix obtained contracts. Usually, since the owner of the site had not yet settled on the land, provisions of food had to be packed along, and nights were spent sleeping under the wagon or plow beam. The stark reality of such lonely employment took on an added dimension when wolves made their appearance, whereupon Dix wisely transferred his sleeping gear inside to the bottom of the wagon bed. As a result of his far-ranging jobs he became attracted to the fertile land and spotted a tract to his liking that he subsequently purchased.[79]

Similar to the surveyor who penetrated new lands, the prairie breaker filled a distinct niche in the vanguard of the frontier in much

76. An English Settler in Pioneer Wisconsin: The Letters of Edwin Bottomley 1842–1850, in Collections, Publications of the State Historical Society of Wisconsin, XXV (Madison, 1918), p. 69. Hereafter cited as Bottomley, Letters 1842–50.

77. Josie Greening Croft, "A Mazomanie Pioneer," Wisconsin History, XXVI (1942), 213.

78. Jasper Packard, History of LaPorte County, Indiana (LaPorte, 1876), p. 101. An English traveler in the Illinois prairies observed a farmer living in a tent when he was cutting open the grass sod. William Ferguson, America by River and Rail (London, 1856), p. 374.

79. Biographical and Genealogical Record of La Salle and Grundy Counties, Illinois (Chicago, 1900), II, pp. 445–47.

the same manner as the set-up hand in the timbered regions. These semi-professional laborers were especially needed in newly settled prairie regions, and they obtained employment so long as virgin grassland remained unbroken. After initial settlement and subsequent cultivation of these areas, many sodbusters turned to other employment or devoted full-time attention to their own farms. Others continued in the prairie-breaking line, although they had to roam greater distances to obtain contracts. These men were also expert teamsters and engaged in frontier hauling jobs for the lack of other employment. By teamstering and sodbusting they gradually worked their way up toward the goal of farm ownership.

Teamstering

His team went in out of sight, but
he kept whipping and hallooing at
the hole, and they eventually came
out all right on the other side.[1]

TEAMSTERING was a vital service occupation in the
1815–60 period, when railroads had not yet achieved predominance
in the field of transportation and movement of goods. The most
prominent teamsters were the drivers of large freight wagons on the
major east-west roads and turnpikes that linked the Atlantic ports to
the inland commercial cities.[2] There existed, however, a lesser-known
category of teamsters who worked primarily in rural areas on a seasonal basis. These "part-timers" of the business were mainly farmers
and common laborers who secured odd-job hauling during the slack
seasons or on a temporary basis. This short-haul teamstering was important because of its relationship to seasonal labor in the countryside.
Many farm hands got their start by working their way up through
part-time teamstering and related employments.

The first step for most settlers as well as farm hands, prior to renting or purchasing a farm, was the acquisition of a team and (if possible) a wagon; these were essential for any successful farming
operation. Ownership of a wagon provided greater flexibility in farming and job situations, and the individual possessing both team and
wagon enjoyed an enviable status in the community. The desirability
—indeed, the necessity—of owning a team was made clear in the let-

1. *History of Jackson County, Michigan* (Chicago, 1881), p. 195. These
lines describe the old Washtenaw Trail between Ann Arbor and Jackson in
territorial Michigan, where travel by wagon through marsh-like lowlands, called
swales, created problems for teamsters. Westward wagon routes through Michigan
were notorious, and John Plumbe's early midwestern guidebook in 1839 advised
travelers to beware of them in spring. *Sketches of Iowa and Wisconsin*, (Iowa
City, 1948), pp. 40–41.
2. Caroline E. MacGill, *History of Transportation in the United States before
1860* (New York, 1948), p. 127.

ters of Horatio Houlton, who worked at various employments, including wood chopping, on the Minnesota frontier in the 1850's. His letters home expressed hope of obtaining his own farm within a year or two, but this depended upon his acquiring a team; otherwise, he concluded, farming was impossible.[3] Similarly, the loss of work animals represented a crisis of the first order for the settler who counted on getting his farm going and a crop in. In 1837 an Indiana farmer summed up his dilemma to a sister back in Ohio, lamenting the loss of his horse prior to planting time. Owing to the scarcity and high price of animals, he was forced to rent out his land and teach school for a while.[4]

To obtain their own team and possibly a wagon, most men were impelled to hire out, a fact which emphasized the relationship between teamstering and farm labor. Since wages were low and prices for animals high, the process obviously required frugality over a period of time—usually from at least one to three years, depending on individual circumstances. The correspondence of George Wilkie, a carpenter and set-up man in Minnesota, reveals the considerable amount of labor needed in order to acquire a team with which to commence farming.[5] Others like Daniel Knisely, raised as a bound-out boy in Ohio in the 1840's, made this the first order of business. Knisely hired out at age twenty for $10.50 per month; these wages made possible the purchase of a yoke of oxen, a nice complement to the 50 acres of woodland he received in Indiana as part of his bound-out contractual agreement.[6] Irish-born John Leemond earned twelve dollars a month as a farm hand and fifty cents a day at husking corn during winter in Illinois. Between 1851 and 1857 he saved enough to buy a team and rent land, besides purchasing a tract of unimproved land in Vermilion County.[7] A twenty-two-year-old Ohio youth hired

3. Horatio Houlton to William Houlton (Monticello, Minn., March 27, 1855). A subsequent letter of June 1, 1855, indicated that he could easily get 160 acres of good prairie land but that he still had no horses, while a letter of October 7, 1855, mentioned that wages were high owing to the fact that people expected to make money. Horatio Houlton Papers.

4. H. W. Bereman to Sally Ann Bereman (Madison County, Ind., April 8, 1837).

5. George M. Wilkie to Mrs. Wilkie (Prairie du Chien, April 4, 1858). His accountbook reveals that during the previous year he went up to Rice County, Minnesota, to erect a cabin on a man's claim; entry of February 5, 1857. George M. Wilkie Papers.

6. *Valley of the Upper Maumee River with Historical Account of Allen County and the City of Fort Wayne, Indiana*, I, p. 364.

7. *Portrait and Biographical Album of Vermilion County, Illinois* (Chicago, 1889), p. 298.

out at ten dollars a month and also chopped wood at thirty-seven and a half cents per day. After one year he invested his wages in a team, rented a farm, and took a bride for himself.[8]

Good horses cost up to $50 each prior to 1830 and increased to $100 by the 1850's, while oxen averaged $50 to $100 per yoke. Essential to any team was a wagon. In 1819 a wagon in southern Illinois cost $35 to $40;[9] however, special circumstances sometimes permitted the acquisition of a team and wagon at below actual value. From Elnathan Kemper, a Cincinnati farmer who employed a number of hands for clearing land, chopping wood, and teamstering, William Bell in 1822 received a wagon and team of horses as compensation for $33 owed him for back wages by Kemper.[10]

In the 1830's a settler on the Illinois prairies sold a wagon for $45, accepting prairie breaking and rail splitting in lieu of cash.[11] During the following decade a Wisconsin pioneer stated that a comfortable two-span wagon cost $45 to $50—a figure comparable to eastern prices, according to Josiah Marshall's *Farmer's and Emigrant's Handbook*.[12] Greater demand for wagons was reflected with a general price increase by the 1850's. In 1851 at Rockford, Illinois, a dealer advertised "first rate" wagons with wooden axles for $65 or iron-axled ones from $80 to $100.[13] A firm at Pekin, Illinois, was reportedly turning them out at the rate of one per day, selling at from $90 to $130 in 1855.[14] In general, teams and draying conveyances were expensive, and after buying land many settlers lacked sufficient funds to acquire them.

8. Charles Blanchard, ed., *Counties of Howard and Tipton, Indiana* (Chicago, 1883), biography section, p. 484. For other examples, see *Biographical Record of Ogle County, Illinois*, p. 431; Thomas Gregg, *History of Hancock County, Illinois* (Chicago, 1880), p. 889.

9. Warden, *Statistical, Political, and Historical Account of the United States of North America*, III, p. 62; see also Henry Bradshaw Fearon, *Sketches of America* (London, 1819), pp. 336–37.

10. Elnathan Kemper Daybook, entry of September 19, 1822. The previous year Kemper had been able to pay Bell in cash (silver); see entry of November 5, 1821. Teams and wagons were used for commerce in the city and for hauling wood from surrounding farms, according to Daniel Drake, *Natural and Statistical View, or Picture of Cincinnati and the Miami Country* (Cincinnati, 1815), p. 140.

11. Richmond, comp., *Centennial History of Decatur and Macon County*, p. 49n.

12. Carl de Haas, *Nordamerika. Wisconsin von Dr. Carl de Haas in Calumet*, I, p. 47; Marshall, *Farmer's and Emigrant's Handbook*, p. 16.

13. *Freeport Journal*, February 21, 1851.

14. Gerhard, *Illinois as It is*, p. 447. At Indianapolis, an Englishman had a wagon constructed for $65, although $9 extra was charged for installing a bed in it. The wagon harness cost $20, and a horse was purchased for $100. J. Richard Beste, *The Wabash* (London, 1855), I, pp. 271, 275–77.

Indeed, possession of a team might be considered more valuable than land. In 1836 a German immigrant located near Ann Arbor, Michigan, where he worked two years as a farm hand. Two years later he and his wife headed west to Indiana with his own team, which he was reluctant to sell in order to buy land; hence he decided to go farther west into Illinois, finding employment near Joliet on the Illinois and Michigan Canal project. In 1841 he returned to buy eighty acres in Indiana.[15]

Settlers moving westward employed young men to assist with the wagons on the journey. Board, basic expenses, and transportation were usually the main compensation, and afforded a comparatively cheap method for getting out west. At age twenty-one Benjamin Carpenter was hired to drive a wagon for a man emigrating to the Western Reserve of Ohio in 1820. Upon arrival at the destination, the young teamster secured employment as a farm hand.[16] But there were disadvantages to this mode of travel for young wanderers. Headed for Illinois in 1838, a twenty-year-old hired himself to two families en route to Jackson, Michigan, and drove one of the teams. Along the way he contracted some debts and stopped briefly to work as a farm hand for several months in Michigan, but his pay proved to be in the form of worthless wildcat bank notes for which the state was notorious during this period.[17]

For these settlers arriving in the West without teams and wagons, the final segment of the journey was made with local or short-haul teamsters. As a form of itinerant employment teamsters conveyed easterners and immigrants from rail heads, river towns, and lake ports like Toledo, Detroit, or Chicago out to new farm sites. The short-haul teamster offered four distinct services. First, he made it possible for many immigrants to complete their journey to new homes in the West. Second, as an occasional prairie breaker or sodbuster, he assisted them with the establishment of the new farm. Third, he might team the harvested produce from the first crop to a regional market or point of shipment on a canal, river, or lake. Finally, his

15. Goodspeed and Blanchard, eds., *Counties of Porter and Lake, Indiana*, p. 725.

16. *History of Geauga and Lake Counties, Ohio*, p. 252.

17. *Portrait and Biographical Album of Peoria County, Illinois*, pp. 966–67. For other examples, see Finley, *History of the Wyandott Mission, at Upper Sandusky, Ohio*, pp. 115–17; Richard Illenden Bonner, ed., *Memoirs of Lenawee County, Michigan* (Madison, 1909), I, pp. 221–26; *History of Stephenson County, Illinois* (Chicago, 1880), pp. 678–79; *Portrait and Biographical Album of Lenawee County, Mich.* (Chicago, 1888), p. 742.

wagon was seldom empty on the return haul, for if he was not conveying new settlers, he hauled the supplies that were always required by earlier inhabitants of the rural community who were unable to get into town.

Many teamsters were naturally interested in ultimately becoming farmers, and they used the opportunities provided by hauling trips to search out choice farm sites, not only for themselves but also for others. Originally from New York, William Lobdell came out to Michigan in the autumn of 1835 and stayed the winter. He owned a team and discovered that there was money to be made in conveying pioneer families to the Grand River area; on one of these hauling trips he located land in Genesee County for his own farm.[18] Not suprisingly, these men were knowledgeable regarding the best routes and locations of choice lands. Diodate Hubbard, an early settler at Oakland County, Michigan, conveyed many settlers to their farm sites while hauling goods and supplies between Detroit and other points during the 1820's and 1830's.[19] A similar individual was Alonzo Chapin, who farmed in Genesee County, sixty miles to the north of Detroit, and who engaged in teamstering over the various parts of the state, transporting goods and settlers as far west as Lake Michigan. Like Diodate Hubbard in Oakland County, Chapin built up a wide range of acquaintances and became familiar with the different sections of the state.[20] These men were clearly in a position to render valuable advice to settlers who had still not chosen a specific location upon their arrival at Detroit.

Movement of settlers involved the transporting of large numbers of people as well as their possessions. Harvey Lee Ross recalled that his father secured men to drive wagons and stock from southwestern Illinois to their new home in the central part of the state in the early 1820's.[21] Migration from the East and the Ohio Valley into northern

18. *History of Genesee County, Michigan,* p. 306.

19. *History of Oakland County, Michigan* (Philadelphia, 1877), p. 237. Settlers in search of farm sites hired men and teams at Detroit. Sometimes prospective land-seekers were disappointed and failed to find a desirable piece of property. William Brown, *America: A Four Years' Residence* (Leeds, 1849), p. 66.

20. *History of Genesee County, Michigan,* pp. 196–97. Teamsters did not necessarily follow any specific route but ranged in all directions. On occasion they might lose their sense of direction, especially in prairie grasslands, according to Caird, *Prairie Farming in America,* p. 66.

21. Harvey Lee Ross, *Early Pioneers and Pioneer Events of the State of Illinois* (Chicago, 1899), pp. 2, 26–27. The *Intelligencer* at Vandalia noted in autumn, 1825, that in a five-week period 250 wagons, with an average of five

Illinois and lower Wisconsin was strong during the 1830's and 1840's. An English traveler reported the National Road through Ohio and Indiana heavy with westward-bound immigrants whose wagons averaged twelve to fifteen miles per day, and along the roadside were log cabins with signs reading "House for Movers."[22] A Wisconsin guide pamphlet in 1838 noted, "Another mode is by land, in large wagons and 4 to 6 horse teams. A gentleman lately from Wisconsin, who travelled through the western states, stated that the roads were crowded with families, and wagons bound for Wisconsin, and emigrating in this manner."[23] The *Courier* at Springfield, Illinois, observed similarly in 1840 that the prairies were filled with moving people and the routes were clogged with "movers' wagons."[24]

By the late 1840's, however, a shift occurred in the population movement, and the influx of settlers and immigrants at the port of Chicago offset the previously dominant stream from the lower Midwest. Moreover, farmers in northern Illinois found it advantageous to convey prospective hands out to farms. Richard and Robert Harrison of Ringwood Prairie in McHenry County arranged for an English farm laborer and his family to come directly to Chicago, where they were met by Harrison's team and conveyed the fifty miles out to the farm. This Englishman worked out at farm labor during the next couple of years until he was able to purchase his own hundred acres.[25]

Others disembarked at Chicago's chief rival, the expanding port of Milwaukee. For some time wagon teams from Galena and southwestern Wisconsin had hauled lead across lower Wisconsin to Milwaukee, where it was shipped east; but by the 1840's lead was being phased out and replaced with agricultural production.[26] Improved

persons to each, passed through the town headed northwards; as cited in *Niles' Register*, XXIX (November 26, 1825), 208. On another occasion, the *Intelligencer* reported the passing of eighty wagons in a two-week period, as cited in the *Ohio State Journal and Columbus Gazette*, November 17, 1825.

22. J[ames] S[ilk] Buckingham, *The Eastern and Western States of America* (London, [1842]), II, pp. 291–93.

23. Henry I. Abel, *Geographical, Geological and Statistical Chart of Wisconsin & Iowa* (Philadelphia, 1838).

24. As cited in *Niles' Register*, LIX (December 5, 1840), 219–20. A young Wisconsin farm boy in 1846 at Dane County, forty miles north of the Illinois-Wisconsin state line, recalled men and teams passing through to points farther north bringing flour and supplies from Illinois. C. E. Jones, *Madison, Dane County and Surrounding Towns* (Madison, 1877), p. 478.

25. Bateman and Selby, eds., *Historical Encyclopedia of Illinois Including Genealogy, Family Records and Biography of McHenry County Citizens*, II, pp. 992–93. For a similar case, see *History of McLean County, Illinois*, pp. 1029–30.

26. Joseph Schafer, *Wisconsin Domesday Book: General Studies: Volume*

roads and the impending construction of railroads also signaled the approaching end of this form of transportation. The *Galena Gazette* in 1851 paid tribute to the teamsters whose ox-drawn wagons had long served as the sole connecting link to the outside world:

Their's is a wild, nomadic life, most of them being residents of middle and southern Illinois and Indiana, starting at the season when the first spring grass will support their teams, and reaching here in April and May, and not returning till the grass is so far destroyed by approach of winter as to render it impossible to keep their teams on the prairie —for these teams and teamsters generally do not put up, except by the road-side, turning their teams off to feed at night, while they build a fire, bake their bread, cook their bacon, wrap themselves up in their blankets, and sleep in their wagon or under a shady tree. Years ago, these teamsters made their business a most profitable one, for they sometimes obtained as high as $5 a ton, for bringing lead from Mineral Point—a distance of some 40 miles. . . . As the roads grow better by further increase of population and great communications between towns, and particularly on the completion of Railroads, these pioneers of transportation will disappear, but they will be long remembered by all old citizens of the Mineral Region, as an interesting and worthy class of hard working men. . . .[27]

Milwaukee's importance as a teamstering center for the immigrant traffic was apparent by the foreign-born themselves who engaged in this line of work. An Englishman, working several years in Wisconsin as a farm hand, bought a team and wagon and hauled immigrants and merchandise from Milwaukee to all parts of the state for several years until he settled down permanently at farming in 1852.[28] A fellow Englishman during the 1850's worked in Monroe County, hiring out at farm labor, mill work, and even carrying mail. Later he worked as a surveyor's assistant—an occupation which gave many men an ex-

---

III: The Wisconsin Lead Region (Madison, 1932), pp. 107–9. Farming was practical in this area, observed an astute land speculator in 1846: "You may perhaps think that as this is a good mining country it is a poor farming country. The contrary is true. Everything that can be raised in this latitude is raised here in abundance and with little labor." Larry Gara, "A Glimpse of the Galena Lead Region in 1846," *Illinois Historical Journal*, L (1957), 88. A good example was nearby Green County, where farmers at first shipped their surplus to the mines but later hauled it by teams and wagons to Lake Michigan. *History of Green County, Wisconsin*, pp. 1008–9, 1136.

27. *Galena Gazette*, as cited in *Freeport Journal*, July 11, 1851.

28. *History of Crawford and Richland Counties, Wisconsin* (Springfield, 1884), p. 1034; for additional reference to Englishmen arriving at Milwaukee who hired teamsters' wagons, see Sarah M. Maury, *An Englishwoman in America* (London, 1848), p. 196.

cellent knowledge of where choice lands were located—and, not surprisingly, he began hauling settlers out to new farm sites.[29] This form
of teamstering—conveying settlers to new farmsteads—was a good
source of employment but eventually tapered off when an area became established. Yet, other opportunities existed for itinerant teamsters within farming communities.

One alternative was hauling produce to markets, although it was
not always sufficiently remunerative. Prices fluctuated so much that
farmers often did not bother to ship grain to distant markets. The key
factor was the weight-size distribution. Bulk farm produce in un-
processed form was expensive to ship, especially when the market
prices were depressed. Many farmers simply could not ship their
agricultural commodities to market because it was unprofitable; consequently, near-subsistence farming served as the economic basis in
settlements remote from markets.[30]

Henry County in northwestern Illinois, for example, was settled
during 1830–50. Its agricultural production was near-subsistence oriented because the markets of Chicago and Galena were distant, while
Peoria in the central part of the state was at best a limited market.
Occasionally when good crops occurred, some wagon loads were
hauled over a distance of 150 miles to Chicago, although farmers debated whether or not such long-distance hauling was worth it.[31] The
geographical position of Carroll County, also in the western part of
the state, posed a similar dilemma for its farmers; they could take
their produce either to Savanna (on the Mississippi River) or to Chicago. In the 1840's the price differential of wheat for Chicago and
Savanna was considerable: Chicago paid ninety cents to one dollar
per bushel, but Savanna markets yielded only forty-five to fifty cents
per bushel.[32]

This price differential was not peculiar to Illinois; rather, it pre-

29. *Biographical History of La Crosse, Monroe and Juneau Counties, Wisconsin* (Chicago, 1892), p. 699.

30. For reference to transportation rates and general prices, see Taylor,
Transportation Revolution, pp. 132–34; Thomas S. Berry, *Western Prices before
1861: A Study of the Cincinnati Market* (Cambridge, 1943); John G. Clark,
The Grain Trade in the Old Northwest (Urbana, 1966); Henrietta M. Larson,
The Wheat Market and the Farmer in Minnesota, 1858–1900, Columbia Univer-
sity Studies in History, Economics and Public Law, CXXII (New York, 1926).

31. Henry L. Kiner, ed., *History of Henry County, Illinois* (Chicago, 1910),
I, p. 206.

32. *Portrait and Biographical Album of Jo Daviess and Carroll Counties,
Illinois* (Chicago, 1889), p. 850.

vailed widely and followed an approximate 50 percent break-off in price determination of the produce as far as the farmer was concerned. At Logan County, in north central Ohio, the price of wheat in the settlements was fifty cents a bushel—but if hauled to Portland, Ohio, one hundred miles distance and nine days traveling time with wagon, it brought one dollar per bushel. Usually a load amounted to about twenty-five bushels; sugar and salt were taken in trade and brought back on the return trip.[33] Sometimes in periods of economic depression farmers did not bother to haul produce. This situation occurred in the early 1840's in western Ohio and eastern Indiana, where markets were readily available at nearby Cincinnati and Columbus.[34]

Despite poor prices and lack of decent roads, some farmers continued to team to various urban markets. The advent of canals, especially in Ohio and Indiana, expanded the short-haul teamstering business. As canals were completed in northern Ohio and Indiana, roads linked up with them at terminal or feeder points, facilitating the movement of farm produce to primary market centers.[35] In the area north of Fort Wayne where the state lines of Indiana, Ohio, and Michigan converged, grain and other goods were hauled by oxen to one of three locations in the 1830's: Fort Wayne at the Wabash Canal, across northern Ohio to Toledo, or north to Hillsdale in southern Michigan.[36] Roads stretched south from Michigan into northern Indiana, and with the opening of the Wabash Canal during 1832–35 the flow of commerce increased.[37] For example, in nearby Kosciusko County barreled flour was hauled to Fort Wayne at the cost of twenty-five cents per barrel. The trip required three and one-half days, and the driver paid his own expenses. Lumber from Kosciusko County sold in Fort Wayne at an attractive price of $5 per thousand feet, but it cost $2.50 for hauling charges.[38] From the Wabash Canal teams ran

33. *History of Logan County and Ohio* (Chicago, 1880), p. 469. A similar differential rate existed in Minnesota as late as the 1850's and 1860's, according to Larson, *The Wheat Market and the Farmer in Minnesota*, p. 53.

34. *History of Delaware County and Ohio* (Chicago, 1880), p. 62.

35. Elbert Jay Benton, *The Wabash Trade Route in the Development of the Old Northwest*, Johns Hopkins University Studies, Historical and Political Science Series, XXI (Baltimore, 1903), p. 96.

36. Ira Ford, ed., *History of Northeast Indiana: La Grange, Steuben, Noble and De Kalb Counties* (Chicago and New York, 1920), I, pp. 469, 486.

37. Benton, *Wabash Trade Route*, pp. 100–101.

38. *Biographical and Historical Record of Kosciusko County, Indiana*, pp. 216–17. See also *Annual Report of Commissioner of Patents of the Year 1848*, 30th Cong., 2nd sess., H.R. Ex. Doc. 59, 693.

north from Logansport to Michigan City via LaPorte. The canal increased the demand for teamsters who transshipped goods on feeder roads to and from the canal. This fact was evident in the career of William Douglas, who started out as a farm hand in the area, but by the late 1830's and in the 1840's was working at various jobs including driving a team between Logansport and Michigan City.[39]

Given the scarcity of money, it is reasonable to assume that those men owning a team and wagon preferred to make hauls into markets despite low rates instead of sitting about idle. Community cooperation dictated many of the hauling jobs whereby a farmer with a team made the rounds of the neighborhood, inquiring if anything had to be hauled to market, and if staple items such as salt or sugar were needed on the return run. Rarely would the teamster have charged his neighbors a commercial rate, yet it would be naive to believe that he should not expect some small but reasonable recompense for his efforts. In short, he did not "gouge" his neighbors, but it was no gratis trip at his expense.[40] Agreements were informal, which explains the lack of precision in determining rates and costs for local short-hauls.

Contemporary sources provide some information on the teamster and hauling rates. The *Peoria Register* in 1841 commented on the price of wheat and hauling to Chicago markets. Located on the Illinois River, Peoria was becoming a relatively important commercial center in central Illinois, although wheat prices there were only fifty cents per bushel or one-half of what was paid at Chicago. A Knox County farmer, thirty-five miles from Peoria, loaded his two wagons with thirty bushels of wheat in each and set off in September for Chicago. He and his son averaged twenty-eight miles per day; after arriving at Chicago and inspecting the market prices, he decided to sell at $1.10 per bushel. He collected a return load of salt, fish, and other goods and followed the practice of many teamsters by securing a load of household goods for a family which had just landed at Chicago and was bound for French Grove, located only half a day's drive from his farm. On this portion of the load he received 75 cents per hundred pounds, making $16.50. He figured his expenses coming and going at sixteen dollars, paying usually twenty-five cents for a meal with lodging at an additional twelve and a half cents per night. Sta-

39. Thomas B. Helm, ed., *History of Cass County, Indiana* (Chicago, 1886), part II, p. 502.

40. Describing his early childhood in Michigan, Eugene Davenport recalled that a wealthy neighbor, owning the first horse team in the area, charged his neighbors for running an errand in town, much to their annoyance. *Timberland Times* (Urbana, 1950), p. 205.

bling of the teams cost twelve and a half cents; however, to save money, he tied out the teams most of the time en route.

With the local interests of Peoria markets in mind, the *Register* concluded that there was a fifty-dollar profit by going to Chicago; however, if the farmer sold in Peoria, twenty-five dollars worth of traveling time could be saved. Hence, he was only twenty-five dollars ahead by this calculation. Moreover, as a result of the decline in wheat prices in Chicago since the farmer's trip, the *Register* could safely state that although wheat commanded only fifty cents per bushel in Peoria, area farmers were advised to come there instead of going to Chicago, where the market had plummeted to eighty cents a bushel.[41] In fact, a distinct risk was involved for those who arrived at a market following a drop in prices, sometimes to the point where the grain was actually sold at a loss.

The uncertainty of market conditions produced an anxiety-filled trip in 1842, when a group of Knox County men hauled their wheat to Chicago. Deciding to enter the city early the next morning, they camped the night before on the outskirts. In the early hours a man passing in a team called out to them that they had better start into the city and get an early place in line, should the price of wheat decline. Often these lines were very long, and farmers waited hours to have their wheat dropped into the hoppers.[42]

Cincinnati similarly attracted a good deal of short hauling, and as early as 1815 the farmers' trade was an important segment of the city's marketing activities.[43] Farmers in the lower Midwest found it profitable to haul produce to the "Queen City" on the Ohio River. Part of this trade included itinerant teamsters and hucksters from the surrounding agricultural area. According to the *Cincinnati Gazette* in 1844, huckster wagons monopolized the market square and filled the adjoining streets. On one occasion almost six hundred produce-laden wagons from the countryside were counted on one street. Some of this traffic came from the Hamilton County area and surrounding region, where farmers from thirty to fifty miles away easily drove into Cincinnati to sell truck produce; the opinion of the *Gazette*

41. *Peoria Register*, as cited in *Hazard's United States Commercial and Statistical Register*, V (October 20, 1841), 262. Hereafter cited as *Hazard's Register*. See also *Annual Report of Commissioner of Patents for the Year 1848*, 694.

42. *History of Knox County, Illinois* (Chicago, 1878), pp. 117–19.

43. Background information on early Cincinnati is found in Richard T. Farrell, "Cincinnati, 1800–1830: Economic Development through Trade and Industry," *Ohio History*, LXXVII (1968), 111–29.

was that these farmers enjoyed an advantage over others who came from greater distances.[44]

For central and northern Ohio the ports of Toledo, Cleveland, and Sandusky at Lake Erie served a similar role.[45] The *Cleveland Plain Dealer* observed in 1847 that few of the city's citizens appreciated the immense amounts of produce being shipped into Cleveland from the mills in the countryside. It was calculated that 391,821 bushels of wheat were brought into the city at the rate of 35 bushels per wagon; within the city at any one time there were 11,000 teams. The breweries alone consumed 30,000 bushels of barley. Such estimates indicate that Cleveland, like other port cities, attracted considerable teamster traffic, of which a fair percentage was either itinerant or short-haul.[46] In addition, the northwestern part of Ohio was tied into the network of the Wabash and Erie Canal, with its linkage to the Miami and Erie Canal; feeder routes of plank roads interlaced the area, covering 38 counties in Indiana and a 22,000 square mile area of northwestern Ohio and southern Michigan.[47]

In northwestern Indiana and the upper half of Illinois, the pattern of teamstering underwent an important shift toward Chicago. By the late 1830's and early 1840's farmers were hauling to Chicago from points as far south as central Indiana.[48] Chicago newspapers kept an eagle eye on this trade, and correlation between agriculture and transportation vis-à-vis the city received solicitous attention in the press. The *Chicago Democrat* indicated proper awareness for the agricultural situation; for example, one reader at Boone County in northwestern Illinois predicted a 150,000 bushel crop for the 1845 season but noted a shortage of harvest laborers and teams. It was estimated

44. *Cincinnati Daily Gazette*, August 17, 1844; August 20, 1845; August 11, 1848. Some cities attempted to regulate vegetable truck farmers who teamed their produce into town for sale on the streets or in the marketplaces. For an example of such an ordinance in the city of Sandusky in northern Ohio, see *Daily Commercial Register*, June 7, 1852.

45. *History of Delaware County and Ohio*, p. 826; *History of Hardin County, Ohio* (Chicago, 1883), pp. 310–12, 462.

46. *Cleveland Plain Dealer*, as cited in *Cist's Weekly Advertiser*, September 28, 1847.

47. Benton, *Wabash Trade Route*, pp. 100–101.

48. H. W. Beckwith, *History of Montgomery County, Together with Historic Notes on the Wabash Valley* (Chicago, 1881), pp. 364–65. See also Beckwith, *History of Vermilion County* (Chicago, 1879), p. 657; A. A. Parker, *Trip to the West and Texas* (Concord and Boston, 1836), pp. 60–61. For early newspaper reports of this activity, see *Chicago Weekly Democrat*, July 9, 1834; *Chicago American*, as cited in *Hazard's Register*, V (October 30, 1841), 247; *Chicago Journal*, as cited in *Cincinnati Daily Gazette*, October 4, 1844.

that every horse and oxen team in the county would have to haul for one month in order to bring the crop to market—which was of course located at Chicago.[49]

Hauling of produce constituted a vital segment of a complex mosaic for Chicago's prosperity. In autumn of 1848 the *Democrat* commented on the large number of farmers' teams and wagons crowding the city streets. Unfortunately, that season farmers had expected higher prices, and because they did not get them, the usual amount of trade at commercial houses had seriously dipped. In short, farmers were not spending freely with merchants.[50] Inadequate teamstering resources could easily produce a similar problem with the same effect on the city's commercial interests.

Other changes occurred in the transportational network of the Midwest. In 1848, when the Illinois-Michigan Canal was in its final stages of completion, the prescient editor of the *Chicago Democrat* predicted a prosperous future for Chicago's growth. But John Wentworth felt that the canal's impact, as well as the approaching railroad link-up with the East, would alter certain basic trade patterns, especially that of the "honest old teamster" who regularly conveyed his two or three tons of goods from the country to city and back. Actually Wentworth was a bit premature with regard to the supposed demise of the teamsters. Considerable quantities of agricultural produce continued to arrive at Chicago during the 1850's, a portion of which was conveyed by teams and wagons.[51]

Urban centers along major river systems also provided employment for teams which transferred produce and goods to landing points for loading on to boats. In October, 1845, the *Alton Telegraph and Democratic Review* observed large numbers of teams arriving at that

49. *Chicago Daily Democrat*, July 16, 1845. Merchants in country towns were also grain buyers, and ultimately they shipped the grain to Chicago markets. These local middlemen depended on the services of local teamsters, as indicated in an advertisement of a Freeport, Illinois, merchant: "CASH paid for HAULING WHEAT to Chicago. 60 teams wanted immediately to which the highest price will be paid by D A KNOWLTON Freeport, December 12, 1848." *Freeport Journal*, December 13, 1848; see also March 14, 1849.

50. *Chicago Daily Democrat*, October 12, 1848. Chicago was not a safe place for any teamster, inexperienced or professional. Teamsters did become involved in dangerous situations with gamblers and prostitutes, while the risk of being waylaid on roads into the city was not uncommon. See *ibid.*, August 17, 1849; December 16, 1857.

51. *Ibid.*, February 28, 1848. See list of produce imports into the city by rail, canal, and teams during 1852: *Hunt's Merchant Magazine and Commercial Review*, XXVIII (March 1853), 362. Hereafter cited as *Hunt's Merchant Magazine*.

Illinois city on the Mississippi. Flour normally conveyed downstream on the Illinois River was temporarily being hauled overland from Springfield to Alton because the water was too low for navigation. This was seen as an opportunity to reinforce a plea for the construction of a southwest railroad; but for local farmers and men with teams, the low water on the Illinois coincided with the start of their off-season, when teamstering employment was welcomed.[52] Similarly, the transfer of mercantile goods from river points to inland locations provided employment for men with teams and wagons.[53]

Alton attracted itinerant laborers such as John McNail, who worked on nearby farms, drove cattle to Alton slaughterhouses, and for a while handled a team in the city.[54] Alton served as a market center for southwestern Illinois, but business interests there deplored the impossible condition of roads and bridges leading into the city. The *Alton Commercial Gazette* cautioned in 1839 that farmers and waggoners who came to Alton for supplies, as well as the country merchants who made their wholesale purchases in the city, might be compelled to go greater distances to St. Louis if the roads and bridges were not repaired.[55]

Some entered the teamstering line casually and ended up working for merchants. Elisha Smart brought his wife and small son out to Chicago in 1838 with no particular destination in mind and hired out at rail splitting in Du Page County, west of Chicago, at the rate of three dollars per hundred. He made good wages and purchased a piece of land, simultaneously engaging in hauling meat and supplies from Chicago to a local Du Page merchant.[56] Country merchants in

52. *Alton Telegraph and Democratic Review*, October 18, 1845. When floods damaged Ohio's canal system, goods and produce were hauled overland by teamster wagons. Teamsters enjoyed a profitable situation by increasing their rates in such circumstances. *Annual Report of Commissioner of Patents for the Year 1848*, 694.

53. For examples, see Nelson W. Evans, *A History of Scioto County, Ohio* (Portsmouth, 1903), pp. 117–19; *History of Knox and Daviess Counties, Indiana* (Chicago, 1886), pp. 809–10.

54. *History of Greene and Jersey Counties, Illinois*, p. 1124.

55. *Alton Commercial Gazette*, October 16, 1839. The traffic of teamster wagons into the Alton-St. Louis area was heavy, especially coming from the rural part of southwestern Illinois, according to Oliver, *Eight Months in Illinois*, p. 88. Poor roads created hazardous conditions; one teamster hauling produce to St. Louis slipped off his wagon, and his head was crushed by the passing wheels. *Sparta Gazette*, as cited in *Chicago Daily Democrat*, March 10, 1849.

56. Bateman and Selby, eds., *Historical Encyclopedia of Illinois and History of Du Page County* (Chicago, 1913), II, p. 1034. For a similar example of an early Illinois farmer who worked at freighting for merchants, see *History of McLean County, Illinois*, p. 958.

this period were involved in two-way commerce, shipping grain to urban markets while obtaining most of their mercantile goods from urban wholesale houses. For example, a merchant at Freeport in northwestern Illinois advertised in the local press for forty teams to haul his wheat to Chicago and bring back merchandise which he had ordered from the East.[57]

Midwestern store accounts are a good source of information on short-haul teamstering, because merchants were often farmers themselves in need of hauling services. John H. Young's daybook of his farm and general store, located at Clearcreek Township, Fairfield County, in southwestern Ohio, provides information on hauling and the use of teams during 1821–35. The accounts indicate that he relied on day labor of his customers, who credited their bills with hauling work. Whereas men without teams earned only thirty-seven and a half to fifty cents per day, those with teams were in the position to command a dollar or more per day.[58] And if a storekeeper operated a diversified business, including a stage and freighting line, he hired men to teamster by the month, in addition to working at his store and on the farm.[59]

Specialization in teamstering services held out a profitable advantage, as in the case of a Michigan storekeeper. Detroit was the natural port of entry for many Easterners who arrived without teams, and the demand for hauling services in the lower part of the state enabled men like Asa Rice at Ann Arbor to develop an operation involving a farm, store, and boardinghouse, as well as teamstering and rental of dray animals, during the 1830's and 1840's. Rice had access to a number of men who performed all varieties of work: for example, an individual ran up debits on his account for repairing boots and for the purchase of gloves. His account was credited with work done on Rice's shed and twenty-two days driving a team, for which he received eleven dollars. Rice hired hands by the month at fourteen dollars, although this was mostly for summer work. One hand worked the harvest season but also teamstered on several occasions; however,

57. *Freeport Journal*, August 15, 1849. Frontier merchants exercised considerable economic leverage over the local grain trade: see Larson, *The Wheat Market and the Farmer in Minnesota*, p. 20.

58. John H. Young Daybook of Farm and General Store Accounts, 1821–35, p. 75, entry of November 11, 1824; see also p. 102, entries of July 18–19, 1826; p. 104, entry of September 1826; p. 106, entry of December 8, 1826; p. 130, entry of March 4, 1831; p. 133, entry of May 5, 1832.

59. Merrick Ely Accountbook, 1832–39, p. 19, and entry of December 6, 1833; p. 21, entries of March 18, July 18, August 12, 1833; see also entries for Daniel Strong and John Sharpe; p. 38, entry of April 1, 1838.

during winter he was employed at a lower rate of pay. Rice also ran a boarding house of sorts in which he picked up cheap farm labor on an occasional day-labor basis.[60]

Rental of animals and equipment was part of Rice's operation. These early business records reveal a basic problem for many settlers in a newly settled region—scarcity of teams and equipment. Some men relied on Rice's rental service of teams over a considerable period. The account sheet for a James Grant, commencing in 1839 and running through 1845, contained debits for hay, oxen, horses, and the use of a gig. In one instance he hired a horse for four days at the cost of $1.50. This individual made good on his debts with Rice by haying and hoeing work, and by 1845 he was able to pay cash. Rice also made advances of grain and seed to people, simultaneously providing them with hauling services, although men like Josiah Norris in 1845 repaid debts for grain and hauling by doing repair work on Rice's wagon.[61] By the late 1840's this activity tapered off, coinciding with the completion of the railroads through lower Michigan and the overall establishment of the region.[62] Teamstering was a limited occupation in the sense that it was surpassed in time by better means of transportation.

Farming as a seasonal activity produced alternating periods of employment and unemployment. Whereas winter months often forced idleness upon farm hands, teamsters were seemingly less affected.[63] Some in fact teamstered only in winter while following other lines of work, such as prairie breaking, in summer.[64] Even in the upper Mid-

60. Asa Rice Accountbook, 1827–66, p. 2, entry of September 27, 1836; p. 13, entry of March 16, 1844.

61. *Ibid.*, p. 15, entry of 1842; p. 36, entry of 1838; pp. 36, 43, entries for James Grant during 1839–45; p. 61, entry of June, 1845. The owner of teams and drays often made a nice profit in renting them. At the town of Ravenna in northern Ohio during 1848–49, the household accounts of Darius Lyman show that he rented on occasion a team and wagon, usually for $2 to $2.50 per day. As a luxury item, a horse and buggy were somewhat more expensive at $3 per day. Darius Lyman Accountbook, 1848–59, p. 4, entry of July 15, 1848; p. 5, entry of August 14, 1848; p. 19, entry of August 4, 1849.

62. MacGill, *History of Transportation*, pp. 503–5. For a similar situation in rural Pennsylvania, see Stevenson W. Fletcher, *Pennsylvania Agriculture and Country Life, 1640–1940* (Harrisburg, 1950), I, pp. 260–62.

63. "Teaming affords good employment for young men the year round," observed a traveler in Minnesota, adding that the roads west of St. Paul were heavy with wagons hauling furniture and provisions. C. C. Andrews, *Minnesota and Decotah: In Letters Descriptive of a Tour through the North-West, in the Autumn of 1856* (Washington, 1857), pp. 130, 158.

64. For examples, see *Portrait and Biographical Album of Stephenson County, Ill.* (Chicago, 1888), p. 598; *History of Knox County, Illinois* (Chicago, 1912), II, p. 635; *History of Macoupin County, Illinois*, pp. 193–94.

west winter did not necessarily impose a halt to teamstering. At the frontier port of Milwaukee, Nelson Olin secured a variety of jobs: construction, digging and clearing lots, opening cellars, and cutting logs during the summer of 1835, with time out in July to work in the harvest fields or at plowing. In the autumn and winter of 1835–36 he teamstered goods between Chicago and Milwaukee but returned to his former common labor tasks in the spring.[65] Another Wisconsin teamster who did prairie breaking in summer wrote to his uncle back east that during the winter of 1845–46 he had made seven trips between Janesville and Milwaukee, hauling wheat by ox team and bringing back lumber at five dollars per thousand feet.[66]

Winter months found men cutting and hauling wood. A Scotch immigrant, shortly after arrival in Ohio, write in February, 1830: "The people here are very busy just now, while the snow will last, hauling fire wood, which is very laborious work—"[67] Loads of firewood were hauled to town markets on ricks and sleds, standard equipment in winter. In the early 1820's at Zanesville in central Ohio the town's first merchant obtained most of his mercantile goods from Sandusky. Wintertime, when the ground was covered with snow, was a preferred season of travel. He hired a man with a sled and two horses to make the drive up to Lake Erie. En route the sled broke, but since both men were handy with axes they repaired it on the spot.[68] Teamsters probably used both sleds and wagons, depending on the depth of the snow. A farmer near Detroit noted in the spring of 1847 that teamsters were hauling flour, using "wagons" and "wheels," adding that it was still good sleighing in the backwoods and fields.[69] A Michigan

65. Nelson Olin, "Reminiscences of Milwaukee in 1835–36," *Wisconsin History*, XIII (1930), 206–9, 213, 215, 220.
66. Luke Cheseboro to Cyrus Williams (Janesville, Wis., April 10, 1846), Wisconsin Territorial Letter Collection. The *Milwaukee Courier* noted in 1841 that shipments of lead overland were drawn in winter by teams and sledges. Teamsters returned with salt purchased in Milwaukee for $2.50 a barrel and sold it at the mines for $7. As cited in *Niles' Register*, VI (November 11, 1841), 23. In 1835 George Featherstonhaugh reported that wagon teams brought large quantities of goods to the mining area, and profits were considerable: flour that cost $5–6 a barrel in the East sold for $14 at the mines. *A Canoe Voyage Up the Minnay Sotor* (London, 1847), reprint, (St. Paul, 1970), II, p. 71.
67. Charles Rose to John Rose (Scotch Settlement, Columbiana County, Ohio, February 2, 1830).
68. *History of Logan County and Ohio*, pp. 416–17.
69. David Palmer Diary, entry of March 13, 1847. A sufficient snow usually brought teamsters and farmers to town, for hauling was easier with sleds and sleighs on snow rather than wagons on frozen, rutted roads. The newspaper editor at Sandusky, Ohio, welcomed a snowfall: "Farmers take advantage of the time to do their hauling, marketing and visiting; and the consequence is that

farm hand wrote in January, 1853, that he found the drawing of lumber by teams to be very tedious but not severe work. He was also hauling cord wood, and several weeks before he had made a wagon trip into Indiana to obtain a load of corn.[70]

Considerable distance might be involved in winter teamstering. A young tanner drifted west in November, 1836, and met a "teamster of sorts" en route to Michigan, where he had a job to help move a man down into neighboring Indiana. William Sherman, the young tanner, hitched a ride as far as the Raisin River, despite the approach of winter.[71] For others who spent their winters teamstering, a related trade might be pursued: a Michigan settler worked on his farm in summer but in winter went to Pontiac, where he teamstered and constructed wagons.[72] Farmers in the upper Midwest (such as northern Michigan) often hauled produce to the lumber camps in autumn and then stayed through the winter, hiring themselves and their teams to haul logs.[73]

Naturally, settlers pursued teamstering to raise capital. Establishment of a farm required physical stamina, wrote an Indiana pioneer who frankly found farm-making difficult and demanding. Fortunately, he owned a wagon and secured hauling jobs that gave him extra money to hire hands to work on his farm—a vital necessity, since his little sons were still going to school and could not help on the farm.[74] In a similar case Isaac Mitchell settled in McLean County, Illinois, and rented land for a while; in 1843 he took out a government claim for eighty acres and bought an additional eighty with security put up by a lawyer. During the subsequent years this debt was paid off by breaking prairie and hauling grain and supplies to Chicago. After the prairie on his own land was broken, he rented the farm out while working elsewhere at teamstering. The fact was that

---

our town is filled during the day, with everything from a 'bob' to a four horse 'fancy.' Glad to see it, and hope our business men will be much profited." *Daily Commercial Register*, December 23, 1854.

70. Myron W. Wright to Allen G. Wright (Fredonia, Mich., January 7, 1853), Allen G. Wright Papers.

71. "William Sherman Reminiscences of His Journey and Move to Wisconsin in 1836 and Farming in Waukesha County," p. 10. It was not unusual for boys to hitch a ride during treks across the country; see *History of Delaware County and Ohio*, p. 821.

72. *Portrait and Biographical Album of Oakland County, Michigan* (Chicago, 1891), p. 760.

73. *History of Tuscola and Bay Counties, Mich.* (Chicago, 1883), p. 17.

74. Samuel McCutchan to William McCutchan (Floyd County, Ind., July 19, 1832).

he could make money and pay off his debt faster with teamstering than if he applied his own labor to the operation of the farm.[75]

Those who had to work out at the beginning apparently found it advantageous to continue doing so, and this delayed their entry into full-time farming. An Illinois settler in the 1840's without sufficient capital hired out as a farm hand for ten dollars per month, saving his money to purchase a team of oxen for sodbusting. In time he broke several hundred acres and then switched over to driving teams, going as far as Dubuque, Iowa. He teamstered for twenty years before settling down.[76] Here again was a classic case of starting out at the bottom of the ladder as a farm hand and working upward with the acquisition of a team.

Hauling work was also a common way of settling previously acquired short-term debts—an arrangement advantageous to both parties. The Van Horn family, consisting of the father and several sons, secured occasional employment from their affluent neighbor, Nathan Pierce, who farmed a large tract in Calhoun County, Michigan. In May, 1850, Pierce sold Van Horn five bushels of wheat, to be paid back during the coming summer at the fixed value of five dollars; however, it was not until September that a son finally came along with oxen and worked five days to balance out the debt.[77] Labor exchange in absence of money was a common method of paying debts on the frontier.

An individual did not have to be a farmer *per se* to engage in hauling work on the frontier. An excellent example was a cooper who owned land in Clinton County, Michigan: Joseph Sperry in the late 1840's possessed the only team and wagon in the area. Besides his coopering trade, he did general hauling for his neighbors, and this service was reimbursed by labor rendered on his farm. The arrangement gave him a double advantage because he had additional time to work at his trade, while agricultural improvements with his farm proceeded.[78]

On the other hand, tradesmen themselves might have need of haul-

75. *Portrait and Biographical Album of McLean County, Ill.* . . . (Chicago, 1887), pp. 374–75.

76. *Portrait and Biographical Record of Lee County, Illinois* (Chicago, 1892), p. 194.

77. Nathan Pierce Accountbook, 1848–60, p. 13, entries of May 3, September 30, 1850. Pierce also arranged for men to plow land for crops and later to perform hauling services at harvest time: see Accountbook, 1842–61, pp. 56–57, entries of July 9, 16, 1860.

78. *History of Shiawasee and Clinton Counties, Michigan* (Philadelphia, 1880), pp. 382–83.

ing services from those with such equipment. The daybook of William Hunt, a carpenter in Portage County, Ohio, during the 1840's and 1850's, showed him working at construction and logging. Hunt pursued his trade during the cold months: in the winter of 1842 he made buckets for a man who paid for them with produce and "one day and a half of self and team, hauling." As a carpenter engaged in construction work, Hunt depended on those who could haul lumber and timber to the project sites.[79]

While information is admittedly sparse, public construction projects—laying out roads, digging canals, and railroading—drew teamsters and their teams away from less lucrative hauling jobs. The demand for teams and wagons was widespread even in rural areas. Road building in the vicinity of frontier Indianapolis during the early 1830's prompted an advertisement in the *Indiana Journal* calling for fifty or sixty teams to haul rock for bridges. Given the extent of settlement in central Indiana at this time, an appeal of this sort was directed mainly to local farmers or settlers.[80] Work on public roads also enticed men with teams who otherwise worked on farms. In Fulton County, east of Toledo in the Maumee River Valley, a farmer wrote to his son in the California gold fields about the lack of farm help in Ohio. This farmer was awaiting the arrival of a man whom he hired to work on the farm; one of the incentives included a promise that a team would be made available to the hired hand. Apparently this farm hand had a team which he hired out to contractors on road construction. The farmer admitted that contractors did everything, even offering advances in wages, to keep men with teams on the job.[81]

Canal and railroad construction offered similar temptations to men with teams. Previously mentioned was Henry von Hollen, a German immigrant who wanted to settle in Lake County, Indiana, but not at the price of selling his team. He wisely went farther west to Illinois, working at Joliet on canal construction, and it is not unlikely that he hired his team out for hauling materials.[82] In the case of railroad construction, James Hock came over from Indiana to Ford County (in east central Illinois) during the laying out of the Illinois Central Railroad. Part of the time he worked hauling timber for bridge and

79. William Hunt Accountbook, 1841–54, p. 2, entries for 1842–43.
80. *Indiana Journal*, July 23, 1831.
81. Elisha Huntington to William R. Huntington (Delta, Fulton County, Ohio, March 26, 1854).
82. Goodspeed and Blanchard eds., *Counties of Porter and Lake, Indiana*, p. 725.

culvert construction, but in 1853 he went into adjacent Iroquois County, working a spell on a farm before returning to settle in Ford County.[83] Here teamstering work, as well as farm labor in a nearby county, influenced an outsider to take up land and settle in a specific area.

Whether or not they owned their own animals and equipment, teamsters on construction projects usually received better wages than farm hands.[84] Also, men who worked as farm hands by the month commanded good rates when their skills included knowledge of transportation equipment; unfortunately, there is a lack of information on these semi-skilled persons. One indication of their value appears in the diary of an Illinois farmer near Jacksonville who hired a man at twenty dollars per month, a higher than average rate for the times. Handy with tools, this individual worked on the timbers of the stable, hauled corn, and repaired a wagon bed. Indeed, a hired hand with such skills might be a better bargain than the average hand at twelve to fifteen dollars per month.[85]

Hauling rates, rather than wages, provide the best index of what teamsters earned. The short-haul teamster earned about $1.50 to $2.00 per day, although jobs were sporadic or very infrequent.[86] In his study of American transportation during 1815–60, George Rogers Taylor admitted that summarization of teamsters' rates and costs posed a number of problems which made each situation different: condition of roads, cost of labor, tolls, and competitive conditions. Based on a price unit of 100 pounds per weight, the figure of 75

83. *Portrait and Biographical Record of Ford County, Illinois* (Chicago, 1892), p. 244. The Illinois Central employed about 10,000 laborers for the construction of its line during the 1850's, especially German and Irish immigrants who hoped to earn money for the purchase of farms. Some achieved this goal, but many continued as construction laborers or railroad employees, according to David L. Lightner, "Construction Labor on the Illinois Central Railroad," *Illinois Historical Journal*, LXVI (1973), 285–301.

84. Evans, *History of Scioto County, Ohio*, p. 1003.

85. Sewall, *Diary*, p. 239. The fact that skilled farm hands were worth more was confirmed by the observations of a Swedish visitor in the 1830's: "Masons, carpenters, and joiners, are as much wanted in the country as in towns, owing to the number of buildings continually being erected. An able workman of that class earns at least one dollar per diem, and in many places in the country even two dollars and a half." Arfwedson, *United States and Canada, in 1832, 1833, and 1834*, I, p. 207.

86. "History of Wages in the United States from Colonial Times to 1928," *United States Department of Labor, Bureau of Labor Statistics: Bulletin No. 499* (Washington, 1929), p. 448. Hereafter cited as *U.S. Department of Labor Bulletin No. 499*.

cents to $1.50 prevailed as the low-to-moderate average in the 1820's and 1830's.[87] According to *Niles' Register* in 1827 the cost of wagoning hogsheads of tobacco from central Ohio to the port of Sandusky seventy-five miles away was 75 cents per hundred pounds.[88] As late as 1841 a similar figure was reported by central Illinois farmers who hauled goods to and from Chicago.[89]

This 75 cents per 100 pound rate rose to $1.25 and $1.50 in Michigan, where teamstering was much in demand, especially by the 1830's. In Lenawee County merchants and hotelkeepers regularly brought supplies from Detroit, using a differential rate: heavy goods were figured at $1.00, while dry goods were billed at $1.50 per 100 pounds weight.[90] At Genesee County, north of Detroit, hauling rates in 1835 stood roughly at $1.25 per 100 pounds. Through the remainder of that decade provisions hauled into Livingston County (west of Detroit) ranged between $1.00 and $2.00 per 100 pounds, with the bulk of the goods in the form of beef, pork, and flour provisions for new settlers.[91]

Speculation in the teamstering line—i.e., "gouging the newly arrived settlers"—may explain the increase in rates for hauling. Certainly the large influx of settlers in pre-1837 years to Michigan, as well as to other parts of the Midwest, increased the demand for this basic service similar to all other necessities of life. The hauling rate advanced in some cases to four dollars per hundred pounds or higher. Benjamin Chamberlain came out from New York in September, 1836, arranging with two men living in Calhoun County (in central Michigan) to meet him at Detroit with their covered wagons. After his belongings, consisting of provisions and sundries, were weighed, they were loaded on several wagons and driven out to the farm site at the rate of four dollars per hundred pounds.[92]

Another New Yorker also came via ship to Detroit in 1836; he was bound for Genesee County, a sixty-mile haul from the port city. Teamsters swooped in like hawks on the naive newcomers; one teamster offered to convey him out to the farm site for a forty-dollar fee. Declining this offer, he negotiated with another teamster and obtained a better deal than from the first, but with a nominal three dol-

87. Taylor, *Transportation Revolution*, pp. 132–34.
88. *Niles' Register*, XXXII (July 14, 1827), 323.
89. *Peoria Register and North-Western Gazetteer*, as cited in *Hazard's Register*, V (October 20, 1841), 262.
90. Bonner, ed., *Memoirs of Lenawee County, Michigan*, I, p. 439.
91. *History of Livingston County, Michigan*, pp. 22–23.
92. *History of Calhoun County, Michigan* (Philadelphia, 1877), p. 175.

lars extra per woman in the party.[93] It might be assumed from this incident that when rates were figured for families, the men who could either walk or help with the teams were not charged in the head count of costs. And the number of people to be hauled in the wagons was always figured in the teamster's cost-conscious calculations. The family of George Ferguson landed at Toledo, where a man agreed to bring the family and their possessions up to Lenawee County, a short distance to the northwest and just across the Michigan-Ohio state line. Presumably to spare his draft animals any extra burden, this teamster compelled the children in the family to walk much of the way to the farm.[94] Teamsters did not remain after they had deposited their passengers and loads at the desired locations or farm sites; most probably started the return trip the next morning.

Teamsters were flexible businessmen and open to compromises when it came to hauling costs. A New York man and his family who arrived at Detroit in 1831 were charged only ten dollars, and the teamsters agreed to accept an ax as partial payment for conveying the party of six and their belongings. Although the family had exhausted their money in getting west, they had arrived![95] Sometimes fellow settlers undertook the task of teamstering money-short immigrants who needed a helping hand to complete the last leg of their journey. Michael Brown, an Irishman who came to the United States via Canada with a wife and four children, arrived at Chicago. A settler in town with his wagon charged him only five dollars to haul the entire family the fifty miles to Kendall County. Because he was en route to his own farm in the same area, this settler charged only a nominal fee for the money-pressed family.[96]

Others were not so lucky and paid a higher fee—in one case a flat rate of eighteen dollars. Eric Norelius noted in his diary in 1850 that the Swedish immigrant party of which he was a member had taken a packet boat south on the Illinois-Michigan Canal from Chicago to

93. *History of Genesee County, Michigan*, p. 186.

94. *Portrait and Biographical Album of Lenawee County, Michigan*, p. 635. In most instances, teamsters demanded hard cash for their services; for example, see *History of Livingston County, Michigan*, pp. 191–92.

95. *History of Macomb County, Michigan* (Chicago, 1882), p. 843.

96. Bateman and Selby, eds., *Historical Encyclopedia of Illinois and History of Kendall County* (Chicago, 1914), II, pp. 952–53. Some teamsters were never paid or had to wait a considerable time for their money. An Ohio farmer moved from Fairfield to Van Wert County in 1849 but had to promise the teamsters that they would get their money eventually—and in this case it was many years before he paid them! *History of Van Wert and Mercer Counties, Ohio* (Wapakoneta, 1882), p. 207.

Peru in central Illinois. At that point they were still sixty miles from
their destination of Henry County, at the western edge of the state
near the Mississippi River. Those who still had money left to hire
livery teams paid eighteen dollars to have their belongings conveyed
out to their homesteads; otherwise they had to store their things at a
warehouse.[97]

Short-haul teamsters were important to the agricultural frontier in
the period before railroads. Hauling jobs were not confined solely to
goods and produce, but included the movement of settlers to new
farm sites. These part-timers in frontier transportation were sometimes farmers or prospective farmers raising money for the eventual
purchase of a piece of land. Others were formerly farm hands who
invested their carefully saved earnings in a team and wagon and perhaps a breaking plow. With such equipment they were in a position
to earn good money for several years before entering the full-time
business of farming.

97. *Early Life of Eric Norelius (1833–1862). Journal of a Swedish Immigrant
in the Middle West* (Rock Island, 1934), p. 112. Hereafter cited as Norelius,
Journal. This was the identical route taken by Hans Mattson, a Swedish immigrant boy, who worked as a farm hand in 1852. He specifically mentioned traveling from the canal overland to western Illinois by "farmers wagons." Hans
Mattson, *Reminiscences, The Story of an Emigrant* (St. Paul, 1892), p. 28.
According to William Oliver in the 1840's, a wagon load consisting of 3 to 4
persons with baggage cost $15. *Eight Months in Illinois*, p. 124.

Harvesting

We had one man to cradle, another to rake and bind, and two to reap with sickles. We had a big dinner and lunches in the forenoon and afternoon, and the longest imaginable stories told at intervals of rest and during the thunder-storm. But we got the wheat duly housed, after which came the threshing and cleaning. The usual way of threshing then was with a flail, and the tenth bushel was the common price for that work.[1]

HARVEST LABOR was a basic requirement on midwestern farms during the critical months of July, August, and September, when grain ripened and hay became ready for cutting. Less urgent was the demand for this labor during threshing and corn-picking operations in autumn and early winter. Despite premium wages, the summer harvesting cycle was short in duration but set in motion a vast army of men from diverse backgrounds: skilled and unskilled, immigrant and free black, as well as thousands of common farm laborers. This migration raises basic questions about harvest labor, its high wages, and why men pursued this brief, exhausting occupation.

Harvesting of grain, including wheat, rye, and oats, and the cutting of hay, was done with the sickle prior to the 1830's. The stalks of grain or hay were grasped in the left hand while the right drew the sickle close to where the hand was holding the bunched stalks. Most harvesters in this period bore a tell-tale scar, usually on the small finger where the sickle made a close shave; sometimes the lower part of the left hand was covered with these scars from the sickle blades. The sickles were usually slung over the shoulder or hung on waist belts when the harvesters stopped to bind up the sheaves. With a sickle the harvester could cut on an average three-quarters of an acre per day.[2]

An improvement over the sickle was a larger implement, the scythe,

1. William Cooper Howells, *Recollections of Life in Ohio from 1813 to 1840* (Cincinnati, 1895), p. 62.
2. *History of Champaign County, Ohio* (Chicago, 1881), p. 222; "Early Reminiscences of Parke County [Indiana] by Ira Mater," p. 2; Martin Welker, *Farm Life in Central Ohio Sixty Years Ago* (Cleveland, 1895), pp. 32–33; Rogin, *Introduction of Farm Machinery*, p. 130.

with its curved blade attached to a long-handled pole held with both hands and swung in a long, lazy arch through the grass or grain. Its razor-sharp blade moved through the grain with a swinging motion, cutting the stalks just above the ground. In time, the scythe was modified into the cradle, similar in appearance but with a frame of slender rods or curved finger-like projections. As the blade made a swath, the cut grain fell back upon this framework of rods. At the end of the swing the cradle was tilted slightly forward to allow the gathered grain to fall out in small clusters for the binders to tie and stack.[3] Increased speed and greater efficiency of the cradle necessitated the employment of two or three extra hands to follow and rake up the grain and tie it into sheaves. A single cradler and two binders could harvest approximately two acres per day, and record amounts of as much as four acres per day were attained.[4]

While the cradle represented a slight improvement in harvesting efficiency and in fact remained the primary harvesting implement before the Civil War, the most important mechanical innovation was the horse-drawn reaper. The McCormick and Hussey reapers which appeared in the early 1830's provided the basic mechanical substitute for the backbreaking labor of cutting wheat and hay with a scythe or cradle. In simple terms, it was a device with a horizontal set of cutting teeth mounted on a wheeled carriage pulled by a team of horses. As the reaper cut the wheat or grass, a raker on the rear platform pulled off the swaths of loose grain for the binders following on foot.

Farmers were naturally impressed with this new harvesting machinery. A farmer's wife near De Kalb, Illinois, reported in July, 1853, that seven hands and a McCormick reaper harvested fifteen acres per day; within five days seventy-five acres of wheat had been cut and stacked.[5] The mechanical reaper reduced both harvesting time and manpower requirements. The advantages of the mechanical

3. Charles W. Burkett, *History of Ohio Agriculture* (Concord, N.H., 1900), pp. 168–69. With either the scythe or cradle it was a matter of conserving energy, and the mower was advised to swing the cutting edge only so far as to cut through the grass or grain, letting the blade stop the instant it had done its work. *Ohio Cultivator*, I (June 15, 1845), 91–92. "Point-in" and "point-out" were the positions of the blade at the beginning and end of each sweep: see Ocie Lybarger, "Every Day Life on the Southern Illinois Frontier" (M.A. thesis, Southern Illinois University, 1951), 25–26.

4. William Henry Smith, *The History of the State of Indiana* (Indianapolis, 1897), II, p. 657; William T. Hutchinson, *Cyrus Hall McCormick: Seed-Time, 1809–1856* (New York, 1930), I, pp. 71–72; Rogin, *Introduction of Farm Machinery*, pp. 126–28.

5. E. Currier to Friend Nathan (South Grove, De Kalb County, Ill., July 25, 1853), E. Currier Letter Collection.

reaper over the hand cradle were convincing to a central Illinois farmer in 1855. His fifty acres of hay were cut with a mechanical reaper within one week at a cost of $24, whereas with the hand cradle this task had previously required two or three weeks with a corresponding labor cost of $92.[6]

Yet many farmers did not purchase these labor-saving devices, and the use of mechanical reapers did not solve the problem of labor shortages which occurred every season. According to a recent study by Paul David, the employment of the mechanical reaper was not widely accepted prior to 1850, but over 50 percent of the wheat crop was harvested with machines by 1860. Mechanized harvesting equipment did not make the hand cradler obsolete, nor was it necessarily profitable for all farmers to switch over to machines; rather, those with less than fifty acres of grain were well advised not to make the investment in a reaper during the late 1840's and 1850's.[7] Not until the impact of the Civil War forced thousands of farm laborers into the ranks of the Union Army was the importance of farm machinery completely realized.[8]

Identification as a harvest hand applied loosely to all field harvest labor: cradleman, reaper, binder, raker, stacker, etc. Top wages went to those who swung the cradle or scythe; the others earned proportionately less, but in general harvesters earned more than common farm laborers. They were usually employed on a day basis and retained as long as the fields required harvesting.

Ohio men in the early decades earned 50 to 75 cents per day, a standard rate up to the 1840's.[9] By the late 1840's it rose to $1 per day and remained level during the 1850's, although local demand sometimes caused it to advance to $1.25 and $1.50. The farm records of Martin Grey, who cultivated wheat, rye, oats, and potatoes near

6. *Daily Commercial Register*, September 1, 1855. These figures are similar to those reported by New York wheat farmers: see *Cultivator*, VI (May, 1849), 143–44.

7. Paul A. David, "The Mechanization of Reaping in the Ante-Bellum Midwest," in Henry Rosovsky, ed., *Industrialization in Two Systems* (New York, 1966), pp. 3–39, esp. pp. 23–27.

8. Rogin, *Introduction of Farm Machinery*, pp. 72–79, 91.

9. Young Daybook of Farm and General Store Accounts, p. 54, entries of April 26, May 3, 1823; p. 58, entry of July 16, 1823; p. 63, entry of October 14, 1823; p. 68, entry of July 1, 1824; Thomas J. Y. Hart Store and Farm Records, 1819–50, entries during July, 1819, under Edward Phelps; John Brown Daybook, 1832–53, p. 31, entry of September 5, 1835, in Nessly-deSellem Papers; Caleb Walters Farm Accounts, pp. 1, 4, 14, 20, 22; see also entries of July 15, 1843, July 13, 1844, August, 1845, February 6, 1846; Rufus W. Howe Ledger, 1830–66, pp. 1, 16, 34, 67, 69.

Cleveland, show that he regularly paid $1 per day for potato digging, wages similar to those for reaping and mowing. A slight increase was evident in harvesting a field of rye: cradlers earned $1.25 per day, although the rakers and binders received the customary $1.[10] Overall farm wages in Ohio by 1857 were averaging over $1 per day with board, and in some areas like Darke County they reached as high as $1.50 per day.[11] In a survey two years later farmers reported the harvest wage between $1 and $1.25 per day.[12]

In Indiana the wage levels were similar to those in Ohio up to the 1840's. Local boys supplied much of the harvest labor in the early decades and at low rates: "It was a habit in those days for farmers to help each other, and their sons to work in the harvest field. . . . This was a source of wealth to the sons of the early settlers and to those farmers who were unable to purchase a home. They received from 25 to 50 cents per day and their board. That was wealth, the foundation of their future prosperity. It was the first egg laid to hatch them a farm. . . ."[13]

By 1836 Calvin Fletcher was paying mowers $1 per day on his farm adjacent to Indianapolis;[14] three years later a German immigrant farmer wrote from Marshall County that newly arrived Germans could easily find work in the grain fields at 62.5 cents per day, while experienced cradlers received $1 per day.[15] Day harvest rates rose sharply in Indiana during the late 1840's and in the 1850's. In 1846 the *Western Farmer and Gardener* reported that harvest hands in Wayne County earned $1.25 per day.[16] A decade later rakers were receiving $1 per day, binders $1.50, and cradlers $2.50. Rumors circulated that cradlers in some Indiana locales commanded as much as $3 per day.[17]

10. Martin E. Grey Farm Record, 1854–74; see accounts for years 1854, 1855, and 1856.

11. *Annual Report of the Commissioner of Statistics, to the General Assembly of Ohio, For the Year 1857* (Columbus, 1858), I, 75–86. Hereafter cited as *Ohio Statistics*. See also *Annual Report of Commissioner of Patents for the Year 1848*, 689.

12. *Hunt's Merchant Magazine*, XLI (1859), 759.

13. *History of Wayne County, Indiana* (Chicago, 1884), I, pp. 369–70.

14. Fletcher Diary, entry of July 12, 1836.

15. Donald Carmony, "Document Letter written by Mr. Johann Wolfgang Schreyer," *Indiana History*, XL (1944), 287.

16. *Western Farmer and Gardener* (Indianapolis), II (October 17, 1846), 296. See also *Annual Report of Commissioner of Patents for the Year 1845*, 29th Cong., 1st sess., *H.R. Doc. 140*, Appendix 34, 1149–54.

17. David Francisco to Horace Cochran (Jacksonburg [Wayne County, Ind.?], June 28, 1857), Henry F. Strong Papers.

Harvest wages in Michigan were similar to those in Ohio and
Indiana during the 1830's and 1840's but rose in the 1850's. A harvest
hand in Van Buren County wrote to his brother in New York during
1844 that $1 per day was the rate in harvest and 75 cents per day in
haying season.[18] By 1849 Nathan Pierce at Calhoun County paid his
hands $1.25 per day for cradling, raking, and binding wheat;[19] ac-
cording to the report of a Branch County farmer, in 1859 the average
daily harvest wage had reached $1.38.[20]

Harvest wages in Illinois appeared more attractive in comparison
to Ohio, Indiana, and Michigan. Even as early as the 1820's 75 cents
a day was offered in the English settlement of Morris Birkbeck, especially for immigrants: "Many of them without money, and some in
debt for their passage, they at first hired out at the usual price of
fifty cents a-day without board, and seventy-five for hay-time and
harvest."[21] According to John Mason Peck, who traveled extensively
on horseback through the state in the 1830's, a good harvest cradler
earned $1.50 to $2 per day.[22] William Sewall paid cradlers, binders,
and rakers on his farm near Jacksonville during the 1830's at $1.25
per day, but only $1 for his hands at hay mowing in 1837, indicative
of either the effects of the Panic or lower wages for hay cutting.[23]
During the hard times of 1838–45 an Ogle County farmer paid harvest hands $1 per day, which compared to what Matthias Dunlap, a
farmer and nurseryman just west of Chicago, was paying in the early
1840's for his harvest labor.[24] These rates rose in the 1850's; according
to a popular guidebook, $1.25 was paid for binding and shocking
hands, while $1.50 was paid to stackers.[25] In 1856 Matthew T. Scott
was paying his harvest hands $1.25 in central Illinois,[26] while two
years later the *Chicago Democrat* reported farmers hiring harvest

18. Joel P. Barlow to Elijah P. Barlow (Van Buren County, Mich., May 27,
1844).
19. Nathan Pierce Accountbook, 1848–60, p. 8, entry of July 21, 1849. See
also *Annual Report of Commissioner of Patents for the Year 1848*, 691.
20. *Hunt's Merchant Magazine*, XLI (1859), 759.
21. George Flower, *History of the English Settlement in Edwards County.
Illinois*, I (Chicago, 1909), p. 222.
22. John Mason Peck, as cited in Henry Lewis, *The Valley of the Mississippi
Illustrated* (St. Paul, 1967), pp. 275–76.
23. Sewall, *Diary*, pp. 150, 185.
24. Bateman and Selby, eds., *Historical Encyclopedia of Illinois and History
of Ogle County*, II, p. 718; Dunlap Account and Ledger Book 1839–47, pp. 69,
108–9.
25. Gerhard, *Illinois as It is*, p. 296.
26. Scott Memorandum Book and Index, 1856–58, p. 4, entry of September
6, 1856.

hands at rates of $2.50 and $3 per day.[27] Wisconsin farm harvest rates
experienced a similar increase during the 1850's. According to a popular guidebook in 1860, "Men who are good with the cradle, in harvest-
time will get $2, some as high as $2.50 per day for their work; the
reaping-machines drawn by horses, however, are fast superseding
manual labor."[28]

Payment in kind in lieu of cash wages was a common practice, more
so in the early decades than by the Civil War.[29] An English settler in
Illinois wrote in the 1820's: "During the harvest, the custom here is
to give two bushels per day for reaping, including meat."[30] Others
were paid on a daily basis, like Thomas West, who was hired to work
on an Ohio farm during the summer of 1831 at the rate of one bushel
of wheat per day. During his employment the price of wheat rose
from forty cents to one dollar per bushel. His employer tried to pay
him in cash according to the wheat's value when the work was begun,
but West refused to agree to this switch in the terms and instead took
the wheat.[31] Yet it was in the greater interest of harvest hands to get
their wages in cash rather than produce, and instances occurred when
men refused to accept substitutes. For example, in the 1820's at Fairfield County, Ohio, harvesters demanded cash wages of fifty cents
per day, and ". . . farmers usually contrived some means of getting
money to pay the harvest hands."[32] Unless wheat unexpectedly rose
in price, harvesters were well advised to demand cash wages, thus

27. *Chicago Daily Democrat*, July 12, 1858.
28. Thomas Spence, *The Settler's Guide in the United States and British
North American Provinces* (New York, 1862), p. 163. See also Hiram Nourse
Accountbook, I, p. 23, entries under July–November, 1850; p. 32, entries of
1851; p. 45, entries of 1857.
29. An English traveler reported that labor in northern Ohio during the 1840's
was expensive, which made cash wages difficult. As a result, farmers were willing
to split the hay or grain harvest in half with the harvester, which was a form of
payment in kind. Brown, *America*, p. 41.
30. S. H. Collins, *The Emigrant's Guide to and Description of the United
States* (Hull, 1830), pp. 153–54.
31. Charles A. Hanna, *Historical Collections of Harrison County, in the
State of Ohio* (New York, 1900), pp. 65–66; for similar examples of payment in
kind, see A. J. Baughman, *History of Ashland County, Ohio* (Chicago, 1909),
p. 53; *Biographical Record of Bureau, Marshall and Putnam Counties, Illinois*
(Chicago, 1896), p. 53.
32. Hervey Scott, *A Complete History of Fairfield County, Ohio* (Columbus,
1877), pp. 257, 277. For a similar case, see *History of Brown County, Ohio*
(Chicago, 1883), p. 372. Farmers were urged to pay their hands promptly at
the end of each day, according to advice in the *Prairie Farmer*, III (May, 1843),
97–100. Harvesters and threshers often sewed their money into the lining of
shirts or coats for safe-keeping: see *Portrait and Biographical Album of McLean
County, Ill.*, p. 871.

avoiding the inconvenience of marketing the grain. The latter process could easily prevent the harvesters keeping apace with the ripening fields and securing additional harvesting jobs.

Problems of this kind, as well as labor shortages, were minimized by arrangements in advance to have sufficient help available for the harvest. Farmers employed regular farm hands for an annual period or for a half year's time by the month. By employing a man for several months or the entire year, the farmer in effect guaranteed himself a permanent harvest hand during July and August. Because competition for harvest hands was keen (a fact which both employer and employee recognized), farmers hired their hands early in the season and agreed to increase the monthly wage rate during the harvest months as an incentive for reliable work and as an inducement to remain on the farm. An Ohio farmer at Waynesville wrote this type of contract into his accountbook in 1836: "Benjamin Whiteacre set in to work one year with Benjamin Ninde this first day of the second month 1836 on the following termes.[sic] to wit, eight Dollars per month for the five first months and the five last months of the time, and fourteen Dollars per months for July and August. for the performance of which we subscribe our names."[33]

A farmer at Huntington County, Indiana, during the 1850's executed a contract with his hired hand, who received increased pay during eight months of the year and was assured of winter employment but at a lower rate: "Commenced work for one year at 14 dolls [sic] per month for 8 summer months and 10 dollars for 4 winter months to commence on the 1st of 12m [i.e., December 1] and end on the 1st of 4m [April 1]."[34] This agreement was mutually advantageous: the farmer gained a year 'round hand, and in turn the hired hand received a higher wage in harvest time and had winter employment with a place to stay.

Extra wages were an important incentive according to the accountbook of a farmer in Clark County, Ohio, who hired George Deel in March, 1846, to work for six dollars per month. According to the stipulation, if there was a harvest that year, Deel was to have $6.50 per month. Apparently this was not attractive to the hired hand, for in June it was recorded that George had quit![35] Others were more suc-

---

33. Andrew Whiteacre Farm Accountbook, p. 22, Box 6, Folder 2, in Andrew Whiteacre Records.

34. Benjamin Coale Daybook, Accountbook and Diary, 1845–58, Ledger section entitled "Cash Book," John Feagle Agreement of 1855.

35. Lewis Lesher Farm Accounts, 1841–49, entries of March 30, June 28, 1846.

cessful at negotiating a new rate: in January, 1842, Nathan Pierce of Calhoun County, Michigan, hired David Wright for four months at twelve dollars each. At the end of the period Wright and his employer came to a new understanding. Pierce agreed to hire him for one more month at thirteen dollars. A subsequent extension occurred in June; Wright agreed to work four additional months, including haying and harvest up to October at fifteen dollars per month.[36]

Hands also signed on to work in harvest with the option of staying on the farm for the winter at a reduced wage rate if the employment was suitable. An Ohio farmer near Defiance secured a man late in the harvest season during September, 1848. This hand apparently came on a recommendation to William Holgate, who recorded in his accountbook: "Major's hand began work for me Sept. 18th at noon (Monday)—at 10$ per month 1st month, winter at 9$, if he stays." During July, 1847, Holgate hired several hands to cradle and harvest his wheat field, paying them fifty to seventy-five cents per day, including "Irish Mike," presumably an immigrant. Although most of the harvest work was completed by the following month, Holgate hired a hand on a monthly rate: "This morning early Hermann began work for me for three months at $10 per month, the next 3 to be at $9 per month. He came in yesterday. He began boarding at my own house."[37] Sufficient work existed on the farm following the harvest to warrant retention of hands, claimed Solon Robinson, who deplored the common practice of discharging them after the seasonal rush.[38]

Farmers with extensive grain and hay fields found it advantageous to hire the harvesting work by the acre on a contract basis. Contract rates for harvesting by the acre varied according to the times and locale, what the cradler could accomplish in a day's period, and the heaviness of the crop. In 1814 a farmer in southern Ohio hired his wheat and oats cradled at the rate of 37.5 cents per acre. Assuming that one man could cradle two acres per day, the basic daily earnings

36. Nathan Pierce Accountbook, 1842–61, p. 7, entry of January 22, 1842. In a similar case, a farmer outside Cincinnati hired a man for eight dollars per month to work from June to December, but during harvest his monthly wage was increased to nine dollars. Hugh Fulton Kemper Accountbook, entry of June 26, 1847.

37. Holgate Accountbook, p. 6, entry of August 11, 1847; pp. 33–34, entry of September 17, 1848. According to a survey in 1859, the monthly wage during summer harvesting averaged eighteen to twenty-two dollars in parts of Ohio, Michigan, and Illinois; however, these rates were reduced to ten to fifteen dollars per month in the slack winter season. Hunt's Merchant Magazine, XLI (1859), 759.

38. Solon Robinson, Facts for Farmers (New York, 1866), pp. 682–84.

approximated 75 cents, a figure in line with what harvest hands were paid in daily wages.[39] An Illinois farmer in the 1830's was putting up hay but encountering labor difficulties. He offered mowers 75 cents per acre; they regarded this as insufficient and therefore quit. Ultimately he conceded, for his diary recorded that a man was cutting hay for him at the rate of $1 per acre.[40] By the early 1840's, a popular guidebook advised Illinois settlers to pay $1.25 per acre.[41] However, when times were poor and jobs scarce, harvest hands willingly accepted lower rates. In the summer of 1840, an Indiana farmer hired men to cut his clover: "It is understood that they can cut by the acre or by the day at 62½ [cents] per day or 75 [cents] per acre & put up the same ready to be hauled." Despite the low pay, the men were glad to have the work: "We can get any number of hands at 62½ [cents] per day. Mony [sic] is very scarce—"[42]

Hay was a cheaper and easier commodity to harvest than wheat. An Ohio farmer's accountbook during the mid-1840's provides basic information on the different rates paid for harvesting hay and wheat on an acre basis. In 1846 he paid 50 to 75 cents "per acre according to the grass" for hay mowing, whereas wheat harvesting commanded a higher rate of $1.50 to $1.75 per acre. In hay-mowing jobs he supplied the harvester with meals at the rate of twenty-five to thirty-one cents, while the wheat harvester supplied his own board. A local man, George Castleman, agreed to mow hay for him at seventy-five cents an acre, with the stipulation that the job was to be finished as soon as practical. He was not required to cut near the fence corners, for the farm was probably enclosed with rail fences which by their design ran along a zig-zag line.[43]

Others did wheat harvesting for this Stark County farmer: "Let out

39. E. Kemper Daybook, entry of June 18, 1814.
40. Sewall, Diary, pp. 158–59.
41. Oliver, *Eight Months in Illinois*, p. 135.
42. Fletcher Diary, entries of June 15, 18, 1840. It was common for men in debt to work for comparatively low rates. A Coshocton County, Ohio, farmer in the summer of 1845 had several men mowing hay at sixty-two and a half cents per acre in order to credit advances of cash, seed, and hay. Jeremiah Cooper Accounts of Produce, Daybook, 1844–50, entries of August 3, 14, 1845.
43. Farmer's Memorandum Book, Stark County, Ohio, entries of June 10, 13, 17, 19, 1846. Apparently it was standard practice not to cut hay near fences and corners. An Ohio farmer related how an itinerant mower profited by cutting left-over places: "Last year a German laborer mowed some of the fence corners, and small runs on this place, from which he got about one ton of hay, for which he might have got $10. I think there are many boys who read the *Cultivator*, who might make a few dollars every year by securing this grass, and by it improve the appearance of their farms." *Ohio Cultivator*, VIII (July 1, 1852), 195.

7 acres field of wheat, to cut and put upp [*sic*] in shock, for 162½ [$1.62½] per acre to Jonathan Miller. Measured 7 acres 16 perches $11.53¾." Not all wheat was contracted out on this basis, and harvest hands were hired on a regular rate in the wheat field: "This day had Tho. Oliver and William Castleman, cradling wheat, paid them in full each $1.25, 3 rakers and binders, 3 dollars each a dollar for this day's work." Obviously he could not rely exclusively upon harvest hands or those who contracted to cut wheat by the acre, for a hired man in his regular employ negotiated a wage increase from him during the harvest season: "Bargained with Richard Cole to continue to work." Cole, who started at eight dollars per month, was raised to ten dollars in August.[44] Farmers were under considerable pressure to complete their harvest and thus resorted to either method of employing men. The larger operator was in a better position to contract the job out on a flat rate per acre, whereas the farmer of a small tract tended to hire men only for a specific number of days. Since circumstances varied from one locale to another, some farmers employed both methods during the same season.

Country merchants were the economic center of the community, especially in matters pertaining to the annual harvest. Some early merchants were also farmers, and it is difficult to determine which was economically more important: store or farm.[45] In terms of labor, the storekeeper was in a position to fulfill his own harvest needs with cheap help. Elijah Wadsworth, a storekeeper and farmer near Youngstown in northeastern Ohio during 1813–21, enjoyed considerable local farm trade. Purchases made on credit from his store were repaid with labor by his customers. In July, 1815, a man was credited with work "by yourself and boy's two days at haying," indicating that debtors also had their children assist in the fields, with their work applied toward the reduction of outstanding bills at the store. Wadsworth exercised latitude in determining the amount of work rendered: "William Hooly cr. by work cradling oat[s]—say ½ day."[46] Some

44. Farmer's Memorandum Book, Stark County, Ohio, entries of June 19, August 15, 1846.

45. For additional information on frontier merchants, see Lewis E. Atherton, "The Services of the Frontier Merchant," *Mississippi Valley Historical Review*, XXIV (1937), 153–70.

46. Elijah Wadsworth Farm Accounts, 1813–21, p. 54, entry of August 2, 1815; p. 56, entry of August 22, 1815; p. 59, entry of September 18, 1815; p. 73, entry of July 26, 1816; p. 74, entry of July 29, 1816. For similar examples, see Young Daybook Farm and General Store Accounts, p. 54, entries of April 26, 1823; May 3, 1823; p. 58, entry of July 16, 1823; p. 63, entry of October 14, 1823; Hart Store and Farm Records, entries of 1819 for Edward Phelps.

storekeepers were quite specific in demanding harvest labor: an Ohio storekeeper in the 1840's sold a barrel of flour and stipulated that it was to be repaid in harvest labor figured at the rate of fifty cents per day.[47]

Merchants also fulfilled crediting functions when cash was scarce. Sometimes farmers arranged the payment of their harvest hands through the local storekeeper, from whom the laborers obtained wages either in cash or store pay. For the farmer it was convenient if not mandatory—especially when the grain was sold to the merchant, who deducted the payments of cash or goods for the hands from the total credit of the farmer's account. Crediting of harvest wages was a sophisticated arrangement. One harvest hand who had a series of debts with a local storekeeper never saw the cash, which was applied instead to his debits. During 1828 Arthur Flynn accumulated debts with Charles Phillips, a merchant at Princeton, Indiana. A farmer hired Flynn to harvest grain and mow hay at fifty cents per day. Payment was in the form of a cash order which Flynn endorsed and gave to the merchant to be applied to the debts. While it is impossible to determine the originator of this arrangement, the crediting transaction indicates that the merchant was flexible in his financial dealings and that itinerants were able to work summer harvests and have their wages transferred to the local merchant.[48]

The daybooks and ledgers of John Williams, a Springfield, Illinois, merchant, offer conclusive proof of the relationship between storekeepers and local harvesting. Williams was both a successful merchant and a land dealer; while he did not involve himself directly in the operation of farm land, he had financial dealings with many farmers in the area. Hired hands on area farms came into Springfield to trade at his store. During the summer months Williams debited the accounts of local farmers in his ledgers to pay the farm hands who came in for their wages.[49] It was advantageous for Williams to make cash advances in the form of wages to farm hands: when they came

47. Johnston Thurston Farm Accounts, 1832–57, entry of April 10, 1844.
48. Charles Phillips Accountbook, 1826–31, see cash slip dated June 26, 1829, payable to Charles Phillips, attached to account sheet of Arthur Flynn. Elisha Embree Business Papers.
49. Journal, 1851–54, pp. 150, 217; Petty Ledger, 1854–58, p. 169; Cashbook, February, 1851–August, 1856, p. 15, entry of July 12, 1851; for similar accounts, see pp. 16, 21, 22, 24, 47, 48, 56, 57, John Williams Business Papers. For similar mercantile activity, see the store records of Nicholas McCarthy at Indianapolis during 1829–30: Store Daybook-Ledger, 1829–30, p. 77, entry of July 7, 1829; p. 133, entry of August 3, 1829, as well as subsequent daybook entries during August–October, Nicholas McCarty Records.

to town for their pay, they undoubtedly patronized his store. In short, the merchant became a middleman or agent between the farmer and his hands regarding financial matters.

Tradesmen and artisans were essential to the agricultural frontier, not only to provide specialized skills and services, but also to help in the harvest fields during season.[50] According to John Lorain, "Labourers of all descriptions as well as most mechanics must assist in the harvest."[51] Tradesmen working in the harvest were fairly common, and many were in the process of acquiring or establishing their own farms.[52] Hiram Moulton was such a man of diverse skills: shoemaking, carpentering, and farm labor. Working in Ashtabula County, Ohio, during the 1830's and 1840's, he was available to farmers at all times for plowing, sheep shearing, butchering, and even fashioning implements. He mowed hay in summer, picked corn in late autumn, and threshed grain in winter.[53] Similarly, carpenters who came in season to do minor construction and repair work on farms also assisted in the harvest fields. The farm accountbook of Nathan Pierce at Calhoun County, Michigan, in 1851 shows that Pierce hired Marquis Griffith

50. Some tradesmen, of course, owned land or farms; and like storekeepers they obtained cheap labor in return for services. Blacksmiths and shoemakers, for example, were often able to demand help in the harvest as repayment for their services. See Frank Robbins, "The Personal Reminiscences of General Chauncey Eggleston," *Ohio History*, XLI (1932), 300–309. For other examples, see William D. Gribbens Shoemaker Accountbook, 1831–46, pp. 47, 112; Augustin Williamson Tanner's Accountbook, 1823–45, p. 62, and account entries for John Martin during 1837–39; W. W. Hamelle, *A Standard History of White County, Indiana* (Chicago and New York, 1915), I, pp. 218–19; Bateman and Selby, eds., *Historical Encyclopedia of Illinois Including Genealogy, Family Records and Biography* of McHenry County Citizens, I, p. 1052. According to one individual who grew up on the Michigan frontier in the 1850's, settlers did not easily forgive the skilled tradesman who required them to pitch hay in return for services. Davenport, *Timberland Times*, p. 210.

51. John Lorain, *Hints to Emigrants* (Philadelphia, 1819), p. 11.

52. This desire was poetically summed up in an Ohio carpenter's ledger in 1828:

"I wish I had a little land
Sufficient my grain to raise
Likewise a little paster [sic] lot
in which my cow might graze."

Samuel and William Henry Egbert Accountbook, 1828–45.

53. Hiram Moulton Ledgerbook, p. 3, entry of January, 1832; p. 5, entry of February, 1832; p. 10, entry of February, 1841; p. 17, entry of June–July, 1838; p. 20, entry of August, 1842; p. 24, entries of January 21 and February 19, 1840; p. 36, entry of May 31, 1842; p. 38, entry of June 27, 1842; p. 58, entry of June 28, 1846. A similar case of a multi-skilled tradesman was Conrad Winter, who hired out at haying season and repairing grain cradles in Fairfield County, Ohio. Conrad Winter Farm Accounts, 1838–52, pp. 10–11, 14–15, 32–33.

to come from Washtenaw and do carpenter-joiner work on his buildings in April; by mid-July he completed the lathing job, helped hoe
corn and potatoes, and then worked several days harvesting wheat.[54]

Tradesmen went as far north as the Minnesota Territory in the
1850's. John Shumway, a carpenter who came up to Minneapolis in
1855 from Connecticut, had in mind the establishment of a farm on
a land claim. During the first year he worked out at monthly wages
of twenty and twenty-five dollars; with the approach of winter his
employer requested him to remain and chop wood for board, with
the provision that he was free to spend his time otherwise at whatever he chose. The following summer Shumway wrote that he was
hired out to a farmer at twenty-six dollars per month, working as one
of five binders who followed the reaper in the field. Although work
was easy to obtain, he planned to devote himself to improvements of
his own claim in the fall, along with cutting hay and plowing.[55]

An English traveler in the United States during the late 1840's
reported that town laborers, artisans, and mechanics annually turned
out in the harvest fields. Aside from the fact that the work was easy
to learn and wages high, it was in the interest of this working class
to support and assist the farmer, for the latter's success in crop harvesting had an immediate bearing on the amount of money he spent
in town for labor and services. If the farmer suffered, the artisans and
mechanics were equally at a loss.[56]

The local blacksmith shop appeared to be the logical place where
loiterers and common laborers could be secured for harvest employ-

54. Nathan Pierce Accountbook, 1848–60, p. 65, entries of April 29, May 24,
June 21, July 7, 17, 1851. In a similar case a carpenter worked on a farm at
Oakland County, Michigan, in 1855. Besides constructing gates, he also threshed
clover and stacked wheat. C. F. Morley Accountbook, p. 12; see also pp. 4,
50, 74 for accounts pertaining to wagon repair, construction of gates and wood
racks, and fashioning of ladders and ax halves. See also the carpenter records
of William Hunt, Accountbook, p. 4, entry in 1842 account for Mr. Dormand; p.
6, entry of September, 1842, and account for Freeman Damond.

55. John Shumway to Miss Amoret Louisa (Minneapolis, March 9, [1855],
November 25, 1855, and August 9, 1856), John Shumway Letters. A similar
case of a blacksmith trekking over long distances was John Reife, who, during
the 1850's in Ohio, worked the harvest fields cutting wheat with a cradle for
62.5 cents per acre and usually making $2 or more per day. Portrait and
Biographical Album of Greene and Clark Counties, Ohio (Chicago, 1890), pp.
211–12. For a similar example, see Pictorial and Biographical Memoirs of Elkhart
and St. Joseph Counties, Indiana (Chicago, 1893), p. 462.

56. W. M. Stewart, Eleven Years' Experience in the Western States of
America (London, 1870), pp. 78–80. For other examples of townspeople
seeking employment in the harvest fields, see History of Crawford County and
Ohio (Chicago, 1881), pp. 804–5; Lyle S. Evans, ed., A Standard History of
Ross County, Ohio (Chicago and New York, 1917), II, p. 523.

ment. Henry Parker Smith, son of a farmer near Schoolcraft, Michigan, was ill with diarrhea during the July harvest of 1848 and had to secure a replacement: "I went to the blacksmithshop and hired a hand to take my place. . . ."[57] A poem of the 1850's extolled the conviviality of the blacksmith shop for various itinerants:

> The village idlers lounge about.
> And talk the country gossip o'er;
> And now and then a farmer's man
> Drives up on horseback to the door;
> And reapers come from pastures near. . . .[58]

When mechanics or tradesmen themselves did not take time off to work in the fields for farmers, they at least allowed or gave tacit approval for their assistants and apprentices to do so.[59] The records of Jonathan Gordon, an Ohio blacksmith, indicate such a situation: one of his employees, William Lutzin, worked at the shop for $140 per year. Various notations attached to his account show time lost from work, including camp meetings and militia training; particularly outstanding were the large number of days lost at harvesting in midsummer. Gordon also hired an apprentice or assistant in April, 1819, at ninety dollars per year. This individual apparently had worked on a farm prior to his employment at the blacksmith shop: in May he took off a day from work to shear sheep for "his old master," and again during July to cradle grain.[60]

A sixteen-year-old Ohio youth was apprenticed to a blacksmith during 1849–52. Every year at harvest season the boy was given two weeks leave to work in the harvest fields, and these earnings sufficed as his personal spending money during the remainder of the year.[61]

57. Henry Parker Smith Diary, entry of July 14, 1848. A mechanic at Rock County, Wisconsin, closed his shop for the lack of business and hired out during the summer on a nearby farm. George W. Ogden Diary, 1837–41, entry of June 20, 1838.

58. *Watchman of the Prairies*, January 20, 1852.

59. John Reife, the above-mentioned blacksmith who followed the harvest circuit, ultimately settled at Springfield, Ohio, and established a blacksmith shop; yet each season he turned out into the fields and worked for area farmers. *Portrait and Biographical Album of Greene and Clark Counties, Ohio*, pp. 211–12.

60. Jonathan Gordon Daybook, see back cover listing employees' records, especially entries for William Lutzin of April, 1816, and July 8–11, 1816; see also entries of April 19, May 31, July 7–8, 11, 1819. During 1823, one of his assistants lost twelve days at harvest and haying; entry of July 23, 1823. A blacksmith at Manchester, Michigan, in the 1850's lost the services of his assistant for twenty days during the harvest. See Manchester Blacksmith Shop Ledger, 1854–61, p. 47.

61. *History of Allen County, Ohio* (Chicago, 1885), p. 665.

While evidence of this kind is admittedly sparse, the practice was apparently common with the trades in the early Midwest. John Craft apprenticed himself out to a planemaker who also ran a farm in conjunction with his trade near Charlottesville in Hancock County, Indiana. The boy's pay during apprenticeship was board and lodging only, except when he was paid one dollar per day to work in the harvest fields of his employer.[62] A summary conclusion is that both farmers and tradesmen alike benefited from this temporary summer employment: farmers obtained necessary help in harvests, while tradesmen and apprentices had the opportunity to make extra pocket money.

Employment in the summer harvest fields was a boon to schoolteachers, enabling them to make good cash wages when school was not in session; many in fact worked the entire summer as farm hands on a daily or monthly wage. Not surprisingly, wages received as a prime farm hand sometimes exceeded the winter salary as a schoolteacher.[63] Rare was the teacher who earned higher wages than a farm hand, although Almon Frost, who taught school in Oakland County, Michigan, during the 1840's for thirteen dollars per month in winter, earned only ten dollars per month on summer vacations working on farms. Farmers grumbled that he obtained such high pay for teaching in comparison to manual labor wages.[64] At Kendall County, Illinois, the school board in 1847 viewed the teacher on the same level as a farm hand: "One man thought $8, the wages of a farm hand, sufficient, but the more educated knew that it was impossible to secure a competent man for any such money." The result was that no teacher could be hired that year.[65] A. D. Van Buren taught school, worked harvests, and tended a threshing machine at Oakland County, Michigan, in

62. George Hazzard, *Hazzard's History of Henry County, Indiana 1822–1906* (New Castle, Ind., 1906), I, p. 410.

63. For examples, see *History of Kalamazoo County, Michigan*, p. 476; Samuel Harden, *Early Life and Times of Boone County, Indiana* (Lebanon, 1887), pp. 328–29.

64. *Portrait and Biographical Album of Oakland County, Michigan*, p. 346.

65. Bateman and Selby, eds., *Historical Encyclopedia of Illinois and History of Kendall County*, II, p. 810. The problem was common in the Midwest: " 'The occupation of a teacher is too often compared with that of a common laborer. A laborer can be employed for from $6.00 to $10.00 a month and why should not a man teach school for as little, since teaching school is not as hard as mauling rails, grubbing, plowing, etc. I once heard a farmer say while talking about the price of teaching, that if he were making $10.00 a month he would think he was doing good business, and to give a teacher $20 and $25 a month was entirely too exorbitant.' " Remarks at a Monroe County, Indiana, teachers' association meeting in 1843, as cited in James A. Woodburn, "James Woodburn: Hoosier Schoolmaster," *Indiana History*, XXXII (1936), 245.

the 1840's. During the school session of 1847 he administered stern discipline to an unruly class of boys who had thrown the teacher out the previous term. The potential crisis was checked when he let it be known that "I have been used to tending a threshing machine, and know how to bring out the wheat."[66] Although many schoolteachers served as seasonal farm laborers, especially in peak harvest periods, they were not always held in high respect as mentors for young minds!

Harvest labor was an introduction to American farming for many newly arrived immigrants who welcomed the opportunity to make attractive wages. Typical of many Irishmen was John Cass, who arrived at Chicago in 1849 with only a few cents to his name. He worked in the harvest fields of nearby Grundy and Kendall counties, afterward securing employment in Iowa on public construction—in all likelihood digging work on roads and railroads. The following spring Cass was back in Illinois, working on canal boats along the Illinois-Michigan Canal. This employment then gave way to work in the harvest fields once more, although he stayed on as a hired hand during the year for ten dollars per month.[67] The Reverend Gustaf Unonius, who settled in the 1840's at Waukesha County, Wisconsin, hired a Swedish sailor who similarly worked about in different locales. This itinerant had worked on farms in the Midwest and at odd jobs, traveling sometimes as far south as New Orleans:

> For such perambulating laborers harvest time is a golden season when wages are high and farmers have difficulty in getting the help they need. I hardly know what sort of man it would be that could not count on employment and earnings then. After working on various farms our Swedish sailor had now earned a sum of ready cash for travel and was preparing, not to pack up his possessions, for he had no baggage to pack, but as usual to depart for some other market.[68]

Less astute immigrants were sometimes tricked and shamefully exploited at harvest. Arend Jan Brusse, a young Dutch lad, came to

66. *Michigan Pioneer Collections*, XIV, p. 361. Schoolteachers were often viewed with little respect. Men whose occupations did not require work with their hands were suspect in the eyes of the local populace: "Frequently they volunteered to show their mettle by acts of manual labor in order to receive favor at the hands of the people." William Vogel, "Home Life in Early Indiana," *Indiana History*, X (1914), 299.

67. *History of Grundy County, Illinois* (Chicago, 1882), part II, p. 47. For examples of other immigrants whose first employment was harvesting grain, see *History of St. Clair County, Illinois* (Philadelphia, 1881), p. 272; Bateman and Selby, eds., *Historical Encyclopedia of Illinois and History of Carroll County* (Chicago, 1913), II, pp. 774–75.

68. Unonius, *Memoirs*, I, pp. 332–33.

the United States in 1846 with his parents, brother, and sister. The family took the traditional route of many immigrants during this period: by ship to Boston, then over to Albany to take the Erie Canal westward to Buffalo, and a ship via the Great Lakes to Milwaukee. Work was available in the nearby countryside, and a farmer promised to provide employment throughout the harvest for all members of the family with the option to continue working for him afterward on a share-crop basis. The family was conveyed out to the farm by a hired team and wagon. Brusse described what happened:

> This farmer had a large field of wheat. He was to give every one of the family work, or to those of us that could work. He tried us, to see what we could do. My brother Gerrit did not like the appearance of things; so he went to work for another farmer. The rest of us were set to work. I and two other hands were sent into the fields with cradles to cut grain; it was the hardest work I ever did. I found that this farmer was a dishonest rascal. When his grain was cut, we had to leave, without getting a cent for our hard and honest work. We again hired teams and went back to Milwaukee.[69]

Without knowledge of English and reliable advice from fellow countrymen, some immigrants were taken advantage of during their first year in America; but it must be assumed that a greater number were employed in the harvest fields and were honestly compensated for their work.

Historical evidence pertaining to farm labor in general is not abundant, and the role of northern black farm laborers is even more obscure. In 1851 an English traveler in the United States put the matter in strikingly blunt and almost modern terms when speaking of the infrequency of Negro agricultural labor:

> 'Wherever the interests of the white man and the black come into collision in the United States, the black man goes to the wall.' Such is the statement of those who, in America, profess to be the coloured man's friend. It is certain that wherever labour is scarce, there he is readily employed; when it becomes plentiful, he is the first to be discharged. The whites are employed in preference, from sympathy with their colour, on account of their votes, through fear of their political or other influence.[70]

69. Henry S. Lucas, "Reminiscences of Arend Jan Brusse on the Early Dutch Settlement in Milwaukee," *Wisconsin History*, XXX (1946), 87. Following this unfortunate experience, Brusse found work in another common itinerant occupation: brickyard labor.

70. James F. W. Johnston, *Notes on North America Agricultural, Economical, and Social* (Boston, 1851), II, pp. 314–15. For studies dealing with the Negro

Blacks were in fact used when labor was in short supply. An early example occurred during the War of 1812 at Youngstown, Ohio, where storekeeper Elijah Wadsworth hired a black named Peter during August and September, 1813. The following spring another black named Frank was employed on the farm at corn planting. Frank seemingly lived in the area but worked on a day labor basis; during July, 1814, he mowed hay several days, while in the spring of 1815 he threshed oats and worked on Wadsworth's ice house.[71] Troop requirements for the War of 1812 had reduced the number of white men available for harvesting in Ross County, Ohio; Henry Miskel, a black, was credited with assisting the women and children in the harvest, working both day and night.[72]

Like southern Ohio, southern Indiana attracted a heavy concentration of Negroes. At Princeton in Gibson County two blacks worked in the early 1820's as hired hands on the farm of William Embree, located several miles from town. They were described as good hands, living in a small log cabin on the farm. One was educated and often borrowed books from residents in the neighborhood. Both worked in corn planting season and chopped wood during the interim period before corn picking and harvesting. For two years they resided on the farm until they suddenly disappeared. It was common opinion that slave catchers kidnapped them and took them across the Ohio River.[73]

By the 1830's and 1840's Indianapolis attracted a sizable number of blacks, many of them finding employment on area farms. In July, 1845, the issue of available jobs and hiring of blacks exploded in an

in the North prior to 1860, see Lorenzo J. Greene and Carter G. Woodson, *The Negro Wage Earner* (Washington, 1930); Leon F. Litwack, *North of Slavery: The Negro in the Free States, 1790–1860* (Chicago, 1961); Eugene H. Berwanger, *The Frontier against Slavery: Western Anti-Negro Prejudice and the Slavery Extension Controversy* (Urbana, 1967); and Emma Lou Thornbrough, *The Negro in Indiana: A Study of a Minority* (Indianapolis, 1957). Thornbrough states that the 1850 census showed 2,150 Negroes, 976 being listed under the occupation of farming while 720 were enumerated as laborers who ". . . were in many cases farm laborers. In clearing the forest and transforming the state from a wilderness into a prosperous agricultural society these Negroes played a part." P. 133.

71. Wadsworth Farm Accounts, pp. 1, 3, entries of August 23, September 28, 1813. He identified his black employees as, e.g., "Frank the Negro," p. 17, entry of May 10, 1814; p. 23, entries of July 22, 23, 25, 28, 1814; p. 43, entries of March 6–7, 14, 1815.

72. Isaac J. Finley and Rufus Putnam, *Pioneer Record and Reminiscences of the Early Settlers and Settlement of Ross County, Ohio* (Cincinnati, 1871), p. 13.

73. William Cockrum, *Pioneer History of Indiana Including Stories, Incidents and Customs of the Early Settlers* (Oakland City, Ind., 1907), p. 571.

ugly racial incident when a black farm hand was brutally murdered. John Tucker, once a slave in Kentucky who had honorably obtained his freedom, worked on a farm near Indianapolis and was generally known as a quiet man. When an argument between him and several whites came to physical blows, Tucker attempted to defend himself, but was fatally injured when one of the whites struck him and fractured his skull. The affair was all the more disgraceful since it occurred in the presence of 200 onlookers whose language and mood were "get the damned nigger, they are too thick about here. . . ." It is significant that the victim in this tragedy was a black farm hand in times that were still not prosperous.[74]

Negroes were employed on farms in the Indianapolis area, and Calvin Fletcher's diary not only documents their work but also proves conclusively that they were hired in instances when white hands could not be secured. This confirms what Johnston observed: Negroes received employment when work was not scarce—they were the last hired and the first fired. In July, 1847, Fletcher employed three blacks at hay mowing on land belonging to one of his tenants; and a week later they were cutting hay on another part of his property. Their terms of employment were stipulated: ". . . I now pay 75c per day & 87½ per acre for mowing grass & they feed themselves." A possible explanation, aside for the need of hands, was illness of his foreman and "Coy the cradler." The following harvest season blacks were again employed: Joe Sanders and another Negro worked in the clover field, and a week later Fletcher had them cradling and binding grain.[75]

The harvests in the early 1850's were marked by excessive heat and a local epidemic of cholera. Fletcher's harvest hands were so sick and exhausted that they demanded a holiday as a relief; reluctantly he had to settle and pay them off. The harvesting was clearly carried out under extraordinary conditions when a threat of disease caused

74. *Indianapolis Sentinel*, as cited in *Cincinnati Daily Gazette*, July 11, 14, 17, 21, 23, 1845. Calvin Fletcher was among those who spoke out for a vigorous prosecution of the white men involved in the incident; *ibid.*, July 17, 23, 1845. An excellent study of the anti-black attitude in the Midwest is James H. Rodabaugh's "The Negro in the Old Northwest," in O. Fritiof Ander, ed., *In the Trek of the Immigrants: Essays Presented to Carl Wittke* (Rock Island, 1964), pp. 219–39. The problem of blacks competing against whites for employment was present in other parts of the North prior to 1860: see E. S. Abdy, *Journal of a Residence and Tour in the United States of North America, from April, 1833, to October, 1834* (New York, 1969), I, pp. 116–17; III, p. 330.

75. Fletcher Diary, entries of July 1, 9, 18–24, 27–31, 1847; June 15, 24, 1848. See also entry of July 22, 1848, regarding "Harrison the negro" working at one of the tenant farms.

a major labor shortage, but Fletcher's own statement reveals the fact
that blacks were welcomed harvest hands when white harvesters
were either unavailable or walked off the job:

> When [the] harvest arrivd & we had some 200 of acres or more to
> harvest. . . [;] a general sickness prevaile[d] throghout [sic] the
> country call[e]d Flux . . . Some of my hands took [sick?] & others
> could not be hired—My wheat 1/5 of it prostrated & could not be
> cradled[.] We had a number of colored men hired[.] But Curt[i]s
> Potts & Jud Bolin could do much more & th[e]y all except one gave
> out—Harvest hands command[e]d from one to one & a half dollars
> per day—My hands left the down[ed] wheat & passed over it[.] we
> had some 75 or 80 acres of v[er]ly heavy wheat—Many people did not
> cut their down[ed] wheat but turn[e]d their hogs upon it[.] In order
> to save mine I had to take the sickle & Keep up with the hands with
> 2 other reapers making 3 & 4 cradlers & 3 reapers[.] At length we got
> thro' [through]—got ½ stacked—[.][76]

A similar dearth of labor occurred in the summer of 1853, when
sickness among Fletcher's hands again necessitated employment of
blacks in the harvest field. In that year he used a reaping machine
which, according to him, did a good day's work. Unfortunately,
Fletcher did not state if the black harvest hands were actually connected with the operation of the machines or if they were simply left
with the raking and binding tasks. He did express regret that the harvest was not completed and that in his absence the hands did not
perform their work well; nonetheless, he held a large harvest dinner
for the neighbors, tenants, and hired hands at the completion of the
work.[77]

It should be mentioned that black harvest hands were employed
elsewhere in the Midwest. In late autumn of 1857 Edward Robbins,
a farmer outside Milwaukee, employed a "Black Boy" in plowing and
corn husking.[78] At Dearborn in eastern Michigan, William Nowlin
recalled that three or four Negroes were employed in 1857 on the
farm to help in the haying and harvesting operations. One of the
blacks brought his sister, who was hired to assist in the kitchen with
the cooking. After the harvest the blacks returned across the border
to Windsor, Canada, on account of their fear of remaining too long

76. *Ibid.*, entries of August 10, 21, 22, 1850, and December 31, 1851. During
the cholera epidemic of 1849, the owner of a large farm at Pickaway County,
Ohio, reported the death of thirty-four hired hands, owing in part to a lack of
medical help. *Ohio State Journal*, as cited in *Daily Sanduskian*, August 28, 1849.
77. Fletcher Diary, entries of June 29, 30, July 2, 5, 25, 30, 1853.
78. Edward Robbins Diary, I, entry of November 4, 1857.

in the United States and risking recapture by slave hunters.[79] From these traces of evidence of Negro harvest labor it is not easy to draw firm conclusions, save that Negroes, except in certain areas, were not used extensively in this work. When they were employed in the harvest field, it was because of a lack of white men to perform this type of labor.

The shortage of harvest hands, even with the utilization of harvesting machinery, remained a problem. Wheat production increased during the decades prior to the Civil War in excess of either available manpower or machinery to handle the task.[80] The dilemma was summed up by an Illinois farmer in 1855:

> The wheat crop has been very large indeed and the country did not afford help enough to harvest it in season. I do not believe that there was more than two thirds of the wheat that grew in this country saved. Wages were two dollars a day for binders. The wheat and oats in this country are all reaped by machines. A machine is drawn by four horses and will reap from 10 to 20 acres per day. Wheat has been so heavy this year that it has taken 9 or 10 hands to bind after one machine when 7 or 8 were sufficient last year.[81]

This labor shortage became apparent in the 1840's. The *Prairie Farmer* of Chicago offered a logical explanation: manpower had been drained off when the Mexican War broke out in 1846, compounded by a subsequent exodus of harvest workers for the gold fields of California. Yet the report was optimistic that this loss could be offset by the employment of immigrants and the use of labor-saving devices.[82] The 1850's were basically no different. A disgruntled Ohio

79. William Nowlin, *The Bark Covered House, or Back in the Woods Again* (Detroit, 1876), pp. 220–22. The presence of blacks in northern Ohio and at Detroit was viewed by a newspaper editor in negative terms. Employment opportunities were scarce, and blacks were advised to remain at Cincinnati and the lower parts of the state. *Daily Commercial Register*, August 4, 1853.

80. When farmers converted to mechanized harvesting equipment in the 1850's, the primary reason was the rising cost of harvest labor rather than the overall expansion of wheat production, according to Paul David's "Mechanization of Reaping in the Ante-Bellum Midwest," in Rosovsky, ed., *Industrialization in Two Systems*, pp. 25–28.

81. Angle, "Story of an Ordinary Man," 221. That same season, the *Illinois Daily Journal* observed on August 13, 1855: "A Gentleman whose business has recently led him among the farmers in every county in Southern Illinois and Indiana, informs us that large quantities of grain have been lost the present season from the inability of farmers to produce sufficient harvesting machines and laborers. . . ."

82. *Prairie Farmer*, IX (July, 1849), 212. This same situation prevailed in the late 1850's, according to Wayne Temple, "The Pike's Peak Gold Rush," *Illinois Historical Journal*, XLIV (1951), 147–48, 159.

farmer complained to the *Ohio Cultivator* about the lack of harvest hands and the incompetence of those who were employed.[83] An Illinois farmer had encountered the same problem in 1845–46. Efficient harvest hands were not to be found anywhere, and he recalled swinging the cradle himself for twenty-seven consecutive days, including Sundays, because of the unavailability of men: "Hence, I had to do my own harvesting which decided me to quit farming for a living."[84]

Farmers often had to search for harvest help and occasionally met with no success. William Sewall of Jacksonville, Illinois, rode through the entire neighborhood looking for hands to help cut his hay: "Cutting grass myself, not being able to get help. Putting up hay."[85] Competition for harvest help was keen, and the farmer with sufficient capital controlled the local labor market. Another Illinois farmer described the dilemma confronting him and his fellow farmers, who were unable to match the high wages offered by a wealthy landowner named Shillaber: ". . . hands very scarce—worth $1.50 in cash at ie what Mr. Shillaber gives & he monopolizes them—shall lose some of my grain most probably—"[86] Farmers in proximity to cities enjoyed an advantage over their more remotely situated fellow cultivators; their diaries contain occasional reference to trips into town, where unemployed laborers were secured.[87]

83. *Ohio Cultivator*, XIII (September 1, 1857), 260–61.
84. Bateman and Selby, eds., *Historical Encyclopedia of Illinois and History of Tazewell County* (Chicago, 1905), II, p. 911.
85. Sewall, *Diary*, p. 173; at another instance he noted: "Went up the bottom to hunt for hands for harvest time." P. 247. See also William Wallace Wright Memoirs: Diary, p. 62, entry of July 19, 1841; and Spencer and Emily Carrier Diaries, 1847–54, entry of September 17, 1849.
86. Charles Hubbard Farm Diary, 1842–52, p. 162, entry of July 22, 1845. On occasions, however, farm hands had to search for employment in harvests. Formerly a schoolteacher in Indiana, Jabez Brown came out via wagon to Baraboo, Wisconsin. In July, 1855, his first employment was cradling wheat for half a day; he noted the following day: "Went to see a man named Kelly to get work in harvest, and failed, then I went to see a man named All. and cut wheat for him about half the day." Jabez Brown Diary, entries of July 23, 24, 1855.
87. Samuel Skewes Diaries, 1839–70, IV, p. 99, entries of July 15, 21, 1856; Francis Larpenteur Diary, 1856–61, entry of July 21, 1856. The letter of a harvest hand at Chicago in 1836 reveals the ease which men had at hiring for a job in the countryside: "I left town near four weeks ago and went into the country 25 miles South west to help the man I Board with here in town to do his haying and harvest. I expected to be gone but 2 weeks[;] this has caused my neglect [to write]. I worked 26 days at haying and harvest and in the time I had but ½ days rest for wet weather. . . ." Letter of James Hanks (Chicago, September 6, 1836), as cited in R. Waite Joslyn and Frank W. Joslyn, *History of Kane County, Ill.* (Chicago, 1908), I, p. 86.

Men without work frequently turned to the cities, where employment agencies recruited them for jobs in various locales.[88] An army of common laborers flourished in numbers and without steady work to warrant the following advice from a Cleveland newspaper in July, 1848: "The season of Harvesting and haying is just commencing, and we would say to those if any such there be (of laborers) in our city, go into the country and you can get good wages and plenty of work. There are thousands of acres of grass and grain to cut this month. The fields are ready for the harvest, and laborers are in good cash demand, and fragrant is the new mown hay, and the rich ripe wheat."[89] The situation was similar several years later, in 1855: "If there is no work in the city, go to the country where hosts of sheaves of grain are awaiting the fork. One may as well be dead as idle."[90]

Urban unemployment was obviously a problem even in good times, but it became worse with the depression of 1857. Paradoxically, the ranks of urban unemployed increased, while harvest and general farm jobs in the surrounding countryside went unfilled. The *Cleveland Leader* in August, 1857, urged common laborers to turn out to the farms:

> During the past week, we have visited Cuyahoga, Lake, Portage, Trumbull, and Ashtabula counties and inspected the crops. . . . Wheat is now being harvested, and a good yield is in sight. The weather has been very good to the farmer, the rain and sunshine have been just right, making grains of the earlier type ripen before time. The only problem seems to be getting labor in the fields. Farmers are unable to do all the work themselves, and they can not hire help for love or

88. An advertisement for this type of agency appeared in a Cleveland newspaper: "A hired man wanted—A young man well acquainted with the farming business, wishing to hire out for the season, will find a favorable opportunity by calling at this office. Liberal wages will be paid to a good faithful hand—none other need apply." *Cleveland Herald and Gazette,* June 19, 1838, as cited in *Annals of Cleveland, 1818–1935: A Digest and Index of the Newspaper Record of Events and Opinions* (Cleveland, 1937–38), XXI, p. 99. Hereafter cited as *Annals of Cleveland.* These agencies operated in other cities. Harriet Martineau described an employment office at New York which catered especially to immigrants. The number of job opportunities exceeded the number of available applicants at a ratio of six to one. Harriet Martineau, *Society in America* (London, 1837), II, pp. 97–98.

89. *Cleveland True Democrat,* July 12, 1848, as cited in *Annals of Cleveland,* XXXI, p. 46.

90. *Cleveland Leader,* August 3, 1855, as cited *ibid.,* XXXVIII, p. 129. The same situation for urban laborers existed at Sandusky. In response to a tradesman's complaint of a lack of work, the editor suggested to this individual and his co-workers that ". . . 'farmers would gladly give them employment in their harvest fields' at high wages. . . ." *Daily Commercial Register,* July 20, 1855.

money. Men, who, in the city, complain they can find nothing to do, can easily earn from $1.50 to $1.75 per day in the fields.[91]

Clearly, many laborers in the cities were reluctant to obtain temporary employment. In a letter to the *Ohio Cultivator* in September, 1857, an angry farmer criticized the unemployed in towns and cities who turned up their noses at the idea of working in the harvest fields yet bemoaned "hard times."[92]

Reluctance of laborers to leave the city was a problem elsewhere in the Midwest. In western Illinois, the *Moline Independent* reported that farmers could not obtain men to assist in corn harvesting during November, 1857. When a farmer tried to get help to harvest his corn at $1.25 per day, the laborers complained that they wanted $1.50 and refused to work for less. "Let such men starve" was the conclusion.[93] The *Illinois Farmer* adopted a similarly critical attitude and urged greater implementation of labor-saving machinery so the farmer might not have to be confronted in the future with such tactics on the part of laboring classes: "Hired Help for Harvest—The lazy idlers, who loaf about the towns, and want double prices when they work in the harvest fields,—are miserable help when they get there. What is to be done? The Reaper and Stacker offers [sic] some relief. Our farmers cannot get along without agricultural machinery, and those machines which require the fewest hands to tend them, are very likely to be the best."[94]

The effects from the 1857 economic panic lingered over the next several years in the Midwest. The plight of unemployed laborers became critical at places like Chicago, where charitable relief funds were soon exhausted. Newspapers urged the jobless to go to the farms and work if necessary not for wages but board and lodging. "SEND THE POOR INTO THE COUNTRY" was the advice.[95] Unemployment was also a problem at nearby Milwaukee as late as the summer of 1860, when men were urged to work either on railroad construction or in

91. *Cleveland Leader,* August 10, 1857, as cited in *Annals of Cleveland,* XL, p. 101.
92. *Ohio Cultivator,* XIII (September 1, 1857), 259.
93. *Moline Independent,* as cited in *Chicago Daily Democrat,* December 4, 1857.
94. *Illinois Farmer,* III (August, 1858), 120. Matthias Dunlap, who maintained a distrust of farm laborers, claimed that there was a class distinction between the worthy mechanic and the lowly farm hand. The farmer was advised to mechanize his farming operation and establish a firm alliance with the mechanic, rather than with the undependable hired hand. Dunlap Clippings Book, September, 1853–September, 1858, article dated May 22, 1854.
95. *Chicago Daily Democrat,* October 27, November 19, December 9, 1857.

the harvest fields. According to the *Milwaukee Sentinel*, harvest hands were reportedly needed at Waukesha, Jefferson, Rock, Dane, and Dodge counties in the central part of the state; those wanting harvest work were transported at half fare on the railroad.[96]

By the 1840's and 1850's it was apparent that an itinerant labor force was concentrated in urban centers, while agricultural areas suffered from a lack of manpower, especially during the critical harvest season. It is not entirely clear why these individuals came to the cities, though several reasons help explain their refusal or inability to go out into the countryside at harvest time. These include the brevity of the harvest, occasionally low pay, and the cost of transportation to the harvest areas. After considering all the factors, many probably concluded that this gruelling work was not worth the time, effort, and expense.

Harvesting offered seasonal employment as long as grain remained in the field to be cut. The working season could be long or short, depending on the distance harvesters were willing to travel for continuous employment. Once the job was finished, laborers either returned to their former pursuits or moved to a different locale to continue harvesting. In a sense harvesters were the true migratory laborers, in comparison to regular farm hands who remained for several months or a year, often on the same farm or at least in the general area. Every season, noticeably in the earlier decades in Ohio, Indiana, and Illinois, men made seasonal treks, beginning in the southern counties of the state and moving northward as the grain ripened. An Indiana source recalled: "In early days, these bands of reapers, with their sickles, composed of a dozen or two young, stalwart men, together would begin their work in the south part of the State, where wheat first ripened, and reap the fields northward, thus catching on to the maturing fields as they ripened. The best reapers were paid 37½ cents per day, or a bushel of wheat, then reckoned an equivalent."[97]

These men were semi-professionals in this south-to-north sweep through the midwestern grain fields and pursued this seasonal work each year:

> Laborers were abundant, and the farmer had little or no difficulty in supplying himself with "hands," either for the season or for an emergency. Almost every one could swing the cradle or scythe, or perform

96. *Milwaukee Sentinel*, July 18, 1860, as cited *ibid.*, July 19, 1860.
97. John B. Conner, *Indiana Agriculture* (Indianapolis, 1893), pp. 7–8; see also Smith, *History of the State of Indiana*, II, p. 657.

any other work in the harvest field. Before the introduction of the reaping machine, expert hands from settlements in the northern counties would go to some of the lower counties, and continue along with the ripening grain on their return trip. Journeymen and others working at trades in the towns, would also go to the country in harvest and take a hand in the field.[98]

Champaign County in southwestern Ohio was one of many starting points for these northward-moving bands of cradlers. The *Ohio Cultivator* reported in 1847 that it was common for dairy farm hands at the Western Reserve to come down to the southern part of the state and then work their way north with the ripening harvest fields.[99]

Young men willing to wander in any direction seemed to have no difficulty in obtaining farm work, especially in harvest. A farmer at Kane County, Illinois, wrote in June, 1838: "I am now alone and shall not hire any until haying and Harvesting comes on and then I shall want one or two hands for a month or two. I think I can get what help I shall want here as there is a number of young men who come into the place this spring."[100] Typical of such young men was Isaac Hatch, who arrived without money at Chicago in 1837. Departing from the city, he stopped off at a farmer's house for lodging and work, and remained several days to cut prairie hay for one dollar per day. Ultimately he made his way to Kane County, where he split rails for one dollar per hundred and then obtained work at threshing wheat and oats.[101]

The individual farmer determined the standard of employment, not only in terms of wages but also setting the work pace, the type of meals provided, and how long his harvest hands had to remain in the field. The *Prairie Farmer* identified three types of farmer employers whom the harvest hand might encounter: 1) the sharp Yankee New

98. *History of Champaign County, Ohio,* p. 225.

99. *Ohio Cultivator,* III (1847), 107, as cited in Robert L. Jones, "The Introduction of Farm Machinery into Ohio prior to 1865," *Ohio History,* LVIII (1949), 4. For similar examples, see Andrew W. Young, *History of Wayne County, Indiana* (Cincinnati, 1872), pp. 78–79; *History of Hardin County, Ohio,* p. 796; *History of Henry County, Indiana* (Chicago, 1884), p. 554; *History of Shiawassee and Clinton Counties, Michigan,* p. 385; *History of Kent County, Michigan* (Chicago, 1881), p. 753; Bateman and Selby, eds., *Historical Encyclopedia of Illinois and History of Peoria County* (Chicago and Peoria, 1902), II, p. 792; *Biographical Record of Bureau, Marshall and Putnam Counties, Illinois,* pp. 71, 364–65.

100. Joslyn, *History of Kane County, Ill.,* I, p. 111.

101. *Commemorative Biographical and Historical Record of Kane County, Illinois,* pp. 730–35; for a similar example, see *Portrait and Biographical Album of McLean County, Ill.,* II, pp. 1142–43.

Englander, 2) the farmer of a large operation, 3) the farmer of a small or average farm.

The sharp Yankee New Englander was generally not an extensive farmer but hired several hands in the busy season and during haying. In the morning he would arrive at the field around 10:30, forgetting to bring the mid-morning lunch so that the hands had to wait until the noon dinner. He cleverly urged races among the men to see who could cut the best and fastest. When the dinner horn sounded at noon, he might call out: "Let us have one more round before we go, boys." At three in the afternoon the trick was repeated and again at sunset with "one more round" urged, telling the men how good it was to cut hay during the coolness of the evening. It was observed that he changed his hands every season and sometimes oftener, but his hay was probably not done quicker or better than the harvest of his neighbors.

The farmer of a large operation made certain to get his hands up early in the morning and saw that nothing obstructed their work or efficiency. He complimented his men when a good swath was cut and laid; and on long, hot summer days he was careful to provide his harvest hands with their mid-morning lunch between ten and eleven o'clock. When harvest work lasted until after sundown, he paid his men extra wages. The conclusion of the *Prairie Farmer* was that this type of farmer had no difficulty in hiring men, but that it was doubtful if many could endure the pressure of such a rigorous regimen.

The small farmer approached the matter casually but sensibly. The men did not have to be called in the morning, for the farmer himself set an example by getting up for a prompt start in the fields. The day's work was carefully laid out so that each work day was utilized yet paced so that all could be completed by the end of the season. At five in the afternoon he promptly called a halt to the work in the field; if the hands had worked hard and well, they were not expected to milk the cows prior to dinner. If an individual harvest hand was idle or lazy by this system, the farmer simply counted out his dollars and gave the man his walking papers. With this method the farmer always got his haying done on time and as easily as his neighbors who pressured their hands with a faster pace. The editor of the *Prairie Farmer* concluded that each farmer had to determine what was best for his own operation, inferring that something was to be learned from each of these examples.[102]

102. *Prairie Farmer*, VI (February, 1846), 54.

The work followed a demanding pace during the critical hay and wheat harvesting. A day's work was understood to be from sun-up to sundown, and the farmer did not sit on the side of the field; rather, he set the pace by working with the men in the field.[103] He made an effort to engage his harvest hands early in the season; good men were readily hired, while the shirks were hired as a last resort. Men who gathered and bound the most sheaves were accorded respect, and those who signed on to work but did not perform to their ability encountered subtle ostracization. Harvest hands were normally expected to handle the chores in the evening following a full day in the field.[104]

Contemporary accounts mention the intense strain and exhaustion of harvest labor. Sunday was considered as any other day of the week during this critical period, and seventeen-hour days were not uncommon. John Muir, raised on the Wisconsin frontier in the 1850's, recalled the summer harvest labor with a touch of bitterness. He questioned the excessively exhausting work in harvesting the wheat in such quantity and under such pressure of speed that it endangered men's health. He foolishly tried to keep ahead of the hired men in the blazing sunlit field—in his words, all for the vice of overproduction. Men rose at four in the morning and labored the entire day in sweat-damp clothes, and sometimes into the evening hours until darkness required a halt.[105]

A German traveler who tested his strength and stamina for the sake of experience described an Illinois harvest field:

During the harvest season I worked for a farmer without pay. For this purpose I had made for myself several sets of working clothes out of rough linen, and mingled with laborers in the hayfields. In the beginning I worked only two hours daily, one hour in the morning and one in the afternoon. I did the easiest work: raking hay. Easy as the work was, the burning sun was intolerable. The thermometer rose to 100 and over. After an hour's work I was completely soaked with

103. "Autobiography of Alexis Crane Hart covering the period of his childhood spent in Jefferson and Trempealeau counties," pp. 17–18.

104. *History of Clinton County, Ohio* (Chicago, 1882), p. 274; *History of Crawford County and Ohio*, p. 686; *History of Hardin County, Ohio*, pp. 462–63.

105. Muir, *Story of My Boyhood and Youth*, pp. 201–2, 222–24. For additional reference to working conditions in the harvest fields, see *Michigan Pioneer Collections*, XVIII, p. 421; Daniel Thomas Diary, 1851–55, entries of July 26, August 20, 1853; Edwin Benjamin to John Benjamin (Belvidere, Ill., [1850?]), Box 1, folder of undated correspondence, John Benjamin Papers. The scarcity of harvest laborers was emphasized by a hired hand who worked in Michigan and Illinois: Myron Wright to Allen G. Wright (Marshall, Mich., August 7, 1852; Downers Grove, Du Page County, Ill., July 24, 1853), Allen G. Wright Papers.

perspiration. I had to change my clothes several times daily. Other kinds of work which I was able to do were turning the swath with a wooden fork, cocking it when dry, piling up the hay, loading it on the wagon, then unloading the wagon onto the haystacks. Stacking hay with an iron fork is very tiring, and even if one works without a shirt and drinks water constantly, it is almost unbearable.[106]

Summer harvest in the Midwest coincided with the hot months of July and August, when combinations of excessive heat and rain produced high humidity, to the distress of those prone to fevers and the ague. An early settler at Morgan County, Indiana, described the ideal months as April and May, as opposed to fever-ridden July and August. Harvest work had to be done at these times, and farmers in poor health, sometimes without hired help, struggled with the harvest themselves.[107] In 1842 at Spoon River in central Illinois, wheat harvesting was conducted in temperatures hovering about the 120° mark, and labor was scarce![108] During harvest a farmer at Fond du lac, Wisconsin, became so ill with diarrhea, known as the flux, that he was unable to work in the fields with his hired hands.[109]

During the wheat harvest in July, 1839, near Indianapolis, Calvin Fletcher was faced with a "muitany," to use his term, on the part of harvest hands who refused to work in the excessive heat: "At 1 P M went to the farm [and] found that the 4 hands I had supp^d w [supposed would] cradle & bind my wheat had nearly given out & wanted to retire from the field in consequence of the heat and dust &c. I c^d [could] have prevented this muitany [sic] had I been with [them] during the A M."[110] The *Prairie Farmer* cautioned farm laborers to wear light clothing as protection from the excessive sun, while the *Ohio Cultivator* recommended the purchase of a palm leaf hat to

106. Gustorf, "Frontier Perils Told by an Early Illinois Visitor," 142–43.
107. Esarey, "The Pioneers of Morgan County: The Memoirs of Noah J. Major," 303–4.
108. John Regan, *The Western Wilds of America, or Backwoods and Prairies* (Edinburgh, 1859), pp. 165–66. Exhaustion from the heat was common during harvesting: see *Ohio Valley Farmer*, I (June, 1856), 17–19; (July, 1856), 34–35.
109. Carrier Diaries, entry of July 29, [1853 or 1854?]. For a similar complaint of a Michigan farmer, see Smith Diary, entry of July 14, 1848.
110. Fletcher Diary, entry of July 29, 1839. This statement underlines the importance of the farmer working in the field with his men. On another occasion, he was infuriated with the progress of work in haying. His son who was supposed to direct the work was missing, and the hands had spent three hours in the morning loading only two wagons. "I felt impatient," was Fletcher's reaction, and he joined the men in the field to speed up the work. Entry of July 11, 1856. In the summer of 1847 Fletcher had other problems with his harvest hands: "They were bad & Slow mowers—vagrants to some extent not wish[ing] to work more than a day or 2 at a time in one place." Entry of August 9, 1847.

shield the harvester's head.[111] "Green hands" were especially cautioned to take it easy when working for the first time in the harvest fields, for in the western states work was harder and the temperature higher.[112] Harvest fields were hot and dusty in summer, especially when threshing work was conducted in the fields. Threshing hands were advised to cover their mouths and noses with a hollowed sponge. The sponge, after being dipped in water and squeezed out, afforded protection against inhaling the dust and fine particles while working near a mechanical thresher or reaper.[113]

Thunderstorms provided an opportunity to take a break. William Howells recalled instances in Ohio during the 1820's when long stories and jokes were exchanged until work could be resumed. The open field was not a safe place during a storm because of the risk of lightning. Death from lightning bolts was a major hazard for individuals on the farm. Protection in the barn was not always adequate; in 1836 at Washtenaw County, Michigan, a young farm boy witnessed as lightning struck his father and the hired hand while both were in the barn unloading hay.[114]

Another hazard in the harvest fields was the presence of snakes, including poisonous rattlers. Harvesters encountered them when cutting marsh or prairie hay; they wrapped bindings or ropes around their legs as protection against snake bites.[115] Snakes were also a problem in the fields after cutting wheat, as in the case of an early Illinois settler at Cass County who raised oats on bottomlands. One year the snakes were so numerous that he was unable to procure harvest help because the reptiles often concealed themselves under the bound bundles and sheaves of grain that had to be lifted into a wagon.[116]

111. *Prairie Farmer*, X (July, 1850), 201; *Ohio Cultivator*, X (July 1, 1854), 191.

112. Stewart, *Eleven Years' Experience*, p. 83. John Young, a farmer at Menard County, Illinois, had hands cutting wheat and stacking hay during the first week of July, 1859; all were severely affected by the heat. John Young Diary, 1859–62, entries of July 7–8, 1859.

113. *Ohio Cultivator*, III (August 1, 1847), 113; *Cincinnati Daily Gazette*, August 28, 1847.

114. Howells, *Recollections of Life in Ohio from 1813 to 1840*, p. 62; Samuel W. Beakes, *Past and Present of Washtenaw County, Michigan* (Chicago, 1906), p. 815.

115. *History of Crawford County and Ohio*, p. 814.

116. William Henry Perrin, ed., *History of Cass County, Illinois* (Chicago, 1882), pp. 162–63; for other examples, see *Biographical and Genealogical Record of La Salle and Grundy Counties, Illinois*, II, p. 579; Lowell Joseph Ragatz, "Memoirs of a Sauk Swiss by Rev. Oswald Ragatz," *Wisconsin History*, XIX (1935), 215.

Harvesting was strenuous work, and the hands were accustomed to large amounts of good, wholesome food which was sometimes served in the field. An indication of men's appetites during a full day's work is readily appreciated in the following description from the *American Agriculturist* in 1849:

> For Breakfast—Coffee or tea, with cream and sugar, just as much as is desired. Fried bacon, and in the season, eggs always. Cold beef or hash, or perhaps fish, and often fresh meat. Irish or sweet potatoes, good butter, and plenty of it; cheese, ditto; pickles, stewed dried fruit, light and white flour bread, cornbread, or hot cakes, hot biscuit, often pies or cakes. For Dinner—Coffee, sweet milk, or sour, or buttermilk, as may be preferred. Boiled pork, beef, potatoes, turnips, cabbages, beets, &c. White loaf bread and butter, cheese, pickles, stewed fruit, and almost always pie or pastry. Supper—The cold meats and vegetables from dinner, or perhaps a hot dish of meats or fish, or some broiled chickens, and coffee or tea, of course, with bread, as before, to which add a little 'tea cake.' At each meal, all the condiments and provocatives of appetite, such as mustard, catchup vinegar, pepper, salt, pickles, &c., are usually on the table. During harvest time, a lunch in the forenoon and afternoon, of cold meats or fowls, with fresh wheaten loaves or biscuits, cakes or pies, and often accompanied by hot coffee, with cream and sugar, always as a matter of course.[117]

The forenoon and afternoon lunches were considered standard procedure, and allowed the harvesters to take an appropriate break from the work. The farmer who always included this treat was well thought of by his men: "Most farmers who have a proper respect for the health and comfort of their 'help' in harvest-time, provide the harvesters with an 'ice-can,' or a can with skim milk and ice to use, instead of 'water and poor whisky.' This first drink is good in its kind, and with some good cheese and *short-cake* inspires the laborer and strengthens him under the fatigues of the warm season. . . ."[118]

A Rock River Valley farmer in northern Illinois described an elaborate arrangement in the field for feeding the hands during a harvest in the early 1840's. Illness hampered his efforts to hire hands, and those who worked for him were either sick from the beginning or

117. *American Agriculturist*, VIII (June, 1849), 181–82.
118. Spence, *Settler's Guide in the United States and British North American Provinces*, p. 73; see also Smith, *Recollections of the Pioneers of Lee County*, pp. 440–50. Small boys and old men were also used to assist in carrying food out to the field and keeping the water pail filled. Ben Douglass, *History of Wayne County, Ohio* (Indianapolis, 1878), p. 429; *History of Clinton County, Ohio*, p. 274; Bateman and Selby, eds., *Historical Encyclopedia of Illinois and History of Kendall County*, II, p. 711.

became so after indulging in the quantities of food along with rum and whisky: "We had put in large crops which had grown as they only do in a new country, but with the harvest came the fever. We had a large tent raised in the field with a table spread with cold meat, rum, whiskey, iced waters, etc., which was undoubtedly appreciated by the few harvesters we succeeded in hiring, for they spent a good part of the time in it; but they got too sick and the cradled grain lay unbound in the harvest field. . . ."[119]

Consumption of alcohol by farm hands was more obvious at harvest time than during other periods of the year. The custom is traceable to the beginnings of the Old Northwest. John Melish observed in 1811: "There is unquestionably too much spiritous liquors drank in the newly settled parts of America, but a very good reason can be assigned for it. The labour of clearing the land is rugged and severe, and the summer heats are sometimes so great that it would be dangerous to drink cold water."[120] Early American farmers were known for their proclivity to the home manufacture and consumption of diverse hard liquors, and prospective farm hands were in fact cautioned to be on guard against such employers.[121] George Hollenbeck, recalling his boyhood days in Kendall County, Illinois, during the 1830's, was delegated with the harvest task of taking the whisky jug and water pail out to the hands in the field.[122]

The temperance movement had its beginnings in the 1820's and increased in tempo during the next three decades.[123] The harvest

119. Smith, Recollections of the Pioneers of Lee County, p. 490.
120. John Melish, Travels through the United States of America (Belfast, 1818), pp. 312–13.
121. John Bradbury, Travels in the Interior of America in the Years 1809, 1810, and 1811 (Liverpool, 1817), pp. 318–19; see also Kingdom, America and the British Colonies, p. 3. This advice appeared in guide books as late as the 1830's: see William Cobbett, The Emigrant's Guide; in Ten Letters (London, 1829), pp. 150–52; Collins, Emigrant's Guide to and Description of the United States of America, pp. 86–87.
122. Bateman and Selby, eds., Historical Encyclopedia of Illinois and History of Kendall County, II, p. 711. According to a Swiss settler at Madison County, Illinois, in 1832, farm hands unfortunately allowed themselves too much liquor, and at the expense of their health. "Letters from New Switzerland, 1831–1832," Illinois Historical Journal, XLIX (1956), 436. John Blake advised against liquor for farm hands who, in his opinion, were men without a sense of responsibility; under the influence of alcohol they might be tempted for a few dollars to set afire the property of their employers. The Farmer's Every-Day Book (New York and Auburn, 1855), p. 108.
123. William Warren Sweet, Circuit-Rider Days in Indiana (Indianapolis, 1916), p. 70; see also Fletcher, Pennsylvania Agriculture and Country Life, 1640–1940, I, p. 121. For views of the farm press on this issue in other parts of the nation, see New England Farmer, XVIII (May 6, 1840), 370; XIX

became a critical test for local temperance advocates, according to an American Home missionary assigned to Pike County in southwestern Illinois.[124] At Kendall County in northern Illinois in 1834, a minister sponsored a temperance pledge which most of the settlers signed, promising to deny themselves and their hired hands the use of liquor; among the signatories was an Edward Ament, formerly a hired hand in the area.[125] Although these public affirmations were common throughout the Midwest, it is questionable whether their influence was permanent. For example, at Jefferson in Ashtabula County, Ohio, a temperance society was formed in 1841; its pledge contained an impressive list of signatures of those who promised not to serve liquor to men in their employment. The society flourished for several years until 1846, when local enthusiasm for its noble intentions seemed to wane.[126]

Some farmers adopted the letter of the law in the pledge and assuaged their disgruntled harvest laborers with additional wages in lieu of whisky. A proud preacher on the Indiana frontier reported in 1829 that farmers denied alcohol to their hands and correspondingly paid them six and one-quarter cents additional per day as compensation for abstaining from the whisky jug.[127] Benjamin Harris, a large farmer and cattle raiser in Champaign County, Illinois, described how he held the line on harvest hands during the 1840's: "I remember when I had my first wheat and hay harvest[;] the men I highered to help do the work they wanted the whisky as that had bene the custom I told them I would not have whsky but would give each man twelve & a half cents extry in place of whsiky they growled a while

(August 19, 1840), 52; XX (September 8, 1841), 75; *Boston Cultivator*, III (March 27, 1841), 1; *Moore's Rural New Yorker*, II (July 24, 1851), 233; *Southern Cultivator*, I (April 12, 1843), 45.

124. Reverend Warren Nichols to A. Peters (Atlas, Pike County, Ill., August 1, 1835), American Home Missionary Letters. A similar report came from Michigan attesting to the decline of alcohol in the harvest fields: Alonson Darwin to A. Peters (Tecumseh, Mich., September 10, 1829), American Home Missionary Letters.

125. Hicks, *History of Kendall County, Illinois*, pp. 60–61, 138–39. A German visitor to Ohio in the early 1830's made reference to efforts to prevent laborers from drinking; see August Witte, *Kurze Schilderung der Vereinigten Staaten von Nord-Amerika* (Hannover, 1833), p. 18.

126. *Condensed History of Jefferson, Ashtabula County, Ohio*, p. 52. Early religious leaders in the Midwest were aware of this temporary zeal; see Reverend B. Messenger to A. Peters (Edwardsville, Ill., February 24, 1832), American Home Missionary Letters.

127. Reverend A. Craig to A. Peters (Mt. Carmel, Franklin County, Ind., August 4, 1829), American Home Missionary Letters. For a similar occurrence, see *History of Delaware County and Ohio*, p. 679.

and finalley agreed to the proposition. . . ."[128] Since harvest hands did not take kindly to their employers' temperance notions, the issue was probably debated in many instances. Proof of this appears in the travel memoirs of a German who, during the early 1830's in Michigan, had personally observed harvest hands spending half the night in heated argument over the question: "Half a dozen farmhands, working here during harvest time, slept in the same room with us. They argued half the night about temperance associations, and it seemed that our host, a strong supporter of the temperance movement, was definitely unsuccessful in persuading his workers of the practicality of his views. Sleep was impossible under these circumstances, and we were glad when morning came."[129] Some harvest hands were adamant on this issue. In the 1850's, when an Ohio farmer withheld the whisky and promised extra money, the hands put their scythes down and walked from the field.[130]

It is questionable if the custom of liquor in the harvest field was seriously jeopardized prior to the Civil War. A reader of the *Indiana Farmer* in 1853, commenting on the harvest in the central part of the state, observed caustically: ". . . the grain and hay were unusually hard to cut, judging from the amount of stinking whisky that was used on the occasion."[131] The *Ohio Cultivator* conceded the presence of alcohol as an integral aspect of harvest in that state, but in a one-sided view blamed foreign rather than native-born American laborers. "Unfortunately the great majority of foreign laborers are more or less addicted to the use of strong drinks, and consequently they either refuse to labor on farms, or continue their evil habits when there, so that farmers cannot safely rely upon them, and hence many refuse to

128. Mary Vose Harris, "The Autobiography of Benjamin Franklin Harris. Edited with Introduction and Notes" (M.A. thesis, University of Illinois, 1923), appendix, 43–44. Farmers did provide a variety of substitutes for alcohol, including hop beer, tansy or bitters, metheglin, boiled honey and water, ginger beer, chocolate and boiled rice, and coffee. For reference to these items and their use, see *Cleveland Register*, August 24, 1819, as cited in *Annals of Cleveland*, I, pp. 726–27; Fletcher Diary, entries of July 17, 18, 1846; *History of Dearborn and Ohio Counties, Indiana* (Chicago, 1885), p. 135. William Henry Perrin, ed., *History of Stark County, with an Outline Sketch of Ohio* (Chicago, 1881), pp. 544–45; *History of Crawford County and Ohio*, pp. 575–76; Charles Eames, comp., *Historic Morgan and Classic Jacksonville* (Jacksonville, Ill., 1885), p. 58; *New England Farmer*, XX (September 8, 1841), 75; *Prairie Farmer*, VIII (May, 1848), 159–60.
129. Frank Braun and Robert B. Brown, "Karl Neidhard's Reise nach Michigan," *Michigan History*, XXXV (1951), 51.
130. Moritz Busch, *Travels between the Hudson & the Mississippi 1851–1852* (Lexington, 1971), p. 257.
131. *Indiana Farmer*, IV (August 15, 1853), 372.

employ them. But let the means of gratifying this habit be removed from all our towns and cities, and laborers would be not only more willing to work on farms, but more reliable and serviceable when there."[132]

Although corn picking and husking were minor harvesting activities in comparison to the feverished pace of wheat and hay cutting, they provided employment for men when the summer harvest rush was past. Moreover, corn was a substantial crop during 1815–60, especially in Ohio, Indiana, and Illinois.[133] It was planted in spring or early summer, before the oppressive heat, and required little attention during the growing season. The penchant for corn cultivation in Indiana, according to Chamberlain's *Indiana Gazetteer*, glutted local markets without flexibility to promote diversified crops. It was estimated that farmers grew from twenty to one hundred acres, and that one hand could prepare and work twenty to twenty-five acres in a season. The yield was thirty-five to seventy-five bushels per acre with an average of forty-five bushels.[134]

The work force for this activity, when not conducted in community husking bees, was made up of farm laborers and other itinerants who took whatever job was available in winter for low wages or merely for board and lodging.[135] Local farmers hired their less affluent neigh-

132. *Ohio Cultivator*, IX (October 1, 1853), 299. The *Cultivator's* remarks reflect rural resentment toward cities and a latent anti-foreign tone.

133.
Corn (bushels)

	1840	1850	1860
Ohio	33,668,144	59,078,695	73,543,190
Indiana	28,155,887	52,964,363	71,588,919
Illinois	22,634,211	57,646,984	115,174,777
Michigan	2,277,039	5,641,420	12,444,676
Wisconsin	379,359	1,988,979	7,517,300
Minnesota	—	16,725	2,941,952

Statistical View of the United States, p. 171; *Agriculture of the United States in 1860*, p. 185.

134. E. Chamberlain, *The Indiana Gazetteer* (Indianapolis, 1849), pp. 35–36. Corn was relatively immune to damage or weather after ripening, unlike wheat, whose harvest requirements were critical, according to George Flower, *The Errors of Emigrants* (London, 1841), p. 31. Cutting, stacking, and husking corn were activities easily deferred to the winter months. Some midwestern farmers avoided harvest labor by turning their livestock loose in both wheat and corn fields, a practice popularly known as "hogging down." See Fletcher Diary, entry of December 31, 1851; William Baxter, *America and the Americans* (London, 1855), p. 219; Robert Russell, *North America, Its Agriculture and Climate* (Edinburgh, 1857), p. 116; Caird, *Prairie Farming in America*, p. 83.

135. A colorful description of corn husking for this period is found in Buley, *The Old Northwest*, I, pp. 322–23; see also pp. 175–176 for discussion of early corn production and its importance to the Midwest.

bors on a wage basis or by contract with payment frequently made in
kind, as in grain harvesting. In the fall of 1828 at Sangamon County,
Illinois, a settler hired himself out to cut corn at five cents per shock
or an equivalent of fifty cents a day, which doubtless included stacking and tying the shocks.[136] This rate varied little during the period.
In the autumn of 1860 a farmer at Menard County, Illinois, hired a
hand to cut and set up corn in the field at six cents per shock, assembling 182 shocks in the course of one month.[137]

Wages for corn husking were similar to cutting and stacking work
in the fields; for example, an Ohio farmer paid a husking hand six
and one-quarter cents per shock. But generally most farmers preferred to avoid cash wages and pay for the work in kind.[138] At Pike
County, Illinois, in 1840, a newly arrived settler husked corn and took
every fifth load as compensation for his labor.[139] Similarly, Benjamin
Cox, who settled at Kane County in 1843, worked for local farmers
husking corn at the rate of fifty cents per day with payment in kind.[140]
At McLean County in central Illinois an early settler worked twenty
days at corn husking; he received ten bushels of corn per day as
wages.[141] Although corn was not as important in Wisconsin as in
other parts of the Midwest, one settler near Elkhorn walked ten to
twelve miles for husking work, receiving the tenth bushel as pay.[142]
Similar was the case of an Illinois farm hand who worked during the
winter at husking corn for fifty cents a day and took his pay in corn
worth ten cents a bushel.[143]

Young boys were also employed in corn husking. Daniel Brush left
a vivid picture of such work during the 1820's in southern Illinois,
noting a division of labor in which the boy or inexperienced hand

136. *History of Sangamon County, Illinois*, p. 693; John Carroll Power,
History of the Early Settlers of Sangamon County, Illinois (Springfield, 1876),
p. 447.
137. Young Diary, entries of September 25, October 4, 1860. This work was
also performed according to a fixed rate per acre: "Cutting, hauling home, and
setting up corn, at 1 dollar 50 cents per acre." Oliver, *Eight Months in Illinois*,
p. 135.
138. Virgil D. Moore Ledger, p. 97.
139. M. D. Massie, *Past and Present of Pike County, Illinois* (Chicago,
1906), p. 108.
140. *Biographical Record of Kane County, Illinois* (Chicago, 1898), pp.
173–75.
141. Duis, *The Good Old Times in McLean County, Illinois*, p. 212.
142. "Recollections of Harvey Brown, Elkhorn, Wisconsin," pp. 6–7. For
a similar example, see Lewis M. Gross, *Past and Present of De Kalb County,
Illinois* (Chicago, 1907), II, pp. 372–75.
143. *Portrait and Biographical Album of Warren County, Illinois* (Chicago,
1886), p. 547.

covered the "down-row." The down-row or center row was where the wagon passed through the corn field. A single wagon was slowly drawn through the field with the huskers working on either side, shucking the corn and flipping the ears into the wagon. Young Brush followed behind the wagon and took the down-rows. The movement of the wagon was gauged by the speed of the huskers—which in turn determined the speed of work for the boy, who sometimes found himself behind or ahead of the overall progress of the work.[144]

The agricultural press debated whether or not it was preferable to let huskers throw the corn ears to the ground and have followers pick them up to load into the wagons. A farmer in the Little Miami River Valley of Ohio stated his objections to this method: dirt and mud were easily mixed with the corn. The preferred method, he contended, was for the hands to husk and throw the corn directly into the wagon; when full, the first wagon was taken to the crib, while a second took its place in the field.[145] Figuring an average acre with 9,600 ears of corn, the *Indiana Farmer* estimated that in a ten-hour day an ordinary farm hand could handle half an acre: "This is fast work but there is no doubt it has been repeatedly done." Like the *Ohio Cultivator*, this editor advised against piling the corn in the field after husking, for the ears got covered with mud. Use a team and wagon, urged the *Indiana Farmer*, but cover no more than seven rows at once. With a wagon, a hired man could work a full acre per day.[146]

Corn production in parts of the Midwest necessitated considerable hired labor. Large cattle raisers, in particular, recognized the value of lands in central Illinois where this commodity was raised for feeding stock.[147] A description of one of these operations in *Hunt's Merchant Magazine* shows the importance of labor for corn production, and that hands were employed to assist in the winter feeding:

144. Brush, *Growing Up with Southern Illinois 1820 to 1861*, pp. 31–33.
145. *Ohio Cultivator*, V (January 15, 1849), 25. Although a good farm hand could harvest ten bushels of corn per day (measured after it was shelled), it was claimed that farm hands in Tennessee were reportedly able to husk fifty bushels per day! *Ibid.*, V (January 1, 1849), 6.
146. *Indiana Farmer*, III (November 15, 1853), 56. The main disadvantage of husking in the field late in the season was exposure to the cold, especially in the northern Midwest. Despite early winters in areas like Minnesota, farmers did their husking as late as November and December: see *Massachusetts Ploughman*, December 26, 1857, in "Minnesota Agriculture File," and Larpenteur Diary, 1856–61, entry of November 10, 1856.
147. See Paul Gates, "Cattle Kings in the Prairies," *Mississippi Valley Historical Review*, XXXV (1948), 379–412; and Richard Bardolph, "Illinois Agriculture in Transition, 1820–1870," *Illinois Historical Journal*, XLI (1948), 244–64.

Mr. Boardman, of Lincoln, Illinois, says:—The general practice in
Central Illinois is to hire about the 1st of April for the 'crop(corn)
season,' or until after harvest, which includes wheat, oats, hay, &c.
Corn-cutting is nearly all done by the shock. We pay from 7 to 10
cents a shock for putting up shocks from 44 to 46 hills square—shocks
not tied—at which work hands make from $1 25 [sic] to $2 per day.
A great share of the corn planting in this State is now done with two-
horse planters, which plant two rows at once, and are managed by two
hands, both riding on the machine, one driving, the other operating
the dropping. The past season, hands were hired through the corn-
crop for from $13 to $18 per month; and at from $15 to $18 through
harvest. Until last season I have paid first-rate hands $20 per month
through the summer, and as high as $25 and $30 for feeding in the
winter. Feeding includes Sundays, and all weather. By the team
[term?] 'feeding' is understood, in this State, hauling out shock-corn
for 100 to 150 cattle, or 1,000 to 1,700 sheep. This is paid for at from
$25 to $30 a month.[148]

Allied to harvest work and corn picking was threshing of grain, a
task which provided employment for itinerant laborers and farm
hands during autumn and winter. After harvesting, the bound sheaves
were removed from the field to the barn, where it was a full winter's
task for the lone farmer to thresh and clean a crop of wheat from ten
acres. The standard procedure for separating or threshing the wheat
grains was flailing with a stout stick several feet long and joined by
thongs to a handle of equal length. During the 1830's in central Ohio
a professional class of wintertime threshers or flailers performed this
labor.[149] An alternate method was placing the bundles of grain on the
barn floor and driving horses and oxen over them to tread out the
grain head. An Illinois pioneer in the 1830's recalled: "We thrashed
our grain by arranging the bundles in a circle on the ground, the
heads all leaning the same way and then driving both horses and

148. *Hunt's Merchant Magazine*, XLI (December, 1859), 760. Wintering
cattle was inexpensive, observed the *Chicago Weekly Democrat*, February 18,
1834. In July, 1835, a herd of about 800 cattle were driven to Philadelphia
markets, according to the *Sangamon Journal*, July 2, 1835, as cited in *Niles'
Register*, XLVIII (August 1, 1835), 378. Matthias Dunlap in 1852 urged
Illinois farmers not to take their corn to railroads for shipment but to use it for
feeding operations. His advice was "Ship Cattle rather than Corn!" Dunlap
Letterbook, 1852–53, pp. 2–5, communication addressed to *Prairie Farmer*,
January 12, 1852. For reference to farm laborers who worked on these cattle
farms for twelve to twenty dollars per month, see *Portrait and Biographical
Album of McLean County, Ill.*, pp. 1154–55; J. G. Kohl, *Reisen im Nordwestern
der Vereinigten Staaten* (New York, 1857), pp. 483–84.
149. Welker, *Farm Life in Central Ohio Sixty Years Ago*, p. 31.

oxen against them on the circle, one person constantly tossing up the straw with a fork while another drove the animals."[150]

Winnowing or fanning was the necessary and final cleaning process for the grain. A common method employed by the pioneers was to shake the grain up and down on a drawn sheet held between two men on a windy day. The straw and chaff were blown away, while the heavy grain settled back in the sheet. On a windy day a single person could also winnow wheat simply by pouring the grain over and over until most of the chaff had been blown free: "Until we were able to obtain a fanning mill the grain was separated from the chaff by pouring it through the wind. A common expression of excellence then was 'the head of the heap.' This originated from the fact that when grain was cleaned in this way the heaviest and best fell first and constituted the head of the heap."[151] Fanning mills of diverse designs appeared and in time replaced the former hand methods of tossing with a sheet or pouring in the wind.[152]

An early pioneer of Fairfield County, Ohio, recalled in the 1820's when eight to ten bushels per day were threshed out by flails or tramped out by the feet of horses. This also included time spent in sieving the grain free of large straw matter and then winnowing it in the wind with a sheet. Three hands were required to go over the wheat several times in order to assure a clean load.[153] Near Steubenville, Ohio, in the same decade William Cooper Howells observed that ten bushels of threshed wheat were a full day's work for one hand. Rye, barley, and oats were easier to thresh; a good hand could turn out twenty to twenty-five bushels of the latter in a day's work, with pay figured at one bushel per ten threshed.[154] In Indiana prior to 1840, grain was usually threshed with a flail or tramped out by horses: two men could flail and winnow twelve bushels a day, while two men and a boy with horses could tramp out and clean twenty bushels.[155]

150. George H. Weaver, "Autobiography of Dr. Ephraim Ingals," *Illinois Historical Journal*, XXVIII (1936), 288.

151. *Ibid.*

152. For a discussion of the various devices for threshing and winnowing, see Rogin, *Introduction of Farm Machinery*, pp. 154–68.

153. Scott, *Complete History of Fairfield County, Ohio*, p. 247.

154. Howells, *Recollections of Life in Ohio from 1813 to 1840*, pp. 62, 155; *Commemorative Biographical Record of the Counties of Harrison and Carroll, Ohio* (Chicago, 1891), pp. 395–96. In a slightly different case, an English immigrant at McHenry County, Illinois, in 1851 raised money for his land by threshing with a flail at the rate of one-eighth of each bushel; *History of McHenry County, Illinois* (Chicago, 1885), p. 527.

155. Smith, *History of the State of Indiana*, II, p. 657.

The situation varied from locale to locale. As early as the 1840's in Wisconsin there was a traveling class of professional threshers who brought their own oxen and also used the farmer's. Grain was stacked in a rough circle, using sometimes a plot of hard frozen ground. Fifty to sixty bushels of wheat were threshed in this rather crude manner, probably not including the winnowing of the chaff and loose straw bits. The threshers took their daily pay in the form of four bushels of wheat.[156] Others worked by the day; Joshua Shinn at Mahoning County, Ohio, paid thirty-one and one-quarter cents per day for threshing in the summer of 1830, indicating that he preferred to thresh his grain shortly after harvesting.[157] A farmer at Licking County paid fifty cents per day for threshing in November, 1844, a fairly representative figure for winter day labor on the farm.[158]

Threshers were regularly sought out by farmers in wintertime and acquired a local reputation. A colorful example at Wheelersburg in southern Ohio was Peter Chabot; he lived in a cabin-like shanty and hunted wild game in his spare time. During the years prior to mechanization Chabot performed much of the flailing and winnowing of wheat in the neighborhood. For the final cleaning of the flailed wheatheads he employed a fanning mill, a three-sided box with a hoop fan attached to one end. The wheat was poured through, and as the fan blew the chaff out, the heavy grain heads fell to the bottom of the box.[159] An even more unusual case was Samuel Birdsall, who worked as a thresher from 1829 to 1856 at Huron County in the Firelands region of northern Ohio. Birdsall had been a schoolteacher in New York until an accidental gunshot deprived him of his eyesight. Despite his handicap, he was self-sufficient and made a living at threshing grain with a flail for farmers in the area.[160]

156. Benjamin H. Hibbard, *The History of Agriculture in Dane County, Wisconsin* (Madison, 1905), p. 123. Hibbard's study is quite valuable because it was based on conversations with veterans of this occupation.

157. Joshua Shinn Ledger, p. 4, entry of June 21, 1830. Threshing and winnowing of grain in summer were hot, dusty tasks; for a vivid depiction of this type of work, along with other itinerant labor by a Swedish immigrant, see Norelius, *Journal*, pp. 146–48, 171, 173–74.

158. Thurston Farm Accounts, entry of November 9, 1844; see also S. Larkin Store and Farm Accounts, p. 40, entry of October, 1840; Moulton Ledgerbook, p. 5, entry of February, 1832; p. 24, entry of January 21, 1840. Generally, fifty cents per day was the prevailing wage for threshing in these accounts.

159. "Pioneer Sketches," pp. 15–16, 230.

160. *Firelands Pioneer*, n.s., I (June, 1882), 155–56. For other examples, see Harden, *Early Life and Times of Boone County, Indiana*, pp. 97–98; *History of the Early Life and Business Interests of the Village and Township of Leslie, Ingham County, Michigan* (n.p., 1914), pp. 35–36.

Mechanical threshing machines, designed to eliminate the arduous flailing, were patented as early as 1791. Horse-powered machines, employing a treadmill, were larger and preferable to the smaller devices that were hand powered with a crank. Steam-powered threshers also made their initial appearance in the antebellum years. Although threshing machinery was complicated, the basic principle involved a series of rollers that crushed the straw and extracted the grain; and some models were also developed to clean the grain as it was processed. Their efficiency was obvious in comparison to the old flailing and winnowing techniques: a ten-horse-powered thresher, constructed at Chillicothe, Ohio, in the 1850's, was employed in the harvest field. Three men operated the machinery with the assistance of farm hands, performing the work of seventy flails and threshing one hundred bushels per hour.[161] William Oliver cited a threshing machine in Illinois in the 1840's which processed one hundred bushels of wheat per day at a cost of six and one-quarter cents per bushel and averaged twenty-two bushels per acre,[162] although a Wisconsin farmer gave a different threshing cost in 1851 (ten cents per bushel or two dollars per acre).[163]

Mechanical threshing machines did not eliminate the need for harvest laborers. In fact, larger harvests with ever increasing yields only necessitated more laborers, especially those who could work with machines. Usually the farmer had to provide the necessary extra hands to help operate these labor-saving devices. Farmers in a neighborhood also joined together and contracted to have a thresher bring his machine into an area, going from one farm to the next. Larger operators of course owned their own machines and threshed in the fields as the wheat was harvested. Many who did harvest labor in summer also worked in threshing operations, which became an integral aspect of the overall harvest.[164]

161. *Preliminary Report on the Eighth Census*, see esp. pp. 96–100, which provide the historical background of mechanization in threshing. A more technical treatment is found in Rogin, *Introduction of Farm Machinery*, pp. 154–76. These machines were expensive, often exceeding $300, while the less efficient hand-powered devices were about $100. Rogin cites a model in 1820 for $80: see pp. 161–62. An Illinois farmer in 1851 complained of the high costs of mechanization in wheat cultivation, mentioning the threshing machine at $300 while the reaper was comparatively less at $125. *U.S. Pat. Office Report, 1851* (Washington, 1852), 443.

162. Oliver, *Eight Months in Illinois*, p. 135.

163. *U.S. Pat. Office Report, 1851*, 460.

164. The small farmer frequently relied on the services of the professional thresher who owned his own machine: see "Knure Steernson's Recollections: The Story of a Pioneer," *Minnesota History*, IV (1921), 135–36. Solon Robinson

As in present-day agriculture, farm machinery involved some risk to employees. An Irish immigrant hired out as a farm hand for ten dollars per month in Kendall County, Illinois, in 1843. Employed but three weeks, he met with an accident—his foot was caught in the mechanism and had to be amputated. Despite the fact that he was basically a hired farm hand and new to the area, settlers were kind to his family and built a log cabin for him.[165] Similar was the case of a man who came from New York to Rock County, Wisconsin, in 1844, secured work on a farm in October, and a month later lost his foot in a threshing machine accident.[166] Carelessness could be fatal: a German, hired to work on a farm near Chicago in the summer of 1857, accidentally stumbled and his hand and foot became tangled in the mowing machine's sickles. The only other person in the field with him was the farmer's young son, who ran one and a half miles to obtain assistance. Despite surgery and amputation, the man died two hours later.[167]

Information on harvest laborers' attitude toward mechanization is sparse. It has been suggested that as machinery threw men out of employment, farm laborers reacted, although not with the violence of the English Luddites who destroyed machines in the early nineteenth century.[168] According to a report by the Ohio State Board of Agriculture in 1859, a class of laborers depended on winter employment in flailing, threshing, and cleaning grain prior to the 1830's. Introduction of threshing machines displaced workers who were often members of the community; some harvesters reacted to the use of the McCormick reaper by walking out of the fields in protest rather than working with the devices. This report also cited the low wages of agricultural laborers who were present in large numbers before 1830. But twenty years later, when farm wages had increased, help was still

---

spoke out against mechanical threshers and claimed that they destroyed winter-time employment opportunities for unemployed farm hands. *Facts for Farmers*, pp. 682–84. During the 1830's in the wheat-producing regions of New York, professional threshers with mechanical devices replaced laborers who flailed by hand; however, small farmers benefited by obtaining their threshing at a lower labor cost and with greater speed. See E. T. Coke, *A Subaltern's Furlough* (New York, 1833), II, p. 17.

165. Bateman and Selby, eds., *Historical Encyclopedia of Illinois and History of Kendall County*, II, pp. 952–53.

166. Sarah Pratt Diary, 1844–47, p. 33, entry of October–November, 1844; see also Charles Bartlett Diary, entry of July 22, 1850, when one of his harvest laborers lost his hand in an accident with the machinery at Lake County, Illinois.

167. *Chicago Daily Democrat*, September 29, 1857.

168. Jones, "Introduction of Farm Machinery into Ohio prior to 1865," 12.

scarce, despite greater mechanization. The explanation was based on a fairly accurate premise: laborers had not passed out of existence; rather, they had "simply found a demand for their abilities in other and new directions."[169] Farm laborers were drained off for employment in other occupations or to different areas, including urban life, the gold fields of the West, canal and railroad construction, as well as ownership of their own farms.

The introduction of farm machinery did not cause unemployment among farm laborers, except for some dislocation on the local level. Job dislocation involved a change in the type of work but did not lessen the need for harvest workers. The demand for farm laborers remained keen, according to newspaper reports, despite the use of harvesting machines.[170] Farmers did not mechanize their operations until during and after the Civil War: reluctance to make costly changeovers to mechanization was related to the shortage of competent hands to operate the machines, and raking, binding, and stacking remained basic hand tasks. An Illinois farmer compared the benefit of technological improvement in relation to labor competence: "How often do we find it to be the case that the new inventions are hard to be understood by the usual, intelligent laborers on the farm."[171] Despite farm machinery, harvest help remained scarce, largely owing to the massive expansion of wheat production, especially in the prairie states during the 1850's.

Men followed the ripening tide of grain. Harvest work was strenuous and exhausting, more so than other tasks on the farm. If the pressure of concentrated effort did not debilitate men, the blazing heat, fevers, and consumption of alcohol took their toll in human energy and fortitude. Greater harvest yields and scarcity of help raised wages, gradually at first, but to unprecedented heights in the prairie states of Illinois, Wisconsin, and Minnesota by the 1850's, when men earned two and three dollars per day. But high acreage yields produced a labor imbalance, with men who had been needed

169. *Fourteenth Annual Report of Ohio State Board of Agriculture* (Columbus, 1860), 484–85; see also *Ohio Cultivator*, III (September 1, 1857), 123, for harvest laborers' resentment of the mowing machine. At Delaware County in southwestern Ohio, such resentment resulted in damage to the machinery: see *History of Delaware County and Ohio*, p. 161. At Peoria County, Illinois, it was claimed that "traveling men" who worked the south-to-north sweep of harvests were left without employment. See Bateman and Selby, eds., *Historical Encyclopedia of Illinois and History of Peoria County*, II, p. 792.

170. *Chicago Daily Democrat*, July 18, 1848; August 1, 1850.

171. *Illinois Farmer*, III (March, 1858), 44; for a similar observation, see *U.S. Pat. Office Report, 1851*, 462.

in midsummer turned loose at the end of the season. Unless they were regularly employed as farm hands, worked at other occupations, or were in the process of acquiring their own farms, harvest laborers were in an unstable market that provided high wages for a brief period but little security in the long run.

Drainage, Well, and
Cellar Digging

The surface of this region, whether wooded or woodless, is generally undulating or level, and scarcely anywhere broken into hills and ravines. The rigid grasses of the prairies retard the escape of rains and melted snows, while their long wiry roots bind the soil, and prevent the waters from excavating trenches through which they might flow off. Thus, extensive tracts of wet or marshy prairie are formed and maintained. Between these (many of which will be rendered dry by ditching, when the population becomes denser), and the low bottoms, which are irreclaimable, the whole of this extensive and fertile portion of the Wabash Basin is infested with autumnal fever, of which many cases assume a malignant and fatal character.[1]

MEN CAPABLE of handling a spade found ready employment in the unattractive tasks of digging and ditching, tasks that an ax-oriented American viewed as foreign and unpleasant. Native-born Americans willingly performed farm labor, observed an English traveler, but they disliked digging work of all forms, often leaving this occupation to the Irish immigrants.[2] Three specialized types of this agricultural labor were found on midwestern farms: drainage ditching, well digging, and cellar excavating. Although these activities seem unusual in the frontier context, thousands of men nonetheless followed these lines and were in keen demand to perform these dirty, back-breaking, and sometimes dangerous jobs.

Techniques of drainage ditching were practiced as early as 1818 at the English settlement of Morris Birkbeck and George Flower on the southern Illinois prairie. Initially Birkbeck prepared to settle on

1. Daniel Drake, *Malaria in the Interior Valley of North America* (Urbana, 1964), p. 319.
2. Charles MacKay, *Life and Liberty in America: or, Sketches of a Tour in the United States and Canada, in 1857–8* (London, 1859), I, pp. 177–78.

timbered land in Ohio but altered his plans upon the advice of Edward Coles, later a governor of Illinois in the 1820's, who observed that English laborers brought to America were poorly trained in handling the ax, a basic tool for establishing a farm in timbered areas. Such laborers were well equipped, however, to work in low, marshy regions, digging ditches and building trenches by which fertile soil might be made useful for cultivation.[3]

Birkbeck and Flower established their settlement on Illinois prairie land which required drainage, and during the next several years English laborers, single or with families, migrated to America and took employment at the settlement. According to Flower, their skills coincided with his own agricultural requirements:

> . . . from time to time little parties came in year after year, chiefly small-tradesmen and farm-laborers. The latter, a most valuable class, came from all parts of England. . . . Three brothers, Joseph, Thomas, and Kelsey Crackles, able-bodied farm-laborers, from Lincolnshire, came with a full experience in the cultivation of flat, wet land; and brought with them the light fly-tool for digging ditches and drains, by which a practised hand can do double the work that can be done by a heavy steel spade. They lived with me three years before going on farms of their own. Their experience has shown us that the flat, wet prairies, generally shunned, are the most valuable wheat lands we possess.[4]

The early activity of the English settlement in draining prairie lands was not widely imitated, at least for several decades, since settlers generally preferred to establish themselves in or near timber. Fear of open prairies with their damp, swamp-like conditions influenced many to avoid these regions. But the techniques and methods of Birkbeck in the 1820's were in fact no different from those applied to wet lands during 1830-60, when many farmers began to experiment and construct crude ditches and drains for the improvement of their land. This increased interest in ditching during the later period

3. E. B. Washburne, *Sketch of Edward Coles, Second Governor of Illinois, and of the Slavery Struggle of 1823-4*, in Clarence W. Alvord, Collections of the Illinois State Historical Library, XVI (Springfield, 1920), pp. 367-68. For similar advice, see *Niles' Register*, II (May 30, 1818), 229-32; III (September 12, 1818), 33.

4. Flower, *History of the English Settlement*, I, pp. 130-31. Morris Birkbeck's interest in ditching was described by his son in a letter of December 29, 1819: "Ditching, if you recollect, was my father's favourite operation, and he would never rest until he had completely secured any spot which *appeared* even likely to be ever wet." As cited in Gladys S. Thomson, *A Pioneer Family: The Birkbecks in Illinois, 1818-1827* (London, 1953), p. 64.

coincided with the large number of Irish and English laborers who flocked to America.

Federal legislation in 1850 made available large tracts of swamp-lands to the individual states, including prairies within Illinois, Indiana, Michigan, and Wisconsin. According to one authority on the Swamp Land Act, Illinois received 1,500,000 acres; Indiana 1,250,000 acres; Michigan 5,500,000 acres; and Wisconsin 3,250,000 acres. Much of this land was acquired by speculators and remained unsettled, but interest was generated in the concepts of drainage as more settlers penetrated the prairie lands. The agricultural press in the late 1840's and throughout the 1850's devoted articles to the topic, elaborate in detail and embellished with cross-cut illustrations of ditch designs. Some machinery was developed by the 1850's, but it was not widely adopted until after the Civil War.[5]

Even such established agricultural regions as Ohio were experimenting with ditching and drainage on the local farm level. The *Ohio Cultivator* in 1847 advised its readers of the advantages to be derived from drainage. It recommended plows, especially in cutting open ditches, but saw no substitute for the hand labor of spading which remained the specialty of skilled hands. The *Cultivator* conceded that Americans willingly chopped and plowed on farms but exhibited no fondness for work with digging tools; obvious was the inference for the recruitment of foreigners to perform this task. Several years later the magazine reported that men were now available for this work: "A Ditch Digger.—If any of our readers, not too far from Columbus, wish to employ a man to make ditches for draining wet lands, we know of one in this city, a true 'son o' the sod.' who would like work of that kind. He offers to take jobs on contract, by the rod, and will shovel dirt a little faster and cheaper than any other man excepting a steam engine!"[6]

The process required considerable time and was not cheap. A Guernsey County farmer in east central Ohio assumed ownership of a farm in 1841; in 1845 he began ditching improvements which were

5. Margaret Beattie Bogue, "The Swamp Land Act and Wet Land Utilization in Illinois, 1850–1890," *Agricultural History*, XXV (1951), 170–71, 178.
6. *Ohio Cultivator*, III (January 15, 1847), 9–10; V (March 1, 1849), 72. Extensive drainage was reported at Hancock and Wood counties in northwestern Ohio; for example, 800 miles of drains had been laid in Wood County by 1856. *Ibid.*, XIII (April, 1857), 99. Much of this drainage work in the 1850's occurred in the vicinity of the famous Black Swamp, according to John H. Klippart, *The Principles and Practice of Land Drainage* (Cincinnati, 1888), p. 38.

conducted over the following five-year period. The tract amounted to 320 acres and covered a number of creek beds. He hired a professional ditcher to shorten the course of small waterways with cut-off drains, the cost of the project amounting to $750 over a five-year period. In addition, the farmer's regular hands, it may be assumed, worked at times on the ditches or assisted the professional digger.[7]

Farmers realized that ditching of land—wet or dry—made good sense, for it prevented collection of water in low spaces and assured a level field for cultivation.[8] The first step was a simple open ditch to drain off standing water. The elaborateness of ditch construction was determined by the amount of water to be drained, according to an Indiana farmer at Franklin County in 1852:

> By making the outlets quite deep, sufficient fall can be obtained for the desired purpose. If the amount of water discharged by this be large, it should be a wide, open ditch; if the amount be small, the ditch may be narrow, and covered. Into these outlets lead several main branches, and the small ditches into these, connected with each other as a river and its tributaries, or forming a system like the veins in the human body. The small ditches, running in every direction where desired, are usually cut from 2 to 4 feet deep, according to the position and character of the ground, and from 1 to 2 feet wide, according to the amount of water to be discharged.[9]

This type of ditch was the easiest to construct and did not necessarily require a skilled ditcher, but could be cut by available hired hands to facilitate the water run-off. Once the surface water had been drained, the next step was to achieve moisture consistency of the acreage.[10] Construction of permanent drains in order to achieve this effect necessitated the skills of trained laborers. Because of this type of job and its tedious nature, the cost factor figured prominently in the extent of the ditch laid. It was not simply a matter of slashing open a line on the surface of the soil, but constructing a ditch according to specific size, proportions, and design. William Sewall, an Illinois farmer near Jacksonville (in the central part of the state), had

7. *Ohio Cultivator*, VI (March 1, 1850), 81–82.
8. Cut-offs and intercept ditches channeled water away from low places where it easily collected. Deepening of creek beds also facilitated adequate water run-off: see letter of Morris Birkbeck (Wansborough, Edwards County, Ill., October 22, 1820), in *Edwardsville Spectator*, November 28, 1820.
9. *U.S. Pat. Office Report, 1852* (Washington, 1853), 301; see also *Second Annual Report of the Indiana State Board of Agriculture for the year 1852* (Indianapolis, 1853), 320–28.
10. *U.S. Pat. Office Report, 1852*, 302.

part of his land ditched during 1831–32. The stipulations regarding the work were specific: the ditcher was to have the assistance of two hired hands, provided by Sewall, in cutting a ditch two and one-half feet wide at the top and eighteen inches at the bottom, and be paid according to the rate of thirty-one and one-quarter cents per rod.[11]

The size and depth of the ditch varied according to personal desire. The deeper ditch dictated a higher price per rod, along with other factors of neatness and precision of work. A Michigan farmer in 1856 described a network of ditches built by a Joseph Hawley, whose name suggests that he was of English birth. Open ditches four to five feet deep were constructed at the rate of thirty-seven and a half cents per rod. The ditcher first laid out lines in survey fashion, using a chain guide. Employing a long, sharp knife, he made straight line cuts into the sod, repeating a parallel line some distance on the other side of the chain. The ditcher and his assistant then went down the two spaced parallel lines, making cross cuts to form square wedges or one-foot cubes. The initial lifting of the sod was performed in teamwork, one man using a dung fork with curved tines to lift up the wedge, while the other dug out the center portion. This process was repeated several times, making more cuts lengthwise and crosswise with the long blade knife in order to free deeper wedges until the desired depth was achieved.[12]

A slightly different approach was to attach a sharpened plowshare to the axle of a wagon and plow open a line in the sod. The farmer and his regular hands could fork out the cut sod, and labor costs were less because ordinary hired hands on the farm could be used. Ditching costs averaged about one dollar per day when regular ditchers were employed, but with the plowshare method it only cost fifty cents a rod and involved men with no previous experience.[13] Darius Pierce at Farmington, Michigan, contracted two men to ditch at the rate of seventy-five cents per rod. The work commenced in July, 1852, and was terminated by December with the completion of 231 rods of ditch.[14]

A properly constructed ditch was reinforced and covered. Various theories prevailed as to the best type of lined and covered drain. Once

11. Sewall, *Diary*, pp. 137, 142.
12. *Michigan Farmer*, XIV (November, 1856), 334–35.
13. *Ibid.*, VIII (June, 1850), 163–64. A plow could also be run directly along the inside of the ditch, with the plowshare set at an angle to scrape out a V-shaped wedge. *U.S. Pat. Office Report, 1852,* 301.
14. Darius Pierce Accountbook, 1566 AA, entries during July and December, 1852.

the ditch was opened and the proper dimensions achieved, the bottom
and sides were lined with stone or wood. This final phase after ditching was described in the *Patent Office Report* of 1852. The ditches

> . . . are then finished in various manners. The most approved method,
> and the one more employed than all others, where stones are plentiful,
> is to build a narrow, dry wall from the bottom of the ditch, on each
> side, to the height of 10 to 15 inches; then cover the aperture with
> large stones; then fill in with earth over the whole to the level of the
> ground on either side. A little straw may be thrown in on the covering
> stones to prevent the loose earth from falling through; as soon as the
> earth becomes compact, it will retain its place, and not fall through
> into the open ditch.[15]

Bricks and stones were often simply cast loosely into the ditch and
then covered over with soil. In timbered areas, wood staves were
utilized, but it was necessary ". . . to cut oak or some other lasting
kind 18 inches or 2 feet in length; then split it into staves 2 or 3 inches
in thickness, and the wider the better. Place one end of them at the
bottom of the ditch on one side, and lean the other end against the
opposite side, breaking the joints. Cover them as before. This will
last most surprisingly."[16]

The type of tools employed by Irish and English ditchers reflected
the specialized art of digging, and these implements were analyzed
by Henry F. French, a New Hampshire farmer, who published *Farm
Drainage* in 1859.[17] The shovel or spade was the primary instrument
for the average ditching job. The New England spade or shovel,
similar to the present-day garden spade, was short-handled in comparison to those used by Irish and English diggers. French conceded
that the long-handled spade was highly efficient, but only in the
skilled hands of Irishmen. Its eighteen-inch blade weighed five
pounds, while the handle fashioned of tough ash gave the imple-

15. *U.S. Pat. Office Report, 1852*, 301. Klippart claimed that considerable
drainage ditching in Ohio was constructed of stones. On off days farmers
employed their hands to gather loose stones that were hauled to the ditching
sites and distributed along the proposed ditch lines. *Principles and Practice of
Land Drainage*, pp. 258–59.

16. *U.S. Pat. Office Report, 1852*, 301. Prior to the Civil War some farmers
laid baked tile drains. The pipes were two to four inches in diameter and cost
eight to twelve dollars per thousand. Cleveland was an important center for the
tile industry. Klippart, *Principles and Practice of Land Drainage*, pp. 38, 296,
314.

17. Henry F. French, *Farm Drainage* (New York, 1859); on the topic of
tools, see pp. 235–46. Klippart also devotes a chapter to the various types of
hand implements, *Principles and Practice of Land Drainage*, pp. 387–93.

ment an overall length of four feet. The blade had a large curve which was highly polished and sharpened almost like a chopping ax. The ditcher adjusted the curve to his own preference by putting the blade under a rock or log and bending it to the desired pitch.

In skilled hands, this Irish spade was a powerful tool that cut off one to two inch roots with complete ease. One side of the upper portion of the blade projected outwards to form a wedge, allowing the digger to strike the blade into the sod with one thrust of the right foot. Americans found it difficult to understand how the Irish could prefer such a narrow-bladed tool. But where the broad American spade was useless in gravel or hard clay below the surface, the Irish spade was exceedingly versatile. French observed his Irish farm hand using one of these spades:

> There is no digging on the farm that his spade is not adapted to. To mark out a drain in the turf by a line, he mounts his spade with one foot, and hops backward on the other, with a celerity surprising to behold. Then he cuts the sod in squares, and, with a sleight of hand . . . throws out the first spit. When he comes on to the gravel or hard clay, where another man would use a pick-axe, his heavy boot comes down upon the treader, and drives the spade a foot or more deep; and if a root is encountered, a blow or two easily severs it. . . . On the whole, though the Irish spade does wonders on our farm, we recommend it only for Irishmen, who know how to handle it. In our own hands, it is as awkward a thing as we ever took hold of, and we never saw any man but an Irishman, who could use it gracefully and effectively.[18]

When digging a deep drain with a narrow base, the ditcher employed an English bottoming tool. Basically a long-handled implement, its narrow blade was bent in the shape of a scoop to cut and lift out narrow chunks of sod from the bottom of the drain. This instrument was superior to the American pick, which was awkward to use in the narrow confines of the drain's base where little space was permitted for swinging and striking. French concluded, after observing his own Irish farm hand, that the Irish digger should use the tools he best understood.[19]

Men worked at ditching during the spring, summer, and autumn, although in the lower parts of the Midwest this work was done also in wintertime.[20] An Indiana farmer, John Goodwin, conducted ex-

18. French, *Farm Drainage*, pp. 237–39.
19. *Ibid.*, pp. 239–40.
20. Robinson, *Facts for Farmers*, pp. 1006–9.

tensive ditching operations on his farm near Brookville in Franklin
County; the seasonal demarcations were fairly clear, according to
the entries in his diary. In March, 1854, he employed ditchers in his
fields, identifying them as the "Irishmen." These itinerants were assisted by regular hands on the farm at the digging. Split timber was
used for lining the ditches, and during the winter of 1855–56 frequent
notations mentioned the hands cutting timber in the woods. In March,
1856, all were involved at one time or another in helping to ditch the
clover field.[21]

An owner of farm tracts adjacent to Indianapolis, Calvin Fletcher
made similar reference in his diary about the men who performed
ditching services for him during 1849–53. At this time Fletcher and
his son were clearing timber off the land, part of which was swampy,
intended for future grazing operations. Besides Irish and German
ditchers, free blacks in the Indianapolis area worked as farm hands
and occasionally at drainage digging on the farm. In September, 1849,
Fletcher mused aloud in his diary as to whether all this clearing and
land improvement was in fact worth the effort and expense. Several
days later two more Germans were hired to ditch the wheat field,
and then they worked with one of Fletcher's hired hands at sowing
a field of timothy. The planting work was performed during the time
they were hired to ditch, indicating that ditchers (like other specialized farm workers, including prairie breakers) stopped their work
to assist with the routine farm tasks and harvesting. Several days later
they completed the job, and Fletcher recorded in the diary that the
men were paid five dollars for six days work. This lawyer-farmer expressed satisfaction that the land's value had been enhanced.[22]

Fletcher resorted to the employment of blacks on his farm when
white laborers were hard to obtain. During the fall of 1851 more
drainage work was carried out amid the press of other activities.
Large numbers of hogs and cattle were being driven to market, which
explained the shortage of farm hands. Several Negro hands dug out
a pond while another hauled manure. Additional reasons for the employment of the blacks were that one of his regular hands got drunk,
while the others were busy cutting cord wood for the approaching
winter. A month later Fletcher's son hired a regular ditcher—an
Irishman—to straighten and shorten the courseway of a creek run-

21. John R. Goodwin Diary, 1848–61, entries of March 16, 1854, December
20, 1855, February 28, March 6, 26, 1856. Goodwin's regular hands were hired
at conventional rates of eight to ten dollars per month: see entries of March
1, June 14, October 8, 1855.
22. Fletcher Diary, entries of May 24, September 5, 14, 18, 1849.

ning through their land.[23] Ditching was continued over the following years, resulting in the drainage of swampland by 1853.[24]

The scarcity of timber in prairie regions prompted the construction of ditches which served a dual purpose of drainage and, more important, as a form of fencing. In 1837, according to Henry Ellsworth of the Patent Office, sod fences were more practical and cheaper than those constructed of rails, especially on the open prairies. At Peoria County in central Illinois in the 1840's, settlers relied on ditch fences constructed from sod. Usually it was a ditch three feet deep with a constructed embankment of the same height, and sides matted with sod. When wood or timber was later procured, the sod fence was replaced.[25]

A farmer in Whiteside County in northwestern Illinois described the specifications of a sod fence: the ditch was three and one-half feet high, five feet wide on the bottom, and two and one-half feet wide at the top. The sides of the ditch were sodded over an area three and one-half feet wide and three feet high.[26] Of the men who built this type of fence on the Illinois prairies during the 1830's, an early settler claimed: "Our first fences were sod and ditch; made by Englishmen who were accustomed to that work. who made their way to the then far west. and were gladly employed by the settlers. Many more of these had now taken up land and like ourselves were making homes."[27]

These men who engaged in ditching and digging during 1830–60

23. *Ibid.*, entries of September 20, October 27, November 25, 1851. An indication of the size of Fletcher's farm was provided in an entry of August 6, 1851, listing 300 hogs, 100 cattle, 200 acres of corn, and 90 acres of hay.

24. *Ibid.*, entry of December 10, 1853.

25. *Peoria Register and North-Western Gazetteer*, April 29, 1842; Ellsworth's observations are cited in A. D. Jones, *Illinois and the West* (Boston, 1838), p. 193. A valuable survey of the fencing issue is Clarence Danhof, "The Fencing Problem in the Eighteen-Fifties," *Agricultural History*, XVIII (1944), 168–86.

26. *Chicago Weekly Democrat*, February 9, 1842. An obvious disadvantage to these open ditch-fences was the constant problem of cattle falling into the trench and being unable to get out.

27. "Reminiscences of a 92 Year Old Woman," pp. 4–5, in La Salle County Pioneer File. According to an Englishman who constructed these fences in Illinois during the 1840's, it was possible to dig as much as ten rods per day. Bateman and Selby, eds., *Historical Encyclopedia of Illinois and History of Du Page County*, II, pp. 983–84. For additional reference to ditch and sod fences, see Plumbe, *Sketches of Iowa and Wisconsin*, pp. 33–34; Ellsworth, *Valley of the Upper Wabash, Indiana*, pp. 35, 60–62; James Logan, *Notes of a Journey through Canada, the United States of America, and the West Indies* (Edinburgh, 1838), p. 112; Jacob Ferris, *The States and Territories of the Great West* (New York, 1856), p. 209. The feasibility of this type of fencing is strongly questioned by Bogue, *From Prairie to Corn Belt*, pp. 74–75.

were usually emigrants from the British Isles in pursuit of a better life and a new start in America; many were part of the massive influx of Irish to whom fell manual construction jobs requiring spade labor. While many were employed in canal digging and later at railroad construction, they also found work as conventional farm hands, even though their skills were not always as versatile as the American farm hand who was a jack of all trades. Yet with the growing interest in land drainage, the demand increased for their talent at handling a spade in ditching and trenching operations.[28]

The relationship between drainage ditching and construction work was apparent in the case of English-born John Sleight, who went on foot from job to job, including work on the Wabash and Erie Canal before turning westward to Dodge County, Wisconsin, in 1845. Although a landowner himself, his first nine years found him employed for others at ditching; he apparently found the work suitable to his training and sufficiently remunerative.[29] So did James Grawcock, who worked at Fort Wayne, Indiana, and then headed to the northern part of the state to work at ditching. By 1854 he had saved $150, which he applied to the purchase of a farm. His brother also came to this area and obtained employment on railroad construction projects.[30]

Not all these immigrants were itinerants who worked from job to job. Some were bona fide settlers whose economic situation compelled them to work at this line in their immediate neighborhood. A Scotch immigrant with an impressive name of John Dollar settled in Coles County in southern Illinois, where he filed a claim to eighty acres. During the 1840's, while his own farm was being established, Dollar did ditching work in his spare time for other farmers in the area.[31] Similar was the situation for another Scotsman who brought his wife and children to Wisconsin Territory in 1846 and settled in Green

28. *American Agriculturist*, VI (June, 1847), 181–83. Irish were urged not to stay in the cities but to seek employment in the countryside away from urban vices. Agricultural employment, including ditching, was strongly recommended, and they were told to expect wages of ten to sixteen dollars per month. Indiana, Illinois, Missouri, and Iowa had the best openings for farm hands, while the South was to be avoided whenever possible. John O'Hanlon, *The Irish Emigrant's Guide for the United States* (Boston, 1851), pp. 90–92.

29. Homer Bishop Hubbell, *Dodge County, Wisconsin. Past and Present* (Chicago, 1913), II, p. 314.

30. *Counties of La Grange and Noble, Indiana* (Chicago, 1882), pp. 482–83. For other examples, see *ibid.*, p. 326; Kiner, ed. *History of Henry County, Illinois*, II, p. 344; Beckwith, *History of Montgomery County, Together with Historic Notes on the Wabash Valley*, p. 428; Goodspeed and Blanchard, eds., *Counties of Porter and Lake, Indiana*, p. 738.

31. *History of Coles County, Illinois* (Chicago, 1879), p. 565.

County with fourteen dollars and a land warrant to his name. During the next three years he raised money by digging ditches, wells, and cellars. He often took livestock in payment for his services; even after the first crop was raised on his farm, this specialist with a spade continued to work at such jobs.[32]

Well digging, as a segment of farm-making, was an important occupation that attracted both professional and itinerant, and many well diggers were often native Americans, white or black. They also performed basic foundation work, digging out cellars for houses and barns. Reliance on well water was not common in all parts of the Midwest. Access to a natural flowing spring spared many settlers the cost and labor of digging a well, while Scandinavian settlements in the upper Midwest tended to rely on water from streams or in rain barrels. Both sources were poor: bacteria bred in the stagnant rain water and streams were not always reliable for human consumption.[33] In southern Illinois during the 1850's, a traveler stopped at a small cabin for a drink of water. The woman replied that whisky was preferred to water, and at ten cents a quart was cheaper than the process of digging a well.[34] The cost of constructing a well was directly related to the availability of men to perform this work. Labor for well and cellar digging was scarce, according to a letter of an early Wisconsin settler in the 1840's: "Last Summer there was a great Number of New Houses Built around us and could not get hands enough to dig Cellars and Wells and stone them up. . . ."[35]

The first step in digging a well was to choose a location, and opinions ranged far and wide on how to find water. A well digger with seventeen years' experience in the business discussed various methods to determine a likely water source for a well. Some adhered to the use of a forked stick—preferably witch hazel, willow, or peach, he said. Another method, especially in dry weather, was to observe the surface of the land just before sunrise: green streaks or spots in the grass suggested water below; additional proof was the presence of spiders in such places! On plowed surfaces, moist areas readily stood out in contrast to dry ones. If these methods seemed speculative or some-

32. *History of Green County, Wisconsin*, pp. 702–5.

33. Knut Gjertset and Ludvid Hektoen, "Health Conditions and the Early Practice of Medicine among the Early Norwegian Settlers, 1825–1865," *Norwegian-American Historical Association: Studies and Records*, I (1926), 29.

34. *Alton Telegraph and Democratic Review*, as cited in *Cist's Weekly Advertiser*, June 25, 1852.

35. Georgia Dow Townsend, "Letters of James Stark, 1841–42, Friend and 'Most Ob. Servant,'" *Wisconsin History*, XXXIII (1949), 210.

what occult, the well digger's final advice contained the most common sense and probably was the only realistic way of going about the matter: "Keep digging and boring in different places till you find water."[36]

The condition of the substrata—rocky, sandy, or clay—determined how the well was to be dug. George Flower recounted the struggle to sink a well in rocky subsoil in the 1820's at Edwards County, Illinois:

> One of my first undertakings was to dig a well, two persons attracted by my location came on in quest of employment, and agreed to dig a well; I had first to build a small cabin for their residence. Five feet from the surface of the ground the well diggers came to a solid sand stone rock, we had to peck through that rock thirty two feet, and every other day I had to send a man and horse thirty miles to a blacksmith's shop to get the tools sharpened, until the job was completed.[37]

Most wells in the Midwest were sunk in soft soil or sand rather than rock in order to avoid the problem encountered by Flower. Letters appearing in the *Michigan Farmer* during the 1850's describe several methods of well construction, primarily in average soil conditions. Two professional well diggers contracted to put in a well on a farm at Livingston County, Michigan. They agreed to dig, stone, and finish up a well which was to draw three feet of water for the price of twenty-four dollars, provided the well depth did not exceed forty feet. The farmer himself had calculated that water might be struck at the thirty-four-foot level. The first eight feet were dug and thrown out by hand. For the rest of the way, a frame with a pulley attached over the mouth of the well site and a rope rigged to a harnessed horse provided the power to raise a tub containing the earth dug from the well. In response to voice commands, the horse either backed up to lower the tub or moved forward to raise it. Because the soil was loose and sandy, the well diggers in this instance curbed the shaft as they dug downward.

For the curbing, oak timber was split into five-foot lengths, five to six inches wide, notched and then placed along the sides in log-cabin manner. When the appearance of quicksand indicated closeness to

36. *Farmer's Companion and Horticultural Gazette*, II (October 1, 1853), 70.
37. Flower, *Errors of Emigrants*, p. 24. The average depth of wells was twenty to thirty feet: see Oliver, *Eight Months in Illinois*, p. 134; Parker, *Trip to the West and Texas*, p. 58.

the water level, the men selected a white oak tree whose trunk was about three feet in diameter. Sawing out a section, they carefully split off the sides in stave-like fashion, marking the pieces in the order they were removed. The inside was then chiseled out, and the staves were bolted back together. This barrel-shaped oak frame was then pushed down into the quicksand. Dipping out the sand, the diggers pushed the barrel frame deeper, eventually leaving it at the bottom of the well to filter out sand and stones. The oak did not readily rot and prevented seepage of sand into the water. By the end of six months, the water in the well was crystal clear, and the farmer satisfied with the job.[38]

This description of well-digging attracted the interest and criticism of another Michigan farmer who suggested an alternate method. He hired an Irishman to construct a well by a faster, cheaper technique on his farm at Lenawee County. A three-foot, four-inch diameter hole was opened up, with the Irishman digging downward until he reached water. A curb of half-inch-thick boards in six-foot lengths was nailed to a frame which sat at the base of the shaft. Against this frame he laid a wall of bricks—not stones, which were presumably too irregular in shape. As the Irish digger proceeded deeper, scooping out the sand, clay, and earth, the brick wall settled down gradually to the desired depth. It was claimed that a thirty-foot well of this design, achieving a water depth of four feet, could be constructed in a single day. The Irishman's charge was twelve dollars in sandy soil and fifteen dollars in clay. In terms of labor, the cost was half that of the oak-staved model, although the cost of bricks was an additional factor to be considered.[39]

Such wells were constructed on a flat job rate, but this was not the only way of computing the labor cost. When a farmer-storekeeper in the 1820's at Fairfield County, Ohio, hired laborers to dig a well on his property, one hand, Henry Christy, worked two days on the digging of the well at fifty cents per day, while another who had the main responsibility for the work was paid on the basis of a contract. Ac-

38. *Michigan Farmer*, XIV (July, 1856), 199–200.
39. *Ibid.*, XIV (September, 1856), 267–68. The amount of time needed to dig a well varied according to the depth, type of soil, and the siding of the shaft. With ready-made brick, the job required less time, although an Illinois guidebook estimated four to five days for well construction: Mitchell, *Illinois in 1837*, pp. 70–71. Stones were used more than brick, and the farmer had the responsibility of gathering and supplying this material for the well digger. For example, see George Jenkins Diary, entries of October 13–14, 1857.

cording to the daybook, Jacob Hunt, a professional well-digger, dug at the rate of twelve and a half cents per foot, and the job took six days.[40]

The single flat rate was common and often appeared in early farm records. For example, in northern Ohio a well digger charged a farmer the simple fee of five dollars to dig a well in 1815.[41] Men in need of employment took whatever pay was offered, as did Samuel Wayman; he came to the Chicago area in 1843, purchased land in nearby Lake County, but worked at well digging for seventy-five cents a day.[42] Possibly men like Wayman were employed to assist the professional digger who actually worked in the well and who needed day laborers to hoist the refuse dirt from the pit. Large landholders like Matthew T. Scott in central Illinois in the 1850's hired tenants. In June, 1855, a man named Fisk was recorded digging nine feet of a well, and in July another individual was reimbursed twenty-five dollars for digging a well in addition to setting out posts.[43]

Wages based on a per foot rate varied with the locale and the type of soil. When the county poor farm was established in Stark County, Ohio, in 1834, John Shank received the job of sinking a well at the rate of $1.50 per foot.[44] In 1839 several Norwegians found day labor employment at fifty cents per day near Chicago. They then went to Jefferson Prairie in southern Wisconsin and worked at well digging at fifty cents a foot.[45] An even lower rate, based on the number of feet dug, was paid by Fielding Beeler, a farmer near Indianapolis. He employed one of his hired hands to do this work on an extra basis: William Darnell, a twelve-dollars-per-month hand, agreed to dig a well thirteen feet deep at the rate of twelve and a half cents per foot. The job entailed more than what his employer anticipated, for seventy-five cents additional was credited to Darnell's account for "digging well deeper."[46]

40. Young Daybook of Farm and General Store Accounts, p. 112, entries of August 18, 25, 1827.
41. Gordon Daybook, p. 54, entry of June, 1815, for Joseph Paton.
42. A. T. Andreas, *History of Cook County, Illinois* (Chicago, 1884), p. 510.
43. Scott Notebook and 3 Papers from Pocket, 1855–56, p. 23, entry of June 23, 1855; p. 35, entry of July 23, 1855.
44. Perrin, ed., *History of Stark County, with an Outline Sketch of Ohio*, p. 212.
45. Rasmus Anderson, *The First Chapter of Norwegian Immigration, (1821–1840) Its Causes and Results* (Madison, 1906), p. 256.
46. Fielding Beeler Farm Diary, p. 72, account of William Darnell, 1850. A physician at Schoolcraft, Michigan, Dr. Nathan Thomas, obtained a good deal of cheap labor for his farm, especially patients who worked off their medical bills. One individual excavated a cellar for $6, while another dug two wells

In the early 1840's William Oliver gave an accurate and informative set of cost estimates for the construction of a thirty-foot well on the Illinois prairie. The cost of digging the well shaft, made as narrow as conveniently possible, totaled $7.50, based on a rate of twenty-five cents for each perpendicular foot. Hauling of the stone involved fifteen loads, an average of one load per day with oxen rented at two dollars daily, or approximately thirty dollars. The labor of building the stone into the sides of the thirty-foot well shaft cost twenty-five cents per foot, and the furnishing of the well with a roller, rope, and bucket added another five dollars. Thus the total cost of labor, equipment, stones, and well accessories approximated fifty dollars, a sizable investment in the overall expenditures of establishing a farm.[47]

Well digging was a hazardous occupation in comparison to ditching and general farm labor. Professionals were cold realists or outright fatalists who ran the constant risk of being trapped and buried alive. Thomas Anderson was a hardened veteran who performed digging and well cleaning services in Champaign County, Ohio. In 1828 he and a young assistant were cleaning and enlarging an old well when the sides caved in and temporarily trapped them. The accident did not daunt this tough gladiator, who was described as being a crusty old character addicted to strong drinks and a staunch belief in General Andrew Jackson.[48] A similar accident but with fatal results occurred at Brown County in western Illinois; a digger was working in sandy soil without erecting a siding to prevent the sliding of sand and soil. Repeatedly warned of a possible collapse, the well digger only laughed at the advice. Eight feet of earth smothered him.[49]

Death in a well accident recognized no color line. In 1847 a Negro well digger was trapped by a cave-in at Franklin County, Ohio. Ef-

costing $9.25 and $8.50 respectively. Nathan Thomas Ledger from January 10, 1832, pp. 41, 157.

47. Oliver, *Eight Months in Illinois*, p. 134.

48. "Pioneer Sketches," p. 48.

49. *Daily Rock Islander*, as cited in *Chicago Daily Democrat*, September 8, 1857. At Kane County, Illinois, a well digger was trapped for nine hours at a depth of twenty-five feet. When he was rescued and given a drink, he was ready to undertake the next well-digging job! *Aurora Beacon*, as cited in *Alton Telegraph and Democratic Review*, July 14, 1848. Diaries and letters of early settlers expressed shock and horror when such accidents occurred: see Pratt Diary, entry of December 25, 1845; Bottomley, *Letters 1842–1850*, p. 112. Well-digging accidents were common throughout the country: see *Niles' Register*, XXX (August 19, 1826), 432.

forts to rescue him continued for fifty hours, but the gravel kept sliding back down and hampered the work of the many rescuers.[50] An
accident in this area twenty years before had also involved an illit-
erate Negro who made his living digging wells. Richard Stanup had
reached a depth of sixty feet when the sides caved in. He was able to
pull himself up halfway on a rope before twenty feet of soil buried
him. When his rescuers finally reached him, he seemed lifeless at
first but revived, to the suprise of those who saved him.[51]

An equally common danger associated with well digging was the
collection of gas in the shaft of the well. Traces of this gas were
often present without warning; many succumbed before being able
to get out of the well. The danger was no less for those who attempted
to rescue these victims. George Flower related the details of a double
tragedy at the English settlement at Edwards County, Illinois, in
1819:

> The hands engaged in digging a well for Mr. Lawrence, in the Village
> Prairie, met, with a fatal accident. The well had proceeded to a con-
> siderable depth. As usual, in the morning, a man was let down; he
> was seen to stagger and fall. Another was let down to assist him; he
> fell also. With difficulty, others were saved, who went down to bring
> these up. Richard Kniffer and Thomas Clem, two active and able-
> bodied laborers, full of life and health, a quarter-of-an-hour before,
> were now brought up corpses. They were carried to their graves, and
> interred with solumn rites of burial by their sorrowing companions.
> They had incautiously descended, and fell victims to the noxious
> vapor at the bottom of the well.[52]

Wells posed sanitation problems and, for diggers, often unpleasant
and unhealthy work situations. A man near Pittsfield in southwestern
Illinois wondered why the water tasted so poorly until a cleaning job
revealed 482 dead frogs in the bottom of the well![53] Illness was sometimes traceable to well water sources, as in the case of an entire farm
household near Alton, Illinois. It was speculated that the well was the
origin of the malady when David Ashton, the family hired hand, be-

50. *Cist's Weekly Advertiser*, August 24, 1847.

51. Joshua Antrim, *The History of Champaign and Logan Counties* (Bellefontaine, Ohio, 1872), pp. 401–3.

52. Flower, *History of the English Settlement*, I, pp. 123. For similar examples,
see Scott, *Complete History of Fairfield County, Ohio*, p. 281; *History of
Seneca County, Ohio* (Chicago, 1886), p. 590. Even digging a shallow pit for
a privy posed a danger; a newspaper reported the death of a German digger
from the gas while working in the pit. *Daily Sanduskian*, August 14, 1849.

53. *Pittsfield Sun*, as cited in *Chicago Daily Democrat*, March 26, 1858.

came deathly ill only hours after having worked at cleaning out his employer's well.[54]

Bizarre accidents also occurred in this line of work. A Stark County, Ohio, well digger was killed when his hoisting rope broke and caused him to plunge to the bottom.[55] In 1851 Patrick Galvin came close to losing his life while digging a well in La Salle County, Illinois. Galvin was at the bottom when the chain on the bucket used for hauling up dirt broke. The bucket came sailing down at full force, grazed the man's temples, and completely severed his foot.[56] The stamina and nine-lives character of well diggers seemed legendary; old Nate Baily was the local well digger in Genesee County, Michigan, during the 1830's and 1840's. While he worked at the bottom of a well, a tubload of stones fell down on his back—but the accident did not impair this tough professional, who continued to follow his trade.[57] Animals frequently slipped into uncovered wells, but William Truscott probably considered the event unique while he was at the bottom of the shaft. He heard a noise and looked up to see a hog which had partially slipped over the edge, trying desperately to pull itself back up. Realizing the hopelessness of the brute's struggle, the well digger took the only course available and flattened himself against the wall. Down came the hog with a smashing thud, just missing the frightened digger, who was gratefully hauled out of the shaft.[58]

Minor excavating jobs on the farm were routinely performed by whatever labor was available. Such tasks as cellar digging, laying out small trenches for foundation walls, or scooping out soil for an icehouse were less specialized and clearly without the hazards associated with well digging, so that farmers could delegate these tasks to their regular hands. If a cellar was to be dug and then lined with brick or stone, the actual digging part of the project could be prepared by the hired hands in advance of the mason who came specifically to perform the brick work. According to the *Wisconsin Farmer* in 1851, cellar construction in the cities was costly. But the opposite prevailed in the countryside, where a cheap form of labor already

54. *Alton Telegraph and Democratic Review*, as cited *ibid.*, January 26, 1858.
55. Perrin, ed., *History of Stark County, with an Outline Sketch of Ohio*, p. 456.
56. *La Salle County Democrat*, August 20, 1851, as cited in *Chicago Daily Democrat*, September 5, 1851. This type of accident killed a black well digger at Xenia, Ohio: see *Daily Sanduskian*, August 2, 1850.
57. *History of Genesee County, Michigan*, p. 208.
58. *Combined History of Edwards, Lawrence and Wabash Counties, Illinois* (Philadelphia, 1883), p. 65.

existed on the farm: ". . . common farm laborers can do the principal part of the work on the cellar, and at odd jobs when business is not pressing. Not much skill is required to lay a cellar wall—one master workman for a few days will be the whole outlay for a cellar 30 by 40."[59]

A farmer at Sheboygan, Wisconsin, employed hands at the rate of twelve to sixteen dollars per month during the summer of 1855. The men dug out the cellar for his barn, and then a mason was brought in to lay the walls.[60] Masons sometimes worked at the digging, too; a Michigan farmer employed one to construct brick chimneys and excavate a cellar, in addition to helping with the grain threshing.[61] Hired hands and tenants who performed these tasks occasionally received extra compensation: William Brown, a Minnesota farmer in the 1850's, hired a man at eighteen dollars per month but also paid him seven dollars for cellar digging.[62] The employment background and economic circumstances of itinerant diggers were in many instances fairly identical to those of agricultural laborers, since most of them were at times farm hands or performed farm-related tasks.[63]

The three related occupations of well digging, cellar-foundation digging, and drainage ditching provided itinerants with seasonal employment on farms. Excavation work was tedious and sometimes hazardous, especially in connection with well digging. Cellar and foundation tasks involving less risk were carried out by average farm

59. *Wisconsin Farmer*, III (April, 1851), 89. Cellar digging was more important in the cities; and according to Charles Cist of Cincinnati, these men were seasonal laborers who worked in the packing houses in winter. *Sketches and Statistics of Cincinnati in 1851* (Cincinnati, 1851), pp. 287–88. A newspaper editor at Sandusky, however, called for property owners to hire unemployed laborers at cellar digging, excavating, ditching, and fencing during winter. *Daily Commercial Register*, January 31, 1855.
60. Asel G. Dye Diary, entries of May 2, June 21–22, July 5, 1855.
61. Nathan Pierce Accountbook, 1848–60, p. 28, entries during 1848–52.
62. William Brown Farm Journal, p. 15; see also Lathrop Burgess Diary, entries of January 2, March 26, 1844; Burgess Accountbook, 1849–60, p. 20. For other references to minor excavating, see Elhannah Morris Accountbook, 1818–19, sheet entitled "Account of hands Employed at the Mill, May 25, 1818–"; also entries of June 11, 27, 1818; *History of Oakland County, Michigan*, p. 86.
63. For examples, see Jones, *Madison, Dane County and Surrounding Towns*, p. 560; *History of Union County, Ohio* (Chicago, 1883), p. 344; Calkins, ed., *Log City Days*, p. 45; *History of Greene County, Illinois* (Chicago, 1879), pp. 699–700; Bateman and Selby, eds., *Historical Encyclopedia of Illinois and History of Ogle County*, II, pp. 833–34; *History of Washtenaw County, Michigan* (Chicago, 1881), p. 992; *Portrait and Biographical Record of Christian County, Illinois* (Chicago, 1893), p. 284.

hands. Drainage ditching became increasingly prevalent during 1830–60, a period coinciding with the influx of emigrants from the British Isles. Despite American scorn for those laboring in these employments, these newcomers to the United States found immediate and available employment in an aspect of agriculture for which they were well suited and well trained.

Farm Labor and Horticulture

> In almost all locations there are difficulties to encounter. One
> of these is that of securing efficient laborers. American laborers
> of the right sort are rarely to be found. American blood is fast,
> and fast blood is impatient with a hoe among carrots.[1]

HORTICULTURE was a specialized aspect of agricultural production and included nurseries, garden farms, and vineyards. Patient preparation of soil, delicate grafting and properly
timed transplanting were seemingly inappropriate to a wood chopping, sodbusting frontier where the monotony was broken with rough
sports of fighting, shooting matches, horse races, and whisky drinking. While strictly horticultural production required less acreage than
conventional crops, most horticulturists operated farms which necessitated the employment of hired laborers.[2]

Pioneers established modest orchards as early as the 1790's near
the Ohio River, but gradually over the years horticulture and garden
farming expanded along commercial lines.[3] This development coincided with the movement of settlers into the upper Midwest, while
rising cities emerged as shipping outlets and markets for fruit and
truck vegetables. The port city of Cleveland on the edge of Lake
Erie became an export center for fruit, especially peaches to Detroit and Buffalo.[4] By the 1840's Chicago assumed a similar position
of importance; the famed Illinois horticulturist John A. Kennicott
counted fifty horticultural farms in northern Illinois which produced
in total 30,000 to 80,000 trees.[5] Kenosha, Racine, and Milwaukee in

1. Edmund Morris, *Ten Acres Enough* (New York, 1916), pp. 250–51.
2. Ulysses Prentiss Hedrick, *A History of Horticulture in America to 1860*
(New York, 1950), pp. 230, 244; Gates, *Farmer's Age*, pp. 255–61.
3. *History of Washington County, Ohio* (Cleveland, 1881), p. 514; *History
of Wayne County, Indiana*, I, pp. 618–23.
4. *Western Horticultural Review*, III (September, 1853), 579–80.
5. *U.S. Pat. Office Report, 1849* (Washington, 1850), 435. The fad for trees
on the prairies is analyzed by Earl W. Hayter, "Horticultural Humbuggery

nearby Wisconsin also became horticultural centers,[6] but Cincinnati remained indeed the "Queen City," occupying a prominent location and situated in a region known for its excellent climate.[7]

Akin to nursery and truck farming was grape culture for the wine industry at Cincinnati. The Catawba grape flourished in areas facing the Ohio River, where the moderating temperatures of the water assured steady, unhampered growth. High hills with southern exposure overlooking the river valley, similar to the Rhine Valley of Germany, afforded a combination of sunlight and warmth to promote the delicate grape vines.[8] The importance of all three horticultural lines was reflected in their increasing value by 1840–60.

TABLE 3. VALUE OF ORCHARD AND MARKET GARDEN PRODUCTION, WINE PRODUCTION (GALLONS), 1840–60

	Value of Orchard Produce			Value of Market Garden Produce		
	1840	1850	1860	1840	1850	1860
Ohio	$494,978	$695,921	$1,929,309	$97,606	$214,004	$907,513
Indiana	127,286	324,940	1,258,942	61,212	72,864	546,153
Illinois	149,746	446,049	1,126,323	71,911	127,494	387,027
Michigan	22,342	132,650	1,122,074	4,051	14,738	145,883
Wisconsin	1,062	4,823	78,690	3,106	32,142	208,730
Minnesota	—	—	649	—	150	174,704

	Wine Production (Gallons)		
	1840	1850	1860
Ohio	11,524	48,207	568,617
Indiana	10,265	14,055	102,895
Illinois	474	2,997	50,690
Michigan	—	1,654	14,427
Wisconsin	—	113	6,278
Minnesota	—	—	412

Sources: *Statistical View of the United States*, pp. 172–74; *Agriculture of the United States in 1860*, pp. 186, 190. The figures for the value of orchard produce in 1840 were combined with the value of nursery produce in the above table.

among the Western Farmers, 1850–1890," *Indiana History*, XLIII (1947), 205–24.

6. *Western Horticultural Review*, II (September, 1852), 540–42.

7. *Cincinnati Daily Gazette*, June 12, 1847; *Western Farmer and Gardener* (Cincinnati), V (September, 1844), 37–38.

8. Robert Buchanan, *A Treatise on Grape Culture in Vineyards in the Vicinity of Cincinnati* (Cincinnati,, 1850), preface, v. Hereafter cited as Buchanan, *Treatise on Grape Culture*. A brief history of grape culture is also found in the 1860 census report: "Vineyards and Wine Making in the United States," *Agriculture of the United States in 1860*, introduction, clix-clxi.

Hired help was essential for the busy nurseryman-farmer who had a thousand and one details to administer. Besides directing the farm, he supervised such aspects of fruit culture as grafting, setting out trees, and filling the orders for the trees and plants to be sent to customers. Accountbooks or memoranda of these operators contain lists of seedlings and plantings, carefully noted for location on charts showing the plots of the nursery. Records covering several years were essential before it could be determined if a particular plant or setting was worth growing on a large scale. The letters of Matthias Dunlap, a horticulturist near Chicago, form a detailed day-by-day account of the nursery business and show his need for competent help for this specialized work: "I am going to attend to matters at home as much as possible & have been to work like a Turk this fall having until a few days only one man. I want a good garden in the spring say in March."[9]

Unlike the hired hand, a gardener in the nursery was a shade or two above average and served in a foreman's capacity. Dunlap was fortunate to have for this position a good hired man who supervised much of the work. In correspondence during 1854 he commented on his present gardener, who had been with him for two years, adding that another hand took care of the farming aspects of the nursery. Later in the same year this gardener took charge of the nursery work, directing the graftings, a precise and tedious task, while Dunlap was off on a trip to Chicago.[10]

A competent gardener or foreman at the nursery was crucial for Dunlap when he shifted his operation in 1856 from Chicago to Champaign County. The recently constructed Illinois Central Railroad passed through Champaign and assured adequate transportation for the shipping of tree orders.[11] While his gardener was setting up the new nursery near Urbana, Dunlap stayed at the old establishment to work with the hired hands, completing 150,000 grafts which consumed considerable time and energy.[12]

The grafting of cuts or slips from one plant or tree to another improved its quality and growing capacity. Roots could also be split

9. Dunlap Letterbook, 1852–53, p. 495, December 23, 1852.
10. Dunlap Letterbook, 1853–55, p. 410, May 12, 1854; p. 547, December 20, 1854. During his absence from the farm, a member of the farmer's family could supervise the hired hands' activities. John Lorain, *Nature and Reason Harmonized in the Practice of Husbandry* (Philadelphia, 1825), p. 425.
11. Richard Cobden, during his travels in the Midwest in 1859, stopped en route to visit Dunlap's establishment. Elizabeth Cawley, ed., *The American Diaries of Richard Cobden* (Princeton, 1952), p. 188.
12. Dunlap Letterbook, 1855–58, pp. 311–14, December 26, 1855.

and similarly grafted to produce new young trees. Illinois became the testing ground for new varieties of orchard trees to ascertain what survived best in a changing climate of extreme summer heat and bitter winter cold. Some nurseries contained, for example, over 150 varieties of apples; this experimentation reached chaotic proportions when some varieties became identified under several different names. The standard was achieved when the various cuttings and grafts yielded a respectable fruit tree of high quality, but the nurseryman spent much time grafting and experimenting to obtain that final result.[13]

An Indiana horticulturist in 1846 deplored the lack of competent hired hands who could perform the grafting of plants: "It is rare that assistants can be had upon whom reliance can be placed. There are men enough to plow, and grub, and clean; but to select buds and grafts, to work the various kinds and plant them safely by themselves, this, usually, must be done by the proprietor. Where a nursery is carried on by assistants, it makes almost no difference how much care is used, mistakes will abound."[14] This discouraging conclusion was shared by a fellow horticulturist: "I wish to sell my nursery. So far, the assistants that I have been able to get have been almost invariably ignorant and irresponsible—which is worse. I have therefore budded and grafted every tree myself; laid and inarched, and potted every plant; seen to the planting and digging every tree, and attended to or have done all other miscellaneous work which no one else would or could do—and I am tired."[15]

Hired help constituted a sizable item in the overall operating costs of a nursery, according to a set of calculations in the *Cultivator* of Albany, New York:

> A brief estimate of the cost of raising a nursery of ten acres, may assist in placing the business in its true light. . . . Taking $28 as the average, the rent of ten acres would be $280 per annum. To keep a nursery of this size in *proper order*, at least four hands on an average, and one horse would be required; with board and feed, the right sort could not be had for less than $750. The materials to stock such a nursery would vary greatly with its character and with circumstances;

13. Hedrick, *History of Horticulture*, pp. 323–25.
14. *Western Farmer and Gardener* (Indianapolis), II (August 1, 1846), 227–28.
15. *Ibid.*, III (May, 1847), 53. Nurserymen were cautioned not to allow their hired hands to bruise or damage the fruit tree limbs by wearing nailed shoes or boots. *Massachusetts Ploughman*, as cited in *Western Cultivator*, I (November, 1844), 242.

but we will call it $500. To manure and drain the land properly, and bring it to a suitable condition, could not be less than $50 per acre. Advertising, printing catalogues, procuring tools, materials for packing trees, &c., would be $100 per year. The yearly cost of seeds and collecting stocks, &c., might vary from $50 to $1,000, according to the circumstances, or the enterprize of the nurseryman, but we call it $200. There are many other items of a smaller nature which we do not take into account.[16]

The first phase of work occurred usually in November, when the plantings were dug up for grafting. For example, in 1852, despite the cold weather, Matthias Dunlap and his hired hand were plowing, spreading manure, and taking up the plants. The actual grafting work was performed in the cellar where the cuttings were stored for the winter.[17] In others years Dunlap commenced grafting about the first of December, as in 1855, when he expected to have a sufficient number of hands at twelve to fifteen dollars per month.[18] These high wages indicate that hired hands at nurseries were often semi-skilled laborers who earned good pay during the winter months—in contrast to average farm laborers, who considered themselves lucky to receive either half wages or simply board and lodging during the off season.

Grafting work lasted through a good portion of the winter months. In March, 1853, Dunlap reported that 26,000 grafts had been set, while an equal number remained untouched, despite the fact that he, his sons, and five hired hands all worked at the task.[19] Several months before, he had complained of pruning work from which, he said, "my back's most broke."[20] The pressure mounted at times; for example, in January, 1856, he had to apologize to a customer because an order was delayed due to preoccupation with a heavy load of grafting chores, compounded by having all new hands for this task. Some division of labor was necessary in grafting time; since Dunlap retained hired hands during the winter season, some were assigned to this work, while others attended to the routine farm operations.[21]

As commercial enterprises, nurseries received orders and shipped

16. *Cultivator* (Albany), n.s. IX (September, 1848), 279.

17. Dunlap Letterbook, 1851–52, pp. 454–57, November 29, 1852; pp. 459–61, November 30, 1852.

18. Dunlap Letterbook, 1855–58, p. 239, November 19, 1855.

19. Dunlap Letterbook, 1852–53, p. 673, March 29, 1853.

20. *Ibid.*, p. 552, January 28, 1853.

21. *Ibid.*, p. 518, January 15, 1853; Letterbook 1855–58, p. 757, January 21, 1856.

plants, cuttings, and small trees by any available means of transportation. While nurserymen had no real control over their product after it was placed in shipment, special care in packing helped assure safe arrival. Poor or sloppy packing of young trees and cuttings resulted in a shriveled item ill suited for planting. Complaints were directed against nursery owners who trusted "hirelings" to pack trees, a task which should be done personally or at least supervised by the owner.[22]

Shipment by river transportation, generally steamboats, offered a number of hazards to young plants and trees; sometimes they were crammed into storage holds or placed too near the steam and heat of the engines. Cincinnati was a prime nursery area and a major shipping point on the Ohio River, and one dissatisfied customer excoriated nurserymen who allowed inexperienced hands not only to pack the trees but also to deliver the items to the shipping point:

> The manner of shipping trees, too, is another abuse which calls loudly for reformation. The nurseryman is too apt to send some stupid numbskull to the river with a load of trees, and bills of lading in hand, which he gets signed by the clerk of a steamboat, when off he goes, leaving the bundles upon the wharf to take care of themselves, instead of explicit orders as to where they should be stowed; or, what would be better still, wait and see that they were put into the right place himself.[23]

As a nurseryman, Matthias Dunlap was keenly aware of the necessity of good packing. Orders came during the spring and summer when purchasers generally planted new trees. In April, 1856, Dunlap expressed regret about a delay and explained that tree packing kept all his available hands occupied. The demand for shipment of trees did not taper off until late in the season. In November another rush of orders kept him and his crew busy, with Dunlap lamenting a lack of what he considered qualified hired men capable of taking up and packing trees in a proper manner.[24] While native American hands were perhaps good men in a nursery, many immigrants were trained in horticulture. Dunlap had a Frenchman and a German packing trees; their work was closely supervised, yet it contained fewer errors than anticipated.[25]

22. *Western Horticultural Review*, III (October, 1852), 23–24; (March, 1853), 266–69.

23. *Cincinnatus*, II (1857), 118.

24. Dunlap Letterbook, 1855–58, p. 517, April 14, 1856; p. 247, November 19, 1855.

25. *Ibid.*, p. 569, June 7, 1856. As an employer, Dunlap was fair with his

The labor force on a nursery farm varied according to the season. Dunlap hired two to four hands during the summer but retained only one or two in the winter to assist him and his full-time gardener with the grafting. Writing in September, 1852, he noted: "Our family is now small ourselves 6 children two hired men & a girl to do house work eleven all counted one of the men will leave in a few days & I do not intend to keep but the one until next spring—"[26] In the summer of 1853 his laboring force numbered four field hands for the farm and nursery: "My nursery is doing first rate & is in good condition. Keep four hired hands two of which are haying the others with myself & Boys [Dunlap's sons] work in the nursery. . . ."[27] Probably like most nurserymen, Dunlap preferred horticultural matters to the dull routine of the farm. In fact, he often delegated the farm work to the hired hands: "My nursery is doing very well considering the little personal attention I have given it, but since the budding season has commenced I have been pretty steady at home & I now intend to give the nursery most of my time. I do not work on the farm myself only look after it have three men at farm work, myself and Hiram [his son] will do the budding we have now set some 4 or 5,000."[28]

As a farmer Dunlap treated his hands like any other agricultural employer; nursery-orchard tasks were all in the line of work for a hired hand, and were no more or less difficult than average farm chores, except that some skill, such as grafting, might be necessary. Specifically he viewed the life of a hired hand: "I think I hear you say you would not like to work for me, nor would you unless you like hard work & plenty of it."[29] All things being relative, earlier in March of the same year he wrote with a slightly different slant of the hired hand's life as being essentially uncomplicated in comparison to his drudgery:

---

hired hands and defended their work against complaints of unreasonable customers. *Ibid.*, p. 1, August 14, 1855.

26. Dunlap Letterbook, 1852–53, p. 385, September 19, 1852. This was standard: a farmer-nurseryman at Quincy in western Illinois reported that for thirty-eight acres of farm and orchard, two men were hired from March to December at twenty dollars per month with board. *Transactions of the Illinois State Agricultural Society*, IV—1859–60 (Springfield, 1861), 233–34. Hereafter cited as *Illinois Agricultural Transactions*.

27. Dunlap Letterbook, 1853–55, p. 89, July 20, 1853; p. 94, July 24, 1853. Earlier in April he had five hands working for him: see Letterbook, 1852–53, p. 680, April 6, 1853.

28. Dunlap Letterbook, March–December, 1851, p. 163, no date [August 22 or 23, 1851?].

29. Dunlap Letterbook, 1853–55, p. 250, December 1, 1853.

I . . . shall now be extremely busy for Some months & must set myself
to work at least 16 hours a day one third of which must be at the desk
pen in hand—have 4 men & two boys to work grafting & the ground
will do to work in the nursery setting out small trees soon. My hired
hands know little of hard work they can go to bed at the close of the
day while 11 & 12 o'clock finds me at the desk. . . . I wish I could
have the privilege of working in the field 'from early morn to setting
sun' the task would be far lighter than now. . . .[30]

Dunlap followed conventional lines with regard to wages for his
hired help, even after moving to Champaign County in 1856. According to the *Transactions* of the Illinois State Agricultural Society, his
operation differed little from that in northern Illinois during 1851–56.
His nursery near Urbana consisted of 240 acres of nursery, wheat,
corn, and potato fields; five hands were employed at a rate of between
ten and twenty dollars per month including board, with the average
at about fourteen dollars per month.[31] Men working in orchards and
nurseries were usually hired at rates comparable to those of farm
hands; in fact, most were probably farm hands of one sort or another. One advantage, however, was that those retained in winter
months earned good wages.

Men who hired out to nurseries were in most respects similar to
farm laborers and went from job to job.[32] Large operators needed an
extensive laboring force, as was the case near Bloomington (in central Illinois), where nursery cultivation began in the late 1840's and
expanded during the 1850's. One owner of 600 acres reportedly had
200 men working under him, and a portion of his land consisted of
orchards and nurseries.[33] Horticulturists also experienced a labor
shortage during the California Gold Rush in 1849 and the early
1850's. A nineteen-year-old Ohio youth headed west into Indiana in
1847 and stopped in Miami County, where he worked for a farmer
and nurseryman. His salary was $120 per year, and he worked for

30. Dunlap Letterbook, 1852–53, pp. 669–70, March 27, 1853.
31. *Illinois Agricultural Transactions*, IV—1859–60, 225–26.
32. Hired hands at nurseries were probably an average lot of humans, and a
"bit of human nature" was revealed in a letter of Robert Kennicott, written from
the family farm-nursery at the "Grove" in Northfield, Illinois. Young Robert
expressed pleasure in the fact that one of the hired hands brought in from the
field six young white mice, apparently aware of the lad's interest in wildlife.
Robert Kennicott to Spencer F. Baird ("The Grove," West Northfield, Ill.,
May 1–2, 1855), Kennicott Papers.
33. J. H. Burnham, comp., *History of Bloomington and Normal in McLean
County, Illinois* (Bloomington, 1879), pp. 78–79; see also *History of McLean
County, Illinois*, pp. 263, 283.

the next two and one-half years, saving his money in the meanwhile
to purchase land. After selling this land for a profit, he proceeded to
California via ship.[34]

Local men also obtained employment at nurseries in order to raise
money for a farm. In 1852 a settler at Lee County, Illinois, took out
a claim to land but lacked funds to develop it. First he went down to
Bureau County and teamstered, followed by a stint in a local nursery
at wages of thirteen dollars per month. He accumulated enough at
this work to tide him over until his first crop.[35] Young children were
sometimes hired by nurserymen. Born and raised in Cincinnati, John
McGowan hired out at age twelve to a friend of the family who
operated a combination dairy farm and nursery outside the city.
His wages were set at three dollars per month; during the winter
months he delivered milk until spring, when the work in the nursery
resumed.[36]

The duties of horticultural workers were not unlike those of the
average farm; but since most nursery owners made farming part of
their operation, availability of competent hands was often a problem. With adequate supervision the hired help could handle many
horticultural tasks, such as pruning and grafting, in addition to the
packing and preparation of plants and trees for shipment. It was impossible for nurserymen to maintain their establishments without this
extra help, especially when the nursery was operated along with a
farm.

Like nursery and orchard production, vegetable or truck farming
yielded specialized crops from concentrated cultivation. The overall
value of truck produce in the midwestern states increased from several hundred thousand dollars in 1840 to over two million dollars by
the Civil War. Truck farming was local and provided seasonal jobs
for itinerant workers who helped townspeople establish fruit and
vegetable gardens adjacent to their homes.

As a thriving urban center in the early Midwest, Cincinnati offered
such opportunities for laborers. An advertisement in the *Liberty Hall
and Cincinnati Gazette* in 1818 called for one or two young, industrious men with good recommendations in market gardening. Applicants should apply to a farm on Mill Creek, an area adjacent to

34. Perrin, ed., *History of Stark County, with an Outline Sketch of Ohio,*
pp. 902–3.

35. Frank E. Stevens, ed., *History of Lee County, Illinois* (Chicago, 1914),
I, pp. 468–69.

36. *History of Cincinnati and Hamilton County, Ohio* (Cincinnati, 1894),
pp. 822–23.

Cincinnati which later became an important horticultural-orchard source supplying the city with fresh produce.[37] A farmer's advertisement in 1821 sought a man good at farming with a wife skilled in cooking.[38] Conversely, trained gardeners placed advertisements for employment; an example was a middle-aged man who listed his qualifications and European training, and voiced no objection to travel in various parts of the country in his job. He was a specialist who was hired not only to establish a horticultural garden, but also to seek out for his employer new seeds, plants, and cuttings to improve what was then available in the West.[39]

The diary of Dr. Asahel Clapp, a physician who resided at New Albany in southern Indiana, provides interesting information. Like many townspeople, Dr. Clapp raised foodstuffs in a garden adjacent to his house. During March and April, 1823, his diary reveals that laborers or itinerants in early midwestern towns were available and hired out to work in gardens in spring, and that Dr. Clapp as a busy professional man depended on such help. Several individuals worked on various days at fencing, carting earth, and spading, while Dr. Clapp personally handled the planting of flowers.[40] Necessary for any garden was a fence, which the average farm hand could construct if he was handy with an ax. A farmer near Chillicothe, Ohio, placed the following advertisement: "To Labourers and Intruders. Two or more sober industrious hands, who understand fencing and working a garden will meet with employment, generous wages and regular pay by applying to the subscriber...."[41]

Some farmers with orchard and garden tracts were large land operators. A representative example was an Ohio Valley farm-fruit-

---

37. *Liberty Hall and Cincinnati Gazette*, November 24, 1818.

38. *Ibid.*, February 14, 1821.

39. *Ibid.*, December 23, 1820.

40. Asahel Clapp Diary, entries of March 21, 24, April 17, 22, 25, 1823. Other professional men required aid in their gardens; one minister complained of a lack of funds for this purpose: "The reason is, in the first place, my family is such that for want of help, which I am not able to hire, I have to spend considerable of my time in domestic affairs; and add to this the cultivation of some two acres of land including a garden, so that I have but a small portion of time for reading and making the necessary preparations for the Sabbath." The Reverend David Smith to Corresponding Secretary of American Home Missionary Society (Lisbon, Ill., July 29, 1840), American Home Missionary Letters.

41. As cited in Marie Dickore, *General Joseph Kerr of Chillicothe, Ohio* (Oxford, 1941), p. 9. A farmer who operated a tavern and store on the outskirts of Columbus, employed men in his garden and orchard. The work included fencing the garden and grafting fruit trees for twenty-five to fifty cents per day. Innkeeper-Tanner Accountbook, entries of April 27, May 4, 1826.

vegetable farmer, William D. Kelly, at Ironton in Lawrence County. His farm won a prize premium as the best-conducted agricultural unit in Ohio and consisted of 300 acres: farm land, gardens, orchards, and pasturage. His own statement reveals the problem of the historian in acquiring substantial data on labor costs. His farm hands were used in all job applications, including the nursery, grape raising, and cultivation of fruits and vegetables,

> . . . all connected with my farming operations—all done by the same laborers, so it is impossible for me to present an exact account of the farming expenses. I have in my employ all the time from 10 to 15 hands. When not at work in the garden, or on the farm, they are clearing up the uncultivated land, or at some other business connected with the farm, so that I cannot very well keep the expense account correctly. I pay my head gardener from $35 to $40 per month. I pay other hands from $12 to $26 per month. My farm shows from $1,000 to $3,000 profit per year.[42]

Fresh fruit for urban dwellers' tables was attractive but not always obtainable, but by the 1840's Cincinnati's residents were receiving strawberries from nearby truck farms. Prior to this time, strawberries were difficult to raise in quantity; but, prompted by the investigation and experiments of Nicholas Longworth, cross-breeding produced greater yields.[43] Cist's Weekly Advertiser, commenting on local production, claimed city sales during 1844–45 averaged 8,000 to 12,000 quarts of berries per day, occasionally more.[44] The operators of these strawberry truck farms were largely concentrated on the banks of the Licking River opposite Cincinnati. A few acres sufficed for strawberry farming, but some cultivated fifteen acres, and one farmer operated fifty acres. It was estimated that 300 hands found employment in this growing area, and one producer alone employed sixty hands at his patches.[45]

The berry season commenced in May, usually around the middle of the month.[46] Labor was both tenant and hired—a realistic approach to a specialized culture. German tenants planted and tended the strawberry fields, but at harvest time proprietors hired additional help, readily available because of the closeness of the city. According

42. *Ohio Valley Farmer*, III (December, 1858), 178–79.
43. For the results of these investigations, see Nicholas Longworth, *The Cultivation of the Grape, and Manufacture of Wine* (Cincinnati, 1846).
44. As cited in *Hunt's Merchant Magazine*, XVIII (September, 1847), 326; see also *Cincinnati Daily Gazette*, June 4, 1846.
45. *Ibid.*; see also *Watchman of the Prairies*, June 6, 1848.
46. *Cincinnati Daily Gazette*, May 20, 1847.

to the *Cincinnati Daily Gazette*, men, women, and children obtained seasonal work at from two to three cents per box: each box held two quarts, and the average daily wage ranged from 37.5 cents to $1.25.[47] It was a lucrative business: a strawberry truck farmer in 1860 near Cincinnati operated ten acres of land; his gross receipts were $2,210; expenses for marketing came to $25; and labor costs, including the hands for picking and their board, amounted to $225.[48]

Who were hired laborers in gardens and on truck farms? Most were of foreign birth, usually German, Irish, or English, and came from backgrounds where such employment had provided experience and training. In 1849 Andrew Jackson Downing, a leading horticulturist, surmised that four-fifths of garden laborers in the eastern and middle states were Irish. Germans were also recommended for trenching, subsoiling, and preparing the ground for orchards and kitchen crops.[49] Charles Lewis Fleischmann, an employee in the Patent Office during the 1840's, advised his German countrymen that although wages were high, opportunities were plentiful.[50] Another writer during this same period specifically advised Germans that easy work circumstances could be found with farmers near large cities in the cultivation of vegetables and fruit, with wages at eight to fifteen dollars per month and board.[51] These Germans wandered considerable distances, reported J. G. Kohl, who observed them as gardeners employed by the United States Army units stationed at Fort Ridgeley, Minnesota, during the 1850's, raising fresh vegetables and greens for the soldiers' messes.[52]

47. *Ibid.*, June 20, 1846.

48. Edmund Morris, *How to Get a Farm, and Where to Find One* (New York, 1864), p. 179. The produce trade in Cincinnati was a good source of income to nearby farmers. *Cincinnati Daily Gazette*, August 14, 1848. Residents of midwestern cities depended on this produce trade for their foodstuffs. Their occasional resentment against high prices prompted the passage of regulatory ordinances such as at Sandusky: See *Daily Commercial Register*, June 7, 1852, September 12, 1853, January 27, 1854.

49. Andrew Jackson Downing, *Rural Essays* (New York, 1860), pp. 56–57.

50. Charles Lewis Fleischmann, *Erwerbszweige, Fabrikwesen und Handel der Vereinigten Staaten von Nordamerika* (Stuttgart, 1850), pp. 295–300. For further information on Fleischmann, see Paul Gates, "Charles Lewis Fleischmann: German-American Agricultural Authority," *Agricultural History*, XXXV (1961), 13–23.

51. Carl Schmidt, *Dies Buch Gehört dem Deutschen Auswanderer* (Leipzig, 1855), p. 26.

52. Kohl, *Reisen im Nordwestern der Vereinigten Staaten*, p. 232. A recent study shows that soldiers were also assigned gardening duties at early frontier forts: see Roger L. Nichols, "Soldiers as Farmers: Army Agriculture in the Missouri Valley, 1818–1827," *Agricultural History*, XLIV (1970), 213–22.

Advertisements appearing in newspapers of large cities made frequent requests for German gardeners: "A German Boy, 15 or 16 years
of age, wanted to go a short distance into country. One that can make
himself generally serviceable will receive fair wages, and become acquainted with the gardening business."[53] Cincinnati was a key area
of employment for German immigrants trained in gardening, especially in the Mill Creek area on the northern edge of the city. Its
topography was almost entirely rural and well suited for agriculture
and horticulture, as witnessed by the location of College Hill, where
the famous Farmer's College was situated. This institution, chartered
in 1846, published *Cincinnatus*, a periodical devoted to horticulture.
In this area German immigrants worked at a variety of occupations,
including gardening, until they settled permanently in the city.[54]

These immigrants exhibited an amazing degree of job adaptibility;
gardening was only one phase of their years as laborers. Peter Kline,
a farm laborer in Germany, came to America in 1852; his first stop
was at Madison, Indiana, on the Ohio River, where work was obtained
at a packing house, followed by a stint as a gardener. Other employment attracted him northward to Indianapolis, where he worked on
a dairy farm, before his wanderings then brought him west to Champaign County, Illinois, working as a cattle drover and handler.[55]

Some faced a rough struggle during the first years of their existence in a new country. In autumn, 1850, a German couple located in
an old roofless log cabin near Grand Detour in western Illinois. The
husband chopped wood throughout the winter at forty cents a cord
and obtained day jobs in the spring with area farmers for seventy-five
cents per day. In addition, he labored at the plow works in Grand
Detour. His wife stayed at home raising garden produce which he
hawked each day from a wheelbarrow to townspeople. By the end of
five years they had saved sufficient money to purchase their own
land.[56]

Agricultural employment was a seasonal occupation, but gardeners

53. *Cincinnati Daily Gazette*, July 4, 1844. A similar situation prevailed in
Chicago, where an advertisement in the *Chicago Daily Democrat*, August 28,
1851, requested a young or middle-aged couple, preferably German, who
understood gardening and farming.
54. Henry A. and Kate B. Ford, comps., *History of Hamilton County, Ohio*
(Cleveland, 1881), pp. 333–45, esp. pp. 418, 424–25. Those from the British
Isles also found employment on farms and at gardening: *ibid.*, p. 418; *Portrait
and Biographical Record of Effingham, Jasper and Richland Counties, Illinois*
(Chicago, 1893), p. 279.
55. *Counties of Warren, Benton, Jasper and Newton, Indiana*, pp. 771–72.
56. Smith, *Recollections of the Pioneers of Lee County*, pp. 430–31.

often found work in the South during winter. August Laser, a German immigrant, came to the United States in 1850 and worked briefly in the East before heading to Ohio, where he was employed as a gardener and greenhouse worker. He then went down to New Orleans; there designing and laying out gardens kept him busy. He also pursued this line of work in Illinois, where a greenhouse was under his supervision. Apparently well trained and skilled in his knowledge of landscaping, Laser obtained additional work of this nature and in time was able to purchase eighty acres as the basis for his own fruit farm.[57]

These garden and landscaping experts made their way into many parts of the Midwest and had no difficulty in securing employment. Calvin Fletcher, whose farm land included nursery and orchard acreage as well as gardens, commented on a Mr. Woodman who came seeking work. According to Fletcher's diary, the man appeared for work the next day with "John," a German who was hired at ten dollars per month to do garden work. Woodman himself ended up working in the nursery, although a subsequent entry notes the two working together in the garden.[58] The following year Fletcher's older son had a Frenchman brought to the place to work in the garden and fix asparagus beds and roses along the walk to the house. He remained a month to prepare the plantings for winter and take up Mrs. Fletcher's roses.[59]

Despite the increased attention to gardening, as witnessed by a comprehensive article in *Patent Office Report* of 1854,[60] most native-born Americans appear to have shunned this type of work unless in connection with their own farms. But there were exceptions: Jacob Shoemaker was employed with several others to open up a farm at Wolf Prairie in Berrien County, Michigan. Following this set-up and prairie-breaking work, Shoemaker turned to boating on the St. Joseph River, alternating with work as a gardener until 1850, when he went farther west.[61] While there is little specific evidence that free Negroes followed this work, especially in small towns, gardening may well have been one of the many odd-job tasks available to them locally. During the 1850's at Princeton, Illinois, it was recalled, the only black

57. *History of Peoria County, Illinois* (Chicago, 1880), pp. 776–77.
58. Fletcher Diary, entries of May 12, 13, 23, 1858.
59. *Ibid.*, entries of October 6, November 13, 1859.
60. *U.S. Pat. Office Report, 1854* (Washington, 1855), 322–93.
61. *History of Berrien and Van Buren Counties, Michigan*, pp. 279–80; for a similar example, see Hubbell, *Dodge County, Wisconsin. Past and Present*, I, p. 93.

in town helped people with their yards and gardens.[62] In general, however, the number of native-born Americans in this occupation was limited.

Related to nursery and garden farming was grape culture and its alliance with wine making, a minor but significant horticultural production in the Ohio Valley. By the 1830's grapes were cultivated in quantity, although statistical data are lacking for the early years from 1825 to 1840. Vitaculture was sufficiently extensive at Cincinnati to merit comment by Harriet Martineau. She met Nicholas Longworth on her western tour in 1835 and visited his vineyards, where four gardeners were employed and twelve different kinds of wine produced. "Mr. Longworth is sanguine as to the prospect of making Ohio a wine-growing region," she reported, "and he has done all that an individual can to enhance the probability."[63]

Ohio indeed became the leader in wine and grape culture, and most of the grape vineyards were located close to Cincinnati. In 1845 the vineyards covered 350 acres and provided employment not only to vine cultivators and dressers, but also to such allied occupations as coopers, who fashioned the wooden barrels for grape fermentation. By 1850 the industry directly and indirectly employed over 2,000 persons, and a visitor in 1852 estimated that 1,000 acres were now devoted to grape culture.[64]

Several years later the *Cincinnati Columbian* presented an updated statistical picture from the Cincinnati Horticultural Society and the Wine Growers' Association: "Within a circle of twenty miles around Cincinnati, about 1,200 acres are planted with the vine, some 800 acres of which were in bearing this year, and produced on an average 400 gallons to the acre—an aggregate of 320,000 gallons of wine. Some of the best vineyards yielded 600 to 800 gallons to the acre. . . ."[65] By 1860, the State of Ohio officially set the total acreage of vineyards at 2,200 acres, with the chief concentration in Hamilton (Cincinnati),

62. "Childhood Reminiscences of Princeton," *Illinois Historical Journal*, XLIX (1956), 109.

63. Harriet Martineau, *Retrospect of Western Travel* (London, 1838), II, p. 244. For information on Longworth, see Louis L. Tucker, "Old Nick Longworth, the Paradoxical Maecenas of Cincinnati," *Cincinnati Historical Society Bulletin*, XXV (1967), 246–59.

64. *Cist's Weekly Advertiser*, May 21, 1852; *DeBow's Review*, XII (February, 1852), 195. Longworth reportedly invested $100,000 in his winery, which set a record in 1852 with 100,000 bottles produced. *Ibid.*, XIII (August, 1852), 199.

65. As cited in *ibid.*, XVIII (January, 1855), 56–57.

Clermont, Brown, and Adams counties, all near the Ohio River.[66] The other primary grape-growing center was Kelley's Island off Sandusky in northern Ohio. By the 1850's grapes had also become popular as table fruit.[67]

Grape culture attracted the specialized labor of German immigrants who were trained for vitaculture in their native country, and whose presence in large numbers contributed to Cincinnati's marked German atmosphere and way of life. Wine produced in the Cincinnati area was locally consumed and offered keen competition to the famed beer gardens: "Before the cultivation of the vine can be carried on extensively and profitably, we must have a sure market for the wine as it comes from the press; so that the vine-dressers can sell their wine as readily as the farmer his wheat. At present it is mostly sold to our German population, at fair prices."[68]

Germans were suited for this work and employed as tenants under a contract system.[69] Nicholas Longworth himself preferred Germans and specifically recommended their employment on this basis. His evaluation of their performance was: "All they know, is hard labour and coarse diet."[70] For example, Longworth negotiated a contract in 1833 with a German who had a wife and three stout sons. The conditions called for the German to trench and wall six acres of grapes with a total of nine acres completed within five years.[71] These contracts sometimes covered a twelve- to fifteen-year period; the immigrant worked the land and planted the vines, which took several years to mature, while Longworth advanced the cuttings or slips for the first two or three acres to get the vineyard going and took half the produce of the harvest. Land parcels were rented out in amounts

66. Hamilton County and Cincinnati accounted for over 70% of the total state production in 1850 and 1860. *Statistical View of the United States*, pp. 207, 295; *Agriculture of the United States in 1860*, pp. 114, 118.

67. *Ohio Statistics, 1859*, III, 12–13. Grapes were first grown on Kelley's Island in 1843, and 230 acres were under cultivation by 1860. *Hunt's Merchant Magazine*, XLIII (November, 1860), 638–40; see also *Firelands Pioneer*, IV (June, 1863), 33–47; *U.S. Pat. Office Report, 1851* (Washington, 1852), 373–74.

68. Buchanan, *A Treatise on Grape Culture*, p. 34. Another contributor to this pamphlet noted: "Heretofore, all the wine made at my vineyards, has been sold to our German coffee houses, and drank in our city." p. 35. The *New York Organ of Temperance* viewed Cincinnati as a Babylon where drunkenness prevailed with 1,200 grog shops, 1,000 of which were operated by Germans. As cited in *Cist's Weekly Advertiser*, February 27, 1850.

69. Downing, *Rural Essays*, pp. 57–58.

70. *Western Tiller*, March 13, 1829; *The Farmer's Guide and Western Agriculturist* (Cincinnati, 1832), p. 309.

71. Longworth, *The Cultivation of the Grape*, pp. 5–6.

usually of fifteen to twenty acres, although smaller areas were equally common.[72]

Labor costs were high in grape cultivation, especially for the initial establishment of a vineyard. The high steep hills, facing south for light, warmth, and exposure, could not accommodate a plow; therefore hand labor with the spade and mattock was required. Brush had to be cleared, the land trenched for water run-off, and benching erected. Benching involved a form of ditching and banking for which tier layers with embankments were constructed to form ledges up the sides of the hill on which the vines and their retaining paling (stakes) were planted. The preparation of a vineyard was performed during winter when other forms of agricultural work were scarce, according to Nicholas Longworth: "On the banks of the Ohio, two miles below our city, I yesterday saw some Germans at work, trenching, banking, and walling one of the most steep, rugged, and stony hills in the county. To have hired the work done by day, would have cost from $300 to $400 per acre. When completed, it will be a lovely spot. The cost to them is trifle, for the work is done during the winter, when they have no employment."[73]

William Resor, a son of an early horticulturist and vineyard owner, was himself a leader in the grape-growing industry in 1845 and produced a set of cost figures for the establishment of a six-acre vineyard:

Trenching, two feet deep, $65 per acre,	390 00
Sodding avenues,	60 00
Cost of 30,000 cuttings, at $2.50 per thousand,	75 00
Planting,	70 00
Fourteen thousand five hundred locust stakes, at $3 per hundred,	435 00
Setting 14,500 stakes,	55 00
	1,085 00
Cost of attending the first year—vine dresser, $216, and a hand for one month, $15, (and board themselves,)	$231 00
Second year—vine dresser, $216, a hand for two months, at $15 per month,	256 00

72. Longworth's comments, as cited in Buchanan, *A Treatise on Grape Culture,* p. 28; see also a description of Longworth's operation in the *Ohio Valley Farmer,* V (February, 1860), 18.

73. Longworth's comments, as cited in Buchanan, *A Treatise on Grape Culture,* p. 31.

Cuttings, after first year, to replace failures, say,	20 00
Hauling, carting, &c.,	68 00
Contingencies, &c.,	150 00
Average cost, say, $300 per acre,	1,800 00[74]

While tenant labor was preferred, wage labor was not uncommon. Robert Buchanan reported that his vineyard, started in 1844 and expanded to six acres, required two hands at twelve dollars per month each to keep the vineyard in order. During vintage season additional help was hired to gather the grapes.[75] A specific labor cost breakdown reflected the need for a permanent hand as well as seasonal help:

Vine-dresser per year, and board himself,	$240 00
Hands to assist in pruning, say,	25 00
″ ″ ″ ″ in spring culture,	40 00
″ ″ ″ ″ in summer culture,	55 00
Or $60 per acre,	$360 00[76]

Men employed in nurseries and vineyards performed other agricultural tasks; for an urban center of commercial importance, Cincinnati was surprisingly farm-oriented. One Cincinnati grape producer reviewed the labor situation and concluded that vineyard workers ought to be able to handle farm work on the nursery-vineyard, effecting a reduction in operation costs. It was too expensive to use vineyard hands solely for grape production while hiring additional help for the routine farm chores.[77]

The *Ohio Cultivator* commented in 1847 that increased numbers of vineyards at Cincinnati necessitated laborers who could also dig ditches, remove stones, and build terraces; much of this common labor, observed the *Cultivator*, was performed by German immigrants.[78] Day laborers were employed, along with trained specialists who were also expected to handle other agricultural tasks. Cincinnati was a large river city that attracted men who sought and accepted jobs in diverse occupations, including nursery and orchard

74. *Ibid.*, p. 28.
75. Cist, *Sketches and Statistics of Cincinnati in 1851*, p. 255.
76. Buchanan, *A Treatise on Grape Culture*, p. 31. Trained vine-dressers were specialists who commanded high wages; see advertisement of T. J. Strait, whose fourteen acres of Catawba grapes and twenty-five acres of farm pasturage were located in Mill Creek Township. *Cist's Weekly Advertiser*, November 28, 1849.
77. *Ohio Cultivator*, I (October 15, 1845), 153–54; these views also appeared in the *Cincinnati Miscellaney*, II (1845), 150–51.
78. *Ohio Cultivator*, III (March 1, 1847), 36.

cultivation, vineyard work, and pork packing. Horticulturists elsewhere in the state felt that Cincinnati's monopoly of the available
labor force was unfair: ". . . they can command any number of cheap
day-laborers when needed, which is very desirable in this business,
and without which a vineyard will be very apt to suffer."[79]

Hired labor, for example, was available to Hugh S. Kemper. He
ran a farm, stone quarry, and vineyard; men and women, including
Germans, were hired to work on his place. In May, 1852, "Henry—A
Dutchman" (i.e., a German) was hired during corn-planting season,
but the most significant entry in Kemper's accountbook was the notation in June when he employed German help for his vineyard with
the stipulation: "Hired George Myers to work for $13 per month and
$7 for his wife when there is work for her in the vineyard."[80]

Women figured prominently in any agreement, whether tenant or
hired. Nicholas Longworth was of the opinion that one method of
reducing labor costs on the farm was to demand labor of women in
grape cultivation. German women, unlike Americans, were accustomed to such work: "Our German emigrants can cultivate the grape
to the most profit, for the greater part of the work in the vineyard is
performed by their wives and daughters, without interfering with
household affairs."[81] And most would agree with the observation of
John A. Warder, editor of the *Western Horticultural Review*, that
Germans in the vineyards practiced greater care and thriftiness than
their American counterparts.[82]

In essence, horticulture was specialized farming and involved
delicate but tedious labor at grafting, pruning, and transplanting.
Horticulturists conducted their nursery, orchard, or vineyard in conjunction with a farm, and hired hands were essential to the horticultural line as well as to conventional farming. Hired help on such farms
worked in the nursery or orchard at various times, although many
horticultural farm operators learned that not all their laborers were
suited for such delicate work. Native-born laborers did not take readily to such assignments, preferring instead conventional farm chores
and chopping with an ax. As a result, European immigrants who were
well trained in horticulture obtained immediate employment.

Although wages of horticultural laborers were comparable to those

79. *U.S. Pat. Office Report, 1853* (Washington, 1854), 305.
80. Hugh Fulton Kemper Accountbook, entries of May 10, June 5, 1852.
81. As cited in Buchanan, *A Treatise on Grape Culture*, p. 32.
82. *Western Horticultural Review*, IV (1854), 149–51.

of conventional farm labor, men skilled in grafting and transplanting were often retained during the winter season to assist in these tasks. In larger horticultural operations, foremen were essential in supervising the various activities in the nursery and orchard as well as the general farm operation.[83] These men were professionals whose additional responsibilities were recompensed with higher wages.

83. Critical of those midwestern farmers who failed to realize the value of competent foremen was the *Michigan Farmer*, XV (April, 1857), 120.

Winter Seasonal Employment

> I have not found a place for the winter yet for it is rather hard
> to hire out to work by the month through the winter season[.]
> though I have not hired out for the winter[,] I have worked
> about a month and have earned eleven dollars and shall work
> some more ether [sic] by the month or chopping some cordwood.[1]

AGRICULTURE was a seasonal occupation, and both
farmers and their hired hands regarded the months from October
through March as slack times. Because farm hands were without
steady employment during these months, they turned to the towns
and cities, where their savings were absorbed for room and board
as well as the pleasures of urban life. More resourceful were those
who sought temporary winter employment in the pork packing houses
or chopping cord wood along river banks and Great Lakes shores.
Sawmill jobs were also available, and the spring rafting of lumber
from northern river areas brought these men down to the lower Midwest in time for the beginning of the farming season.[2]

Prior to 1860, cord wood rather than coal was the main source of
fuel power for steamboats, steam sawmills, and railroad engines. The
standard unit of measurement for wood was the cord, a stacked pile
eight feet long, four feet deep, and four feet wide.[3] The wood fuel
industry was an extensive complex that linked rural and urban areas,
for which the necessary labor force consisted primarily of itinerants

1. Lucian Enos to his parents (Lafayette [County], Wis., October 31, 1843),
Wisconsin Territorial Letter Collection.

2. For a general study of seasonal activity in the early Midwest, see Louis C.
Hunter, "Studies in the Economic History of the Ohio Valley: Seasonal Aspects
of Industry and Commerce before the Age of Big Business," *Smith College
Studies in History*, XIX (1933–34), 1–130.

3. An English traveler commended the Americans for having one standard
of measurement, whereas in England it varied confusingly from one locale to
the next. Henry A. Murray, *Lands of the Slave and the Free: or, Cuba, the
United States, and Canada* (London, 1855), I, p. 244. Lack of historical data is
discussed by Arthur H. Cole, "The Mystery of Fuel Wood Marketing in the
United States," *Business History Review*, XLIV (1970), 339–59.

described variously as choppers, wood scavengers, wood jobbers, wood haulers, and stackers. Not all wood cutters were so easily categorized; those operating lonely wood stations on remote river banks were known as wood hawks.[4] Farmers adjacent to midwestern rivers simultaneously cleared land and sold the wood to passing steamboats, and during the early decades "More than one farm was paid for by the cordwood cut and sold to steamboats for fuel. . . ."[5] Many choppers were wanderers and farm hands who hired out to cut wood for twenty-five to seventy-five cents per day or at a given rate per cord. According to an English traveler in America, hired hands worked on farms from April to November; if they were not lazy, he observed, itinerant employment, including chopping, was available.[6]

Some wood choppers began as individual entrepreneurs and sold the wood directly to steamboats, while others had choppers in their employ and acted as middlemen or retailers of wood.[7] The individual chopper required a base of operations, such as a farm, which he could claim as his own; otherwise his profits might have to be shared with the owner of the timber. After working on a Galena, Illinois, farm in

4. Wood hawks were all-year inhabitants at lone river locations, exercising squatter's rights to the land and its timber. These outcasts of society were frequently mentioned in travelers' accounts: Charles Fenno Hoffman, *A Winter in the West. By a New-Yorker* (New York, 1835), II, p. 118; Frances Trollope, *Domestic Manners of Americans* (New York, 1960), p. 33; Thomas Hamilton, *Men and Manners in America* (Edinburgh, 1833), II, pp. 187–88; Arfwedson, *The United States and Canada, in 1832, 1833, and 1834*, II, pp. 94–96. River wood stations were often devastated by annual spring floods which carried off the corded wood: James Hall, *The West: Its Commerce and Navigation* (Cincinnati, 1848), pp. 57–58; Lauchlan Bollingham MacKinnon, *Atlantic and Transatlantic: Sketches Afloat and Ashore* (New York, 1852), p. 322; *Cincinnati Daily Gazette*, July 2, 1844; *Freeport Journal*, June 13, 1851.

5. Stillman Carter Larkin, *The Pioneer History of Meigs County* (Columbus, 1908), p. 67; see also Evans, *History of Scioto County, Ohio*, p. 717; Cockrum, *Pioneer History of Indiana*, p. 511; *History of Vanderburgh County, Indiana* (Madison, 1889), p. 197; Buckingham, *Eastern and Western States of America*, III, p. 217. In the eastern states, as wood became scarce, farmers were urged to preserve timber tracts. See *Cultivator*, VI (June, 1849), 169–71. For an informative article on farm income from the woodlot, see Paul Gates, "Problems in Agricultural History, 1790–1840," *Agricultural History*, XLVI (1972), 35–39.

6. Stewart, *Eleven Years' Experience in the Western States*, pp. 80–82. Others were skeptical of the notion that wintertime jobs were readily available to common laborers: see Robinson, *Facts for Farmers*, pp. 1006–9; Isaac Holmes, *An Account of the United States of America, derived from actual observation* (London, [1823]), pp. 126–27; Brown, *America*, p. 9.

7. See "Incidents of Early Pioneer Life of Dyar Cobb"; *Michigan Pioneer Collections*, XVIII, pp. 350–52; *History of Sangamon County, Illinois*, pp. 941–42; *Portrait and Biographical Record of Adams County, Illinois*, pp. 156–57; W. S. Blackman, *The Boy of Battle Ford and the Man* (Marion, Ill., 1906), p. 18; Anthony Trollope, *North America* (New York, 1862), p. 144.

1836, Hiram G. Francis spent the winter at Savanna on the Mississippi. He chopped about one hundred cords, but was compelled to turn half over to the person whose land he used for storing the wood.[8]

An alternative was to chop for someone else at a stipulated rate per cord. A Swedish immigrant who had worked briefly as a farm hand in Illinois described such a job near Red Wing, Minnesota, during the winter of 1852–53:

> Our first work was wood chopping, for which we were less fit than almost anything else. We had to go to a place about three miles above Red Wing, where a man had made a contract to bank up fifteen hundred cords of wood for the Mississippi steamers. There was an old wood chopper's cabin which we repaired by thatching it with hay and earth, putting in a door, a small window, and a few rough planks for a floor. . . . We began to chop wood at once. The trees were tall, soft maples and ash, and our pay was fifty-five cents a cord for soft and sixty-five cents for hard wood. At first both of us could not chop over a cord a day together; but within a week we could chop a cord apiece, and before the winter was over we often chopped three cords together in a day. After a few days we were joined by four Norwegian wood choppers for whom we put up a new cabin to sleep in. . . . Those four men were better workmen than we, and one of them, Albert Olson, often chopped three cords a day. They were quiet, industrious, and generous fellows. . . .[9]

The price of wood was subject to considerable fluctuation and depended on the location as well as the demand. Steamboats on midwestern rivers made frequent fueling stops and consumed in normal operation about one-and-a-half to two cords per hour.[10] A traveler through Ohio in 1817–18 reported the sale of cord wood at between $1.50 and $3 per cord.[11] On the Ohio River near Pittsburgh in 1824, another traveler noted the price at $1.25 to $1.50 per cord, and for the same period on the upper Mississippi at northern Illinois a wood yard operator collected $3 per cord from passing steamers.[12] During the

8. *Portrait and Biographical Album of Jo Daviess and Carroll Counties, Illinois*, pp. 803–4; for a similar case where the chopper was in fact driven off the land, see *History of Green County, Wisconsin*, pp. 1065–68.

9. Mattson, *Reminiscences*, pp. 37–38. Winter employment in the northern lumbering areas was available, according to Elizabeth F. Ellet, *Summer Rambles in the West* (New York, 1853), p. 162.

10. J. S. Buckingham, *The Slave States of America* (London, [1842]), I, p. 397.

11. Fearon, *Sketches of America*, p. 220.

12. "Diaries of Donald MacDonald 1824–1826," *Indiana Historical Society Publications*, XIV (1942), 235; *History of Mercer and Henderson Counties* (Chicago, 1882), p. 76. According to an English traveler in the 1820's, the

1830's settlers near St. Louis charged Mississippi River steamboats $2 or $3 per cord.[13] Nathaniel Fish Moore, who traveled the same river in 1845, noted that Galena was the dividing line: north of that point wood cost $2 per cord, but only $1.25 per cord near St. Louis.[14] According to the *Cincinnati Miscellaney* in 1845, wood in that city was available at $2.50 or higher per cord.[15]

The price of wood rose after the 1840's, owing to rapid depletion of timber along the major river routes in the Ohio and Mississippi Valleys. The *Louisville Price Current* in 1855 expressed concern about the high prices for wood, particularly in the South, where they averaged $3.50 per cord.[16] Wood was similarly expensive in the southern counties of Ohio, averaging $2.50 to $3 per cord, and at Cincinnati it reached five and six dollars per cord.[17]

The rates paid wood choppers were low in comparison, however, averaging between 25 and 50 cents per cord during 1815–60. Choppers were able to cut one to two cords per day.[18] In the autumn of 1818 an early Michigan pioneer chopped wood on the Clinton River near Mt. Clemens for twenty-five cents per cord.[19] Wood station owners on the Ohio River also followed this wage rate: James Lodwick, who established a wood yard in the 1820's at Portsmouth, Ohio, sold wood to steamboats for $1 to $1.50 per cord, but his hired boy received only 30 cents a cord for chopping.[20] A. G. deSellem hired men to chop wood for his station and work on his farm near Steubenville, Ohio. During 1837, for example, David Fulks chopped ninety cords of wood at the rate of fifty cents per cord, in addition to his labor in deSellem's orchard. Agricultural work paid better, for he worked at seventy-five cents a day mowing hay.[21] John Brown, an-

---

price of wood decreased at locations further north on the Mississippi. Basil Hall, *Travels in North America, in the Years 1827 and 1828* (Edinburgh, 1829), III, pp. 348–49.

13. "Journal of William Rudolph Smith," *Wisconsin History*, XII (1928), 209–10.

14. Nathaniel Fish Moore, *A Trip from New York to the Falls of St. Anthony in 1845* (Chicago, 1946), p. 43.

15. *Cincinnati Miscellaney*, I (January, 1845), 115–16.

16. As cited in *DeBow's Review*, XIX (December, 1855), 661–68.

17. *Ohio Statistics, 1857*, I, 21, 75–86.

18. Stanley Lebergott, *Manpower in Economic Growth: The American Record since 1800* (New York, 1964), pp. 326–28.

19. *History of Oakland County, Michigan*, p. 86.

20. Evans, *History of Scioto County, Ohio*, pp. 769–70. For an example of a young boy who worked for a farmer-operator of a wood station at Steubenville, Ohio, see Brown Daybook, 1832–53, p. 20, in Nessly-deSellem Papers.

21. A. G. deSellem Daybook, 1832–37, p. 11, entry of May, 1837, Nessly-deSellem Papers.

other wood station operator, paid his cutters rates varying from twenty-five to sixty-five cents per cord. These accounts show that Brown supplied the tools, or at least assumed the costs of repair when a chopper broke an ax.[22]

Steamboat traffic on the Great Lakes occupies a less dramatic niche than that of the Ohio and Mississippi Valleys.[23] Large lake steamers consumed two cords per hour, which meant a daily operating cost of about eighty dollars.[24] Wood was not cheap, and speculation in wood prices caused variations. The *Cleveland Herald* in 1839 reported that fuel suppliers charged as much as four dollars per cord through price-fixing combinations.[25] According to an official report of the State of Ohio in the 1850's, wood averaged three to four dollars per cord at port cities along Lake Erie.[26] Most authorities agreed with *Hunt's Merchant Magazine* in 1854 that future fuel supplies, especially in the Great Lakes cities, had to rely ultimately on the introduction of coal as a substitute.[27]

An early wood station was Kelley's Island off Sandusky, where steamers stopped and discharged their crews to chop fuel during the 1820's. By the 1830's the island's dense forest still had only one hundred acres cleared. During 1836–38 a local inhabitant recalled that twenty-five to thirty men were employed chopping wood for steam-boats in conjunction with clearing land for future farms. In the 1840's ships were stopping regularly at this fueling point. In the record year 1848 there were 400 arrivals and departures, yet the island's popula-tion was only 180 persons.[28]

Like the pioneers along the Ohio and Mississippi Rivers, early set-tlers along the Great Lakes discovered that cording wood for sale as

22. Brown Daybook, 1832–53, see entries in account of Lancaster Sullivan during 1843–44, in Nessly-deSellem Papers.

23. Taylor, *Transportation Revolution*, pp. 61–62.

24. James Cooke Mills, *Our Inland Seas. Their Shipping & Commerce for Three Centuries* (Chicago, 1910), p. 120. Six to eight days approximated the traveling time for a steamer from Buffalo to Milwaukee: see George Taggert Diary, entries of May 22–30, 1838; Maury, *An Englishwoman in America*, p. 196.

25. *Cleveland Herald*, November 16, 1839, as cited in *Annals of Cleveland*, XXII, pp. 93–94. "Syndicates" or price-fixing combinations were not uncommon: for example, a local merchant at Milwaukee attempted to capture control of the cord wood market. See James S. Buck, *Pioneer History of Milwaukee, from 1840 to 1846* (Milwaukee, 1881), II, p. 85.

26. *Ohio Statistics, 1857*, I, 76, 78.

27. *Hunt's Merchant Magazine*, XXXI (October, 1854), 409; for a similar observation, see *Daily Commercial Register*, April 3, 1852.

28. *Firelands Pioneer*, IV (June, 1863), 33, 37–38, 43.

fuel was a profitable operation in conjunction with land clearing.[29] The wood was gathered together and transported in barge-like scows to nearby harbors or fueling stops. Use of lighters or loading scows to convey wood was common on the lakes. These moved wood up and down the shoreline and transferred it from land to waiting steamboats. Their operation began in spring and ended in early winter, when ice closed down the lakes and winter gales made shipping almost impossible. During the 1830's one wood hawk poled his scow along the shoreline near Milwaukee, buying wood from farmers and taking it to Milwaukee for sale to the ships stopped at that port.[30] In the 1850's, a Michigan farmer at New Baltimore on Lake St. Clair operated a fuel wood business. His hired hands were employed both on the farm and handling the wood, and according to his diary, he shipped cord wood on flatboats to markets and customers at Detroit.[31]

By the 1840's and 1850's steamers were regularly making the northern run from Detroit and Port Huron to Mackinaw and down Lake Michigan to Milwaukee and Chicago. Northern wood stations were remote but essential for steam traffic and provided common laborers with employment.[32] Hired hands in these remote locations sometimes performed minor agricultural labor in season. In Michigan's northern peninsula, wood cording, sawmilling, and farming necessitated the hiring of hands on an annual basis. In 1845 an early resident wrote of his intention to get out one hundred cords of wood, and a hired hand worked with him through the winter: "I keep a hired man this winter, and he is now engaged in chopping a fallow. I intend to clear about

29. *Valley of the Upper Maumee River with Historical Account of Allen County and the City of Fort Wayne, Indiana*, I, p. 281; *History of Berrien and Van Buren Counties, Michigan*, p. 536.

30. Amherst Willoughby Kellogg, "Recollections of Life in Early Wisconsin," *Wisconsin History*, VII (1924), 489–91.

31. Cortez Perry Hooker Diary, entries of August 6, October 8, 1859. For reference to scows or lighters at other midwestern port cities, see *Chicago Weekly Democrat*, September 19, 1848; *Daily Commercial Register*, November 6, 1854; January 11, May 30, 1855; May 8, 1858.

32. Early travelers on the Great Lakes noted the importance of fuel stops at various islands, especially the Manitou Islands near Mackinaw: Logan, *Notes of a Journey*, pp. 101–2; S. M. Fuller, *Summer on the Lakes, in 1843* (Boston and New York, 1844), p. 27; Buckingham, *Eastern and Western States of America*, III, p. 349. Choppers who worked on these islands were recruited sometimes by newspaper advertisements: "Wood Choppers Wanted, Eighty cents per cord will be paid for chopping Steam Boat Wood on South Manitou Island." *Cleveland Herald*, June 9, 1847, as cited in *Annals of Cleveland*, XXX, part I, p. 100. For similar ads in Sandusky newspapers, see *Daily Sanduskian*, November 22, 1848; *Daily Commercial Register*, October 17, 1851.

eight acres in the spring. It is my intention to plant about five acres
to potatoes, and the balance to oats. I have an acre and a half of old
ground which I shall sow to Ruta Bagas. If I find as good market for
vegetables next fall as I did this fall I think that I shall make some
money out of them."[33]

Even the early settlers not directly located on the edge of the lakes
could participate in the business by acting as suppliers shipping cord
wood downriver to port locations. At the Grand River Valley, which
drained into Lake Michigan at Grand Haven, an early resident recalled that many settlers cut cord wood near the river or wheelbar-
rowed it to the banks. There it was loaded onto log rafts and taken
downriver to the lake's edge for sale, usually at one dollar per cord
during the 1840's.[34] Further down the shore the area about St. Joseph
also became an important wood and lumber center in the 1830's and
1840's. According to one source, employment was always available,
and men hired out to farmers to chop wood.[35] The port of Waukegan,
Illinois, halfway between Chicago and Milwaukee, also attracted men
to wood chopping jobs in winter. Richard Bishop worked in the harvest fields at $1.50 per day, and afterwards at his blacksmith trade
in autumn. But when blacksmithing jobs were at a lull during the
cold months, he went to Waukegan and chopped wood at fifty cents
per cord for the remainder of the winter.[36]

Commercial dealers in the towns and cities handled fuel or cord
wood. Generally they obtained their wood from two sources, either
imported via river or lake on boats, or from local farmers who teamed

33. Anna Brockway Gray, "Letters from Long Ago," *Michigan History*, XX
(1936), 209–10. At Grand Traverse, early settlers chopped cord wood and sold
it from the beaches at $1.50 per cord. Sailing vessels bound for Chicago
purchased wood which was sold in city markets. *Transactions of the State
Agricultural Society of Michigan for the Year 1854* (Lansing, 1855), 526–28.
Hereafter cited as *Michigan Agricultural Transactions*.

34. Everett, *Memorials of the Grand River Valley*, p. 510. For examples
of farm laborers who chopped wood near rivers in western Michigan, see *History
of Calhoun County, Michigan*, p. 132; *History of Shiawassee and Clinton Counties, Michigan*, p. 246. According to the *Detroit Free Press*, chopping timber in
eastern Michigan was equally important; there quantities of lumber and staves
floated down the St. Clair River. As cited in *Daily Sanduskian*, June 30, 1849.

35. *History of Berrien and Van Buren Counties, Michigan*, pp. 317–18, 330.

36. Bateman and Selby, eds., *Historical Encyclopedia of Illinois Including
Genealogy, Family Records and Biography of McHenry County Citizens*, II, pp.
690–91. Waukegan's rapid growth, especially as a steamboat stop in the 1840's,
attracted considerable attention: see *Hunt's Merchant Magazine*, XII (May,
1845), 478; *Freeport Journal*, June 27, 1849; Elijah M. Haines, *Historical and
Statistical Sketches of Lake County, State of Illinois* (Waukegan, 1852), pp.
103–6.

their wood into town.[37] Itinerant laborers were part of this complex
and worked as handlers, choppers, stackers, and loaders. As a basic
commodity, wood was at times both expensive and scarce in midwestern cities, especially in the winter, when bad roads or frozen
waterways impeded the normal avenues of resupply. As early as 1815
Daniel Drake of Cincinnati commented: "Many teams are constantly
employed in hauling wood into town from the surrounding hills; but
the principal part is rafted and boated down the Ohio and Licking
Rivers. . . ."[38]

One such supplier of cord wood to Cincinnati was Elnathan Kemper, who hired hands to work on his farm near the city and chop cord
wood. The chopping was done in winter, and his daybook registers
an agreement with two men who were to cut the timber in the wood
lot at seventy-five cents a cord and at sixty-two and a half cents a
cord. Probably this difference in rates was owing to the type of wood
and whether it was standing or fallen timber. Kemper deducted one
dollar per week for board. He also outlined the stipulations regarding
such employment; in January, 1817, when he hired two men to cut
wood at sixty-two and a half cents per cord, the agreement required
them to cut what was on the road and then in the meadow. As a middleman or supplier, Kemper also obtained cord wood from neighboring farmers.[39]

No accurate means exist to determine how many farm laborers
drifted into cities like Cincinnati in search of winter employment. In
1851 Charles Cist commented on Cincinnati's population of 115,000,
of which 7,500 were common laborers at undefined occupations.[40] An
earlier unique project had combined a dual solution for the unemployment among common laborers and the rising costs of cord wood

37. Merchants were often retailers of wood obtained from farmers. A whole-
sale-retail storekeeper at Freeport, Illinois, appealed to area farmers: "WOOD!
WOOD!! wanted in exchange for goods at fair prices." *Freeport Journal*, April 18,
1849. At Milwaukee during the 1840's farmers teamstered wood into the city
and sold it for $1.50 to $2 per cord; however, when resold to city residents,
its price was $3-4 per cord in summer and $3.50–6.00 per cord in winter.
Bayrd Still, "Milwaukee in 1833 and 1849: A Contemporary Description,"
Wisconsin History, LIII (1970), 297.

38. Drake, *Natural and Statistical View, or Picture of Cincinnati and the
Miami County*, p. 140. The winter of 1845–46, for example, posed severe
difficulties for Cincinnati where the river froze over; *Cincinnati Miscellaney*, II
(1845–46), 245, 257–58. Similarly, bad roads into Chicago during the winter of
1847–48 caused wood shortages; *Chicago Daily Democrat*, December 6, 1847.

39. E. Kemper Daybook, entries of December 17, 1816; January 17, 1817;
February 14, March 7, 1820.

40. Cist, *Sketches and Statistical of Cincinnati in 1851*, pp. 49–51.

fuel. In the early winter of 1844 the Cincinnati Fire Wood Company was organized to provide unemployed men with work in a wood yard. A man destitute of work was entered on the register with a listing of his occupation, and his wages in the wood yard were deliberately set at a low level, usually fifty cents a day, so as not to tempt individuals who were capable of working elsewhere. The other purpose of the project was to provide inexpensive cord wood for those unable to pay the speculative rates demanded by the hucksters. Many of the poorer Cincinnatians could not purchase cord wood in large amounts at a discount; instead they relied on hucksters who sold wood throughout the city in smaller quantities but at proportionately higher prices. The wood yard undermined this practice by selling wood in any amount without a price-quantity differential.[41]

Chicago experienced its own difficulties in maintaining adequate fuel supplies, especially when money was scarce.[42] Sometimes wet weather made the roads into the city impassable, but later in the winter snow facilitated sleighing of wood. In 1848 maple was selling at $4.75 and hickory at $5 per cord, advised the *Chicago Democrat*, provided conditions for sleighing remained good or roads suitable for wagoning wood.[43] Depending on the greenness of the wood and its weight, the average farm wagon could haul a load of three-quarters to one-and-a-half cords per trip into town.[44]

41. *Cincinnati Daily Gazette*, December 16, 1844; *Cist's Miscellaney*, I (January, 1845), 115–16. At Sandusky, an owner of a timbered tract wanted a thousand cords of wood chopped from his land before spring: "Men out of employment, and good with an ax, can have a chance to pitch in." *Daily Commercial Register*, February 4, 1856.

42. Even the editor reminded his subscribers that cord wood in lieu of cash was always welcomed; *Chicago Daily Democrat*, December 6, 1847; September 26, 1848. At Freeport, the local newspaper made a similar editorial appeal to farmers for cord wood as payment toward their subscriptions; *Freeport Journal*, January 24, 1849.

43. *Chicago Daily Democrat*, November 18, 1848. Farmers tended to wait for snow before attempting to haul wood to town, which was best accomplished with sleds: see *Daily Commercial Register*, February 19, 1853; December 23, 1854; January 24, February 12, 1856. Farmers and their hired hands looked forward to wintertime chopping and hauling of cord wood: see Bottomley, *Letters, 1842–1850*, p. 85; " 'God Raised Us Up Good Friends': English Immigrants in Wisconsin," *Wisconsin History*, XLVII (1964), 226–27.

44. *Chicago Daily Democrat*, June 27, 1851. It was not profitable to haul green wood because of its added weight and lower value in contrast to dried, seasoned wood: see *Niles' Register*, XLVI (June 7, 1834), 256; Brown, *America*, p. 49. Farmers were urged to support the movement for plank roads, which would enable them to haul wood and farm produce more rapidly and at a cheaper rate. W[illiam] Kingsford, *History, Structure, and Statistics of Plank Roads, in the United States and Canada* (Philadelphia, 1851), pp. 15–16; Robert Dale

Information about wood and lumber yards is scanty, although the
Chicago Democrat estimated in 1850 that forty such dealers were
operating in the city.[45] The main activity was cutting the wood into
smaller, more convenient sizes, but by the 1850's commercial wood
yards were replacing choppers by use of steam-powered saws. These
machines were able to prepare three to four cords of wood per hour.[46]
Probably many wood yard workers—choppers, stackers, handlers—
were immigrants who for one reason or another had not heeded the
advice that the city was a poor place to get a start in America.[47] Yet,
some of these newcomers made successful beginnings from itinerant
labor, including work in lumber yards. German-born Henry Wischemeyer arrived at Chicago in June, 1841, without a penny to his name.
He worked briefly on a nearby farm for nine dollars per month, from
which four dollars was deducted for the purchase of boots. During
the autumn and winter of 1841–42 he worked as a laborer on the Illinois-Michigan Canal project. In March, 1842, Wischemeyer worked
once more on a farm, but he soon turned back to the city. There he
was employed in a lumber yard, an occupation which led him eventually to open his own establishment.[48]

Men did not necessarily remain in the Midwest chopping wood or
working in pork packing houses. An annual exodus occurred in autumn when farm and itinerant laborers made their way downriver to
the South. A warm climate and job opportunities awaited them
there.[49] Some of these "snow birds" remained only for the winter and
returned in the spring, while others stayed several years to amass
sufficient money to return and buy a farm. For many, the standard

---

Owen, *A Brief Practical Treatise on the Construction and Management of Plank
Roads* (New Albany, 1850), pp. 5–11.

45. *Chicago Weekly Democrat*, February 2, 1850.

46. *Chicago Daily Democrat*, November 22, 1851. Similar mechanization
was reported at Sandusky: see *Daily Commercial Register*, October 24, 1853.

47. *Chicago Weekly Democrat*, June 26, 1849; *Chicago Daily Democrat*, July
6, 1849. Chicago's immigrant population frequently lived in shanty slums constructed of slabs and boards from lumber yards. Unonius, *Memoirs*, II, pp.
194–95.

48. John Moses, *Illinois Historical and Statistical* (Chicago, 1895), II, pp.
647–49. Other immigrants did not find chopping to be profitable work in the
city and sought different employment. For examples, see *Biographical Record
of Logan County, Illinois*, p. 509; *Portrait and Biographical Album of DeKalb
County, Illinois* (Chicago, 1883), p. 689. Free blacks in the Chicago area also
performed winter chopping; *Chicago Daily Democrat*, June 4, 7, 1851.

49. Cist, *Sketches and Statistics of Cincinnati in 1851*, p. 317; *Cincinnati
Daily Gazette*, November 13, 1848; *Chicago Daily Democrat*, November 7,
1857; November 28, 1859.

employment was chopping cord wood near river landing locations.[50]

An English traveler passing Baton Rouge, Louisiana, in 1835 remarked that the demand for cord wood was so great that "North-country" men from Michigan came regularly to the region. They worked seven months of the year chopping in southern locales, and in the course of four or five seasons earned enough money to buy a midwestern farm.[51] Most were unemployed laborers seeking work for the winter, while others were farmers hoping to make extra cash during the slack season.[52] Some wood choppers who went south were small-scale independent operators. In the 1830's Edward Hitch came out to Cincinnati, where he purchased a flatboat and made his way down the Ohio and Mississippi. He successfully operated his own scowboat, cruising up and down the river with loads of wood for passing steamboats. Eventually his earnings sufficed to bring him back to the Midwest. He bought land and settled in Gibson County, Indiana.[53]

The pay for these men was comparable to wages per cord elsewhere on the Ohio and Mississippi Rivers. Work conditions were rough, and many river locations near swamps were unattractive and unhealthy. Average pay in the winter was fifty to seventy-five cents per cord, and any economic gain might be threatened by disease or

50. Near Natchez, for example, a steam sawmill operated on an annual basis and employed forty to sixty hands. The men could work out several years in the South, if they wanted to remain that long. *DeBow's Review*, V (April, 1848), 380. Several recent studies provide background material on the southern sawmill industry: Nollie Hickman, *Mississippi Harvest* (University, 1962); John H. Moore, *Andrew Brown and Cypress Lumbering in the Old Southwest* (Baton Rouge, 1967); John A. Eisterhold, "Lumber and Trade in the Lower Mississippi Valley and New Orleans, 1800–1860," *Louisiana History*, XIII (1972), 71–91.

51. Tyrone Power, *Impressions of America, During 1833, 1834, and 1835* (London, 1836), II, p. 184. For examples, see *History of Van Wert and Mercer Counties, Ohio*, p. 254; *Biographical Record of Ogle County, Illinois*, p. 22; *History of Green County, Wisconsin*, p. 733; Arthur L. Bodurtha, ed., *History of Miami County, Indiana* (Chicago and New York, 1914), II, p. 586.

52. For examples of farmers who went south, see *History of La Salle County, Illinois* (Chicago, 1886), II, p. 181; *Portrait and Biographical Album of Vermilion and Edgar Counties, Illinois* (Chicago, 1889), p. 1049.

53. Gil R. Stormant, *History of Gibson County, Indiana* (Indianapolis, 1914), p. 511. For additional reference to scowboats on the Ohio and Mississippi Rivers, see Brown Daybook, 1832–52, p. 7, and Brown Account Ledger, 1840–80, p. 4, in Nessly-deSellem Papers; Cockrum, *Pioneer History of Indiana*, p. 511; "Diaries of Donald MacDonald," 234–35; Kohl, *Reisen im Nordwestern der Vereinigten Staaten*, pp. 176–77; A. Oakley Hall, *The Manhattaner in New Orleans; or, Phases of "Crescent City" Life* (New York, 1851), p. 183.

danger in reaching these remote places.[54] By the 1850's the trek south in winter became less profitable. *DeBow's Review* noted the rapidly dwindling wood tracts; in many areas the only available wood came from rafts or was pulled from the river in the form of float (drift) wood—a poor substitute.[55] *DeBow's* strongly recommended conversion to coal at an average cost of sixteen cents a bushel or forty cents a barrel. Since ten bushels of coal equaled one cord of wood, which sold at the medium price of three and a half dollars, coal was by far the cheaper.[56] The high point of downriver chopping came in the 1850's; with the outbreak of the Civil War this regional migration all but ceased.

As the Midwest became settled and developed, it generated demand for cut logs and sawed timber. Mills were soon established, especially in remote locales where timber was plentiful. The Michigan frontier personified the "mill age," especially during 1835–50. Since there was little or no commercial intent behind these mills, they were operated primarily as a part of the farm to facilitate the disposal of timber cleared off the land.[57] As a result, farm hands and itinerant choppers were often employed in the construction and operation of the mills.[58]

The terms of such employment were described in a letter from an English immigrant at Allegan County in western Michigan in 1835. W. Forbes purchased land near the Kalamazoo River in the southwestern portion of the county and wrote his brother for additional money to construct a sawmill. There was a local demand for cut timber; if a successfull sawmill site were established, it could be expanded into a larger milling operation and attract other trades, such

54. *History of Knox and Daviess Counties, Indiana*, p. 815; O. J. Page, *History of Massac County, Illinois* (Metropolis, Ill., 1900), part II, p. 198. In the 1820's a New Yorker established a wood station near Natchez. He employed briefly two Ohio teenagers to cut wood; however, the boys could not adjust to the fever-ridden climate. James Pearse, *A Narrative of the Life of James Pearse* (Chicago, 1962), p. 32.

55. *DeBow's Review*, VIII (April, 1850), 401–4.

56. *Ibid.*, XIX (December, 1855), 661–68.

57. Ormand S. Danford, "The Social and Economic Effects of Lumbering on Michigan, 1835–1890," *Michigan History*, XXVI (1942), 346–64.

58. Numerous biographical sketches include mention of chopping and sawmill labor, along with other itinerant employments. For examples, see *Portrait and Biographical Album of Henry County, Illinois*, p. 457; Bateman and Selby, eds., *Illinois Historical. Effingham County Biographical* (Chicago, 1910), pp. 886–87; *Portrait and Biographical Album of Coles County, Illinois* (Chicago, 1887), pp. 298–99.

as a blacksmith, for the nucleus of a village. A reliable hired hand was already in his employ on the farm, but another would be helpful. If his brother knew of any person who might be willing to come out to Michigan, Forbes could offer him thirty acres of land in return for eighteen months of work.[59]

In areas barely settled and hardly cultivated, the sawmill was a manufacturing unit that converted raw forest products into semi-finished construction materials vital to an expanding frontier area. While most pioneers were farmers or settlers untrained in manufacturing techniques, skilled men with background in mechanical operations did come west and establish sawmills on new farms. John How, formerly an English cotton mill operator, decided to settle at Livingston County, Michigan. He brought his wife, four sons, and a hired hand named William Peel in May, 1834. Teamsters were engaged at Detroit to convey the family and their belongings out to the farm site. Set-up work—the clearing of land and the building of cabins—came first. The following year brought construction of a saw and grist mill, the first mechanical industry in the area. The hired hand in this case engaged in both agricultural and mechanical construction work. According to a list of early land entries, he took up land in 1834, which indicated that these early frontier employees owned land yet found it profitable to work out for others.[60]

A hired hand's contract is preserved in the accountbook of Darius Pierce, who ran a sawmill and owned tracts of land near Farmington, Michigan, in the 1830's and 1840's. During these years Pierce hired men, by both the day and the month, to get out timber. In 1840 he made a contract with a hand who worked at least part of the time in the sawmill:

> Feb. 17th. 1840—Made Contract with B. C. Thompson to work for me at $12 per month for six months washing and mending is to be done in contract[.] 25 dolls [sic] is to be paid by the first of May & the balance when sd. [said] six months labor is performed—it is the understanding that if sd. [said]—Thompson should quit work before the time agreed upon that he is to be paid in the proportion to the worth of labor for the whole time allso [sic] from sickness or other

59. W. Forbes to James Forbe (Plainville, Allegan County, Michigan Territory, April 10, 1835). For examples of laborers at mill construction, see *History of Kalamazoo County, Michigan*, pp. 379, 399; *History of Oakland County, Michigan*, p. 256.

60. *History of Livingston County, Michigan*, pp. 416, 418–20. Hired hands sometimes accompanied their employers from the East and worked in the mills on the farms. Schenck, *History of Ionia and Montcalm Counties, Michigan*, p. 278; *History of Lapeer County, Michigan* (Chicago, 1884), p. 139.

cause there—should [there] be lost time said thompson shall not be subject to damage in consequence of sd. [said] sickness or loss of time.[61]

Considerable migration occurred in the upper regions of the Midwest, where wintertime chopping and logging were conducted in connection with milling.[62] Three kinds of choppers, with specific duties, worked in the northern woods during winter: swampers, choppers, and landing men. Swampers were the first line who cleared the brush. They removed old, worthless timber which might be in the way of the choppers who followed to fell the trees. Third were the landing men who loaded the logs on the sledges which dragged the wood from the forest to the river banks.[63] Local settlers worked in these sawmills and at lumbering while establishing farms. For example, Elbridge G. Fifield took out a land claim at Jefferson County, Wisconsin, in 1837 and worked in sawmills during the next several years while clearing his own land. Part of his income came from rafting lumber and logs down the Rock River that drained from southern Wisconsin into northern Illinois. One of the locations passed en route was Janesville. Fifield established a lumber yard there in 1843.[64]

Rafting of logs and timber was an integral aspect of the lumber

61. Darius Pierce, untitled accountbook, entry of February 17, 1840.

62. Important studies of the lumbering industry in the upper Midwest include George B. Engberg, "Who Were the Lumberjacks?" *Michigan History*, XXXII (1948), 238–46; Robert F. Fries, *Empire in Pine* (Madison, 1951); Agnes M. Larson, *History of the White Pine Industry in Minnesota* (Minneapolis, 1949).

63. Lillian Kimball Stewart, *A Pioneer of Old Superior* (Boston, 1930), p. 83; see also Fries, *Empire in Pine*, pp. 27–32; Larson, *History of the White Pine Industry in Minnesota*, p. 78. Farm boys, transient workers, and tramps often worked in the Wisconsin timber areas during the 1850's, according to Joseph Schafer, *Wisconsin Domesday Book: General Studies: Vol. IV: The Winnebago-Horicon Basin. A Type Study in Western History* (Madison, 1937), pp. 292–93. Early farmers in northern areas faced competition from the lumber industry, which offered higher wages than farmers could afford to give: see L. Hart to Janet Hart (Tuscola, Mich., May 9, 1847), Hart Correspondence. For examples of laborers who worked in sawmills, see *History of Green County, Wisconsin*, pp. 1154–55; Bateman and Selby, eds., *Historical Encyclopedia of Illinois Including Genealogy, Family Records and Biography of McHenry County Citizens*, II, p. 712; Samuel W. Durant, *History of Ingham and Eaton Counties, Michigan* (Philadelphia, 1880), p. 419.

64. Elbridge G. Fifield, "Some Pioneering Experiences in Jefferson County," *Proceedings of the State Historical Society of Wisconsin*, LII (1904), 140–44; see also William Fiske Brown, ed., *Rock County, Wisconsin* (Chicago, 1908), II, p. 536. A farmer at Milton on the Rock River mentioned in his diary the passing of flatboats and rafts of logs down the river. Local settlers picked up employment when help was needed to raft rails and wood. Farmers also cut and hauled wood to Beloit for sale to steamboats. Ogden Diary, entries of August 24, 1838; April 30, July 31, 1839; May 15, 29, 1841.

industry between 1830 and 1870. Especially prominent were the Mississippi River rafters who came down rivers of Wisconsin and Minnesota in spring with immense log floats.[65] Men who worked as farm hands used this route to leave the pineries in spring to go to farm areas. For example, Nels K. Nesgard, a Norwegian immigrant, worked several years as a farm hand in the Rock River area of Wisconsin and chopped wood in winter along the Wisconsin River. In one instance his pay came in the form of timber, a fact which explains why choppers were often forced to become rafters. Hesgard took 160,000 feet of lumber and logs, as well as 30,000 additional feet belonging to his employer, down the Wisconsin River from Wausau with the help of seven hired hands. The long trip ended at Alton, Illinois, just north of St. Louis.[66]

The necessary laboring force for chopping out the timber, handling it at the mills, and rafting the material downriver assumed considerable proportions prior to 1860. Lumber from LaCrosse, Wisconsin, for example, was rafted down the Mississippi to St. Louis, where it was sold for fifteen to twenty dollars per thousand feet. In 1852 the bulk of exports from the upper Mississippi River pineries in Wisconsin, including the St. Croix, Chippewa, and Black Rivers, was valued at over one million dollars, the timber averaging about ten dollars per thousand feet.[67] A reliable source assessed the region as a boon to men seeking work: "The importance of the lumber business of the St. Croix river would hardly be estimated by a stranger. Large quantities are floated down the Mississippi to St. Louis. The business of getting out the timber is carried on in winter, and affords employment to large numbers of young men."[68] Between 1840 and 1860 skilled chop-

65. J. M. Turner, "Rafting on the Mississippi," *Wisconsin History*, XXIV (1940), 59–60. For additional information on rafting, see A. R. Reynolds, "Rafting Down the Chippewa and the Mississippi. Daniel Shaw Lumber Company, A Type Study," *ibid.*, XXXII (1948), 143–52; Walter A. Blair, *A Raft Pilot's Log* (Cleveland, 1930); Charles Edward Russell, *A-Rafting on the Mississip'* (New York, 1928); Larson, *History of the White Pine Industry in Minnesota*, pp. 86–104; Fries, *Empire in Pine*, pp. 55–56, 66–83.

66. Brown, ed., *Rock County, Wisconsin*, II, pp. 1014–16.

67. *U.S. Pat. Office Report, 1851*, 463; *DeBow's Review*, XIV (January, 1853), 26–28; see also Fries, *Empire in Pine*, pp. 19–21.

68. Ritchie, *Wisconsin and Its Resources*, p. 69. A Minnesota visitor observed that these men were generally a sensible lot of individuals who saved their money except in periods of unemployment. They appeared intelligent and spent their evenings in conversation or at story-telling. Andrews, *Minnesota and Dacotah*, pp. 87–88. Yet not all were of this nature, and recent studies emphasize the coarseness of those in this occupation: Wright, *Hawkers and Walkers in*

pers were attracted to the upper Midwest, and by the 1850's they were earning on an average of twenty-six dollars per month with board.[69]

Rafting required from five to sixteen hands.[70] The size varied, but a record raft—described as a "Monster"—was reported at Dubuque, Iowa, in 1860; it consisted of 1,100,000 feet of lumber and 950,000 shingles and lathes.[71] The floating mass of timber was guided by an experienced pilot who supervised the hands, who were stationed at various points on the log rigs and, with the use of oars and poles, maneuvered the raft as it drifted downriver. The men remained on the rafts both day and night until the trip was completed.[72]

The occupational patterns of these rafters differed little from those of farm hands, and agricultural employment was in fact part of the seasonal shift from job to job. Rafting of timber was especially important in the spring, yet some men made it a half-year occupation, going up and down the river several times in one season, while others hired out to raft a single load of timber in order to travel down to waiting farm hand positions.

Economic necessity was a factor for men seeking employment during the slack winter months; immigrants were among those who worked in this line. A twenty-year-old Swede, Jonas Westerlund, worked out initially as a farm hand at Henry County in western Illinois. But in 1851 he began a five-year stint of logging and chopping in Minnesota, and each year three or four raft trips with lumber were made down to St. Louis, with occasional stops to visit his family. He purchased land in Henry County in 1854 but worked out in the piner-

---

Early America, pp. 108–9; Russell, *A-Rafting on the Mississip'*, pp. 95, 135–36, 189–91.

69. Fries, *Empire in Pine*, pp. 12–15; Larson, *History of the White Pine Industry in Minnesota*, pp. 74–77.

70. Brown, ed., *Rock County, Wisconsin*, II, pp. 1014–15; Andrews, *Minnesota and Dacotah*, p. 89; *Chicago Daily Democrat*, October 6, 1857.

71. *Ibid.*, October 2, 1860. Five years earlier at Davenport, Iowa, a newspaper reported a raft 160 feet wide and 192 feet long, containing 500,000 feet of timber worth $10,000. *Daily Commercial Register*, September 8, 1855. For detailed descriptions of how these rafts or cribs of lumber were assembled, see Fries, *Empire in Pine*, pp. 55–56, 66–83; Larson, *History of the White Pine Industry in Minnesota*, pp. 91–93.

72. Turner, "Rafting on the Mississippi," 59–60. The raftsmen sometimes built small cabins, called "cabooses," which sheltered them from the weather. There were work shifts: some rested or slept while others manned the oars. Andrews, *Minnesota and Decotah*, p. 89. For a description of the various problems that might arise on a rafting run down the Mississippi, see Russell, *A-Rafting on the Mississip'*, pp. 109–14; Larson, *History of the White Pine Industry in Minnesota*, pp. 87–89.

ies and at rafting for several more years. Since rafting terminated in the autumn, it may be assumed that he obtained harvest work during the final stop-off visit with his family.[73]

Men without family connections wandered over considerable distances in pursuit of employment. A New York boy lost his parents at age four and was brought to Henry County, Illinois, in 1838 by a man for whom the lad worked until 1851. Then at age seventeen George Buck, who had known only farm work, turned to the nearby Mississippi River and spent the next two years in rafting. At the end of this period he resumed work as a farm hand in Henry County and later followed sodbusting for several seasons.[74] Similar was the case of Thomas Hamilton, who worked as a farm hand in northern Illinois during the late 1830's. In 1842 young Hamilton went to Green County, Wisconsin, where from 1842 to 1845 he worked summers at undisclosed labor in villages and winters in the pineries while rafting timber in season.[75]

Any discussion of wood chopping would be incomplete without mention of the early railroad industry. Railroads, like steamboats, not only sparked a transportation revolution, but also contributed to a gradual depletion of wood as a permanent fuel. Although railroad growth in the Midwest was initially slow, by the 1850's Ohio, Indiana, and Illinois were emerging as leaders in new track laid. By 1860, Ohio's track mileage of 2,946 was greater than that of any other state; railroad fuel consumption approximated 140 cords per mile per year in the pre–Civil War period.[76] The correlation between fuel and farm labor became apparent: fuel was more expensive in the counties through which railroad lines passed, while labor became scarce and expensive. "The laborers easily learn the prices paid in different sections," observed an official Ohio report in 1857, "and go where the labor is highest."[77]

73. *Biographical Record of Henry County, Illinois*, pp. 394–95. Russell documents the importance of harvest labor in autumn, based on the diary of Stephen Hanks, a rafter during the 1840's and 1850's. In addition, Hanks chopped wood in winter along with sawmill labor and accepted "any other light jobs" that came his way. Russell, *A-Rafting on the Mississip'*, pp. 146–47.

74. *Biographical Record of Henry County, Illinois*, p. 206.

75. *History of Green County, Wisconsin*, p. 1070. For similar examples, see *History of Crawford and Richland Counties, Wisconsin*, pp. 1292–93; *Biographical History of La Crosse, Monroe and Juneau Counties, Wisconsin*, p. 621.

76. Taylor, *Transportation Revolution*, p. 79; Cole, "The Mystery of Fuel Wood Marketing in the United States," 352.

77. *Ohio Statistics, 1857*, I, 21–22. Concern was expressed about the rapid depletion of timber land: *Hunt's Merchant Magazine*, IV (January 4, 1841), 62; *Cincinnati Daily Gazette*, October 9, 1846; *Wisconsin Farmer*, VIII (November,

The purpose here is briefly to identify the men who in one way or another supplied cord wood to early midwestern railroads.[78] Some were farmers near the railroad right of way, while others were merely hired hands who wandered in from other locations.[79] Railroads were a major impetus to land clearing and wood chopping in many areas, such as in eastern Michigan, where farmers benefited from the Michigan Central by supplying fuel wood and railroad ties. When work was begun on the railroad at Dearborn in the 1830's, William Nowlin recalled how he and his father chopped and hauled three cords of wood per day from their land to the railroad tracks. They also made railroad ties according to specifications of nine-foot lengths hewed flat in seven-inch diameters.[80]

Farmers who owned extensive timber tracts near railroads contracted wood chopping by the cord rate but employed choppers by the day and month as well. Darius Pierce was a large Michigan landowner with holdings centered at Farmington, west of Detroit near the route of the Michigan Central. He hired men on an annual, monthly, and daily basis for both agricultural labor and wood chopping. During 1841 extensive clearing of timber was performed on his land, and large quantities of wood were sold to the Michigan Central. In October, 1841, he made out a receipt for the cash sum of $310 that was paid to a man for chopping and cutting timber delivered to the "R R Job." Indicative of these choppers' lack of education, Pierce prepared the receipt himself and had the man make his X sign in lieu of a signature. In the same papers for the following day was a receipt signed by Charles Backrus for "ten dollars for labor done in harvesting and work on R R Timber." Other receipts show that Pierce had at least a half-dozen men in his employ doing similar work. One of the signed bills was itemized to show that David Halls in November, 1841, was paid seventy-five cents for scoring timber—

1856), 487–88; *Farmer's Companion and Horticultural Gazette*, IV (July, 1854), 219–21; *U.S. Pat. Office Report*, 1852, 267.

78. For example, two studies dealing with the Illinois Central make little or no mention of labor in connection with cord wood fuel: Howard G. Brownson, *History of the Illinois Central Railroad to 1870* (Urbana, 1915); Paul Gates, *Illinois Central Railroad and Its Colonization Work* (Cambridge, 1934).

79. Travelers reported woodcutters living in small shanties alongside the tracks: Beste, *The Wabash*, I, p. 163; Isabella Lucy Bird Bishop, *The Englishwoman in America* (London, 1856), p. 136.

80. Nowlin, *The Bark Covered House*, pp. 149–50. For other examples of farmers who supplied wood, see Talcott E. Wing, ed., *History of Monroe County, Michigan* (New York, 1890), p. 228; *History of Berrien and Van Buren Counties, Michigan*, p. 336.

probably hewing and smoothing logs for railroad ties—but only fifty cents per day for loading and handling timber.[81] In addition, Pierce sometimes paid his hands with store orders rather than cash.[82] Choppers were not unlike hired hands when it came to loss of time through damage of tools. One of Pierce's choppers had the following notation in the accountbook for his first day of work: "hired Mr. Griffith to hew timber began work on Nov. 26th 1840 about 11.0 clock and broke broad axe handle before night."[83]

A pattern of seasonal work and short-term jobs typified the situation for many of these men, including Menzies Phelps Manley. He started work at a brickyard in April, 1847, at Fulton County, Indiana, an employment which lasted until cold temperatures shut down the operation in October. During the winter he chopped wood at twenty-five cents a cord, while the next summer found him working as a mason. In the fall of 1848 he and a friend trekked to Niles, Michigan. They found no work and spent the winter there cording wood and making railroad ties. Manley worked as a farm hand at Stillwell Prairie in LaPorte County, Indiana, until 1852, when he was offered a job teamstering a wagonload of goods out to Wisconsin. Upon arrival at Wisconsin he secured the most likely available employment in such a region by working in a sawmill.[84]

Typical of seasonal itinerants in the lower Midwest, especially Ohio and Indiana, was Eli Heiny. In the 1840's he worked out on farms at seven dollars per month and corded wood in winter at the rate of twenty-five cents per cord. He combined this work with the seasonal employment of taking hogs to the packing centers, including Cincinnati, then known as the "Porkopolis" of the Midwest. The latter activity commenced in late fall and continued through the packing season until February. He was paid thirty-seven and a half cents per day and two dollars expenses for a ten-day trip, following this sort of winter combination work for six years.[85]

81. Darius Pierce Papers, Folder August-December, 1841, dated receipts and memoranda for October 11, 12, November 8, 1841.

82. Darius Pierce untitled accountbook [Central Railroad], entry of December 22, 1840; undated entry for Craig, *ibid.* See also Folder December, 1840–February, 1841, for signed receipts by Craig.

83. Darius Pierce untitled accountbook [Central Railroad], entry for Griffith, November 26, 1840.

84. *History of Crawford and Richland Counties, Wisconsin*, pp. 1095–97; for other examples, see Durant, *History of Ingham and Eaton Counties, Michigan*, p. 234; *Portrait and Biographical Record of Delaware and Randolph Counties, Ind.* (Chicago, 1894), p. 654.

85. *Pictorial and Biographical Memoirs of Indianapolis and Marion County, Indiana* (Chicago, 1893), p. 368. An early but useful study is Charles T.

Hog slaughtering and pork packing were integral aspects of a wintertime commercial activity and constituted a brief occupation for thousands of men who otherwise had little or no employment until spring. Artificial production of ice was a post–Civil War innovation, and during the antebellum years the packing industry followed the mercurial weather conditions. In the lower Ohio Valley, operations usually commenced either in late October or early November. The high point of activity was reached in December, and the operation terminated by February.[86] At Chicago, the major packing center for the upper Midwest, the season began as early as September—usually after the first frost, which assured lower temperatures. The *Chicago Democrat* stressed an early start and speedy packing procedures, since navigable waters froze early at this northern point and prevented shipment of pork.[87]

This seasonal industry operated during the slack period from late fall, when many farm hands were discharged, until the following spring. Charles Cist, editor of the Cincinnati *Weekly Advertiser*, observed that agriculture, brick-making, and excavation digging were among those employments terminated by winter; were it not for the packing industry and related lines of employment, six thousand men faced unemployment for at least one-third of the year.[88] For farm hands without employment, the cities and towns were places of refuge until spring, and work in the packing houses enabled them to support themselves during the winter.

Cincinnati controlled 80 percent of the pork packing industry in Ohio. It was the largest packing center in the Midwest until the 1860's, when Chicago emerged as the leader; however, smaller cities and towns usually had one or two packing houses to handle the local pork trade.[89] Thousands of men came to these locations during the 1840's and 1850's. No statistics exist for the precise or even approxi-

---

Leavitt, "Some Economic Aspects of the Western Meat-Packing Industry, 1830–60," *Journal of Business of the University of Chicago*, IV (1931), 68–90.

86. *Cincinnati Daily Gazette*, October 29, 1844. The approach of warm weather signaled the end of operations; pork spoiled rapidly at temperatures above freezing. *Niles' Register*, LIV (March 10, 1838), 22–23.

87. *Chicago Weekly Democrat*, September 12, 1848; *Chicago Daily Democrat*, September 26, 1848.

88. *Cist's Weekly Advertiser*, April 11, 1848; Cist, *Sketches and Statistics of Cincinnati in 1851*, p. 228.

89. *Report of the Commissioner of Agriculture for the Year 1866* (Washington, 1867), 384. For a list of midwestern cities and towns where pork packing was conducted, see *Niles' Register*, LXVII (February 15, 1845), 371; LXX (March 14, 1846), 21; *Hunt's Merchant Magazine*, XXX (April, 1854), 457.

mate number, or to indicate how many were farm hands. But it is not unreasonable to assume that many farm hands, especially in southern Ohio and Indiana, fulfilled the final duty to their employers by help- ing to herd and drive the hogs to such markets as Cincinnati and then remained in the city to secure work at the start of the slaughter season. Young men, reportedly from as far afield as Illinois, were hired to drive hogs to packing markets.[90]

Except for Cincinnati, whose packing houses were well described in a variety of reports and travelers' accounts,[91] smaller houses run by merchants in secondary towns are without much documentation. But considerable pork was processed by these smaller operators who gave employment and shelter to farm hands during the winter months. Merchant-owned slaughterhouses were especially prominent in small communities during earlier decades, but they were supplanted in time by the larger and more efficient firms in the cities. Typical of this local trade and handling of pork was that of William Mills, Jr. & Company of Evansville, Indiana, in 1819. During November and De- cember Mills offered merchandise in exchange for corn-fed pork de- livered to his place of business.[92]

In the Hocking River Valley of central Ohio, merchant pork pack- ers predominated in the towns, although farmers usually killed, dressed, and cleaned the hogs themselves, removing the fat and bristles. The slaughtered hogs were then sold to the merchant pack- ers. Meat was processed and packed by the merchants, who employed laborers for this work: "This gave employment to a large number of hands in every village, who would cut and pack pork all winter. The hauling of all this to the river would also give employment to a large number of teams, and the manufacture of pork barrels would keep many coopers employed." Moreover, pork packing in rural towns provided the poor with a low-cost food supply; they were permitted to take gratis those parts of little value from the slaughtered hogs, including the spareribs, heads, and feet. Otherwise this refuse was teamed out of town in wagons and dumped in the surrounding woods.[93]

90. *Cincinnati Miscellaney*, I (1844–45), 172. According to the *Cincinnati Chronicle* in 1843, over four million hogs were driven to the city, indicating the necessity for men to work in this vital herding operation. As cited in *Niles' Register*, LXV (November 25, 1845), 208.

91. See *ibid.*, LI (January 28, 1837), 342; Murray, *Lands of the Slave and the Free*, I, pp. 154–57.

92. *Western Sun and General Advertiser*, December 18, 1819.

93. *History of Hocking Valley, Ohio* (Chicago, 1883), pp. 61–62. It was common in many parts of the Midwest for storekeepers to advance credit, taking

Documentary accounts generally omit mention of personal information on packing house laborers. They worked the eight- to fifteen-week period during the dead of winter when little other employment was available. Presumably this type of work, basically unpleasant and repelling, attracted the coarser elements of society, especially in the river front areas. Regardless of their background, men of all sorts engaged in this work, including immigrants, who found employment in packing houses as a means of getting a start. German-born Simon Weinberg migrated to Cincinnati and found his first winter employment at a pork packing plant; during the following four years he worked also in a stone quarry and at farm labor.[94] Of German birth, too, John Miller followed a similar variety of occupations in southern Ohio, including pork packing and work in a sawmill or as a farm laborer.[95] A young Irish immigrant first worked at railroad construction and pork packing in Illinois, then obtained employment as a hired hand for a farmer who defaulted on his wages. After this experience, this Irish lad headed north to chop wood in the pineries of Wisconsin and Michigan until his return to Illinois, where he again worked out as a farm hand in the 1850's.[96]

Seasonal and itinerant patterns of employment are conveniently summarized in the occupations of Peter Vail during the early 1840's, a period of general depression throughout the Midwest. At Montgomery County, Indiana, Vail teamstered and hauled wheat to Chicago, 140 miles away. However, in 1843 he trekked across Indiana and into southern Ohio, where he obtained work in a pork packing house for fifty cents a day. In summers he worked as a farm hand for $6.50 per month, a handsome amount in depression times. Generalizations should be made cautiously, but Vail's seemed to typify the struggle facing many Midwesterners. He worked at teamstering, farm labor, and pork packing—seasonal employments which in some instances required him to travel considerable distances. He was an itinerant, yet he worked diligently to get ahead. Vail personified an average individual who was content to live out his remaining years on a modest farm of 113 acres in Kosciusko County, Indiana.[97]

---

the hogs in return to balance the debits of their customers. As a result, many merchants became involved with the packing and processing of pork.

94. *Portrait and Biographical Record of Hancock, McDonough, and Henderson Counties, Illinois* (Chicago, 1894), p. 253.

95. Evans, *History of Scioto County, Ohio*, pp. 1072–73.

96. Perrin, ed., *History of Cass County, Illinois*, p. 324.

97. *Biographical and Historical Record of Kosciusko County, Indiana*, pp. 610–11.

A sizable itinerant labor force was employed to supply the fuel requirements for steamboats, railroads, minor industries, and domestic consumption. Seasonal unemployment on farms drove hired hands into cities and towns where the only available employment was in packing houses or at wood chopping. Others headed for the southern states to chop wood, while sawmilling and rafting provided similar employment in the upper regions of the Midwest. Necessity rather than choice set in motion this seasonal migration of men drifting from job to job. For those successful in later life, these brief occupations were a means rather than an end; like farm labor, they were usually performed without due recognition.

Hired Boy

I grew to manhood very much as other boys have done. I
have worked hard, have plowed for twenty-five cents per day,
chopped wood for thirty, reaped wheat for fifty cents per day
and cradled for fifty.[1]

ONE SOLUTION to the labor shortage on the agricultural frontier was the employment of young boys. Whether they
labored on their parents' farm or elsewhere in the neighborhood,
boys of all ages served in a vital capacity as employable hands on both
new and established farms. One view of the farm boy's position was
offered by John L. Blake in the 1850's: "The plough-boy belongs to
another class of humble and toilsome employment; and who, that has
ever shared in the toils or the sports of that vocation, can look back
upon it, from any point in after life, without feelings of complacency
and regret?"[2] Others saw farm youth in a less inspiring but more
realistic light: "Like many other farmer boys he 'mowed and hoed
and held the plow and longed for one-and-twenty.'"[3] Most farm boys
did "mow and hoe" for their fathers until they were twenty-one, and
the frontier father of one or more sons considered himself a lucky man
indeed.[4]

If age twenty-one was the magic turning point, years of arduous
labor stretched between birth and attainment of legal age. Necessity
usually forced a young man to work out; and a common reason in
many cases was the death of the father, who had been the primary
breadwinner. Upon his son fell the main burden of helping the

1. Duis, *The Good Old Times in McLean County, Illinois*, p. 530.
2. John Blake, *Lessons in Modern Farming* (New York, 1852), p. 185.
3. *Portrait and Biographical Record of Winnebago and Boone Counties,
Illinois*, p. 1221.
4. The value of several sons to assist with the farm did not escape the
attention of an early German visitor to Ohio in the 1830's; he equated them in
terms of success or failure for the farm. Witte, *Kurze Schilderung*, p. 22.

widowed mother provide a home and economic base for the family. These boys maintained the family farm with the help of brothers and sisters but also worked on neighborhood farms.[5]

Parents could claim control over their children's labor according to a loosely defined but rigidly enforced custom of time obligation. "Time" allowed the father to claim earned wages of his son until the twenty-first birthday, after which the young man was free of further obligation. To a boy in his late teens, this demand seemed to stretch into eternity. A man with several sons found it advantageous in fact to hire out some of his boys for the purpose of added income.

The farm account of Luther Huston near Piqua, Ohio, during the 1850's reveals such an occurrence. A neighbor, Aaron Goodwin, performed work on Huston's farm to compensate for needed items of corn, cash, tobacco, seed, and slate which Huston advanced him on credit. Goodwin had several sons who, according to the account entries, also came to work. The older one earned the standard daily rate of fifty cents for day labor. A younger son, termed the "little boy," was also sent to help the older brother and father who were plowing corn fields for Huston. The entry for the younger son made a distinction of age by paying a lower rate of thirty-seven and one-half cents per day.[6]

Most boys accepted the obligation of time and usually turned over their earnings when their fathers demanded them. In the 1820's at Trumbull County, Ohio, John Flower and his brothers were hired out with the promise to contribute all earnings toward the family debt. Thirteen-year-old John's share for nine months of labor amounted to twenty-seven dollars, or roughly three dollars per month.[7] Terms of employment as well as wages were negotiable, and boys had some influence in the arrangements. An Ohio lad found himself about to be hired out to a neighbor for the sum of three dollars per month. The boy rebelled, pointing out to his father that such wages were in-

5. *Counties of Warren, Benton, Jasper and Newton, Indiana*, p. 551; *History of Henry County, Indiana*, p. 887; *Portrait and Biographical Record of Adams County, Illinois*, pp. 178–79; *History of Knox and Daviess Counties, Indiana*, p. 492.

6. Luther Huston Account Ledger, p. 17. For a similar circumstance, see Anthony Stranahan Farm Accounts, 1811–26, p. 58, entries for Thomas Walling. Sometimes a boy might be paid as low as 25 cents per day for work such as plowing or harvesting: see J. N. Gridley, *Historical Sketches* (Virginia, 1907), I, p. 48.

7. *History of the Upper Ohio Valley with Historical Account of Columbiana County, Ohio* (Madison, 1891), I, p. 271.

adequate and did not even allow for the purchase of clothes. The matter was ultimately smoothed over with the provision to include a horse, saddle, and bridle.[8]

Farm boys sometimes exercised shrewd insight into their employment situation, as evidenced by the case of Dyar Cobb. He came west with his family in 1819 on a flatboat down the Ohio River, the traditional route of many settlers. Because he was the second son in the family, his father decided to hire him out. Cobb described the arrangement, which paid four dollars per month in wages and involved cleaning out corn fields. Without the father's knowledge or permission, the boy was in turn hired out by the farmer to his brother-in-law at six dollars per month. This was two dollars more than what he paid the boy's father; in effect, he pocketed the extra amount. Young Cobb rebelled against this arrangement and hired himself directly to the brother-in-law so as to receive the full six dollars per month.[9]

The farmer with several sons might release one of them from the obligation of time to earn whatever he could obtain.[10] But the common practice was for the boy to turn over part or all of the earnings to his father until he reached an age of seventeen to twenty-one years. Boys by this time were generally considered full-grown men and accorded equivalent status.[11] Depending upon the relationship of the boy and his father, the time agreement might be partially honored. In the 1840's, Thomas May worked on neighborhood farms in Bartholomew County, Indiana. Prior to his seventeenth birthday, all his earnings went to his parents, while during his seventeenth to twenty-first years he was obliged to give only part of his wages.[12] In contrast, an Illinois farm boy in the 1850's, upon reaching seventeen, was released entirely from the obligation. His father told him to keep his wages and "gave him the balance of the time," to use the common phrase of the period.[13] Here agreement was simple and direct, reflecting an understanding between father and son and a realization of the futility in holding the boy down until his twenty-first birthday. Sometimes a lump sum was negotiated as a final payoff. Seventeen-

8. Scott, *Complete History of Fairfield County, Ohio*, p. 208.

9. "Incidents of Early Pioneer Life of Dyar Cobb."

10. Clarkson W. Weesner, ed., *History of Wabash County, Indiana* (Chicago and New York, 1914), II, p. 836.

11. *Ohio Cultivator*, VII (August 15, 1851), 245–47.

12. *Biographical Record of Bartholomew County, Indiana* (n. p., 1904), p. 335.

13. *History of McLean County, Illinois*, p. 768.

year-old Seth Lytle of Butler County, Ohio, bought time from his father for the sum of sixty-five dollars.[14]

Wages are a good index for both the social and economic position of farm boys in this period. A letter in a midwestern farm periodical declared in 1854 that the boy on the farm was the most abused creature of all, although the editor praised the teenager who could handle farm animals, plow, chop, and earn thirteen dollars per month for a nine-month period while attending school during the other three months. "What a chance here for poor boys!" concluded the editorial.[15]

Perhaps some teenagers commanded such wages before the Civil War, but it is likely that they were in their late teens or fast approaching twenty-one. Farm wages for boys during 1815–60 generally ranged between three dollars per month in the 1820's and eight dollars per month by 1860. The case of a farm boy employed by a semi-urban farmer suggests some of the factors governing the wage rate. Elnathan Kemper owned diversified land which included a farm, quarry, and fuel timber tract adjacent to Cincinnati. In 1816 he hired Chancy Morehouse for four dollars per month, to be paid in anything "that is to eat or wear." Moreover, Kemper could have the boy until his father returned; if the work was satisfactory, the boy might be permitted to go home every Saturday, a welcome treat since it was the only real break in the monotony of the farm.[16] The boy in this case could have come from a nearby farm, or, equally likely, from either Cincinnati itself or a small town nearby. Youths who lived in towns did work on surrounding farms during the busy summer season.[17]

Monthly wages over the decades remained fairly consistent, with no dramatic increase in either cash or "in kind" rates. At Pickaway County, Ohio, the twelve-year-old son of German immigrants worked in the early 1840's for $3.25 per month and gave the wages to his

14. *Portrait and Biographical Record of Ford County, Illinois*, pp. 306–7. Usually in such cases, a legal notice was posted for a time agreement: for example, "I HEREBY give my son, JONATHAN KENISON, his time, until he is of age; and I will not claim any of his earnings, or pay any of his contracting, from this date. DAVID KENISON. April 11, 1850." *Freeport Journal*, July 25, 1851.

15. *Indiana Farmer*, III (May 15, 1854), 249. Abuse and ill-treatment of farm boys in the East were a matter of concern: see *Moore's Rural New Yorker*, V (June 10, 1854), 181.

16. E. Kemper Daybook, entry of February 21, 1816.

17. For examples, see *History of Crawford County and Ohio*, pp. 804–5; Evans, ed., *Standard History of Ross County, Ohio*, II, p. 523.

parents.[18] At the same time farther west in Lawrence County, Illinois, a fifteen-year-old boy from Kentucky worked out seven months for thirty-one dollars, an average of a little over four dollars per month.[19] In terms of a high monthly wage, the *Indiana Farmer and Gardener* reported a farmer in 1842 paying boys seven dollars per month.[20]

During the 1850's the monthly rate shifted slightly upward but still remained basically between four and six dollars. The diary of Henry Parker Smith, a storekeeper and farmer at Schoolcraft, Michigan, noted a hired boy in his employ at five dollars per month.[21] In western Michigan at Ottawa County, a Dutch immigrant boy worked out as a farm chore hand at four dollars per month for a pleasant but poor farmer who proved unable to pay him.[22] In Illinois, where prairies were transformed into farms during the 40's and 50's, wages for hired boys remained fairly uniform. Thomas Wright worked in De Kalb County commencing in 1847 at the rate of four dollars per month,[23] while a Peoria County farmer wrote in a letter to his brother and sister that he had hired a fifteen-year-old boy to work the next three to five months at five dollars per month, with part of the pay to be in hay and "such things as his folks want."[24]

Wages might be increased for various reasons: experience, reliability, and greater capacity for work. If a boy returned to the same farmer the following season, he might expect a slightly higher rate; of course, as he grew older, the increase in pay might rapidly approximate what an adult farm hand received. During the late 1830's in Michigan, Henry Whitford hired out to a neighbor at the busy season for four dollars per month in his ninth year, five dollars in his tenth year, and six dollars in his eleventh year.[25] When a boy worked harvest fields, the monthly rate was one or two dollars more—but for this key season only.

Recently arrived immigrant boys soon discovered that they com-

18. *Portrait and Biographical Album of Woodford County, Illinois* (Chicago, 1889), p. 419.

19. Bateman and Selby, eds., *Illinois Historical. Lawrence County Biographical* (Chicago, 1910), p. 746.

20. *Indiana Farmer and Gardener*, I (September 20, 1845), 280–81.

21. Smith Diary, entry of April 9, 1850.

22. Wynard Wichers, "Autobiography of Jacob Van Zolenburg," *Michigan History*, XLVI (1962), 311–29.

23. Gross, *Past and Present of De Kalb County, Illinois*, II, p. 407.

24. Enoch Huggins to his brother and sister (Arena, Peoria County, Ill., July 22, 1860), Enoch Huggins Letter Collection.

25. *Commemorative Biographical and Historical Record of Kane County, Illinois*, pp. 383–84.

manded a wage less than that of a full hand, even though they might perform commensurate work. Joseph Reichert came to the United States in 1847 from Germany, taking the common route of his countrymen during the 1840's and 1850's via steamboat from the port of New Orleans up the Mississippi River. He arrived at St. Clair County in southwestern Illinois at harvest time and hired out on the second day to a farmer for six dollars per month, getting a few quick lessons in the art of grain cradling. While his pace in the harvest field was equal to the other hands, he learned that boys, by custom, never earned as much as regular hands.[26]

A farmer in central Illinois during the 1840's hired a young German lad at $5 per month; the wage was later increased to $7.50 as age and experience were acquired. His employer appeared eager to retain him, even to the point of paying him extra in the busy season and advancing a sum of money in order for the boy's parents to come to America:

> I am to give him during crop time and harvest, as much per month as young men of his age and experience in this section of the country are paid. I advance him the sum of sixty-five dollars to enable him to bring his father and family to this country, and he gives me his note with William Brink as security for the said sum advanced, which is to draw Int.[erest] at the rate of six per cent per annum from date till paid. . . .[27]

There were jobs for immigrant teenagers, but at lower wages than an American boy would accept. Henry Rudisill, an agent for the Baltimore-based firm of John Barr, directed the latter's holdings in the Fort Wayne area in the early 1830's. Rudisill expressed the need for more immigrants to be placed out where their labor was required to develop farm lands in the company's possession. In a letter to his employer he advised: ". . . hire some Germans from Germany and send them out to me German Emigrants are frequently arriving in Baltimore and would be glad of such an opportunity you can hire them much lower than the Americans and I think they are more to be depended on you can hire a good stout young man for 60 or 70 dols. a year."[28]

Farm boys, whether native born or immigrant, worked for wages

26. *History of St. Clair County, Illinois*, p. 272.
27. Lewis Morrison Ledger, pp. 43, 52, entries for Henry Kasten; p. 67, entry of October 31, 1848, with additional agreement of April, 1849.
28. As cited in Charles R. Poinsatte, "Fort Wayne, Indiana during the Canal Era, 1828–1855; A Study of a Western Community during the Middle Period of American History" (Ph.D. dissertation, University of Notre Dame, 1964), 79.

by the day, month, or year. Although cash might be tendered, wages were frequently in the form of credits to the father's debts or "payment of kind." Both methods were common; in the case of the credit system of payment, it often operated when the employer-farmer was also a tenant landlord or storekeeper. At the Western Reserve in northern Ohio, Thomas Clapp farmed land and ran a store during 1844–64. His account ledger shows that an individual was employed at fifty cents per day, while his son earned only forty-four cents—a good example of the wage differential, here only a few pennies, simply because of the boy's age. Neither father nor son actually saw the cash for the day's labor, since it was applied to credit debts at the store.[29]

Payment in kind prevailed as an acceptable wage substitute. Near Peoria in 1828–29, a fourteen-year-old husked corn the first season after the family's arrival from Ohio. The wages were entirely in corn —more valuable than money, since the seed was required for the family's own planting in the following season.[30] At Edgar County on the Illinois-Indiana state line, eleven-year-old David Collins, a boy who had lost his father, worked out three months for a neighbor in 1835, receiving fifty bushels of corn; the following year he received seventy-five bushels. Corn at this time was worth about ten cents a bushel.[31]

The main disadvantage with such payment occurred when the produce was sold, in many cases to a local storekeeper. One might suspect that a small boy enjoyed little economic leverage in bargaining with a shrewd country merchant. Often the youth ended up with credit toward store goods rather than cash. As a teenager John Smart of Franklin County, Ohio, worked out among farmers for 25 cents per day, or a monthly rate of $7.50 during the 1820's. On one occasion his pay for a day's work was three bushels of oats which he sold for ten cents a bushel, to be taken out in store goods.[32]

The wages for farm boys approximated half of what a regular hand received. Like adult hands, their rate of pay was greater in harvest season, with the increased pressure to get the crops in within a comparatively short time.[33] This was especially the case during the

29. Thomas J. Clapp Farm Accountbook, 1844–64, p. 13, entry of April 29, 1848.
   30. U. J. Hoffman, *History of La Salle County, Illinois* (Chicago, 1906), p. 72.
   31. *History of Edgar County, Illinois* (Chicago, 1879), p. 685.
   32. *History of Union County, Ohio* (Chicago, 1883), part V, p. 144.
   33. As an indication of wages during the harvest season, the prevailing rate

wheat cutting, where a few days meant the difference between a good
harvest or a heavy loss. Corn harvesting, on the other hand, was less
urgent, since the ears could be picked and husked as late as December. In short, if a farm boy hoped to make a "bit extra" for a brief
period, midsummer provided the opportunity. Yet the employer was
not necessarily obligated to give his chore boy anything extra in the
harvest season. As a rule, boys worked an average of six months per
year.[34] Wintertime might include several months of work, which usually dovetailed with the boy's schooling by an understanding in which
he worked during the early mornings, late evenings, or whenever
free.[35]

The orphan or otherwise destitute youth in an agricultural area
found himself in a position similar to that of the chore boy, and with
identical work duties. However, he was categorized as a bound-out
child in a society which met its social responsibility by making him
a public ward to people who promised to raise him and provide for
his basic wants until he reached age twenty-one. Edward Eggleston's
Hoosier Schoolmaster portrayed the negative aspects of this arrangement from the boy's viewpoint, although many orphan children
worked out their childhood with farmers under reasonably acceptable circumstances.[36]

There were good farmers who fulfilled this early civic duty with
clear conscience, and being bound out was not to be scorned, even if
the farmer did obtain an obviously cheap source of labor. Typical in
this period was the notion that the upbringing of a child in an agricultural surrounding was the best preparation for adult life.[37] An

in 1840 in Indiana was $8 per month, $10.50 in 1850, and $21.50 in 1860.
Conner, *Indiana Agriculture*, p. 19. Day wages in Illinois were $1.50 per day
and higher in harvest, according to Gerhard, *Illinois as It is*, pp. 296, 316. The
hired boy could expect one half or less of these amounts.

34. *Illinois Agricultural Transactions*, IV–1859–60, 235. See statement of
Caleb Letton, a farmer near Jacksonville, who worked 50 acres of wheat, corn,
oats, and potatoes: "I employ a boy about 6 months; pay about $12 per month.
This covers my expense besides my own labor."

35. An Indiana farmer had several young boys ages ten to twelve working at
chores during 1856 on his farm at Parke County. See clippings from *Indianapolis
Star*, June 11, 1930, Samuel Chew Madden Papers.

36. Edward Eggleston, *The Hoosier Schoolmaster* (Chicago, 1899), pp.
116–17. Eggleston was master of the vernacular and conveyed a realistic sense
of feeling in terms of a small boy's fears. For further information on the value
and relevance of Eggleston as a primary source, see Clarence A. Brown, "Edward
Eggleston as a Social Historian," *Illinois Historical Journal*, LIV (1961), 415–20.

37. The best source on this attitude is Richard H. Abbott, "The Agricultural
Press Views the Yeoman: 1819–1859," *Agricultural History*, XLII (1968), 35–48.

Illinois preacher in 1851 advised the following course of action for his son: "If I should die soon, you will hire him with a good farmer, or mechanic for a few years before going to college. This will make him independent for life. 16 or 17 is early enough for college."[38]

In attempting to find homes and employment for children the system had both positive and negative aspects, according to an observer in southern Ohio in 1818. Farms were small and hired hands were scarce, because few wished to hire out permanently for any length of time. To fill this labor gap, a child did not have to be an orphan but might instead come from a destitute family where apprenticeship or binding out provided an economic solution:

> Some of the children of the more necessitous families are bound out to labour for other people. The Scotch family, recently mentioned, have a boy and a girl living with them in this way. The indenture of the boy expires when he is twenty-one years of age; that of the girl at eighteen. They are clothed and educated at the expense of the employer. The boy, at the expiry of his contract, is to have a horse and saddle, of value at least 100 dollars. . . .[39]

In northern Ohio in the 1830's an English traveler recorded a similar situation:

> It is frequently very difficult for these farmers, who have much cleared land, to obtain help enough in busy seasons, as there is no class of people in Ohio to be depended upon for permanent labourers; there are no *roundsmen* standing at the corners of their streets all day idle. To secure against the inconveniences resulting from a scarcity of labourers, some of the farmers take children of about six or seven years old as apprentices for a certain term of years. The apprentice is clothed, sent to school, and provided for until he is capable of working on the farm, when his master or boss, as they call him, is amply repaid. Poor Emigrants from Europe frequently dispose of their younger children by apprenticing them to farmers or mechanics, since no premium is required.[40]

38. John Aiton to his wife (Chili, Ill., March, 1851), Aiton Family Papers.

39. James Flint, *Letters from America* (Edinburgh, 1822), in Reuben Gold Thwaites, *Early Western Travels 1748–1846* (Cleveland, 1904), IX, pp. 122–23. A farm background was considered as a healthy form of training, according to the advertisement of a tinner at Vincennes, Indiana. He requested an active lad of good morals and age fourteen to sixteen to be an apprentice: "One from the country would be preferred." *Western Sun and General Advertiser*, January 30, 1819.

40. Griffiths, *Two Years' Residence in the New Settlements of Ohio*, p. 82.

This twofold function served the agricultural frontier community: destitute children were given homes with the prospect of a reasonable start toward an occupation, while the farmer achieved a partial solution to his labor shortage.

Children who were apprentices or bound out on farms did not necessarily come from rural backgrounds. Disease on the "urban frontier" made a contribution of orphaned children to work on farms as public charges. Chicago in particular suffered from repeated waves of cholera during the 1840's and 1850's.[41] Among those hardest hit were the immigrants. For them Chicago served as a mecca in terms of job opportunities, as well as the gateway to the prairie lands in northern Illinois and southern Wisconsin.[42] In 1850 a cholera epidemic struck the city with such force that many children were left without parents. Placement of these orphans in homes was no problem, for they were contracted to foster parents in a region where labor was scarce. The foster parents agreed to raise the children, give them some schooling and ultimately small pieces of land.[43]

While the farmer who accepted a bound-out chore boy acquired a steady and much-needed hand on the farm, he had obligations to the youth for the labor and services rendered. He was expected to present a piece of land as partial remuneration when his charge reached the age of twenty-one. This custom was more common in earlier years when cheap, unimproved lands were still available, and it provided an inexpensive method of meeting obligations to a bound-out boy after years of service.[44] In general, the prevailing agreement for bound-out farm boys called for provision of clothes and board, schooling for a certain number of days or months per year, and a suit of clothes along with a horse, saddle, and bridle upon attaining twenty-one years of age.[45]

Certain aspects of bound-out labor leave a less attractive picture of

41. The disease seemed most prevalent among transients and immigrants, according to the *Chicago Daily Democrat*, July 6, 1849.

42. Norwegians concentrated in Chicago but also migrated to the countryside. Certain Illinois counties had large concentrations of them, including La Salle, Grundy, Kendall, De Kalb, and Lee. In northern Illinois, Boone, Stephenson, and Winnebago counties also experienced a heavy influx. Carlton C. Qualey, *Norwegian Settlement in the United States* (Northfield, 1938); see map facing p. 34, and p. 38.

43. Unonius, *Memoirs*, II, pp. 196–200.

44. *Portrait and Biographical Record of Delaware and Randolph Counties, Ind.*, p. 1067.

45. Bateman and Selby, eds., *Historical Encyclopedia of Illinois and Knox County* (Chicago and New York, 1899), pp. 865–66.

child welfare, especially for farm lads whose legal position as public charges offered little protection except to run away.[46] For example, William Leet, born in 1827 of parents in limited circumstances in Connecticut, was placed in the hands of a man who came to Peoria County, Illinois, to farm. He remained with the farmer for four or five years, but because his treatment was so poor, he left when he was a teenager and worked for a while to make sufficient money for the return trip to the East. Despite the unpleasant aspects of his first employment in the West, he preferred living in Illinois and returned to nearby Bureau County, where he assumed a job as a hired hand for ten dollars per month. His experience suggests one of the various circumstances under which a boy came west, used his employment as a farm hand to become familiar with a new area, and obtained a start.[47]

The treatment of boys varied but could be shocking, even by nineteenth-century standards. A cruel example occurred in Muskingum County, Ohio, where during the 1830's James Harmison was bound out at age nine. His employer was a farmer who hired the boy out to work in a nearby coal mine during the day while burdening him with farm chores in the evening.[48] As responsible guardians for those bound out to them, some farmers exhibited a crassness which bordered on exploitation. In 1836 an Ohio farmer went out to Indiana, bringing with him a ten-year-old boy for whom he was the guardian. The boy helped his employer at clearing the farm. When the farmer's family became ill and returned to Ohio, the lad was given the choice of remaining in Indiana on his own or returning to Ohio. He decided to stay despite his tender years![49]

Bound-out farm boys were not only overworked, but also subjected in some instances to social ostracism. In Illinois during the 1840's a young Yankee lad was bound out by his widowed mother to a farmer originally from South Carolina. The boy was to receive clothing, three months of schooling, and a horse with saddle and bridle at the end of his six-year service. The first five years were sheer misery for

---

46. Farmers might post a legal notice advising of a runaway farm boy for whom a reward was offered. The intent was not so much to get the boy back, but to serve notice that the farmer was no longer legally obligated for whatever happened: for example, see the legal notice of John Regan, a farmer at Lake County, Illinois, in the *Chicago Daily Democrat*, April 14, 1848.

47. *Biographical Record of Kane County, Illinois*, pp. 410–16.

48. *Portrait and Biographical Album of Champaign County, Ill.* (Chicago, 1887), pp. 669–70.

49. *Counties of Warren, Benton, Jasper and Newton, Indiana*, p. 345.

the boy. He was overworked, poorly fed, and provided with a total of forty-one days of schooling. Worse yet was the farmer's refusal to allow the boy to take his meals at the family table, a custom and privilege that hired farm help were normally accorded. When the mother ultimately learned of her son's plight, she had him relocated on another farm, where he worked this time at seven dollars per month.[50]

Comparison of the bound-out boy with the hired farm boy shows that both performed the usual variety of chores and tasks for their employers. The plight of an orphan or bound-out lad afforded little protection against harsh treatment, however, and avenues of recourse were exceedingly limited. In contrast, a neighbor or local boy on wages, when abused, refused to work or requested his parents to remove him from such employment. Whether bound out or working for wages, boys were pretty much the same everywhere: they were individuals with personal aspirations, dislikes, notions about right and wrong, and specific attitudes toward their employers. These boys quickly learned to sense their employers' attitudes toward them, knowing that these were usually an indication of the treatment they expected to receive: "July 1, 1845. Resolved never again to employ boys in planting corn & only such men as I am assured will do the work right."[51]

The northern Ohio farmer who made this observation in his farm ledger not only summed up his opinion of farm boys, but also suggested indirectly that young agricultural workers were not sufficiently enamoured with their tasks to do an outstanding job. Yet most boys came from a background where hard work and discipline were desirable traits. As boys, however, they would naturally prefer an employer who demanded the least of them. It is likely that certain farmers became known among the younger generation of the farm-

50. Bateman and Selby, eds., *Historical Encyclopedia of Illinois and Knox County*, pp. 864–65. The fact that farm help in America usually took their meals at the family table amazed foreign travelers. Typical was Alexander McKay, who observed: "The farmer who works side by side with his servant, tilling the same field with him, and coping with him constantly at the same work, could scarcely sit in one end of the house at his meals whilst the servant sat at his in the other. The farmer, his sons and servants, work together and eat together, living as nearly in a state of equality with each other as can be." *The Western World; or, Travels in the United States in 1846–47* (London, 1849, I, p. 223. The issue of Southerners vs. Yankees in the Midwest is examined by Richard L. Power, "Planting Corn Belt Culture: The Impress of the Upland Southerner and Yankee in the Old Northwest," *Indiana Historical Society Publications*, XVII (1953), 1–196.

51. Clapp Farm Accountbook, entry of July 1, 1845.

ing community as good men to work for, while others had notoriety
for the opposite reasons.

A self-analysis of a farm boy's personality comes from the autobiography of Hosea Stout, later a leader of the Mormon Church in
Utah. During the 1820's Stout was raised in Clinton County in southwestern Ohio, and at the age of fourteen he was hired out by his
father to a nearby farmer. He was poorly treated; when he told his
father so, the latter would not allow him to go back to the farm. Young
Stout was subsequently placed with a wealthy Quaker who proved to
be a stern yet fair-minded employer:

> My first work was to pick and burn brush. He [the Quaker] was a
> pushing man in business and well calculated to learn a 'spoilt child'
> to work I had to work hard earley [sic] and late I generally went home
> every Saturday to see my folks. He was the best man I ever lived with,
> good, kind and obliging [He] would exact all that I could do and no
> more & was a good judge of the amount of work a boy should do. I
> soon found that he only wanted the fair thing and would not be satis-
> fied without it. He never mislead, never repremanded or seemed to
> be dissatisfied with out I was to blame and I soon loved, obeyed, and
> respect[e]d him. . . .[52]

A basic change in the boy's attitude occurred when he was employed
by a man who treated him as a human being, a consideration that
some farmers overlooked or denied.

Poor treatment made an impression on young minds that were
prone to instant resentment. Two Indiana lads in the 1820's were employed on a neighboring farm clearing land and cutting trees. When
the work was finished, the well-to-do farmer refused to pay them, saying that "he was doing a very charitable act in allowing such poor
boys to even work for their board." The adolescent sense of propriety
was "stung to the quick by this harsh treatment"; they overreacted by
leaving home despite the protest of their father.[53] Others exhibited
tough-minded resolve in seeking a farm chore position in order to get
ahead. During the 1850's a sixteen-year-old Ohio boy requested his
father to send him to school. The parental response was that if a better education was desired than at home on the farm, he could "go
out and get it!" The boy took his father at his word and went out to
work among farmers. He ultimately became a schoolteacher, still

52. Reed A. Stout, "Autobiography of Hosea Stout, 1810 to 1835," *Utah
Historical Quarterly*, XXX (1962), 149–51.
53. *Pictorial and Biographical Memoirs of Elkhart and St. Joseph Counties, Indiana*, pp. 772–74.

working as a farm hand in summers until he commenced to read law.[54]

Young men wandered the countryside, going from region to region, and into the cities and out again to farms.[55] Why did they travel about at such a young age? Escapism might be one explanation. In the above case of the two Indiana youths, they were hurt and embittered by the miserly refusal of a neighbor to pay for rendered labor. Their decision to "up and leave home" started them on an odyssey and yet exposed them to a miserable experience. The two brothers set off from their Wayne County farm home with a few clothes, a pair of rude, home-made shoes, and the grand sum of $1.31. They suffered intensely from cold and hunger but refused to admit defeat by going home. At Fort Wayne the only immediately available employment was as a farm hand for two dollars per month; construction labor was then obtained on the Wabash and Erie Canal.[56]

Rivers served as avenues for boys who wandered in pursuit of work. An example of such movement is provided by a thirteen-year-old Indiana youth who was orphaned in 1841. He decided to set off on his own, and he worked at itinerant jobs in Iowa, Illinois, and Wisconsin. Lack of success explained his return to Indiana, where he worked out as a farm hand. After this brief stint he took off again for St. Louis, only to have his clothing stolen. With neither friends nor money it became necessary to get a job on the Mississippi chopping wood. He earned fifteen dollars, which enabled him to return to Indiana.[57]

Farm and itinerant labor was attractive to young boys who wanted to travel and see the region. Fourteen-year-old Joseph Brinton ran away from his foster home in 1852 and headed for Middleburg, Ohio, where he spent the summer working as a farm hand. He then picked up a job driving a herd of cattle from Ohio to Illinois; there he did a medley of jobs and even worked briefly as a carpenter.[58] Possession

54. *History of Clark County, Ohio* (Chicago, 1881), pp. 1037–38. It was quite common for school teachers to work out summers on farms, especially in the haying and grain harvest during July, August, and September.

55. *Cincinnati Daily Gazette*, November 1, 1844. According to this article, young men idled on street corners, engaging in smoking, rioting, and other malicious acts, when obstensibly they had come to the city to learn a trade. It is reasonable to assume that some were of rural origin and left the farm for one reason or another, only to end up in a large city.

56. *Pictorial and Biographical Memoirs of Elkhart and St. Joseph Counties, Indiana*, pp. 772–74.

57. *Counties of Warren, Benton, Jasper and Newton, Indiana*, p. 772.

58. Baughman, *History of Ashland County, Ohio*, p. 791. For a similar example of boys working brief stints at one location as a means of getting to the next, see *Biographical and Historical Record of Kosciusko County, Indiana*, p. 541.

of a horse facilitated the travels of a thirteen-year-old Illinois orphan in the 1850's. He was able to go to Kansas for a year; he then returned on horseback to Illinois, where he worked as a farm hand until the outbreak of the Civil War.[59]

Whatever personally motivated young boys to wander, travel descriptions and numerous guidebooks counseled the opportunities abounding in the West, especially for young, single men, along with the advice not to settle down immediately. Some of these boys migrated at a young age while in the employment of a westward-bound settler.[60] In some locales it was expected that boys in their late teens should go out to work, so that by age twenty-one they could marry and settle down.[61]

Family indifference or domestic strife induced more than one boy to leave home.[62] Not all who left home under a cloud found the situation on the outside any better. Witness the case of a Michigan teenager in the 1840's: Theodore Potter and a neighbor boy started off in the direction of Jackson, Michigan. They obtained employment chopping wood on a tenant farm owned by a Jackson hotelkeeper who refused to grant the boys an increase in wages. The pair made their way toward Ann Arbor but stopped en route at a farm whose owner needed two hired hands. That evening they helped him with the horses; afterward, at the dinner table, the farmer mentioned that he could pay only five dollars per month with board and laundry, too low a figure for the boys. The next morning they helped with the chores to pay for their board and night's lodgings and prepared to leave. The farmer at this point raised his offer to six dollars per month, but the boys went on their way. After seven days they admitted their poor judgment and returned home.[63] Perhaps this was typical of many youthful and short-lived excursions in the farm labor market.

Whatever the motivations for their wanderlust, the employment of boys as farm hands did not escape notice. A writer to the *Ohio Cultivator in* 1850 commented on these "agricultural youth" who left

---

59. *Portrait and Biographical Record of Hancock, McDonough, and Henderson Counties, Illinois,* pp. 474–75. Most biographical sources contain several examples of teenagers or young men who left their farm hand jobs to enlist in the Union Army at the time of the Civil War.

60. *Portrait and Biographical Album of Lenawee County, Mich.,* pp. 1068–69; *Portrait and Biographical Album of Woodford County, Illinois,* pp. 395–96.

61. *Portrait and Biographical Album of Champaign County, Ill.,* pp. 763–64.

62. *History of Menard and Mason Counties, Illinois* (Chicago, 1879), pp. 718–19; *History of Clark County, Ohio;* pp. 1037–38; *Pictorial and Biographical Memoirs of Elkhart and St. Joseph Counties, Indiana,* pp. 772–74.

63. *Michigan Pioneer Collections,* XXXV, pp. 410–11.

the farms and went elsewhere, working about sometimes as clerks or in taverns. He advised that farm chores be lightened in order to minimize the cause for leaving home.[64] His letter did raise a fundamental question about the norm of work expected of a farm boy.

Work days were long and arduous; four o'clock appears to have been a common hour for commencing the day's activities, even in winter. Fourteen-year-old Thomas Tyson in Tazewell County, Illinois, went to work on a farm in 1850. The day began early by going out with the farmer to milk six to eight cows, followed by a trek of ten miles to the timber tract where he and his employer split one hundred rails a day. The monotony of the work was apparent; not surprisingly, an occasional eighteen-mile trip to Pekin came as a welcome interlude.[65] In Clay County, Indiana, during the late 1840's, a youth named Oliver Griffith worked out his school years as a chore boy, apparently getting his board and expenses only. He arose early to do his chores because the school was a good five-mile trek from the farm.[66]

The feelings of a young boy hired out on a strange farm produced mixed emotions. Young Hosea Stout saw it as a lonely existence in Clinton County, Ohio, during the 1820's. Although this employment presented a challenge of new skills, it was admittedly not to his liking; after he went to work for the rich Quaker, conditions improved. His employment with this farmer contained a "wet and dry" agreement; that is, the boy counted the days and "took the weather as it came." If inclement conditions halted farm work, he was not docked pay for essentially workless days. During the course of the day he worked at virtually all tasks, including those normally assigned to a regular hand, with the distinction that the output was somewhat less.[67]

Boys of nine and ten could help in such field work as plowing, while by age fifteen they were expected to labor like an older hand in all kinds of work, including planting, hoeing, harvesting, haying, and husking.[68] Some farm chores were viewed with complete disgust. Just south of Indianapolis, John Duret owned a vegetable truck farm. A portion of his diary covering March through July, 1855, noted that

64. *Ohio Cultivator*, VI (March 1, 1850), 68–69.
65. *Portrait and Biograpical Album of McLean County, Illinois*, p. 756.
66. Travis, *A History of Clay County, Indiana*, II, pp. 54–55. Farmers did consider board as pay and assigned to it a variety of values. For example, in 1849 an Ohio farmer estimated its worth at twenty cents per day. *U.S. Pat. Office Report, 1849*, 186.
67. Stout, "Autobiography of Hosea Stout, 1810 to 1835," 149–50, 160–61.
68. *Ohio Cultivator*, VII (August 15, 1851), 245–47.

his hired boy spent almost all the time hauling manure in the wagon. The unpleasantness of this task was undoubtedly increased by the extreme temperature, for during that time one of the hands employed for spading work quit because he could not stand the sun.[69]

More than other states in the Midwest, Illinois and Indiana produced large amounts of corn. Labor was a factor in its cultivation, especially in the planting phase, commonly called corn dropping. Child labor, usually on a day basis, was important for this work. After the seed was dropped, a cover of earth was hoed over the furrow, while additional hoeing was required in season to remove weeds. According to the account ledger of an Illinois farmer in the 1840's, local children were employed in corn planting season to drop corn at twelve and a half cents per day.[70]

Men who achieved success in later years often mentioned their employment as farm boys, but few saw any importance in preserving a description of the whole process. Fortunately, a Minnesota pioneer left a lucid description of his own experience during the 1850's in Hennepin County. The account is also valuable because it depicts the way of life, in this instance of a hired boy, during the initial period of Minnesota's agricultural expansion for which evidence is otherwise sparse.

In 1858 fourteen-year-old Frank G. O'Brien was hired out by his father to work on a farm seven miles away. The boy was given pocket money for the tramp to the place of employment. Upon arrival Frank was extended the courtesy of the rain barrel, given a tin wash basin, and provided with homemade soap. He then received dinner, which included new potatoes, turnips, cabbage, fried salt pork, biscuits, milk and tea. The house had one story and a small attic; Frank's quarters there were reached by climbing boards nailed to the studding. This attic room served several functions. It was jointly occupied by Frank and several mice, and later in the season it was filled with seed corn, dried pumpkins, and bunches of sage.

The rule of order was "Early to Bed and Early to Rise." Work

69. John B. Duret, Jr., Diary, entries of March 1, 24, April 11, 1855. Operators of truck farms and nurseries hauled manure in carts or wagons from nearby towns and cities. This material was either spread on plots or stockpiled in heaps for future use. See Lorain, *Nature and Reason Harmonized in the Practice of Husbandry*, p. 409; Francis S. Holmes, *The Southern Farmer and Market Gardener* (Charleston, 1842), p. 2.

70. Morrison Ledger, pp. 41, 58, entries for Benjamin Monees, 1846–48, 1849. An authority on early Ohio agriculture notes that children were often used for this task. Jones, "Introduction of Farm Machinery into Ohio prior to 1865," 3.

duties included everything from dish washing to helping with the
threshing machine. His most distasteful job was going into the marshy
swamps for the cows, at the mercy of mosquitoes. Other disagreeable
tasks were churning butter and turning the grindstone for his employer, who made the task especially tiresome for the boy by pressing
the ax head or scythe blade firmly against the spinning stone. While
autumn was a beautiful time of the year, nothing was less enjoyable
than standing in cold marsh water raking hay. When it came to bringing in the hay, it was also Frank's job to clean out the loft so it would
be ready for the new load. Apparently he stayed through the harvest
of the following year, for he described the hired hands getting the
scythes out of storage and sharpening them, a task which occupied a
good portion of one day.[71]

Such was the work routine for many midwestern farm boys. The
farm was never a simple economic unit, but a complex of numerous
small tasks that were invariably handled by hired chore boys. Despite
the youth of these lads, their workload was heavy and tedious. This
brigade of agricultural laborers earned considerably less than the
regular adult hired hands. Boys were sometimes taken advantage of
by employers, with little protection from the farming community except what parents themselves demanded for their sons. Economic
necessity forced many of them into this work; yet they complained
only to a certain point, because the loss of the job meant less money
for the family in debt or dependent on their wages. Like farm girls,
these young hired boys filled a distinct niche among frontier agricultural laborers.

71. Frank G. O'Brien, *Minnesota Pioneer Sketches from the Personal Recollections and Observations of a Pioneer Resident* (Minneapolis, 1904), pp.
48–54. For a similar list of a boy's work duties on a Wisconsin farm in the
1850's, see Muir, *Story of My Boyhood and Youth*, p. 203.

Hired Girl

I am all tired out I have been telling Sylvester this long I
could not do so much housework he got a girl sixteen she staid
a week I did not like her and so I sent her home I had all the
work to do but washing dishes [;] them she did not half wash.[1]

HIRED GIRLS were essential domestic assistants on
farms, especially during spring and summer, when farmers' wives
were burdened with the added toil of cooking huge meals and washing clothes for the hired hands. Usually in their teens and still attending school, local girls obtained immediate employment with
farmers who could afford this help for their wives. The agricultural
press strongly urged the employment of girls, whenever possible, to
lighten the household duties of busy farm wives.[2] Although a common complaint was incompetence, girls were in keen demand, and
most farmers' wives were frankly glad to get them.[3]

This shortage of help was common in most parts of the Midwest.
Early Ohio newspapers appealed to girls to work on farms,[4] while
Michigan pioneers in the first settlements in the 1820's wisely brought
hired girls with them from the East.[5] Settlers in sparsely populated
territories invariably discovered no available help for their wives: a
pioneer wife at Peoria County, Illinois in the 1830's described this
discouraging situation and had little hope of finding any help.[6] The

1. Mary Huggins to My Dear Friends (Farmington, Fulton County, Ill.,
January 29, [1858–60?]), Huggins Letter Collection.
2. *Ohio Cultivator*, V (February 1, 1849), 45–46; *Ohio Valley Farmer*, I
(November, 1856), 105–6; *Michigan Farmer*, as cited in *Indiana Farmer*, III
(September 1, 1854), 366; IV (December 15, 1854), 58.
3. *Ohio Cultivator*, XI (May 1, 1855), 140.
4. Dickore, *General Joseph Kerr of Chillicothe, Ohio*, p. 93.
5. *Michigan Pioneer Collections*, IV, p. 402; for a similar case, see Hubbell,
Dodge County, Wisconsin, I, pp. 69–70.
6. Sarah Aiken to Julia Keese (Peoria County, Ill., January 24, 1834). The
conclusion of Reverend John G. Bergen at Springfield, Illinois, was similar: see
J. Van Fernstermaker, "A Description of Sangamon County, Illinois, in 1830,"
Agricultural History, XXXIX (1965), 139–40.

general shortage of domestic help was obvious in the case of a Wisconsin farmer at Kenosha County in the 1840's. He asked a girl to work on his farm, but as emphasis of her casual concern toward the job, she merely consented at least to discuss the possibility with his wife.[7]

Community assistance for the local family in times of illness or misfortune seemed to be a standard pioneer characteristic. Women of the area assisted their neighbors in such instances, but not over a prolonged period.[8] Farmers whose wives were ill or otherwise incapacitated sought hired girls or women to assist with the domestic duties of the household. Such was the plight of a frontier preacher who farmed as a sideline at St. Clair County, Michigan, during the early 1840's. His wife was quite sick, and it was essential to hire a girl to help with the work. According to his calculations, employment of such a person amounted to eighty dollars a year with board; consequently, his letter to the American Home Missionary Society requested an increase in his allotment to cover this added expense.[9]

Local girls were usually hired on neighboring farms, but farmers also turned to towns and cities for their domestic help on occasions. A Minnesota farmer near Lakeland drove his wagon to St. Paul, where he employed a Swedish immigrant girl of sixteen. Apparently her family was there, for she accompanied him on a trip into the city the following month.[10] So acute was the problem that employment agencies in large midwestern cities channeled girls and women out to jobs on farms where they were needed. An Illinois farmer arranged through a St. Louis agent to have a woman sent up to his place for employment. He originally requested a younger girl but acquiesced in his agent's recommendation of an older woman who had experience among different families. As a domestic in the city for eight dollars

7. Burgess Diary, entry of March 22, 1845.
8. Blanchard, ed., *Counties of Clay and Owen, Indiana*, p. 727; William Henry Perrin, ed., *History of Bond and Montgomery Counties, Illinois* (Chicago, 1882), part I, p. 251.
9. Reverend Luther Shaw to Corresponding Secretary (Algonac, St. Clair County, Mich., December 1, 1842), American Home Missionary Letters. For similar examples, see Farmer's Memorandum Book, Stark County, Ohio, entry of October 26, 1848; Levi Countryman Diary, entries of July 28, August 1, 2, 6, September 14, October 1, 1860.
10. Rodney C. Loeher, *Minnesota Farmers' Diaries* (St. Paul, 1939), III, pp. 184–85. This was also an opportunity for the hired girl to have some recreation and get away from the farm for a spell. When farmers went visiting, such trips might include the hired girl: a farmer at Kent County, Michigan, took his children and the hired girl on a New Year's Day visit to his nearby father. William C. Slayton Diary, entry of January 1, 1859.

per month, this woman could have easily found a job, wrote the agent, but a country position was more to her liking even though it paid only six dollars per month. The agent's bill for this service was two dollars.[11] At the Lake Erie cities of Sandusky and Cleveland, employment agencies specialized in labor requests and placed men, women, and children of all nationalities for jobs in the towns or countryside.[12]

Scarcity of hired girls was critical, both in the countryside and in the cities, observed the *Illinois Daily Journal* in 1853: "Woman's labor is also needed in the West.—Thousands upon thousands of women and girls can find full and profitable employment in families in the cities and country. And they can earn means to make themselves comfortable, and lay up, if they choose. Women who understand house-work need not be out of employment a day in the West."[13] A method of expediting the hiring of girls and women, especially those of foreign birth, was to meet them at ports of entry and arrange their passage westward—in the 1850's, for example, from New York to Illinois: "A merchant of Sangamon County, (who is he?) while in New York recently, engaged a number of German girls, who had recently arrived there in need of situations, to come west and live in the families of Sangamon county farmers, who are equally in need of such help. The merchant paid the passage of the girls to the West, and they were expected by the Eastern cars yesterday on the way to their prairie homes."[14]

It is well known that men outnumbered women on the agricultural frontier—a factor which made young women scarce for employment because they usually married early in life.[15] A German farmer at Calumet County, Wisconsin, in the 1840's advised his countrymen to bring a wife to America rather than looking for one after getting here.[16] And

11. I. B. Burbbayge to David King (St. Louis, June 27, 1843), Folder 34, King Family Papers.

12. *Daily Commercial Register*, April 30, 1858; *Cleveland Herald*, August 22, 1845, as cited in *Annals of Cleveland*, XXVIII, p. 95; *Cleveland True Democrat*, March 8, November 6, 1851, as cited *ibid.*, XXXIV, p. 87; *Cleveland Leader*, April 1, 1858, as cited *ibid.*, XLI, p. 128.

13. *Illinois Daily Journal*, July 12, 1853.

14. *Ibid.*, April 2, 1855. In eastern cities like New York, charitable societies raised funds through donations and financed the westward trip for young girls seeking jobs and homes, especially in the Midwest: see Carter Goodrich and Sol Davison, "The Wage-Earner in the Westward Movement," *Political Science Quarterly*, LI (1936), 95–96.

15. The census report in 1860 made specific mention of this deficiency: Michigan had 40,000 more males than females, while Illinois registered 92,000 more men than women! *Preliminary Report on the Eighth Census*, p. 9.

16. DeHaas, *Nordamerika, Wisconsin*, II, p. 32.

for the bachelor on the frontier it was frankly more practical to marry, when possible, then to hire a woman to care for the domestic aspects of his farm. Droll and without flattery, in the 1830's a young farmer at Lenawee County, Michigan, informed his mother and brother to expect a change in his status with the next letter: "It is very likely that the next letter you receive from me will inform you I am married as I find it difficult to hire a woman to do my work in the house."[17]

For those who could not arrange such a situation by themselves, a general appeal for aid was the solution. In 1857 a lonely Illinois farmer made his wish known to the editor of the *Chicago Daily Democrat*, who obligingly printed it:

> I want a small favor of you, if you are willing to grant it. I am a widower living alone, with two small children to care for. I have no housekeeper, nor do I know of one to be had in these parts suitable for me, and as your city is full of women, I thought you might know of some good housekeeper that would prefer a country life. I want one from 30 to 40 years old, if such can be had, but a younger one would do. I don't want one that can't milk cows and do such out-door work. I am a farmer and live in farmer style, plenty to eat and drink and wear. I will hire or take one for a wife, if we can agree to it; I don't care about riches, only, in the person I get. If you know of any that can be had for love or money, tell them to write to me at this place, or you may write for them and let me know where they can be found, and I will answer them and come see them. . . .[18]

Scarcity of girls and women for hire seemingly became acute by the 1840's and 1850's, at least to the degree that the topic appeared more often in the agricultural press. During this same period, positions came to be filled increasingly by immigrant rather than American girls. Considerable soul-searching accompanied this change: where the traditional, native-born help had often belonged to the community, the foreign born were alien and therefore different in the eyes of many Americans, whose reaction was one of prejudice.[19] Others accepted the changing situation; Josephine Bateham, whose husband edited the *Ohio Cultivator*, declared that since fewer American girls

17. Louis L. Tucker, "The Correspondence of John Fisher," *Michigan History*, XLV (1961), 227–28.

18. *Chicago Daily Democrat*, August 1, 1857.

19. *Cleveland Herald*, October 5, 1847, as cited in *Annals of Cleveland*, XXX, pp. 70–71.

wished to serve as menials on farms, their places would be taken by foreign-born help.[20]

Despite growing employment of foreign girls, it should be emphasized that American girls in many areas continued to work out on farms. This helped to retain an important employer-employee relationship involving the status of the hired girl. Like the hired hand, the farm girl was generally treated as a member of the family. Matthias Dunlap, near Chicago, had his elderly parents living on an adjacent farm with a hired girl to assist them. Subtle appreciation of the relationship is perceived in his casual reference to them and the girl as "Three of them in the family"; this was probably true in countless other cases.[21] Immigrant girls who were new in America soon learned to take their place at the table and eat with the family once the food was served.[22] A sense of fairness and decency ought to be the prevailing standard, suggested the *Michigan Farmer*:

> Why not permit your *hired girls*, when work is over, to sit in the same room with you and your children? There they might learn what is good and useful, and go into the world to make virtuous and useful wives and mothers. . . . None of us know what may be the future situation of our children. They too may at some future day be apprentices and hired domestics, and as we would they should be treated, so should we treat those whom misfortune or necessity has thrown into our employ.[23]

Occasionally there were cases where help was poorly treated on farms: "How cruel and wicked, then, is that prejudice that teaches persons to look down on the *hired girl*, when, in many instances, she is the most important and indispensable member of the family, and not unfrequently the most intelligent!"[24] But the scarcity of girls made it unwise and impractical to take advantage of them for any length of time. Job opportunities were only too plentiful, and girls poorly treated could easily terminate such abuse by quitting.[25]

Spring and summer were the busy seasons, and the wise farmer hired his help early or kept those who had worked through the winter. With an eye to the approaching warm months, a Michigan farmer

20. *Ohio Cultivator*, XI (May 1, 1855), 140.
21. Dunlap Letterbook, 1853–55, p. 232, August 1, 1855; for a similar remark, see Letterbook, 1852–53, p. 713, April 21, 1853.
22. Griffiths, *Two Years' Residence in the New Settlements of Ohio*, pp. 80–82.
23. *Michigan Farmer*, VIII (February, 1850), 59.
24. *Indiana Farmer*, II (March 1, 1853), 206.
25. Ellet, *Summer Rambles in the West*, pp. 222–23.

commented that he had a hired hand and a cook, the latter whom he especially hoped to retain through the summer months despite her announced intent to leave in the spring.[26] Hired girls proved worth their weight in gold during the harvest, when the employment of extra hands increased the workload of the farmer's wife. The harvesting crews had to be fed, and meals were often sent out to the field several times during the day.[27] An Illinois farmer, Charles Bartlett, whose farm was located thirty miles north of Chicago, was fortunate in 1836 to find a girl to work for him during the haying season. But his luck deserted him the following year in July when the wheat was in harvest; "I went up to Lovejoys after a girl got none," he recorded in his diary.[28] When a girl was hired merely for the harvest weeks, the wage rate was slightly higher. During 1855 a farmer in western Illinois employed a hired girl for twenty-three and a half weeks at seventy-five cents per week; however, in late August, when he needed another girl for only a week in peak harvest time, he had to pay her a higher rate of $1.50.[29]

Harvest time was a critical period in the farmer's year, and inadequate help when the wheat was ripe for cradling could be disastrous. Normally women did not engage in field tasks. Harriet Martineau toured the United States, including parts of the Midwest, in 1834–35, and subsequently stated that general custom frowned upon women performing heavy work (except Negro slaves in the South).[30] The *Prairie Farmer* took a similar view of women working the field and claimed that only women of German birth did such labor.[31] Yet it is unreasonable to assume that only immigrant women and girls labored in the fields. The harvest of 1839 in central Michigan was so great, reported a correspondent, that there was not enough help to handle it: "At this moment every man and boy, and even women are actively engaged in cradling, raking, binding and shocking the golden harvest."[32]

26. Charles Fowle to His Brother and Sister (Moscow, Mich., February 10, 1839), Box 1, Folder 1835–43, Benjamin Densmore Papers.
27. Smith, *Recollections of the Pioneers of Lee County*, pp. 449–50.
28. Bartlett Diary, entries of August 3, 1836; July 19, 1837.
29. C. R. Doringh Accountbook, 1852–56, pp. 21–22, entry of September 1, 1855, and sheet of 1855 wages.
30. Martineau, *Society in America*, II, p. 243.
31. *Prairie Farmer*, XI (January, 1851), 38. For examples, see Weesner, ed., *History of Wabash County, Illinois*, II, pp. 721–22; *Biographical Record of Henry County, Illinois*, pp. 345–46.
32. *Western Farmer and Gardener* (Cincinnati), I (October, 1839), 60. Women who performed field work earned varying wages of 31 to 62.5 cents

European-born girls and women often secured farm employment
once they arrived in America; positions were usually filled by those
from Germany or the British Isles.[33] Hired German help, male and
female, were widely acknowledged as competent and hard working,
even by skeptics who subsequently changed their opinion.[34] During
the 1830's Germans were advised of the job opportunities, especially
in the Midwest, and an early guidebook, Heinrich Christian Gerke's
Der Nordamerikanische Rathgeber (1833), pointed out how to make
money while going about to look things over—according to the German expression: "ich muss mich umsehen." Both farm hands and
hired girls engaged in "umsehen" or looking around, said Gerke, but
for the girls it was primarily a case of looking for a future husband
before they became too old.[35]

One guarantee to efficient labor was to engage a farm girl at an
early age. An entry from Calvin Fletcher's diary at Indianapolis in
1840 described how one went about this matter. He approached a
Mr. Bates, who in turn inquired of a German named Frederick in
an effort to locate any German girls twelve to fourteen years old who
were willing to hire out. Fletcher wanted one "to live with us till she
is of age—A large n° of Dutch have recently come to the community—
I must have femal(e) help—& there (is) no better way than to take
a good girl—& pay her well til she is of age—"[36]

German farmers solved their labor shortage by financing the passage of prospective hired help from their native country. In the 1850's
a German near Tipton, Indiana, considered advancing funds for a girl
to be brought over to work on his farm: "If only the Baeder girl were
here to help mother. I don't know, should I pay her passage money
and agree to an annual payment of $10 to the elderly Baeder as long

per day: see Lesher Farm Accounts, Tally Sheet dated July 11, 1846; Samuel
Miller Accountbook, 1831–49, p. 102.

33. Between 1820 and 1860 the predominant age group of girls and women
arriving in America was fifteen to thirty, and many listed themselves as servants.
Preliminary Report on the Eighth Census, pp. 13–18.

34. Christiana Holmes Tillson, *A Woman's Story of Pioneer Illinois* (Chicago,
1919), pp. 110–11. Not all were satisfied with the alleged competence of
Germans: see "Memoirs, Record of Events in the Life and Times of Edward
William West, Belleville, Illinois, A. D. 1895," *Illinois Historical Journal*, XXII
(1929), 244–45; Dunlap Letterbook, 1852–53, p. 598, February 9, 1853.

35. Heinrich Christian Gerke, *Der Nordamerikanische Rathgeber* (Hamburg,
1833), pp. 308–10.

36. Fletcher Diary, entry of July 17, 1840. Another method was the newspaper advertisement: "WANTED—A German Girl to do the work of a small
family. For one steady and trusty a good and permanent situation is offered.
A 'Protestant' girl preferred." *Daily Commercial Register*, September 14, 1854.

as she is in our service. She has repeatedly written us and pleaded that
we pay the passage for her and her aged brother; she would be glad
to work at anything she could do. Both would be useful to us, if they
kept their promise and worked for us several years."[37]

Language was a major barrier until English was learned. A Norwegian minister, the Reverend Duus at Waupaca, Wisconsin, commented on the Scandinavian help in his area: ". . . farmers, craftsmen,
young laborers, and servant girls, especially the last, earn from one
to two dollars per week. As soon as the servant girls can speak some
English and if they are reasonably diligent in their work, they receive
wages of two dollars a week."[38] In southeastern Wisconsin near Milwaukee, Swedish and Norwegian girls were much in demand, the
Norwegians especially because they were considered quicker and
more energetic in their work.[39] The Reverend Duus spoke of his own
problem in obtaining a Scandinavian girl to assist his ill wife: ". . . it
is hard to obtain a reliable hired girl. We have both to beg and to pay,
and pay well. Recently we were very happy at the prospect of getting
a genuine Norwegian girl for a dollar and a half a week, but yesterday we received word that she would rather go to work for some
Americans in order to learn the American language."[40]

Some immigrant girls preferred to work with their own countrymen because of the language difficulty; a fifteen-year-old Norwegian
named Anna Hedalen worked briefly as a house servant in town—an
unpleasant experience, for she fretted about not understanding what
was said. With opportunities prevailing in the countryside, she gladly
went to work for a Norwegian farmer whose language caused her no
worry. From 1857 to 1860 Anna remained with Norwegian farmers
in Wisconsin, and her account indicates what was expected of an immigrant girl hired out to fellow countrymen. From the onset her job
was not so much as a hired girl in the house but as what she termed
"Handy-Andy" for the men in the fields, including manual labor during harvest, when she rode the back of the reaper raking hay on the

37. Andressohn, "The Kothe Letters," 178. Some cautioned against this
approach and recommended the employment of American-born laborers. Nicholas
Hesse, *Das Westliche Nordamerika* (Paderborn, 1838), pp. 153–55.
38. Olaus Frederik Duus, *Frontier Parsonage: The Letters of Olaus Frederik
Duus* (Northfield, 1947), pp. 13–14. Hereafter cited as Duus, *Letters, 1855–
1858*. Norwegian girls were also urged to work for American families so as to
learn more quickly American ways of housekeeping. *Daily Commercial Register*,
July 5, 1849.
39. Unonius, *Memoirs*, II, pp. 112–13.
40. Duus, *Letters, 1855–1858*, pp. 62, 69.

platform like any common harvest hand. Rainy days she devoted to domestic chores like baking and churning.[41]

Whatever the reaction of American society to greater numbers of immigrants working on farms, their presence was important in a period when agriculture was changing. Specialization in farming, which occurred earlier in the eastern states, began in the Midwest during the 1840's and 1850's, a period coinciding with heavy European migration to America. Already the foreign born were proving their worth in such fields as horticulture, nursery cultivation, and truck farming. Dairy production was well suited for the Midwest, especially Illinois and Wisconsin, where experienced women were needed, according to the *Illinois Farmer*: "What we want is a supply of young women from the butter regions of Eastern States to come here and also from the Dairy Districts of England, Scotland, Ireland and Germany. Such women, accustomed to country life, would find full and profitable employment in the families of our farmers—should they choose to accept such situations. . . ."[42]

A common chore on farms was milking the cows. Men from the East and New England assumed this chore, while those with a southern background scorned it. In central Ohio during the 1830's Martin Welker recalled that women generally did the milking—except in Yankee families, where men and boys assumed the task, popularly called "pailing."[43] However, in central Illinois, according to one early observer, southern views were stronger: "No matter if there *were* three or four men about the house, and but one hard worked woman, the former couldn't degrade themselves by adopting this Yankee innovation. I have frequently known young men, when contracting to work by the month on farms, to ask if they were expected to milk. If this was required, either negotiations were broken off, or several dollars were added to the price."[44]

41. Erling Ylvisaker, *Eminent Pioneers: Norwegian-American Pioneer Sketches* (Minneapolis, 1934), pp. 43–45. A Wisconsin boy, raised in Jefferson County during the 1850's described Norwegian girls on his father's farm: 'The girls were strong and buxom, used to hard work, and made excellent help." "Autobiography of Alexis Crane Hart," p. 22.

42. *Illinois Farmer*, II (September, 1857), 209. This article conceded that many girls preferred employment in the city rather than the countryside.

43. Welker, *Farm Life in Central Ohio Sixty Years Ago*, p. 51.

44. *History of Sangamon County, Illinois*, p. 176. An Illinois woman supported the men on this issue: "I milk our cows myself, for I despise to see a man sitting under a cow milking. I think it is a woman's work." Charles Coleman, "Coles County in the 1840's," *Illinois Historical Journal*, XLV (1952), 172.

The question existed in most areas, but lines of demarcation were not always well defined. "A servant girl gets from one to two dollars a week, and has no outside work except to milk the cows," advised Ole Rynning's guidebook for Norwegians, based on personal observations of life in east central Illinois during the late 1830's.[45] A Wisconsin man recalled from his own youth in the 1850's that a girl easily obtained work at seventy-five cents a week, but milking and gardening were required of her.[46] In northern Indiana at LaPorte, a traveler observed: "Girls have an easy time out here. Men carry in the wood and water and even do the milking. Big girls get $1.50 per week, if they do nothing but please the children."[47]

Ultimately, whether or not the hired girl did the milking was a matter of local option, but many assumed the responsibility, especially if the men spent the full day in the field. Still it was a smoldering issue of contention, as revealed in a letter from an Illinois woman:

> The difficulty is with hired hands;—they generally do as little work as possible, always grumble when they are not surfeited with the best cooking we can get up for them—their whole object being to live well, do little work and get high wages;—I say the difficulty is to get these men to do the milking. Oh, they are above that! They will see us picking our way through the mud and weeds to get to the cows, and they will lay about, perhaps smoking, while we milk and afterward get their breakfast or supper for them. Now this is what we do not like.[48]

Most girls signed on with the understanding that milking came with their assigned duties. A letter in 1852 from an Illinois farmer to a prospective hired girl offered the terms of employment, with specific reference to the eight cows on the farm: "We understand that it is your intention to do house work the present spring & summer. Should this be the case we would be pleased to engage you & will pay you $1.50 per week. Should you conclude to come we will send a team over when you are ready besides our own family we have two men & milk some 8 cows—Pleas[e] let us know at your earliest convenience. . . ."[49]

According to medical opinion of the period, only women should milk the cows because the hired hands carried smallpox after working with the horses. Anthony Benezet, *The Family Physician* (Cincinnati, 1826), p. 270.

45. Blegen, "Ole Rynning's True Account of America," 254–55.
46. Roujet D. Marshall, *Autobiography of Roujet D. Marshall* (Madison, 1923), I, pp. 105–6.
47. Sue I. Silliman, "Overland to Michigan in 1846," *Michigan History*, V (1921), 431.
48. *Illinois Farmer*, III (October, 1858), 157.
49. Dunlap Letterbook, 1852–53, p. 198, May 3, 1852.

The activities of the hired girl on the farm are easily summarized, for the work was of standard household routine. The hired girl did not eliminate but reduced the monotony of the farm wife's chores, according to the *Ohio Cultivator* in 1854:

> She was expected to act as a general assistant in all the operations of the kitchen—washing dishes, ironing, baking, sweeping, making beds and cooking meals. On Mondays she was expected to 'take the brunt' of the washing, while the good wife 'did the work.' These, together with helping the boys to milk the cows night and morning, and sitting down to a little sewing in the afternoon, made up the usual circle of her labors.[50]

The hired girl could count on two aspects of her employment with little variation: getting up early and cooking three or more meals each day. Early morning rising was standard, and in harvest the customary hour for beginning the day came at 4:00.[51] The day was long and ended late: "The women work much harder than the men do. A man can get corn & pork enough to last his family a fortnight for a single day's work, while a woman must keep scrubing from morning till night the same in this country as in any other."[52]

The task of cooking for several hired hands and washing their laundry was sheer drudgery in the opinion of an early Illinois farm wife: "Our family then consisted—besides your father, Uncle Robert, and myself—of Loomis, Porter, Plummer, and Horn, who worked on the farm; six hungry men to be fed three times a day; besides which your father had told all but Porter that they could have their washing done in the house. . . ."[53] Washing of clothes was a monopoly of the hired girl—whether she liked it or not.[54] Another chore was looking after the children, which enabled the farm wife to attend to other matters. Matthias Dunlap had six small sons and a daughter who were well, happy, and running about the house, keeping two hired girls busy.[55] Girls rarely stepped into a farm household and assumed extensive responsibility; rather, in the words of the *Ohio Cultivator*,

50. *Ohio Cultivator*, X (August 1, 1854), 234. Others also recommended that the farm wife supervise the girl's work, rather than turning her loose to do whatever she wanted. *Indiana Farmer*, IV (December 15, 1854), 58.

51. *Wisconsin Farmer*, VIII (July, 1856), 291–92.

52. Charles R. Clarke, "Sketch of Charles James Fox Clark, with Letters to His Mother," *Illinois Historical Journal*, XXII (1930), 563.

53. Tillson, *A Woman's Story of Pioneer Illinois*, p. 114.

54. *Ohio Cultivator*, X (August 1, 1854), 234; *History of Sangamon County, Illinois*, pp. 191–92.

55. Dunlap Letterbook, 1852–53, p. 210, November 7, 1853; see also Ylvisaker, *Eminent Pioneers*, p. 5.

they served primarily as general helpers with diverse chores: "Her service was not positively slavish, but still her privileges were not very extensive. During the intervals of work hours, the mistress contrived to have some odd jobs inviting attention, and though she might not have *said* so, yet she *looked* a kind of reproach against allowing any precious time to run to waste."[56]

Measuring the dependability of the hired girl is a wry analysis, for commentary came mostly from one side—that of the employer—and was not always objective. The chief complaint was that girls worked only a short time and then married. A traveler through southern Indiana in 1836 stopped at an inn and inquired about the availability of hired girls in the area: "This Landlady told me that it was hard to keep them. They go away when they please, And never fail when they have earned money enough to buy a piece of finery, to go home to their friends, with the proceeds of their labour, upon their head and shoulders. They are on the constant lookout for husbands, and consequently do not engage to labour, for any one except by the week, or some other short period."[57] Hired girls whose minds were intent on marriage acted highly independent, noted a German traveler in Illinois in the 1850's. Since help was scarce, the farmer was wise not to object strenuously if his hired girl wanted to receive visits from her lover, lasting sometimes to midnight, or if she desired the use of a buggy or riding horse to attend a dance.[58]

The agricultural frontier was always conducive to early marriages. Matches between hired hands and hired girls on local farms were common, according to an Indiana man raised in Bartholomew County in the 1850's. These early working associations provided the opportunity to learn how to get along together; soon the couple began to save their wages for the future.[59] Young farmers occasionally married the help employed on the family farm. At Jefferson County, Wisconsin, during the 1850's, Alexis Hart related how his uncle needed a hired girl on the farm and went to a neighbor three miles up the road,

56. *Ohio Cultivator*, X (August 1, 1854), 234.

57. Herbert A. Kellar, "Diaries of James D. Davidson (1836) and Greenlee Davidson (1857) during Visits to Indiana," *Indiana History*, XXIV (1928), 133. The *Michigan Farmer* estimated that girls remained at a job for only a couple of years and then married; I (August 1, 1843), 95. For an example of a girl who worked only six months, see Nathan Pierce Accountbook, 1848–60, p. 96.

58. Busch, *Travels between the Hudson & the Mississippi 1851–1852*, pp. 256–57.

59. Myrtillus N. Satterthwaite and Martha C. Bishop, *Hoosier Courtships in the Horse and Buggy Days* (Greenfield, 1943), pp. 32–33.

bringing back the daughter. That encounter was the beginning of a romance which finally resulted in matrimony.[60]

Farmers were often irritated with girls who did not work in a steady or competent manner.[61] A frequent notation in farm account-books was "lost time," indicating that a day off was taken by the help. Lewis Morrison, a farmer at Washington, Illinois, hired Louise Bruns in 1851 at one dollar per week. At one point she was planning to leave for St. Louis but apparently changed her mind. Matters had not improved by the next year, when Morrison decided to retain her with some qualifications. A copy of the agreement was transcribed into his ledger with the stipulation that ". . . you are to give us notice of two weeks before leaving such is the full understanding."[62] Some excuses were valid: in May, 1849, Phebe Palmer commenced work by the week for Nathan Pierce in Calhoun County, Michigan. Shortly afterward the girl's sister became ill; when her condition became worse by August, Phebe quit in order to take care of her.[63] Illness of the girl herself was also an unavoidable cause.[64]

The farm girl was well advised to choose her company carefully so as to avoid interference with work. Some actions farmers did not tolerate. In 1853 Matthias Dunlap's German hired girl went to a dance, stayed out all night, and returned at noon the following day. He fired her.[65] The *Indiana Farmer and Gardener* advised farm girls to avoid the dandies and transients; rather, the company of a good farmer's boy or industrious mechanic was worth far more than what easily came along.[66] Such advice sometimes contained more than a degree of sobering truth. A fifteen-year-old farm girl in Lee County, Illinois, in 1849 appeared to have left her job without notice, but eventually it was discovered that she had been murdered. The explanation for

60. "Autobiography of Alexis Crane Hart," p. 23.

61. This was a problem for both farmers and city dwellers who employed girls; one solution was a certification system with a record of previous employment, statement of good character, etc. See *Daily Commercial Register*, July 14, 1853; June 26, 1854.

62. Morrison Ledger, p. 93, entry for Louise Bruns during 1851–52.

63. Nathan Pierce Accountbook, 1848–60, p. 3, entries of May 17, August 11, 1849.

64. For example, see Morrison Ledger, p. 78. entries of September, 1854; December 1, 1854; March, 1855. Local physicians treated the hired help of farmers, including farm girls: see Dr. Orin Sheppard Campbell Accountbook, II, p. 44. Campbell was a doctor in Pike County, Illinois, during the 1840's and 1850's.

65. Dunlap Letterbook, 1852–53, p. 598, February 9, 1853.

66. *Indiana Farmer and Gardener*, I (August 23, 1845), 255; for similar advice, see *Daily Commercial Register*, April 29, 1858.

her death became apparent when it was learned that the locale was
the rendezvous point for a gang of bandits. Public opinion speculated
that she was silenced because of her acquaintance with some of the
gang members.[67] A newspaper report from Chicago noted the demise
of another hired farm girl of questionable reputation. Estella Smith,
according to the *Chicago Daily Democrat*, was found dead on a street
in the city. She was employed on a nearby farm, and it was her usual
habit after getting wages to come into town for a spree, having long
been addicted to intemperate habits.[68]

While it is not entirely clear how the average girl took steps to protect herself, the most obvious precaution, it would seem, was to locate
with a reputable farmer and his family, preferably in the immediate
locale. Bachelor farmers had the most difficulty in obtaining help unless an older woman was available. A German guidebook stated the
matter in blunt terms: "Batchelors are virtually compelled to do their
own housekeeping for seldom will any decent girl go to reside with
them."[69] Improprieties of this sort were circumvented in the case of
a Wisconsin pioneer: Charles Thompson's letter to relatives back east
noted that he had a fourteen-year-old German girl come over in the
morning and evening to work without staying; apparently the girl's
mother accompanied her to do Thompson's laundry.[70]

Girls hired out for a variety of reasons, and a commonly held view
was that they wished to get out and look things over for themselves.
It is clear that many of them were interested in marriage, and in a
related way, this employment provided the opportunity to obtain
luxuries they could not otherwise afford. Busy as they were with work
on the farm, young girls nonetheless liked to purchase dresses and
other small finery which, in a sense, were diversions that broke the
drab monotony of farm life.

Patrick Shirreff, an English traveler during the early 1830's, passed
through Springfield, Illinois. In conversation with people he learned
that hired labor of all kinds was expensive—especially hired girls, who
received one to two dollars per week, depending on whether they
worked in the country or town. A desire for fine clothes, remarked the

67. *History of Lee County*, pp. 633–39; Stevens, ed., *History of Lee County,
Illinois*, I, p. 355.
68. *Chicago Daily Democrat*, September 29, 1857.
69. De Haas, *Nordamerika, Wisconsin*, II, p. 33. Translation of "Junggesellen
sind gleichsam gezwungen, die Hauswirthschaft selbst zu führen; denn selten
entschiesst sich ein ordentliches Mädchen zu ihnen zu ziehen."
70. Charles H. Thompson to relatives (Kewaskum, Washington County,
Wis., August 31, 1856).

hotelkeeper, was a major motivation for girls to work.[71] Shirreff's impressions were similar to those of Swedish-born Gustaf Unonius for the Wisconsin frontier in the 1850's. Scandinavian girls made good wages but spent their money on finery to wear during leisure hours on Sunday; to the distress of his conservative Lutheran background, they were exceedingly prone to this vanity.[72]

There were valid differences of opinion on this matter. In a letter to the *Ohio Cultivator* in 1854, a woman claimed that farm work caused considerable wear and tear on clothing, especially with the dragging of dresses through the grass in order to milk the cows on wet days. According to her observation, girls on the farm had little free time to sew; yet they were expected to dress well. The editor of the *Cultivator* differed with her and claimed that wages for German and Irish hired girls were quite adequate (at seventy-five cents to one dollar per week) to compensate for clothing expenses.[73] This seventy-five cents to one dollar wage was low, in the opinion of Roujet Marshall, who was raised on the Wisconsin frontier in Sauk County during the 1850's. He did concede that it was possible for a girl to get along on such a wage because expenses were small, with a dress usually costing only $1 and shoes $1.50.[74]

Farm records indicate what girls purchased and charged to their employers' accounts at the local merchants; farmers in turn deducted the cost of these items from the final wage settlements. The credit power of the farmer enhanced the buying power of young girls on the frontier where hard cash was not readily available. Economic necessity sometimes prompted a girl to hire out in order to assume some of her own expenses while attending school, although employers were not always convinced of the advantages of such arrangements. After her husband had found a replacement for one such hired girl, a woman in Fulton County, Illinois, still retained her basic skepticism. "He got another girl of the same age to board here and go to school," she wrote, "she is a very pretty girl but we all know how much such girls can do besides going to school."[75] But the practice was a common

71. Patrick Shirreff, *A Tour through North America* (Edinburgh, 1835), p. 250.

72. Unonius, *Memoirs*, II, pp. 112–13.

73. *Ohio Cultivator*, X (June 1, 1854), 172.

74. Marshall, *Autobiography*, I, pp. 105–6.

75. Mary Huggins to My Dear Friends (Farmington, Fulton County, Ill., January 29, [1858–60?]), Huggins Letter Collection. A German immigrant in Wisconsin in the 1840's remarked that numerous positions were available for girls to work on farms and simultaneously attend school. Jack J. Detzler, " 'I Live

one, and it enabled girls like Eliza Kingdom of Trumbull County, Ohio, to buy not only paper for school, but also a bonnet at $4.50, a pair of gaiters at $1.62½, brass buttons for 50 cents, a collar for 18 cents, cotton cloth for 20 cents, and ribbon for 32 cents.[76]

These were typical of the items a hired girl might purchase. Like Letitia Gibson, who worked for Joshua Shinn at fifty cents a week on his Canfield, Ohio, farm, a teenager attending school might thus meet most of her own obligations. In Letitia's case, her employer paid her debts to shoemakers, merchants, and others and charged these to her account in his ledger.[77] Since many girls were inordinately fond of clothes and finery, their wage credits were often balanced by debits from store purchases. At Lebanon, Indiana, in 1847, Jane Hacker worked for Samuel Strong. She bought calico, shoes, handkerchief, ribbons, and other sundries; when she quit at the end of seventeen weeks, her employer owed her seventy-eight cents—the rest had been absorbed by her purchases.[78]

As a rule, farm girls were hired and paid on a weekly basis, in contrast to male hired hands, whose rate of pay and tenure of employment were computed by the month or year. Sources do not make clear the distinction between farm and town employment, but usually hired girls in towns earned slightly more than those in the country. Moreover, wages of girls reflected seasonal demands. A contract negotiated with an Ohio farmer reveals this wage differential: "Bloomfield march the 29th. 1855 Sarah Jackson commenced to work for me She agrees to work seven months for which I agree to pay her one Dollar and twenty-five Cents for four months and one Dollar and twelve and a half Cents for three months."[79]

The average weekly rate gradually increased over the decades. Dur-

---

Here Happily': A German Immigrant in Territorial Wisconsin," *Wisconsin History*, L (1967), 257.

76. John Fenton Accountbook, 1845–58, entry of March 23, 1857, for Eliza Kingdam, and insert sheets at back of ledger. Sarah Jackson also worked for Fenton; similar were her expenditures, entry of March 29, 1855. For other examples of hired girls' expenditures, see Lesher Farm Accounts, entries of March 30, July 22, 1846; Burgess Diary, entry of March 22, 1845.

77. Shinn Ledger, p. 58, account ledger entries of Letitia Gibson. Some of the items included: shoes, leather for shoes, shoe taps, candle stand cover, thread, Indian Medicine, stocking yarn, chince, linen, calico, muslin, linsey.

78. Samuel Strong Ledger, p. 212. At Washington, Illinois, the hired girl of Lewis Morrison earned fourteen dollars, which was neatly balanced out by an identical sum of debits for sundry items. Morrison Ledger, p. 89.

79. Fenton Accountbook, entry of March 29, 1855.

ing the 1830's in Trumbull County, Ohio, an early pioneer recalled her childhood, when wages for girls were fifty cents to one dollar per week.[80] An authority on the Wisconsin frontier estimated the weekly rate in that region at fifty to seventy-five cents in the 1840's.[81] According to a survey by the U.S. Commissioner of Patents in 1848, the average weekly wage of a female domestic with board in the various states was: Ohio, 96 cents; Illinois, $1.14; Michigan, $1.10; Wisconsin, $1.27; and Minnesota, $2.25.[82]

By the 1850's the wage rate was advancing. The *Ohio Cultivator* reported in 1854 that wages in that state reached one dollar per week; according to a state survey several years later they were averaging between $1.25 and $1.50.[83] These figures parallel those in Illinois, Michigan, and Wisconsin.[84] But in the Minnesota Territory the shortage of farm girls was especially acute. A letter from Minnesota in 1854 praised the region's prospects but lamented dearth of good stout girls who understood farm-house work and who could easily command eight dollars per month![85] Girls were paid $1.50 to $3 per week —an average of $2.25—which was equivalent to what farm hands in the lower Midwest were receiving at the $8–10 monthly rate.[86] Nevertheless, few girls remained single for very long in the Minnesota Territory.[87]

Farm girls were in demand throughout the period, as reflected by the steady increase in wages. For most girls the work lasted only a few years; unless economic necessity required them to work, they were marking time until they found a suitable husband. The daily

80. Mrs. W. H. Beebe, "Historical Manuscript, 1896. Incidents of the Early Settlement of the northeastern portion of Howland Township, Trumbull County, Ohio."

81. Lillian Krueger, "Motherhood on the Wisconsin Frontier," *Wisconsin History*, XXIX (1945), 169–72.

82. *Statistical View of the United States*, p. 164.

83. *Ohio Cultivator*, X (June 1, 1854), 172; *Ohio Statistics, 1857*, I, 75–86.

84. See Marshall, *Autobiography*, I, pp. 105–6; Duus, *Letters, 1855–58*, pp. 13–14; Nathan Pierce Accountbook, 1848–60, p. 96 entry of May 26, 1852; Enoch Higgins to Joseph Huggins (Orange Prairie, Peoria County, Ill., June 3, 1860), Huggins Letter Collection.

85. *Farmer's Companion and Horticultural Gazette*, III (June, 1854), 190.

86. *The Immigrants' Guide to Minnesota in 1856. By an Old Resident* (St. Anthony, 1856), pp. 67–68. A farmer at Manomin County, Minnesota, hired a girl at the top rate of three dollars per week. Henry C. Friedley Diary, entries of April 27, June 4, 1856.

87. *Minnesota Chronicle*, as cited in *Daily Sanduskian*, March 9, 1850: "Bring on your girls if you want them well settled in life. This is the best market extant."

routine on farms led to boredom and loneliness. Unless they went to the city for employment (a questionable step), the only escape was an early marriage. An equally persuasive element in American society was the image of women married and with a family, rather than single and independent.

The Hired Hand
in Society and His Contract
of Employment

Both duty and interest require you to regard their rights. They
may demand, at reasonable times, as much palatable and wholesome food as is needed to preserve unimpaired their health and
strength. They may demand as many hours for rest and sleep
as the human constitution ordinarily requires. They may demand
comfortable beds, in rooms not unhealthy. They may refuse such
excessive efforts or great exposure, as would prematurely break
down the constitution. They may claim kindness and civility in
all your language towards them, and in all your treatment of
them.[1]

HOW WERE farm hands treated as employees? What
respect was accorded them as members of society? Despite the lowly
status of agricultural laborers, farmers were urged to deal with them
as human beings;[2] unfortunately, not all of them extended the open
hand of friendship and understanding. "I can remember when my
proffered hand was not received—when my nod of recognition was
unreturned," wrote one farm worker. "I have treasured memories of
slights shown, and thrusts given, when I was only John, our hired
man."[3] Scarcity of labor, adverse economic conditions, and growing
urbanization cast fear into the agricultural community of America.
The increasing numbers of immigrant agricultural laborers prompted
a supercilious attitude: "We don't speak of or to the common farm-

1. *New Genesee Farmer*, II (June, 1841), 91. A traveler in the Midwest
during the 1830's observed: "Farm-hired men, or by whatever other name
they may be distinguished, are to be had in all old settled districts, and also in
many of the new ones. In most cases their reward is ample, and their treatment
good, living on the same kind of fare and often associating with their employers."
Shirreff, *A Tour through North America*, p. 341.
2. *Ohio Cultivator*, IV (April 15, 1848), 62.
3. *Indiana Farmer*, III (October 1, 1853), 7.

laborer any more than of the journeyman dyer. Both may be as ignorant as an ass, and, like an ass, be employed in the lowest drudgery,
content to labor and be fed from day to day."[4]

American attitudes toward farm labor changed in the decade prior
to the Civil War. In 1860 the *Illinois Farmer* urged farmers to replace
hired men with tenant farm laborers. Meals and laundry work would
no longer be demanded of farmers' wives, and the wives and daughters of the tenants could be available to assist in the busy seasons.
This same article labeled farm hands as mere "birds of passage" who
traveled through the countryside without aim or purpose—a char-
acterization that was not necessarily fair or accurate, despite the
migratory nature of the occupation.[5] Yet a few years earlier, in 1856,
the *Illinois Farmer* had described decent young farm hands in glow-
ing terms:

> A short time after, a full breasted, stout young man, entered our sanc-
> tum. He wanted employment. 'What can you do?' 'I have worked at
> farming four years in Vermont, and six in New York.' 'You want to
> work on a farm?' 'Yes,' 'Well you are just the man wanted—and I
> would like to engage half a dozen more like you. I will give you a
> letter to James Curtis, Esq, at West Urbana, Champaign county. He
> wants several good farm hands. Can you go to him—and when?' 'I will
> go in the first cars.' We gave him a letter, and he was off in two hours.
> Now this man, if we mistake not greatly, will have his own farm in
> two years.[6]

As it was, the observations of the *Illinois Farmer* in 1856 were no
more accurate than those of 1860. The truth lay somewhere between
the divergent viewpoints.

Farm laborers were generally average human beings despite their
diverse origin and background. In times of adversity and illness, some
served their employers as if they were members of the family while
performing the routine chores.[7] The dedicated assistance of a loyal
farm hand was crucial to many settlers who arrived in the West with
a less than perfect understanding of what had to be done. A letter

4. *Monthly Journal of Agriculture*, II (February, 1847) 340. Others recalled
with nostalgia the reliable New England farm hand; *Ohio Cultivator*, X (July
15, 1854), 218–19.
5. *Illinois Farmer*, V (November 11, 1860), 181.
6. *Ibid.*, I (May, 1856), 111–12.
7. Brush, *Growing Up with Southern Illinois 1820 to 1860*, p. 23; Eliza
Farnham, *Life in the Prairie Land* (New York, 1846), pp. 86–87; F. A.
McCarty, "Memoir of James Knowles Kellogg," *Illinois Historical Journal*, XII
(1920), 507–8.

from a pioneer couple at Marquette County, Wisconsin, in 1852 expressed gratitude for a reliable farm hand. With no experience or knowledge in farming, it was their good fortune to obtain a hired man who was diligent and well acquainted with agriculture.[8]

Farm hands were probably no more or less honest than other individuals. According to a Wisconsin settler, locks on the cupboard were essential to keep "honest hands" out of them;[9] but an English traveler passing through Illinois observed that pilfering by farm hands was not a problem, American hired men being more honest than those in England.[10] This statement is borne out in the example of a livestock farmer in Sangamon County, Illinois, during the 1830's and 1840's. Cash from the sale of cattle was kept in a desk drawer without the protection of lock and key. Often the drawer was open to full view while hired hands were about the house, but not a single dollar was ever missing.[11] Loyalty in matters involving money was essential to a farmer. An Illinois farm hand in the 1850's went into town with the other hired men to obtain supplies. While there they became intoxicated, but this reliable hand returned with them, the supplies, and the balance of the money from the purchases. His grateful employer rewarded him with an immediate wage increase.[12]

How well the hired hand performed his job might depend on the treatment received from his employer. The farmer had to be firm yet fair-minded, compensating his men honestly on all occasions:

> Be sure to get your hands to bed by seven o'clock, and they will be compelled to rise early by the force of circumstances. Pay a hand—if he is a poor hand—all you promised him; if he is a good hand pay him a little more; it will encourage him to do still better. . . . Extra pay is appreciated by a good young man much. Always feed them as well as you feed yourselves, for the laboring men are the bone and sinew of the world, and ought to be well treated.[13]

8. *Michigan Farmer*, XI (January, 1853), 15.

9. James Start to George Dow (postmarked Fort Atkinson, Wis., August 23, 1841), George Dow Papers.

10. James Stuart, *Three Years in North America* (Edinburgh, 1833), II, p. 392.

11. Power, *History of the Early Settlers of Sangamon County, Illinois*, p. 500.

12. Bateman and Selby, eds., *Historical Encyclopedia of Illinois and History of McLean County* (Chicago, 1908), II, p. 979. Hired hands were used to run errands: a farmer's wife at Fond du Lac, Wisconsin, had the hired hand take trips to town, carry bank bills, and convey her and the children to different places. Carrier Diaries, entries from November 13, 1854, to January, 1855.

13. *Illinois Farmer*, IV (April 4, 1859), 243; see also *Ohio Cultivator*, XV (May 1, 1859), 134.

Sensible advice called for the treatment of hired hands as members
of the family, and this gesture was usually appreciated by common
laborers. Concern for their welfare in hot summer months was reflected by granting a "nooning" period. Work was started early in the
cool of morning, and the men were allowed to rest at midday in the
shade without the annoyance of petty chores. When the main work
resumed in the afternoon, they were refreshed and ready to work.[14]

Except in harvest, hands were not required to work in the evenings.
Sundays were similarly regarded as a free time once the minor chores
were completed.[15] Farmers who requested their hands to work during
the off hours compensated such "over-work" (overtime) with additional wage credits.[16] A satisfied hired hand in Du Page County, Illinois, weighed these factors in his decision not to seek employment
elsewhere:

> I shall stay here untill next fall for I have got into a good place to
> work for at least it does seem so far and where they appear to be
> friendly to me[.] Mr. Lyman is a Ministers son which is a man that
> will not work but six days in a week (which in Mich they work 7) and
> not very early or late or hard and his wife is a good cook (which you
> know ades a great deal to the comforts of a man that is a work by the
> month) and as for having any one to bother you while at work you
> will not find it here for they have but one child and that is but one
> year old and as for him he letes me work as I am a mind to[.] I get
> up about 6 am out to the barn and feede 4 horses and a Durham Bull
> their grain and then let out the sheep (for we have to yard the sheep
> every night on account of the woolves) feede the cattle their hay[,]
> milk and feede the calves [;] clean the stables curry the horses and
> by that time Mr. Lyman has got up and the bell rings for Breakfast
> which I am very glad to here[;] after I have eaten as much as 2 men
> aught to I then prepare myself for a days work such as plowing[,]
> Draying[,] making fence and the like I do not intend to work very
> hard this summer for I get as much pay not to as I would to kill my-
> self for some other man.[17]

14. *Wisconsin Farmer*, VIII (July, 1856), 290–91.
15. "Early Letters to Erland Carlsson from a File for the Years 1853 to
1857," *Augustana Historical Society Publications*, V (1935), 115.
16. Nathan Pierce Accountbook, 1848–60, p. 2, entry of April 14, 1849.
17. Myron Wright to Allen G. Wright (Downers Grove, Du Page County,
Ill., April 24, 1853), A. G. Wright Papers. For examples of former farm hands
who spoke highly of their employers, see *History of Delaware County, Indiana*
(Chicago, 1881), p. 265; William Henry Perrin, ed., *History of Effingham
County, Illinois* (Chicago, 1883), 220–21; *History of Defiance County, Ohio*
(Chicago, 1883), pp. 213–14; Bateman and Selby, eds., *Historical Encyclopedia
of Illinois and History of Kendall County*, II, p. 965. One farmer even advanced

Farm labor was hardly glamorous, but in an agriculturally oriented society this was no stumbling block. The issue was not so much that a man had once been a hired hand as that he should not remain in this occupation after marrying.[18] Romance between the farmer's daughter and the hired hand was not uncommon, and a reliable hired hand was occasionally a providential blessing to the farmer with several daughters:

> The farmer's girls were satisfied, because the hired man, having the sole disposal of his own earnings, was generally in possession of a fair extra suit, with a few loose dollars which he was willing to invest in any reasonable amusement which would secure the favor of the daughters aforesaid, and being gallant withal, was a convenient and eligible beau, not to be overlooked in a time of such general dearth of excitement. And this last availability of the hired man was equally agreeable to all parties. The farmer liked it, because he would rather his girls should be courted by a fellow that knew how to get a living for himself, and his only idea of that capability was, in earning so much a day. The farmer's wife liked it for the same reason, and because she looked upon a tolerably early settlement in life as a manifest destiny, and a desirable necessity. The farmer's boys liked it, because, while it relieved them from the unsentimental necessity of gallanting their own sisters, it left them free to choose more sentimental companions among their neighbors. And finally, the farmer's girls liked it, because—because, why, just because they did! which was reason enough for any girl. . . .[19]

The impending marriage of the hired hand and farmer's daughter was advantageous to the farmer for several reasons. Before the marriage he had the opportunity to assess his prospective son-in-law's character and, equally important, his ability to do well at farming. Moreover, a young man in a romantic attitude was not apt to change jobs and look for a better position, and the farmer was guaranteed of a reliable hand who stayed close to the farm. So that the young bache-

---

his hired man the necessary money to secure a land claim and provided time off to hunt for a land site. E. Kemper Daybook, entries of June 1, 4, October 5, 1818.

18. Satterthwaite and Bishop, *Hoosier Courtships in the Horse and Buggy Days*, pp. 95–96. This observation is confirmed by numerous references in county and biographical histories regarding young men who worked on farms until their marriage, at which time they commenced renting land or bought a tract.

19. *Ohio Cultivator*, X (July 15, 1854), 218–19. The reliable farm hand could prove his worth and simultaneously win the affection of the farmer's daughter, according to a fictionalized version in the *Cincinnati Daily Gazette*, December 2, 1848.

lor would not be tempted to reconsider his imminent loss of independence, the wise farmer might promise the future couple a farm of
their own, usually a parcel of land adjacent to the family farm or in
the immediate neighborhood. The bride and groom could also count
on getting a generous helping start in the way of household goods
and farm equipment.[20]

Occasionally the hired hand was obliged to work dearly to gain the
farmer's approval before marrying the daughter. A wealthy Illinois
farmer had several daughters whose fetching beauty had caught the
eyes of more than one man. A shrewd judge of individuals and human nature, John Strawn required prospective suitors to work long
and hard as hired hands at low wages to prove their worth. An interest in one of Strawn's daughters provided the incentive for Jesse
Bane: "It was a pleasant picture, and though the wages were low and
the labor severe, it was Jesse toiling for Rachel and cheerily he
worked."[21] Sometimes the farmer was powerless to dictate in matters
of love. After a very short romance, a young hired hand and farmer's
daughter eloped. What was done could not be undone, and the father
duly presented the new couple with forty acres of farm land as a
start.[22]

Farm hands had genuine grievances against their employers, but
evidence of this sort is unfortunately sparse or onesided and reflects
mainly the viewpoint of the farmer or employer. Farmers were sometimes accused of demanding too much work. A letter of an Ohio farm
laborer in 1852 described the plight of conscientious hired hands who
were working to get ahead without being brutalized by the strain of
work. His comments raised basic questions about the alleged bene-
fits of agrarian life and the employment it afforded:

> We are without means. We are looking forward, or endeavouring to
> look forward, in order to shape our future course. Suppose we con-
> clude to become farmers. As we cannot do this without farms we must
> engage to work out until we get some capital of our own. Very well.
> If we happen to be stout, hearty fellows, of strong constitutions, and
> great physical power, with energy sufficient to keep it constantly ap-

20. *Portrait and Biographical Album of McLean County, Ill.*, pp. 265–66;
History of Jackson County, Illinois (Philadelphia, 1878), p. 108; *History of
Wayne County, Indiana*, II, p. 288; *Portrait and Biographical Record of Adams
County, Illinois*, pp. 421–22.

21. Spencer Ellsworth, ed., *Records of the Olden Time; or, Fifty Years on
the Prairies* (Lacon, Ill., 1880), pp. 687, 695.

22. Bateman and Selby, eds., *Historical Encyclopedia of Illinois and History
of Fulton County* (Chicago, 1908), 940–41.

plying, we may be so fortunate as to get $15 per month, or $180 per year. But if we happen to be of smaller statues, as many of us are, and possessing some desire for mental improvement, &c., we are put at, say about $12 per month, or $144 per year, making an average of about $165 per year. In order to secure the above wages we must labor from sunrise till sunset in summer, and from early morn till bed-time in winter, and then where is the time for mental improvement, &c., which constitute so prominent a place in the beauties of a farm-er's life? We know that the farmers will not hire us if we take an hour or two each day for reading, writing and study; we are bound to toil constantly or toil at very reduced wages. In fact the subject assumes about this form—you must work all the time that you are able, or we will not hire you.[23]

This sentiment was echoed by a foreign observer in 1860. Anthony Trollope was impressed with the thriving economic condition of the United States but critical of Americans who employed their fellow countrymen and demanded the "nth" degree of work. Trollope's com-ments embrace both town and rural labor in the Midwest; it was his opinion that little protection existed for the laborer in requiring the employer to fulfill his part of the agreement.[24] When the hired hand failed to obtain his wages, it was difficult or impossible to enforce a claim against the defaulting employer. Farmers might decide to abandon their partially worked farm or simply declare their tem-porary inability to make payment.[25] Even large farmers like Calvin Fletcher at Indianapolis faced embarrassing situations. The elder Fletcher noted with concern: "Calvin [Jr.] owes several laborers & it grieves me much that we can't promptly pay them."[26] Owing to the lack of a sound money system prior to the Civil War, farm hands were occasional victims of payment in worthless bank notes.[27]

Hired hands had their own faults. By the 1840's and 1850's, farmers seemingly regarded the old-fashioned hired hand as something of the

23. *Ohio Cultivator*, VIII (July 1, 1852), 195.
24. Trollope, *North America*, pp. 120–22. Similar advice cautioned farmers not to overwork their hired hands: *Wisconsin Farmer*, VIII (January, 1856), 41.
25. *History of Mercer and Henderson Counties*, p. 1185; *Portrait and Biographical Record of Delaware and Randolph Counties, Indiana*, pp. 732–33; *Biographical Record of Bureau, Marshall and Putnam Counties, Illinois*, p. 625.
26. Fletcher Diary, entry of March 28, 1857. The elder Fletcher sometimes disapproved of his son's methods in directing the farm, especially the assignment of excessive tasks which the hands could not reasonably complete. For example, see entry of October 19–20, 1852.
27. *History of De Kalb County, Indiana*, p. 1023; *Portrait and Biographical Record of Lee County, Illinois*, pp. 780–81.

past who was replaced by men with less respect and appreciation for traditional values.[28] Yet criticism of farm hands was raised in earlier decades, and it was applied even to native-born laborers. A traveler in the lower Midwest during 1819 described the type of men available to farmers:

> Western labourers, some of whom are quarter-section farmers, very poor, dirty, and wretched, because idle and semi-barbarians, work about half the day and camp out all night, in all seasons and weathers. They surround a large fire, and lie on leaves under a clapboard tent, or wooden umbrella, wrapped in a blanket, with their clothes on. Their houses and families (if any) are perhaps, from 12 to 20 miles off, to whom they go when the job is done, or their shirts are rotting off their backs. They rarely shave, but clip off the beard, and their flesh is never washed; they look pale, wan, yellow, and smoke-dried. . . . These labourers, though complete workmen when they like, are pests to the English farmers for whom they work, generally, at meals, haunting the fire-side, where they stand in pairs with their backs towards the fire, to the exclusion of the family, at whom they gaze, expecting to be asked to dinner, breakfast, or supper. They come too, for work, and brush in at meal times with their hats on, expecting to be fed; but they never invite themselves, nor express thanks if invited; and if requested to reach this or that to the host, they do it ungraciously, saying, 'Why, I can, I guess.'[29]

Such dissatisfaction was widespread judging by the appeals for reliable help. A farmer near Chicago in 1834 issued a curious but specific request for a farm hand: "Wanted. A Man who has some knowledge of Gardening, and can plant potatoes, make fence, drive a yoke of well broken cattle occasionally, and shut a gate after him, whenever he passes through it."[30]

Knowledgeable opinion conceded that farm hands left much to be desired, but the tactful farmer could influence his men by setting a proper example. There was a distinct correlation between hired hands who were lazy time-wasters and an employer who was miserly and

28. *Cleveland Herald*, October 5, 1847, as cited in *Annals of Cleveland*, XXX, pp. 70–71.

29. W. Faux, *Memorable Days in America, Being a Journal of a Tour to the United States* (London, 1823), in Thwaites, *Early Western Travels*, XI, pp. 291–92.

30. *Chicago Weekly Democrat*, April 23, 1834. Laborers answering this advertisement were to report to the post office, indicating that men in search of employment frequented such places where information regarding positions was available. For a similar advertisement, see *Chicago Daily Democrat*, January 23, 1849.

contemptible in his own habits. From such an atmosphere arose a mounting sense of strife; both parties attempted to defy each other until violence ensued with hand-to-hand combat. A reasonable alternative was to deal with the men on a fair basis and thereby exercise subtle control over them. The wise farmer treated them as human beings, gave words of encouragement, but avoided embarrassing fault-finding of individual hands in the presence of the others.[31] Farm hands who maintained a downtrodden attitude viewed the farmer as some sort of oppressor. The result was that hands endeavored to do the least possible work, because they did not possess property themselves and had no appreciation of the farmer's interests. Some reacted maliciously by willful destruction of their employers' property and were known as barn-burners.[32] Although this attitude was not present among all farm hands, it was cause for concern in the opinion of many individuals.[33]

Hands were not always conscientious, but supervision assured the farmer that his men kept at the job. Isaac Funk, a large land operator in central Illinois, personally looked after every phase of his farm, allowing not even details to be handled by his hired hands without direct supervision.[34] Similarly, Calvin Fletcher checked on the hands at his Indianapolis farm and found tools lying about in general chaos: "I see plainly a wasteful disposition [and] I have requested them to do less & that better."[35] Waste occurred when hired hands performed their work with indifference to the point that the farmer was advised to do the work himself. The *Farmer's Companion and Horticultural Gazette* deplored, for example, haphazardness in feeding the cattle on the farm, "the more especially if we leave the foddering to hired men."[36] The agricultural press advised large farmers, employing more than one hand, to exercise constant watch over their men, either by working with them personally to set the pace, or by returning several times to see that they did not shirk their job:

31. *American Agriculturist*, XVIII (June, 1859), 169–70; see also *Prairie Farmer*, XI (December, 1851), 574–75.

32. Brown, *America*, p. 24.

33. Blake, *Farmer's Every-Day Book*, pp. 260–63. Blake urged the discharge of a hand who was untrustworthy, despite the temporary inconvenience.

34. *History of McLean County, Illinois*, p. 621.

35. Fletcher Diary, entry of November 1, 1847.

36. *Farmer's Companion and Horticultural Gazette*, I (January 1, 1853), 4–5. Calvin Fletcher encountered this problem: "I have felt bad this day in consequence of my hands b[e]i[n]g out & my stock in the wet—The hands rebell[e]d today & refused to feed the stock cattle—This gave me great pain—& I resolved that another winter I shall not be thus troubled. . . ." Fletcher Diary, entry of February 27, 1853.

The old adage is a good one—that 'the owner's eye is worth more than his hands.' The only exception that now occurs to us, is in the case of a large field of grass or grain, when it happens, as it rarely does, that the owner is the best mower or cradler on his farm; he can then to advantage lead the gang. But in almost every other operation of a large farm, while the farmer is sweating like a bull at one extremity of the farm, his more prudent 'hands' are lying under the shade of a tree; or discussing interesting topics in the corn-field, with a halt every three minutes to gesticulate and lay down the law on their side a little stronger. This is no fancy sketch. Every farmer knows how great a difference it makes, with the best help he can hire, whether he himself is in sight or out of sight.[37]

The best single statement came from an Indiana farmer who encountered this problem and decided as a result to switch from hired farm laborers to tenants: "I find it just as you said, and as I knew, before hand, it would be, unless one is present to say 'come on boys' it is very unprofitable to hire."[38]

An Illinois farmer thought highly of the hands working for him but retained a cautious attitude: ". . . but that I should have faithful hands & such I most usually manage to get, a man gets his discharge at once when he fails to obey orders promptly & faithfully."[39] Most disagreements were caused by either a personality clash or a failure to perform work in a satisfactory manner.[40] William Sewall employed a hand on his central Illinois farm in 1842, but the arrangement did not last: "Plowing up North cut of corn. Peter Whitlow having displeased me, his conduct being such as I cannot endure, I therefore settled and discharged him. He has worked 26 days at $11.00 per month."[41] In another case, an Ohio farmer hired a hand who ran up three dollars worth of debts for cash advances and tobacco during his brief employment. On the credit side of the ledger the farmer drew a long angry slash with the pen and tersely remarked: ". . . pidle about the horse would not work much."[42]

The old adage of one bad apple spoiling the others was particularly true on farms where several hands were employed. One individual could easily be a disruptive protagonist or cause difficulties for the employer. In the fall of 1848, Calvin Fletcher mentioned difficulties

37. *Boston Journal of Agriculture*, as cited in *Southern Planter*, XII (February, 1852), 39.
38. John L. Ketcham to Hazen Merrill (Indianapolis, December 9, 1847).
39. Dunlap Letterbook, 1853–55, p. 4, April 25, 1853.
40. For example, see E. Kemper Daybook, entry of August 20, 1817.
41. Sewall, *Diary*, p. 245.
42. Huston Account Ledger, p. 24.

during visits by a relative of one of his hired hands. Whenever this person came to the farm, problems inevitably arose with the other hands. Despite the presence of a foreman, Fletcher felt that had he been present, the affair might have been checked immediately. Several years later he employed a down-and-out Scotch immigrant at his place in Indianapolis and on the nearby farm: "At home I have had an ungrateful Scotsman John whom I took from the poor house—He has done mischief to all my hands." Fletcher tolerated the situation briefly and then fired the man.[43]

The farmer obviously faced an unpleasant situation if he allowed his hands to dictate what they would or would not do. A German immigrant, farming in central Indiana during the 1850's, depended on hired hands from his native country who were friends of the family. His letters back to Germany reveal the perils of employing countrymen as an act of kindness. Justus Meyer could not pay his hands in advance for fear that they would not complete honest and fair work in return. None of the men were well versed in American farm labor techniques, and one in particular not only resented farm labor but even encouraged laziness among the other hands.[44]

Shirking work was a problem experienced by most farmers who hired help. Henry Parker Smith at Schoolcraft, Michigan, offered his hired hand ten dollars per month but stipulated that the monthly wage would be docked if Sam failed in his duties.[45] No less vexing to the busy farmer was the hand who decided not to work and simply drifted away. A farmer in northern Illinois gave the following advice in 1838: "If you can get a good hand to work that wants to come to this country encourage him to come[;] we shall want a good hand[;] my man that I hired for $12 per month has left me after working a month got homesick. I have hired another for a month but he is good for nothing. . . ."[46] Farmers were also irritated when their men claimed inability to perform certain strenuous tasks.[47]

While this occupation attracted the indolent and lazy, there is a surprising lack of direct evidence to indicate crime and violence on

43. Fletcher Diary, entries of October 31, 1848, and March 2, 11, 1853. Foresight helped prevent altercations: "I have 6 or 7 hands 3 here & 3 at [the] farm—It will require great discretion to have them profitably imployed [sic]. . . . I must see that my hands have their work laid out right." Entry of March 19, 1849.
44. Andressohn, "The Kothe Letters," 176–77. For an example of a Swedish immigrant unsuited for rough farm work in Ohio, see Norelius, Journal, p. 185.
45. Smith Diary, entry of March 7, 1856.
46. Joslyn, History of Kane County, Ill., I, p. 109.
47. Stevens, ed., History of Lee County, Illinois, I p. 508.

the part of these men. Problems were usually resolved by either an exchange of words or the discharge of the hired hand from the farm. One probable reason for the lack of violent or major crimes is the fact that farm hands were often local people who were considered part of the neighborhood, despite having to labor for wages. Moreover, those who worked at farm and itinerant occupations did not necessarily come from the lowest ranks of society. The best overall explanation appeared in Reverend William C. Smith's *Indiana Miscellany* (1867). Smith made the reasonable deduction that people on farms were first of all busily engaged in the hard work of farmmaking, and second, that the vices and crime of the cities were generally not close at hand. He balanced this assessment with shrewd insight: "And yet the people were not all pious."[48]

Some violence did occur occasionally with hired hands. Quite unusual was the attempt at claim jumping by a hired hand at Lee County, Illinois, in the early 1840's: "A settler gave employment to a lad until he could earn enough to start for himself. This lad jumped one of his employer's two forties. The committee came to the premises. The lad defied them in a set speech from the top of a barrel. The captain kicked the barrel from under him; others produced a rope. The youngster then begged for mercy and left the county. Floggings too, were used. They were all successful."[49] An unpleasant category of crime was the molesting and assaulting of children. Out of respect to the innocent parties involved, crime of this nature was rarely publicized; yet farmers and particularly their wives no doubt worried in private about this danger when strangers were employed on the farm.[50] The *American Agriculturist* cautioned farmers with families to hire only men of good character: "A faithful, trustworthy man, though inferior in physical strength or in skill, will prove more valuable than a reckless character, whatever may be his other qualifications. Especially is this true where there are children in the family. Their welfare is superior to every consideration of mere profit; and association with profane or immoral hired men has corrupted many a promising youth."[51]

More common was the fight in the field where men were tired or working under pressure. In the summer of 1851 in Mercer County,

48. William C. Smith, *Indiana Miscellaney* (Cincinnati, 1867), pp. 41–42.
49. Stevens, ed., *History of Lee County, Illinois*, I, p. 525.
50. The details of this type of crime were reported in the *Chicago Daily Democrat*, April 5, 1858.
51. *American Agriculturist*, XVIII (February, 1859), 36.

Illinois, Reuben Williams and James Fierman were shelling corn in a farmer's field when an argument erupted. Fierman attacked Williams, who retaliated by breaking Fierman's neck with an accidental blow. He pleaded guilty to manslaughter and was sentenced to a nine-month prison term.[52] Cases of murder sometimes involved the farmer and his hired hand. During the 1840's at St. Clair County, Illinois, a farm hand reappeared in the neighborhood, shot his former employer in the back, and stole a sum of money from him. The reasons for the attack were unknown, but the culprit was apprehended and given "his just punishment" for the crime.[53]

Disagreements and altercations were best avoided by drawing up a contract. Usually the terms were few and specified the length of employment and the monthly rate of pay. These agreements sometimes included an understanding regarding accommodations, board, and whether laundering and mending of clothes were provided. Farmers were cautioned to protect themselves by placing a record of the work agreement in their ledger or accountbook; when payments or advancements of cash were made, the hand was required to initial or sign the book to indicate receipt of wages.[54]

It is not clear how many farmers actually negotiated formal contracts, or whether these agreements always possessed legal power. A Michigan agriculturist observed in 1850 that the traditional sense of obligation was no longer respected: "Custom has almost destroyed the obligation of contracts between the employed and the employer. The first thinks he has a right to leave when he pleases, and the last expects he will go when he likes."[55]

Henry Coleman of the *New England Farmer* claimed that the farm hand was bound by the "morals of labor" to render duty to the farmer. But the bargain was a two-way affair, necessitating the farmer

52. *History of Mercer and Henderson Counties*, p. 162.
53. *Portrait and Biographical Record of St. Clair County, Illinois* (Chicago, 1892), p. 286.
54. *Farmer and Artizan*, I (April, 1852), 27. This advice also cautioned against charging for work on Sunday, which was not a legal day; hence the hand who desired part or all of his wages had to collect them no later than Saturday night. Farm periodicals often urged farmers to keep accurate records as a form of protection: *Western Tiller*, February 27, 1829, 210–12; *Ohio Cultivator*, VI (July 15, 1850), 210; *Indiana Farmer*, VII (August, 1858), 153–54; *Michigan Farmer*, VIII (May, 1850), 150; *Wisconsin Farmer*, VI (January, 1854), 4.
55. *Michigan Agricultural Transactions, 1850*, 501. According to this report, a reward was offered to the best hired hand in the area who labored for at least six months for one farmer and performed his work in a superior manner. The awarded premium varied from four to eight dollars.

to treat his hand with fairness, good food, comfortable lodgings, and reasonable working conditions. Coleman endorsed the right of a farmer to withhold past wages if a hired hand left before completion of the originally agreed period, and courts in Massachusetts strongly enforced such decisions where a farm hand left to work the remainder of the summer, usually in harvest, on another farm for higher wages.[56] Illinois courts similarly ruled that a contract to labor for six months, at a given rate per month, was legally binding. In order for the hand to recover payment for services, he had to perform for the full work period unless released by the farmer or compelled to leave work for a justifiable purpose, which then required the farmer to pay only for the labor rendered up to that point.[57]

Use of the written contract for farm labor agreements was strongly recommended as legal protection for both parties. The hired hand promised to labor for the full term, render honest service, and help protect his employer's property. In return, the employer promised to pay the stipulated wages for the period of the contract. Appended to the contract were requirements of standard behavior, punctuality, neatness in personal appearance, decency in conversation, and obedience to either the farmer or his foreman. No alcohol was allowed at any time. Finally, each job or operation was to be thorough and complete, and tools at the end of each day were to be cleaned and stored away properly.[58]

Matthias Dunlap suggested that contracts should determine farm employment according to projected needs. Writing in January, 1858, Dunlap observed that farmers were in the process of estimating their crops for the coming season in order to gauge the necessary labor requirements. The effects of the recent depression were still lingering,

56. *New England Farmer*, XIX (July 29, 1840), 30. During harvest time, farmers encouraged hands to leave the employment of their neighbors and work for higher wages with them. Calvin Fletcher complained that his neighbor had "seduced" one of his hired hands in this fashion. Fletcher Diary, entry of June 26, 1851. Farmers occasionally tempted railroad construction laborers to desert their jobs for higher wages in the harvest fields: see Lightner, "Construction Labor on the Illinois Central Railroad," 289.

57. Henry Asbury, *Illinois Form-Book; or, Advice concerning the Duties of Justices of the Peace and Constables* (St. Louis, 1858), pp. 172–74. Hired hands enjoyed a legal standing in a locale for certain matters. An Ohio farmer hired a man for day labor but also paid him seventy-five cents for attending court as a witness to a will. Enoch Jones Farm Accounts, 1838–52, entry of October 16, 1840.

58. *Moore's Rural New Yorker*, V (February 25, 1854), 61. For an example of a contract for a foreman of a farm, see H. L. Barnum, *Family Receipts; or Practical Guide for Husbandman and Housewife* (Cincinnati, 1831), pp. 371–74.

and agricultural prices were below previous levels. However, farm hands declined to enter into contracts for wages at anything less than the previous year. The matter rested on the advance of prices during the 1858 season. Dunlap frankly anticipated only a gradual improvement, which meant that the farmer was not about to let out contracts for hired hands at high wages. His advice was ". . . if labor cannot be had at corresponding prices, let the land lay idle."[59]

According to the letters of Edwin Bottomley, a farmer at Racine County, Wisconsin, his hired hand approached him about negotiating a new agreement for the coming season. ". . . I told him I thought I could not make an engagement for another year as things had turned out[.] But I [would] find him as much work as I could and Pay him after the same rate as I had Done before and he might make our house his home and get a little work any where else ocasionally [sic] just as jobs turned up so that it would ease me of my expences a little. . . ." The dissatisfied hand departed and took a job with another farmer. Bottomley retained an open mind and remarked that John was free to return anytime to him.[60]

Once an agreement was negotiated, farmers were strict in making their hands honor the work contract. One of Calvin Fletcher's hands in 1856 actually begged to be released: "Perry the man who had promised to work & set in & plough 10 days of 5 months he had ingaged [sic] for, came to me & begged to be let off to go to Iowa with his 2 brothers & I let him go & paid him for 3 days work & promised to pay the rest if his leaving did me no great injury—"[61] A contract to work at specific wages was binding, and the farm hand was not legally free to change jobs for a better set of wages. A hired hand worked on a Wisconsin farm from April through October, 1856, for ninety-one dollars. Without looking for better wages on a different farm, he hastily agreed to work the 1857 season for the same amount; accord-

59. Dunlap Clippings Book, 1853–58, article of January 6, 1858. The effects of the depression were apparent in other locales. A Minnesota farmer wrote in May, 1858: "I am trying to get along without any paid help this season and so far I do much better than I did the last season with one man & sometimes 2 men." Newton Southworth to Seth Freeman (Belle Plaine, Scott County, Minn., May 27, 1858), Newton Southworth Papers. According to some reports, farmers who hired hands for $20 per month in 1857 were paying only $12–14 per month in 1858. *Daily Commercial Register*, May 4, 1858.

60. Bottomley, *Letters, 1842–1850*, pp. 113–14.

61. Fletcher Diary, entry of April 21, 1846. A Meigs County, Ohio, farmer deducted an amount from the final settlement with his hired hand: "damage for quitting work & receiving balance in cash." Larkin Store and Farm Accounts, p. 61, entry of August 13, 1844.

ing to a member of his family, "If he had waited just two days, he might have had $112 for the same period."[62]

Some agreements indicate that the farmer and his hired hand reserved the right to break the understanding or alter its original terms. A Minnesota farmer recorded briefly in his diary: "Have hired a hand for four weeks if we both are suited, his name is David Huddlestone."[63] Similar was Nathan Pierce's contract with a farm hand in 1843 at Calhoun County, Michigan: George Beegbee commenced work for $120 per year until the parties agreed otherwise.[64] In other instances the farmer reserved the right unilaterally to alter the agreement or retain the hired hand after a trial basis. Calvin Fletcher made the following stipulation in the hiring of an Irish farm hand: "Patrick Branin came to work at $20 per month for one month & if he suit[s] me I am to keep him 6m^s [months] at 22$[,] he will board himself, & if he work[s] at the farm & eat[s] th[e]re we will make it right—"[65]

An essential part of the contract was the method of wage payment. A Michigan farmer at Kent County hired a man in March, 1858, to work eight months for $90—which averaged about $11.25 per month. Written into the memorandum was the agreement of the hand to accept partial payment in the form of one cow and some wheat.[66] Equally common was the requirement of the hand to accept part of his wages in store pay or store goods—a fact which made the storekeeper an important third party in the three-cornered triangle of farmer, farm hand, and merchant. Anthony Stranahan of Coshoctan County, Ohio, made this stipulation a basic part of his contracts with hired help: in 1818 Oliver Kingsbury worked at $10.50 per month, with at least one third of his wages to be drawn in store pay.[67] An Illinois farm contract in 1833 read: "Nicholas Kelly sat [set?] in to work for me at $10.00 per month, half to be paid out of a store, and

62. Letter of Christian and Peter Bovy (Brighton, Kenosha County, Wis., March 5, 1857), as cited in "Documents," *Wisconsin History*, XX (1937), 326.

63. Rollin Notes and Memorandum, IV, entry of September 2, [1860]. For a similar example, see Carrier Diaries, entry for Joseph Roberds during 1851.

64. Nathan Pierce Accountbook, 1842–61, p. 20, entry of April 24, 1843.

65. Fletcher Diary, entry of March 25, 1856. Within one week problems arose, and the hand was fired because of his poor attitude. Entry of April 3, 1856. Fletcher also hired hands with the stipulation of a raise if the work was done well. In February, 1836, he hired a hand for the year at twelve dollars per month, which was to be increased if the work was good. Entry of February 22, 1836.

66. Robert Cornell Daybook, entry of March 7, 1859, in Barber G. Buell Papers.

67. Stranahan Farm Account, p. 60, entry of April 6, 1818.

the other half in cash."[68] Similar was an Ohio farm agreement in
1844: "George Davis Commences work according to agreement for
six months at 8 dollars per month (does his own washing) to be paid
one third cash and balance in store goods, clothing &c."[69] The standard practice was to increase the monthly rate slightly if the hired
hand agreed to accept part of the wages in store pay, which compensated for the merchant's customary mark-up on the goods. For
example, Joseph Kinnet began work for John Henry of Ripley County,
Indiana, in 1843 for five months, agreeing to accept half in cash at the
rate of seven dollars per month and the remainder in trade at eight
dollars per month.[70]

Farmers might specify the line of work and whether the hand was
additionally responsible for other chores. An agreement of this type
was negotiated by an Ohio farmer and cattle raiser: "This is to certify
that I Enoch Pickering agrees to feed a lot of cattle for Johnson
Thurston to the first of march next or work at any other kind of work
that may be needed to take good care of said cattle for which Thurston is to pay him thirteen dollars per month to do his washing. Oct
8th 1855 and boarding."[71] Other contracts were simply a broad dele-
gation of any type of work to be performed: "This is to certify that I
James Watson agrees to labor for Johnson Thurston at any kind of
work one month 30 days to the month to take good care of all property that I may have charge of for which Thurston is to pay me ten
dollars March the 3rd 1856."[72]

Provision was made in the contract for the hand who had his own
horse. Some farmers charged the hand extra for keeping and feeding
the animal, while others made arrangements that the horse could be
used on the farm for work purposes. William Renick at Circleville,
Ohio, recalled that his father paid a farm hand sixteen dollars per
month and board, allowing the hand's horse to be stabled and fed
free during both summer and winter.[73] Other farmers were not so
generous; a hired hand on a farm near Indianapolis was employed at
eight dollars per month, but the farmer deducted fifty cents per week

68. Sewall, *Diary*, p. 151.
69. Larkin Store and Farm Accounts, p. 61, entries of March 13, August 13, 1844.
70. John Henry Notebook, p. 5, entries of February 21, March 1, 1843.
71. Thurston Farm Accounts, entry of October 8, 1855. For a similar contract, see Holgate Accountbook, p. 20, entry of June 4, 1850.
72. Thurston Farm Accounts, entries of March 1–3, 1856.
73. William Renick, *Memoirs, Correspondence and Reminiscences of William Renick* (Circleville, 1880), p. 108.

for the upkeep of the horse.[74] In contrast, an Illinois farmer hired a hand in 1831 and offered not only to board his horse as part of the contract, but also to pay him extra when the animal could be used on the farm in work: "I have this day hired Thomas Thourerman by the month at $15.00, and to keep his horse, and when in actual service, am to pay him 25c per day for it."[75]

A "wet and dry" clause in the contract stipulated whether the hired hand was required to work during inclement weather, and if he received wages on such days. Farm hands were not expected to work on rainy days, maintained the *Michigan Farmer*, and such were instead opportunities for going to town.[76] The *Ohio Valley Farmer* suggested a more practical alternative of a small workshop on the farm where the hands could repair equipment on rainy days.[77] The *American Agriculturist* suggested a combination of leisure reading along with indoor work:

> . . . we think the occasional rest furnished by a rainy day to all workers on the farm—proprietors and boys as well as hired men—is a valuable recuperative of strength and vigor. Rainy days should, in part be devoted to reading and thought; still, as many persons will not improve the time thus, and as work is often pressing, it is well to provide employment for dull weather, by having under cover fence-posts and rails to be fitted, gates, or portable fence to make, muck to be manipulated with manure, grain to thresh or clean, apples to be ground into cider or prepared for drying, and other jobs that can be attended to when field work is impracticable.[78]

The loss of work on the farm owing to rainy weather was figured at fifteen to twenty days per season, according to John Blake, who advised farmers to supply their hands with a coat and trouser set of India rubber over which was worn a tarpaulin cape. Such equipment, he maintained, kept the farm hand dry while pursuing the normal day's work.[79]

According to a wet and dry contract, the farm hand received his

74. Joseph Beeler Accountbook, entry of March, 1844, for Littleton Baker. For a similar example, see Larkin Store and Farm Accounts, p. 61, entry of August 13, 1844, for George Davis.
75. Sewall, *Diary*, pp. 199–200.
76. *Michigan Farmer*, IX (March, 1851), 84–85. Cold weather was also an excuse not to work. Sewall, *Diary*, p. 161.
77. *Ohio Valley Farmer*, II (December, 1857), 186; see also *New England Farmer*, IX (October, 1857), 462; Blake, *Farmer's Every-Day Book*, p. 172.
78. *American Agriculturist*, XVIII (October, 1859), 290.
79. Blake, *Farmer's Every-Day Book*, p. 521. Another source estimated that the average farmer had a 10 percent annual loss from inclement weather; *Michigan Farmer*, XVI (March, 1858), 61–63.

monthly or annual wage regardless of the weather—or, as a Michigan farmer noted in disgust, "Good time for hirelings & ducks."[80] Yet, some farmers determined what their hands did with their free time during rainy weather. William Sewall hired John Elkins in March, 1837, to work one month for fifteen dollars at gathering corn; one rainy day the hand was used instead to help work on the construction of a ferry boat.[81] An ignominious task was given to a Wisconsin farm hand in April, 1852: "Rainy and Snowy day. No plowing, sowing, or dragging, so I had to assist in washing."[82] A Michigan farm hand wrote in a letter that on rainy days he worked in the shop on the farm.[83]

Other farmers adopted a strict line, either working their hands during all kinds of weather or deducting pay. The elder Calvin Fletcher expressed doubt about his son's way of treating the hired hands: "Went to [the] farm Tho[ugh] it rain[e]d neerly [sic] all day y[e]t Calvin & hands work[e]d on the 40 acre field & got all plan[te]d but about 12 or 15 acres[.] Calvin works hard[.] I fear he will make his hands all sick—"[84] William Sewall hired Lucius Spaulding in March, 1843, at nine dollars per month for a six-month period. Shortly afterward he noted in his diary: "Very cold. All stayed indoors near the fire. Spaulding agrees to lose this day, as well as all others not fit to work."[85] According to the diary of Richard Cobden, who visited central Illinois in 1859, Michael Sullivant, an extensive landholder, had a large force of laborers for his 16,000 acres. His arrangements with the hands contained an understanding regarding rainy days: "He pays his laborers $15 a month, & board & lodging—He pays this amount for 26 days of labor, deducting wet days for which he gives food but no wages.—"[86] The wise employer indicated these stipulations when he hired his men so as to avoid subsequent misunderstandings.

80. Smith Diary, entry of August 3, 1848; see also Stout, "Autobiography of Hosea Stout, 1810 to 1835," 160–61. In contrast, urban laborers received no wages or work on rainy days. *Chicago Daily Democrat*, April 22, 1858; *Hunt's Merchant Magazine*, XXXVIII (June, 1858), 766.

81. Sewall, Diary, p. 179.

82. Thomas Diary, entry of April 13, 1852.

83. [Grove Wright?] to Allen G. Wright (Fredonia, Mich., February 15, 1857), A. G. Wright Papers.

84. Fletcher Diary, entry of May 31, 1854.

85. Sewall, *Diary*, p. 253. Sewall did not indicate how the loss was to be made up or if it was to be taken out of the pay. One solution would have been to make the hand work on Sunday. A farmer at Fairfield County, Ohio, in 1837 had a hired hand who lost several days: "He is to make up all lost time." Walters Farm Accounts, p. 22, entry of February 4, 1837.

86. Cawley, ed., *The American Diaries of Richard Cobden*, pp. 184–85.

Accommodations for the hired hands varied from farm to farm, but for many it was merely a matter of having a place to obtain a comfortable night's sleep. Both housing and boarding of hands were however no small concern to the busy, hard-working farm wife:

> It has been truly said that, 'no greater drawback' to the comforts and attractions of country life exists, than in the drudgery and discomfort to which farmers' wives and daughters are subjected in boarding and lodging large numbers of *hired men*. Laborers' and mechanics' wives have a comparative easy life, having but small families to provide for; but the wife of a large farmer, who must supply hearty meals for fifteen or twenty persons at least three times a day, passes a life of hopeless drudgery. . . .' How shall this be remedied, you ask? Every large farmer should provide small and comfortable cottages so that he can employ married men and have them board themselves. He can get better hands, and save the frequent changes often necessary, as well as relieve himself of a portion of loss of rainy days, for such a man could find work about his own premises, when a single man could do little or nothing for his employer. How much more convenient and agreeable to his own family, every farmer can answer, even if he has but one hired man to sit at the table through the season, and his wife finds a still greater difference in the care and labor required.[87]

Married hands were naturally preferred because they were considered reliable and trustworthy, and occasionally farmers were able to employ young couples. Wages were slightly higher than those of single hired men, but the hired hand's wife was expected to assist the farmer's wife with various chores.[88] In the opinion of the *Michigan Farmer*, such employment offered an ideal opportunity to laborers with families, since the farm was supposedly the best place to raise children.[89] But the truth of the matter was that most farm laborers were not married but single men for whom the farmers' wives had to furnish the necessary board and lodging.

Farm hands in pre–Civil War America were usually considered members of the family, or at least treated on a fairly equal basis. They ate at the same table and usually lived under the same roof with their employer and his family. For new farmers the first dwelling was a cabin of logs or a small frame house. The overhead loft was set aside

87. *Genesee Farmer*, XIX (January, 1858), 16.
88. Stewart, *Eleven Years' Experience in the Western States*, p. 86. For examples, see Lovira Hart to Lyman Abbey (Tuscola, Mich., August 4, 1841), Hart Correspondence; Nathan Pierce Accountbook, 1842–61, p. 82, entry of April 2, 1861.
89. *Michigan Farmer*, VIII (July, 1850), 219.

as the sleeping quarters for the hired hand and the farmer's children. Even established farms in the Midwest were known for their cramped quarters; farmers tended to improve their barns and sheds, while the farmhouse was of only secondary importance. As a result, the daughters found themselves sharing the loft or upper room with their brothers and the hired hands, with only a blanket to partition the area between them.[90] To avoid this situation, a Wisconsin settler in the 1830's constructed a log cabin of two rooms separated by a passageway; one room was for his family and the other for the hired help.[91] In another case, where the sod house of an Illinois pioneer was large enough only for his family, the hired hands took their meals in shifts with the family during the day but lodged elsewhere in the neighborhood at night.[92]

One practical solution was to house the hired help in separate cabins which were the equivalent of what eastern farm periodicals termed workers' cottages.[93] Such an arrangement was common even in the early Midwest. Traveling through southern Indiana in 1819, William Faux described an agreement between a farmer and his hired hand: "John Pedley bargained to-day with Mr. Ingle for one year, to receive thirteen dollars a month, and to have a house, and four acres of cleared land, for his use, while he continues in his service."[94] Benjamin Harris, a farmer and cattle raiser on four hundred acres at Champaign County, Illinois, employed eight to ten hands who were housed in three cabins.[95] So advantageous was this form of housing that a Michigan farmer encouraged his hired hand to construct a cabin, supplying the material and additional labor. In October, 1857, according to Nathan Pierce's accountbook, the farm hand agreed to work for the next year at thirteen dollars per month and build a log

90. *Indiana Farmer*, III (September 1, 1854), 366; *Ohio Cultivator*, XI (February 15, 1855), 60; *Michigan Pioneer Collections*, VII, pp. 389–91; "Reminiscences of William Austin Burt, Inventor of the Solar Compass," *Michigan History*, VII (1923), 34–35. Other arrangements were possible; an Illinois farmer housed his hands in the loft of the granary and provided them with cots. *Illinois Agricultural Transactions*, IV (1859–60), 202–3.

91. Brown, ed., *Rock County, Wisconsin*, I, pp. 131–32.

92. *History of Mercer and Henderson Counties*, pp. 174–75.

93. *Genesee Farmer*, X (January, 1849), 20. For additional reference to separate housing for tenant and farm laborers, see *ibid.*, XVII (October, 1856), 311–13; XIX (January, 1858), 16; *Moore's Rural New Yorker*, I (February 21, 1850), 60; *American Agriculturist*, XVII (March, 1858), 73–74; XVIII (June, 1859), 169–70.

94. Faux, *Memorable Days in America*, in Thwaites, *Early Western Travels*, XI, p. 299.

95. Harris, "The Autobiography of Benjamin Franklin Harris," 14.

cabin during the time. Pierce furnished the lumber, nails, window sash, and glass, while the hand completed the construction. Two other hands were provided at the necessary point to assist in rolling up the logs.[96]

The prudent farm hand arranged, when possible, to remain on the farm for the winter, working at less pay or for board and lodging only. But many farm laborers went into the towns and cities, where they used up their wages in board and room, making it difficult to save very much from one year to the next. In Illinois during the 1850's Thomas Bragg worked for wages in summer while accepting a chore job in the winter months. "A great many young men after working for a few months would go to town and board their wages out or spend it foolishly, but Mr. Bragg was not that kind. After the summer's work was done he would do chores in the winter and thus he saved what he had earned and when four years had passed he was able to buy a team and tools and engage in farming for himself."[97] Most farmers preferred to release their hands at the end of the season, but some retained them, either charging a small amount for board and lodging or letting them work at chores.[98]

Agricultural work was arduous, and farm laborers were not in an enviable situation during times of illness or misfortune resulting from an accident. No liability protection was afforded, and hired hands met illness and physical injury as best they could and attempted to get along on their own. Their employers might provide some immediate help but were not expected to assume long-term burdens or obligations. This attitude was clearly apparent in a contract for a farm hand in Illinois during 1845–46: "By beginning to day at 4.00 clock P.M. to work one year for the sum of sixty Dollars and in case of illness I am to charge him moderately for the same—if, the illness should not continue an unreasonable length of time—all days lost in sickness or by holidays are to be made up at the Year's end—he is to have his washing and mending done at his own expense."[99]

Farm hands, particularly those from the East, often fell victim to

96. Nathan Pierce Accountbook, 1848–60, p. 191, entry during October, 1857. For a similar case of a farm hand living in a log cabin, see Portrait and Biographical Album of McLean County, Ill., p. 1046.

97. Hoffman, History of La Salle County, Illinois, pp. 576–77.

98. For examples, see Elnathan and Jane Phelps to Edwin Phelps (Pontiac [Mich.], December 12, 1857), Phelps Family Papers; Clapp Farm Accountbook, entries of November 13, 1848; January 26, September 22, 1849.

99. Morrison Ledger, p. 34, entry of October 28, 1845, for Frederick Bohm.

the effects of the fever or ague in the Midwest.[100] After arriving at Chicago in 1836, Samuel Brown trekked down to Tazewell County, Illinois, where he worked as a farm laborer for several years. During this period he became so seriously ill that all his earnings were wiped out from the disability and related medical expenses. Not until 1843 had he saved enough to obtain a small start of forty acres.[101] Similar was the situation of James Flatt, a Canadian youth who came to Lee County, Illinois, in 1846. During the next seven years he worked out as a farm laborer but suffered bouts of illness that used up his savings; later in the 1850's he returned to Canada until his health was regained.[102]

Accidents were equally disastrous to the farm hand. An Ohio man in his early twenties worked as a farm hand for twelve dollars per month until he injured his leg; it ultimately required amputation. After many months of incapacity he had to accept charity.[103] But he was lucky in receiving aid from local charitable sources, while for others in a similar plight the alternative was less attractive. As a teenager Alfred Hirt worked on farms in Trumbull County, Ohio. When he became ill, his father, also a farm hand, was unable to assist him. The boy stayed at the county poor house until his health recovered. The experience provided a valuable lesson, and the lad resolved to improve his lot by learning the carpenter trade.[104] Farm hands who fell victim to sickness or accidents were placed in a vulnerable position, for their employers might or might not feel obligated to help. Young Hezekiah Brant worked on a farm in Clay County, Illinois, but met with an accident that left him disabled. He approached his employer for his pay, about which there was an apparent disagreement; the man refused to pay his injured farm hand the demanded wage.[105]

The farm hand who worked on a regular basis or was a member of the community possibly received better treatment than a stranger who obtained a job and then happened to become sick. During the sum-

100. For a general discussion of fevers and illness in the Midwest, see Buley, The Old Northwest, I, pp. 240–314.

101. Portrait and Biographical Album of McLean County, Ill., pp. 332–42.

102. Portrait and Biographical Album of Champaign County, Ill., p. 205.

103. George William Hill, History of Ashland County, Ohio (n.p., 1880), p. 214.

104. Jesse W. Weik, Weik's History of Putnam County, Indiana (Indianapolis, 1910), pp. 413–14; in a similar instance, History of Coles County, Illinois, pp. 581–82.

105. Gregg, History of Hancock County, Illinois, pp. 882–85.

mer of 1849, when the cholera epidemic was raging at Chicago, two young sailors headed out from the city and secured work as hired hands on a farm in Du Page County. One of them became ill after a few days in the field, apparently suffering from a fever, and was soon afterward transferred to a Chicago hospital. According to the report in the *Chicago Daily Democrat*, the sick man's removal was prompted by an angry mob. Fear that he was a cholera victim doubtless caused this reaction, but had the individual in question been a local person, such inhuman treatment probably would not have occurred.[106]

Local farm hands usually went home if they were ill for an extensive period. In March, 1852, Nathan Pierce hired Charles Griffith to work on the farm for eight dollars per month, but in May the accountbook read: "Charles Griffith quit work at noon sick and went home with the mumps."[107] Adam Brown, a hired hand in Kent County, Michigan, worked for sixteen dollars per month in 1857. Several times he was ill; he lost twelve and a half days from sickness but remained at his brother's place. When he quit work in June, Brown was debited $1.50 for a bottle of ague medicine purchased during his employment.[108]

Farmers kept track of lost time when their hands were sick and sometimes held this loss against them if they were employed a short period of time. The month was usually figured at twenty-six work days: a six-day work week with four Sundays as free time. A Michigan farmer in the 1850's hired a man to work one month for twelve dollars. He worked twenty-four and one-quarter days, and the farmer accordingly deducted seventy cents for one and three quarter days of sickness.[109] Steady or permanent employees apparently received liberal treatment with regard to lost days. Farmers noted them in the accountbook more or less for the record, and these short-term absences were generally tolerated as long as they were not too numerous or too long.

When the death of a hired hand occurred on the farm, his employer usually assumed responsibility for the final arrangements. William

106. *Chicago Daily Democrat*, August 21, 1849. Rural people maintained a negative view of towns and cities as breeding grounds for disease. Following the summer ravages of cholera in 1850, a Chicago newspaper announced: "As the health of the city is now nearly restored, we shall hope to see our country friends in town at an early day." *Western Citizen*, September 3, 1850.
107. Nathan Pierce Accountbook, 1848–60, p. 91, entries of March 27, May 17, 1852.
108. Cornell Daybook, entry of March 30, 1857, in the Buell Papers.
109. Nathan Pierce Accountbook, 1848–60, p. 44, entry of September 2, 1850.

Sewall's hired hand was killed in an accident on the farm, and the corpse was brought to the house and laid out. The next day Sewall noted in his diary: "Got plank of Mr. Meyers, (40 feet), and Dr. Chandler and I made the coffin, assisted by the neighbors, which occupied most of the day." Sewall had the services for his hired hand at the house and donated the grave plot: "Rev. Robert Leeper performed the funeral rites at my house, after which he was removed not far from here, a place (situated as a burial ground) where he was decently buried."[110] The hired hand unknown locally was given a brief service: the Reverend Samuel Fisk, a Methodist circuit rider, remarked on the passing of an obscure young farm hand in La Salle County, Illinois in 1840, commenting in a melancholy way that the news of the thirty-year-old farm hand's death would probably never come to the attention of his family in far-off Kentucky.[111]

The relationship between the farmer and his hired hand was more personal than that of an employer and common laborer in the town or city. Reasonable treatment and fairness assured the retention of a hand who might take some interest in the farm and its welfare, and this loyalty was often rewarded with appreciation by the farmer. The farmer who demanded too much failed to retain men more than one season. In like manner, the hired hand who was dishonest, shirked his work, or jeopardized the domestic scene was given his walking papers. An agreement or written contract was essential and helped prevent later misunderstandings. But the best advice for farmers who wanted good laborers was: "An underpaid man will frequently make his wages an excuse for neglect, but where full price is paid, you may reasonably demand full work."[112]

110. Sewall, *Diary*, p. 154. For a list of medical and funeral expenses for a Wisconsin farm hand, see Louis Frank, *Pionierjahre der Deutsch-Amerikanischen Familien Frank-Kerler in Wisconsin und Michigan 1849–1864* (Milwaukee, 1911), pp. 74–75.
111. Samuel Fisk Diary, 1840–43, pp. 17–23, entries of August 4–6, 1840.
112. *American Agriculturist*, XVIII (February, 1859), 36.

Leisure Time and Recreation

> Don't confine your attentions to your own boys, include all your
> hirelings in your care. Rainy days are sad ones for the poor,
> uneducated day laborer. . . . If they can find no amusement
> in books, give them something else. If there is no work to keep
> them from being idle while it rains, you had better set them
> pitching quoits or coppers on the barn floor, or under the shed,
> rather than suffer the tedium of "nothing to do." [1]

LEISURE TIME and recreation helped relieve the tedious
monotony of farm work. Although limited in contrast to those of the
town or city, outlets of amusement for the common laborer in rural
areas were available; they included fishing, hunting, and occasional
trips into town. Special events like dances, fairs, exhibitions, political
rallies, and elections also acted as powerful magnets luring the hired
hand off the farm and away from his work. And, of course, Sunday
was always a free day for the farm help. [2]

Fishing was a popular pastime pursued by farmer and hired hand
alike, according to a Minnesota farmer's diary in 1858: "All of us went
fishing." [3] This was cheap and easy fun for the hands, and the wise
farmer knew that it was better for the men than lounging and drinking in town taverns. Some employers viewed fishing excursions as lost
time, while others granted their hands free time from the day's routine, especially in slack periods. [4] In the absence of work, an Indiana
man wrote that he had been fishing and hunting while waiting for the
harvest season to work out as a cradler, binder, or raker. [5]

1. *The Plow*, I (October, 1852), 298.
2. Blake, *Farmer's Every-Day Book*, pp. 166–68. Blake strongly recommended
that hands should have the benefit of recreation and amusement. Sunday was a
good day for these activities; but this statement was qualified with regard to
harvest periods, when the press of work made leisure time impossible.
3. Larpenteur Diary, entry of August 17, 1858. For a similar case, see Fletcher
Diary, entry of June 21, 1856.
4. Jacob Wilson Accountbook, 1851–52, entry of April 28, 1851; Goodwin
Diary, entries of December 6, 1855, June 3, 1856.
5. David Francisco to Horace Cochran (Jacksonburg [Wayne County, Ind.?],
June 28, 1857), Strong Papers.

Hunting was also a popular sport, primarily during the slack winter season. "Now and then a farm servant will have leisure to take a gun and amuse himself for a day or two, without it being look upon as a great favour."[6] Farmers could be quite lenient and understanding in this regard. In the 1840's a Wisconsin farmer granted a number of free days to his hired hand for both fishing and hunting, even purchasing lead for the ammunition shells.[7] A similar understanding existed between a farmer and his hired hand at Lapeer County, Michigan, during 1853–55. Although John Perkins lost a number of days from work, his annual wage was increased from $130 to $140 by 1855. Hunting was a major activity in the autumn of 1855, when he purchased a new double-barreled shotgun—a fact which his employer noted because half a day's work was lost trying out the weapon for the first time. Apparently it was a matter of little concern, for the two men shortly afterward went out together hunting deer.[8]

Barn raisings and corn huskings were popular in rural areas and were usually open to all in the neighborhood, according to an early Ohio observer: "You were sure to see the laboring men of the vicinity out; and the wives of a goodly number of farm hands would be on hand to help in the cooking and serving at the table."[9] Farm hands often attended these community events to partake of the social conviviality, along with liberal amounts of food and drink.[10] House and barn raisings were also viewed as a rural civic duty not to be ignored by able-bodied men. A farm hand at Whitewater, Wisconsin, was hired to work eight months at ten dollars per month in the 1840's, and the only two days he missed from work were in attendance at a town meeting and helping in a house-raising.[11]

Use of a team and the farm wagon or buggy was a means of recre-

6. Regan, *Western Wilds of America, or Backwoods and Prairies*, p. 405. William Nowlin remarked that their hired hand on the farm near Dearborn, Michigan, carried a rifle with him while working in the field. On one occasion a black bear was shot as it entered a cornfield. Nowlin, *The Bark Covered House*, pp. 42–43.

7. Burgess Diary, entries of February 17, March 28, June 15, 1844; see also additional entries in April and May for days lost at hunting and fishing.

8. Warner Wright Goodale Personal Accountbook, entries for John Perkins during 1853–55.

9. Howells, *Recollections of Life in Ohio from 1813 to 1840*, p. 148.

10. For reference to hired hands attending these raisings, see Goodale Personal Accountbook, entries for Perkins in 1855; Burgess Diary, entry of May 21, 1855.

11. *Proceedings of the Home-Coming Festival Held July 4–7, 1907 on the Seventieth Anniversary of the Founding of Whitewater, Wisconsin* (n.p., 1907), p. 14.

ation for the hired hand, especially if he was serious in sparking or wooing a local girl who captured his fancy. A farm periodical advised its readers: "Don't charge your hired man, (if he is a faithful servant,) or your neighbor, on whom you depend for like favors, a few shillings for the hire of a horse or the like. . . ."[12] Yet it was a matter of personal discretion on the part of the farmer if his hired hand was to have the horse and wagon. For example, a Wisconsin farmer deducted $1.50 from the wages of his hired hand for the use of a horse and buggy on the Fourth of July in 1853.[13] Conversely, a Michigan farm hand in the 1850's remarked that his employer granted him permission to take the team at any time with no charge.[14]

Hired hands occasionally abused the trust their employers placed in them; an eleven-dollar-per-month hand at Calhoun County, Michigan, was sent to fetch a girl who was to work on the farm. Instead he used the team and buggy to visit his father in the adjacent county.[15] A farmer close to either a town or city encountered a similar problem, especially when the hired hand appropriated one of the horses on the farm for a jaunt into town. An angry farmer near Cleveland tersely recorded in bold ink strokes that his hired man had taken a horse and gone off to the city for the Fourth of July celebration without permission.[16]

Why was the town so attractive to hired hands? In comparison to the farm, it was a center of bustling activity and provided a degree of amusement. Henry Parker Smith, a farmer and storekeeper at Schoolcraft, Michigan, mentioned the combination of two factors which brought a number of people to town: the arrival of the circus and a rainy day. The streets were filled with a host of drunken men and women, wrote Smith angrily in his diary, the likes and numbers of which he had rarely seen before. Moreover, the rain drove the dirty crowd into the stores where it was popular to congregate.[17] The *Ohio Cultivator* described the lure of the local stores and public houses in town with regard to the farm hand: ". . . sometimes he might be found a mile to two distant at a grocery, eating crackers, dried her-

12. *New Genesee Farmer*, I (April, 1840), 61.
13. Burgess Accountbook, entry of July 4, 1853.
14. Myron Wright to Allen G. Wright (Marshall, Mich., March 7, 1852), A. G. Wright Papers.
15. Nathan Pierce Accountbook, 1848–60, p. 87, entry of March 21, 1852.
16. Ely Accountbook, entry of July 4, 1838.
17. Smith Diary, entry of May 1, 1857.

rings, smoking cigars, &c., and sometimes at public houses, and that is the way the money goes. . . ."[18]

Fairs, circuses, exhibitions, and wandering sideshows were important events in any rural locale, and farm accountbooks make frequent reference to hired hands abandoning work to attend them. These attractions were regarded as lost time from the work duties, and probably most farmers knew it was difficult if not impossible to keep their men on the job. Whether or not specific wage deductions were made for such lost time, the hired hands could usually count on drawing in advance from their wages one or two dollars as spending money.[19] Farmers themselves participated in the fairs and sometimes covered the expenses for their help who went along with the exhibiting livestock. An Indiana farmer entered a horse in the state fair in October, 1854, and paid a hand one dollar per day to care for the stock.[20] However, farm work might suffer if all the hands wanted to attend the fair. Calvin Fletcher complained that work on his farm was neglected; he had secured some Negro hands who deserted from the job, and as a result two of his regular hands were deprived of the chance to attend the fair. Fletcher expressed regret and compensated them with several extra dollars.[21]

Dances, balls, and barbecues were also popular pastimes for the farm help. A farmer near Indianapolis gave his nine-dollar-per-month hand a cash advance to attend a barbecue.[22] Wintertime was often devoted to dances which broke the monotony of the long season. At Kenosha County, Wisconsin, Lathrop Burgess's hired hand lost a half day's work in February, 1844, attending a ball.[23] John Staley, a

18. *Ohio Cultivator*, VIII (September 1, 1852), 267. An English traveler in America during the 1850's made a similar observation: "Often have I seen at the bars of public-houses in country districts, a crowd of idlers or to use the national term, 'loafers,' smoking wretched cigars, unshaven, dirty, meanly clad, and displaying on stoves, counters, and backs of chairs, boots which evidently had not been brushed for a fortnight." Baxter, *America*, p. 29.

19. William Gardner Farm Accounts, entry of June 22, 1845; Fielding Beeler Accountbook, pp. 121–22 and unpaginated entry of March 15, 1852; Joseph Beeler Accountbook, entry in 1852 for Jacob Price; Brown Account Ledger, 1840–80, p. 57, in Nessly-deSellem Papers; Nathan Pierce Accountbook, 1848–60, p. 60, entry for Jerome Burns in 1850; Darius Pierce Accountbook 1566 AA, entry of July 15, 1852. Admission to fairs usually cost twenty-five to fifty cents: see Lyman Accountbook, entries of September 25–26, 1856, September 29, 1857.

20. Fielding Beeler Accountbook, p. 85, entry under October, 1854.

21. Fletcher Diary, entry of October 20, 1852.

22. Joseph Beeler Accountbook, entry of October 4, 1837, for Charles Sparks.

23. Burgess Diary, entry of February 13, 1844.

farm hand near Chillicothe, Ohio, in writing to a friend disclosed that
he was employed on a farm outside the city for eleven dollars per
month including his laundry; in two weeks his time would be up.
His obvious interest in members of the opposite sex and their availability at dances in towns were lucidly described:

> I am now in town with a pocket full of rock as regards to the girl
> business the[re] is lotts of them here of the right stripe[.] I was at a
> part[y] last Tuesday night and I beat then [them?] at a-dancing and
> did not not [sic] try [.] I am going to a party next tuesday night I am
> a going to feel a pritty little girles ribs next Saturday night I think it
> is a chance if I do not take her to Iowa with me. . . .[24]

Fourth of July celebrations and election days brought farm hands
into town. Farmers rarely expected their hands to work on the national commemoration of Independence, and everyone took a holiday.[25] Frederick Augustus Kemper, whose farm was near Cincinnati,
recorded simply in his accountbook: "All hands lost today." John
Duret, who ran a vegetable truck farm south of Indianapolis, made a
similar comment in his diary: "Done nothing today—boys went to
town to celebrate." Affairs on the nursery and farm of Matthias Dunlap came to a complete halt on July 4, 1853: "To day the Boys have
gone to Chicago to celebrate the 4th & the hired men are having a
holiday. . . ." Dunlap added that when his correspondence was finished, the remainder of the day for him would be spent visiting
friends. Calvin Fletcher noted with little comment that on the Fourth
of July in 1856 all his hands were let off and work ceased for the day.[26]
Some probably remained on the farm and took their holiday there
in the form of rest, while local men returned home to visit their
families.[27]

24. John Staley to Jonathan Tutewiler (Chillicothe, Ohio, February 22, 1842).
As a side note of interest, some farm hands had musical talent and played
instruments: see A. O. Huffman and H. H. Hyer, eds., *Biographical Sketches of
Old Settlers and Prominent People of Wisconsin* (Waterloo, 1899), I, p. 36;
W. W. Stevens, *Past and Present of Will County, Illinois* (Chicago, 1907), I,
pp. 358–61; *Portrait and Biographical Album of Rock Island County, Illinois*,
p. 507.
   25. Farmers also came to town on holidays and used the opportunity to hire
extra help for their farms; for an interesting example, see *Portrait and Biographical Album of McLean County, Ill.*, p. 675.
   26. Frederick Augustus Kemper Accountbook, entry of July 4, 1850; Duret
Diary, entry of July 4, 1855; Dunlap Letterbook, 1853–55, p. 71, July 4, 1853;
Fletcher Diary, entry of July 4, 1856.
   27. For example see Nathan Pierce Accountbook, 1848–60, p. 130, entry of
July 4, 1854. Some of his hands took extra days besides the Fourth. Pierce
apparently gave John Wilcox his wages in advance; Wilcox took off from work

Political rallies and election day always sparked attention. Whether or not they voted, hired hands dropped their work to participate in the excitement, speeches, and frivolity, all heightened by the liberal flow of alcohol.[28] Hired hands who headed into the towns for these events probably spent money in one way or another. One of Nathan Pierce's farm hands, working for eleven dollars per month, attended a political rally in 1852, according to an entry in the farm accountbook: "I let Jerome Burns have cash one dollar to go to Kalamazoo whig meeting—"[29] Calvin Fletcher's farm hands put in only a half day on July 15, 1856, and then went into Indianapolis to attend the Fremont ratification meeting, much to their employer's dismay and disgust.[30] An entry in a Minnesota farmer's diary on election day in October, 1858, summed up the extent of labor: "Of course no work."[31]

With regard to voting rights, available evidence indicates that the local men of the community who incidently worked as farm hands were entitled to vote.[32] Whether farm laborers were entitled or qualified to vote could be overlooked in a close local election, but they were expected to cast their votes in an appropriate manner. Use of hired hands for this purpose was not unusual, for the practice of employing day laborers in cities near election time was common.[33] An Illinois Republican described how farm hands were sent down to the central part of the state, where their labor as well as their votes were crucial in the autumn elections of 1860:

"Now I wish to know if you can place a half a dozen good huskers at our disposal. I have made arrangements for the Kane County contingent when to go, and where to go, and what train to go by. Men will meet them on this side of the station where they are expected to leave

---

on July 2 and did not return until after the holiday. Pierce Accountbook, 1842–61 p. 52, entry of July 2, 1860.

28. Words cannot match the depiction of the midwestern election by the midcentury American painter George Caleb Bingham. The drunken scene reveals the cross-section of American society as it poured into the street of a small rural town on election day. A reproduction is found in John F. McDermott, *George Caleb Bingham* (Norman, 1959), pp. 237–39, plates 41–43.

29. Nathan Pierce Accountbook, 1848–60, p. 93, entry of October 29, 1852. For similar activities of Pierce's other hands, see Accountbook, 1842–61, p. 20, entry of July 4, 1843; p. 72, entry of November 6, 1860. See also Williamson Tanner's Accountbook, entries for Isaac Jefferies during 1836.

30. Fletcher Diary, entry of July 15, 1856.

31. Larpenteur Diary, entry of October 12, 1858.

32. See Nathan Pierce Accountbook, 1842–61, p. 20; Harry S. New, "The Importance of a Single Vote," *Indiana History*, XXXI (1935), 104–8.

33. Brown, *America*, p. 61.

the train, and they will find teams all ready to convey them to the neighborhoods where they are expected to work. A small pin stuck in the left lapel of the coat, sticking out about one-half its length, is the sign by which a corn husker is to be known on the train." He placed in my hand $125.00 in nice crisp $5.00 bills . . . and it was not long before we had a half dozen good men and true, to go to Central Illinois, to husk corn, and that voted too.[34]

Local farm hands exercised a more independent political attitude and voted according to personal preference.

Resident farm hands were also obliged to render service on militia muster days. The duty was rarely demanding and sometimes seemed ridiculously unmilitary and confused.[35] Farm accountbooks make it abundantly clear that hired hands participated in this duty, often to the disadvantage of the farmer who lost the men's labor on these days. Elnathan Kemper employed Asa Gloyd for fourteen dollars per month in summer and twelve dollars per month in autumn during 1818. Gloyd lost a day's work attending muster; his employer gave him a cash advance of fifty cents, presumably covering expenses of the day's outing.[36] In time of crisis this type of duty caused a labor shortage. During the Black Hawk War of 1831–32, an Illinois farmer expressed concern that his hired hand was supposedly drafted for duty: "Monday—23rd Indian War. Men were called out and put on the march. Hearing that Lewis was drafted, I hastened to the farm. Lewis was not obliged to go."[37]

Similar to militia duty was the road service obligation. Midwestern roads were kept in repair by local citizens, and usually an average of two to five days per year were required of able-bodied men in the neighborhood. Most farmers preferred this community effort in lieu of a cash road tax, but it was hardly a satisfactory solution. George Flower advised settlers in Illinois to expect to work five days at road labor, not an onerous task. Since many regarded the duty as a local

34. Bateman and Selby, eds., *Historical Encyclopedia of Illinois and History of Kendall County,* II, pp. 735–36.
35. According to George Flower, men were required to serve five days per year at militia muster; attendance was required at camp during the day but not at night! *Errors of Emigrants,* p. 48. The inept character of local military units in Illinois is analyzed by Isabel Jamison, "Independent Military Companies of Sangamon County in the 30's," *Illinois Historical Journal,* III (1911), 22–48.
36. E. Kemper Daybook, entries of August 3, September 3–4, 1818. For similar examples, see Nathan Pierce Accountbook, 1842–61, p. 21, entry of June 26, 1844; Lesher Farm Accounts, entry of March 27, 1847.
37. Sewall, *Diary,* p. 142. For a similar labor problem, see Philander Chase, *Bishop Chase's Reminiscences: An Autobiography* (Boston, 1848), II, pp. 182–85.

holiday, effective repair of the roadway was rarely accomplished. Flower implied that farm hands were obliged to perform this duty, but his statement was probably meant for local resident farm hands.[38] In Ohio, two days were expected of residents, and a reader of the *Ohio Cultivator* voiced objection in 1850 that this work tax fell disproportionately on the poor, those who seldom traveled roads, or individuals with no direct interest in their welfare.[39]

A letter from a German immigrant at Jefferson County, Wisconsin, cited an example of a man with eighty acres of land paying one dollar and rendering two days' service on road repair as his annual taxation. The inference was that property owners or permanent residents, unlike itinerant laborers, were liable for this tax.[40] Lathrop Burgess's hired hand at Kenosha County, Wisconsin, took several days off to work on his road tax; his employer figured this as lost time.[41] Jerome Burns lost time from Nathan Pierce's farm in 1852 to work on the road. According to Pierce's entry this hired hand was specifically working out his tax, even though it meant taking time from his farm employment.[42] Farm hands were sometimes assigned by their employers to public road work. A Wisconsin farm hand recorded in his diary during June, 1853, that he assisted in milking the cows and ". . . then went to work my employer's taxes on road by Norman Wood's in the forenoon and by Mrs. Squire's in the early afternoon. . . ."[43] For most farm hands on wages it made little difference if they spent several days working on the road instead of on the farm—their pay remained the same.

Upon the death of his hired hand in 1834, an Illinois farmer recorded of him in simple fashion: "He never made any profession or pretension of religion."[44] It might be surmised that this description applied to many who were farm hands, but probably these men were

38. Flower, *Errors of Emigrants*, p. 48. In early Michigan, hired hands working off their own road taxes were often given free use of a team and wagon by their employer on such days. Those men who brought such equipment could deduct a day's work. Davenport, *Timberland Times*, pp. 224–25.

39. *Ohio Cultivator*, VI (June 1, 1850), 163.

40. Detzler, " 'I Live Here Happily': A German Immigrant in Territorial Wisconsin," 257–58.

41. Burgess Diary, entry of July 1, 1844.

42. Nathan Pierce Accountbook, 1848–60, p. 93, entry of Jerome Burns in 1852.

43. Thomas Diary, entry of June 10, 1853. For other examples of farmers using hired hands to work the road tax, see Nathan Pierce Accountbook, 1848–60, p. 85, entries of June–October, 1851; Fielding Beeler Accountbook, p. 46.

44. Sewall, *Diary*, p. 154.

no more or less religiously inclined than other individuals in society. William Cooper Howells recalled an Irish farm hand who worked on the family farm in Ohio during the 1820's. Although this man was prone to drinking excessively at times, young Howells was sufficiently impressed with his other traits:

> As we had to hire help in our farming, he frequently worked for us. At any rate, I was a good deal in contact with him, and we always talked when we were together on all manners of subjects, he as a man of fifty and I a boy of fifteen. He would retail [sic] what he had read, and I would inquire and get from him his descriptions of Ireland and his details of experience or tradition. Or, we would discuss some book we had read, or one that he had lent to me or borrowed from me. The books he read were largely theological, of the Presbyterian school, and were generally solid works. So our conversations were seldom useless, and to me they were often a source of a good deal of information. I think it is not saying too much to put to his credit a stock of information equal to many months of school training. Looking back now, it seems to have been a valuable association, though the contact of a boy with a drunken Irishman would not usually be so regarded.[45]

Farmers generally took a dim view of hands who became drunk while in their employment; some used religious arguments to deter or dissuade them from the use of alcohol.[46] An Ohio woman recalled her childhood days in the 1830's when her father employed several hands at his combination farm, brickyard, and stone quarry. After breakfast each day the family and four farm hands listened to a chapter read from the Bible and knelt in prayer. Formerly an alcoholic, one of the hands was converted to sobriety by this religious-minded farmer; so impressed was this laborer that he later named his first child after his employer.[47]

45. Howells, *Recollections of Life in Ohio from 1813 to 1840*, pp. 100–101. Farm hands discussed a surprisingly large range of topics during their leisure time. For examples, see Braun and Brown, "Karl Neidhard's Reise nach Michigan," 51; Soren Bache, *A Chronicle of Old Muskego: The Diary of Soren Bache, 1839–1847* (Northfield, 1951), p. 173.

46. Alvah Brainerd, *A Pioneer History of the Township of Grand Blanc, Genesee County, Michigan* (Flint, 1878), p. 50.

47. Harriet Conner Brown, *Grandmother Brown's Hundred Years 1827–1927* (Boston, 1929), pp. 36–37. These hands were also in sympathy with their employer's sentiments regarding fugitive slaves; when several blacks were pursued by slave catchers, the hired hands blackened their faces and ran in the direction opposite of that taken by the slaves. The decoy was successful, and the slave hunters were thrown off track. Pp. 35–36.

Calvin Fletcher of Indianapolis maintained an adamant stand against alcohol on his farm. In October, 1848, following a visit to his farm on the edge of the city, he recorded in his diary the scene of apparent chaos arising from a drunken hand and declared in a burst of inspiration: "I have resolv[e]d never to have a profane drunken man on my premises again if I possibly can help it—I will also contrive that my men that work with me shall go to Ch[urch]."[48] Fletcher's religious sentiment was not mere lip-service. During the cholera epidemic of 1849 he cooperated with the local clergy who proclaimed a day of fasting and prayer in the midst of the hay-cutting time: "I dismiss[ed] the hands from work & told them I would pay them for the day—Some were all desireous [sic] to be prep[ar]ed to keep the solemn day of fasting & prayer appointed by the Pr[ies]t in consequence of the great calamity the cholera that now pervades the county. . . ."[49]

A certain amount of profanity was common among members of laboring classes, and farm hands were no exception. Farmers themselves were urged to avoid unbecoming language so as to set an example.[50] While for farm hands this was probably an ideal almost impossible to attain, some employers adopted a strict line. An Ohio farmer extended his religious views to this aspect of men's behavior and refused even to tolerate a hired hand swearing at the animals; for this act he fired one of his hands.[51] Religion had some influence in deterring hands from profanity, but the results were not always permanent. Burr W. Jones was raised in Rock County in southern Wisconsin during the 1850's, and he clearly remembered the excellent command of profane vocabulary possessed by the family's hired hands. One of them attended a camp meeting and "got religion," and things were quiet for about a week until an outburst of swearing in the barn dispelled any hope of reform.[52]

Farmers occasionally mentioned attendance of their hired hands at some form of religious service. At Warren County in southern Ohio, a hired hand began work in March, 1835, at ninety dollars per year on the farm of Andrew Whitacre. Various instances of lost time were

48. Fletcher Diary, entry of October 20, 1848.
49. Ibid., entry of July 30, 1849.
50. New England Farmer, as cited in New Genesee Farmer, II (June, 1841), 91.
51. Brown, Grandmother Brown's Hundred Years, p. 28.
52. Burr W. Jones, "Reminiscences of Nine Decades," Wisconsin History, XX (1936), 32.

charged against his account, such as for a sore foot, getting his shoes mended, going to town, and a full day lost at a camp meeting.[53] At Defiance, Ohio, William Holgate's hired man lost half a day attending a Catholic meeting.[54] Robert Hedpeth, a hired hand who worked for ten dollars per month on a farm near Indianapolis, took an active interest by offering to help with the construction of a church building and lost additional time attending religious services.[55] John Goodwin, a farmer in southeastern Indiana, noted that his hired hand went to church with him on Sunday.[56] Nor was it unlikely for farm hands to be more observant than their employers regarding church attendance. A letter written on a Sunday morning by an Illinois farmer mentioned that his wife was still in bed asleep while their children had accompanied the hired hands to the church meeting.[57] In the final analysis, some farm hands attended religious services while others did not. Sunday, at any rate, was free time for the farm help, and they decided how it was to be spent.

Most farm laborers did not acquire many possessions or belongings, except for essentials which were purchased as needed. The standard accessory for farm hands on the move was a large handkerchief or bandana, which was also useful on the job for wiping sweat off the neck and face on warm days. The few possessions were easily bundled into the handkerchief and carried over the shoulder.[58] In Ohio during the 1820's it was common to see many a young man traveling about the countryside with a pack on his back, held in place with two straps passing over his shoulders. The handkerchief was then tied in the front to prevent the straps from sliding off.[59]

A form of recreation was going to town; there various items were purchased, including clothes, boots, socks, handkerchiefs, tobacco, and other sundries. Farm hands without funds had two alternatives: obtain a cash advance from the employer, or request that the purchase be made by the employer, who debited the charged item

53. Whiteacre Farm Accountbook, entry of March 2, 1835.
54. Holgate Accountbook, p. 44, entry of May 29, 1847.
55. Fielding Beeler Accountbook, pp. 82–83, 86.
56. Goodwin Diary, entry of February 3, 1856.
57. Buck, "Pioneer Letters of Gershom Flagg," 181. Insight into the character of a hired hand is seen in Nathan Pierce's accountbook entry for Jerome Burns, a common farm hand working by the month. Pierce gave him fifty cents to attend a lecture, and a week later another fifty cents was advanced so that Burns might make a contribution for a family burned out of their home. Pierce Accountbook, 1848–60, p. 130, entries of May 8, 13, 1854.
58. *Portrait and Biographical Album of Rock Island County, Illinois*, p. 445.
59. *Condensed History of Jefferson, Ashtabula County, Ohio*, pp. 48–49.

against the hand's final wage settlement. Similarly, the farmer sometimes paid the hand's debts for him and later deducted the amounts
from his wages.[60] There is good evidence that farm hands, if known
by the town merchant, also had the privilege of charging purchases
to their employer's account. Usually an informal understanding involving all parties regulated this arrangement. The farm accountbook
of Nathan Pierce noted that his hired hand lost a half day from work
on a Saturday in May, 1851, to go to nearby Marshall, Michigan,
where he traded on "my account" for $3.43 worth of items.[61]

Purchases varied from essentials such as clothes, shoes, and gloves
to more unusual items. Warner Goodale, a farmer at Lapeer County,
Michigan, lent his hired hand the money for a watch and carefully
added in the account that a half day was lost traveling to town for
it.[62] Daniel Thomas, a local hired hand at Kingston, Wisconsin, in
1853 had a store order which he presented for stocking yarn; at the
same time the storekeeper, also a farmer, let him have a hay fork in
consideration for threshing at a later date when the wheat was harvested.[63] And as an indication of a pastime for hired hands, a farm
laborer in Ohio had his account debited for the purchase of an
accordion.[64]

Footgear was an essential expenditure for farm laborers. A thick
pair of shoes cost one dollar for Anthony Stranahan's farm hand in
1822.[65] Joseph Beeler at Indianapolis purchased the shoes for his
hands: in 1836 his twelve-dollar-per-month farm hand was debited
$2.25 for a pair of coarse shoes, while the same account indicated that
shoe repair on one occasion cost 87½ cents. Similarly, a day laborer
on the Beeler farm was debited $1.50 for a pair of shoes, along with
a memorandum for tobacco and boots for $2.75 and $2 for a fur cap.
In 1847, Martin Pierson worked for Beeler at eight dollars per month;
against his account were debits for a chopping ax at $1.50, pair of
shoes $1.25, palm leaf hat 50 cents, cash in town 10 cents, woman's

60. Joseph Beeler Accountbook, undated entry for hired hand named Swain.
Beeler followed this procedure with his other hands: see entries for C. Carter,
a fifteen-dollar-per-month hand. Beeler and Carter went into town, where Beeler
paid "for you in market" and also advanced four dollars to pay a Mr. Campbell.
Entry of May 8, 1837.

61. Nathan Pierce Accountbook, 1848–60, p. 64, entry of May 7, 1851.
Pierce's hands got their footwear when Pierce's family obtained theirs. See p. 23,
entry of April 12, 1850.

62. Goodale Personal Accountbook, entries for John Perkins during 1853–54.

63. Thomas Diary, entries of August 10, 19, 1853.

64. Clapp Farm Accountbook, p. 81, entries for Jacob Turner during 1850–51.

65. Stranahan Farm Accounts, pp. 103–4, entries for Oliver Kingsbury.

shoes 75 cents, "goods at Hubbard's" 75 cents, saddle and bridle $15.50, and an overcoat $9.[66]

An interesting array of expenses appeared in the records of Samuel Fowler, a farmer at Walworth County, Wisconsin, during the late 1840's and 1850's. For example, Andrew Murdock was hired for a year at eight dollars per month; cash was provided to pay his bills, along with an advance of one dollar for a donation party and one dollar for a pair of buckskin mittens. William Gaunt was employed at nine dollars per month, and his account was debited sixty-three cents for seven yards of striped shirting, fifty cents for two shirts, and nineteen cents for a pair of overalls. John Langin, working six months at $12.50 per month, received cash advances for boots and having his teeth pulled.[67] Tobacco appeared frequently in the debit columns of farm accountbooks. Luther Huston's hands on his farm near Piqua, Ohio, consumed varying amounts of this item. A plug cost five cents, but a half pound could be obtained for about twelve and a half cents.[68]

Information on winter wear of farm hands is found in the store ledgers of John Williams, a merchant at Springfield, Illinois. The account of 1852–53 for John Hecker ("Dutchman at Old Farm") included one dollar for buckskin gloves, seven dollars for a blanket coat, thirty cents for socks, and seventy-five cents for a cap. Hecker, who earned thirteen dollars per month, required a cash advance of four dollars to have a coat made.[69] Fine clothes appealed to some farm hands, and store ledgers provide a small but positive indication of

66. Joseph Beeler Accountbook, entries for C. Carter during 1836–37; Fielding Beeler Accountbook, pp. 2–3, 36–37. Palm leaf hats became popular in the 1830's and 1840's. The center for their manufacture was in Massachusetts, where the imported leaf was fashioned into hats by girls and women in their homes under the putting-out system. The price of the hats ranged from twenty-five cents to two dollars. Niles' Register, XL (June 18, 1831), 281; XLVIII (May 23, 1835), 204; LXVI (March 2, 1844), 16.

67. Samuel Fowler Accountbook, III, pp. 57, 73, entries for Andrew Murdock during 1849, 1851; see also entries for William Gaunt of January 15, 1857, and John Langin of April 5, 1859, Nourse Papers.

68. Huston Account Ledger, pp. 6, 14, entries of 1850–51.

69. Williams Business Papers: Journal, 1851–54, p. 50. This same individual did prairie breaking and hauling for Williams amounting to $18.39, which evenly balanced out a list of debits for sundry items at the store, including shoes, boots, pocket knives, etc.; p. 217. Similarly, Luther Huston's hired hand ran up a bill in 1852 for pants, socks, and mittens at stores in Piqua and Troy, Ohio. Huston Account Ledger, p. 9. Buckskin mittens were probably preferred to cloth types. A Minnesota farmer noted in his diary that cloth mittens tended to freeze and stick to the hands in work such as gathering and loading fodder in winter. John R. Cummins Farm Diary, 1857–60, entry of November 18, 1857.

tastes in this regard. In 1835 Williams established an account for a
George Bishop, who ". . . works on A. D. Vaunter Farm." The purchases included a coat for $9, leghorn hat for $1.25, a pair of cashmere
pants with a satin vest for $5.50, along with another pair of pants for
$4.50. This hand was a good credit risk, and he paid for his purchases
with cash and valid notes.[70]

The farmer could provide an alternative to the hired hand's going
to town for clothing by having his wife sew some of the essential
items. This spared the farm hand the expensive mark-up prices of the
storekeeper, especially when the purchase was made on credit. Or the
farm hand could buy material and take it to a woman in the neighborhood to fashion into shirts or basics. Local women were available
to perform sewing services, and some even wove their own cloth.
Cynthia Hatfield, a widow in Huron County, Michigan, continued
operating the farm after the death of her husband in 1846. She employed men by the day rate of fifty cents and arranged to pay them in
cloth, successfully maintaining the farm for ten years until she sold
it in 1856.[71] Similarly, at Jackson, Michigan, Mrs. John Wellman
gained a reputation over the years for making clothes for men and
boys in the neighborhood, doing this sort of work from 1830 until the
Civil War.[72]

The farm hand who arranged with his employer to have clothes
made saved money. In 1851 Spencer Carrier, a farmer at Fond du Lac,
Wisconsin, hired Joseph Roberds. His employment at first was con-
ditional, working the first half-month at four dollars; if both parties
were satisfied, Roberds was to remain for the year at one hundred
dollars. Carrier's wife made several pieces of clothing for Roberds
during the year. Her charges were quite moderate—usually fifty cents
for a set of items such as two overalls, two undershirts, and two regular shirts—the cost of a clothing piece averaging twenty-five cents.[73]
This cost price per garment agreed with similar figures elsewhere in
the Midwest. William Holgate, a farmer at Defiance County in north-
western Ohio, negotiated a specific agreement containing a clause

70. Williams Business Papers: Petty Ledger, 1854–58, p. 169.
71. *Firelands Pioneer*, XVII (December, 1909), 1597.
72. *History of Jackson County, Michigan*, p. 217. A Wisconsin farm hand
in 1844 was debited $2.50 for the purchase of five yards of flannel. Burgess
Diary, 1844–45, entry of January 26, 1844. At Calhoun County, Michigan,
Nathan Pierce debited his hand three dollars for three yards of grey woolen
cloth for pantaloons. Accountbook, 1842–61, p. 21. At Portage County, Ohio,
Merrick Ely's hand was charged two dollars for cloth to be fashioned into
pantaloons. Ely Accountbook, p. 38.
73. Carrier Diaries, entries for Joseph Roberd during 1851.

pertaining to clothes. In 1847 he hired a hand to work for ten dollars per month, including laundering of clothes. In addition, six shirts were to be made for him during this period, not to exceed in cost twenty-five cents each.[74]

Generally laundering and minor mending of clothes were included in the hired hand's agreement. This gave him greater freedom with his leisure time but burdened the farmer's wife; it is not difficult to surmise that many women disliked the added responsibility. An Illinois woman was clearly irritated when her husband casually told three of his four hired hands that they could have their laundry done for them, but she took compassion on the fourth and told him that he might as well have the same privilege.[75] A memorandum in an Ohio farmer's accountbook in 1852 was typical: "He commenced working by the month for me the 12th of the 4th month 1852[,] to work 7 months for 85 dollars first day board and mending and washing the bargain."[76] In other instances farm hands assumed responsibility for their own laundry. Teenaged Justus Griffeth worked out in Pike County, Illinois, during the 1840's, earning seven to ten dollars per month, but he had to take care of his own laundry. Since he was turning his wages over to his mother, she probably washed his clothes for him.[77] Another variation on this arrangement was to charge the hand or deduct a certain amount per month from his wages.[78]

Brief mention should be made of peddlers who sometimes supplied farm hands with sundry items, thereby eliminating the need to make purchases in town.[79] The Indiana farm records of the Beeler family

74. Holgate Accountbook, p. 37, entry of March 10, 1847; see also p. 35, entry of February 2, 1847. At Kent County, Michigan, a farm hand was charged 62 cents for mending shirts and a dollar for cutting and making four pair of jeans. Cornell Daybook, entries in account sheet of John Schaffer, 1856–57, in Buell Papers. A hired hand on a Cuyahoga County farm in northern Ohio was debited $1.50 for four shirts. Clapp Farm Accountbook, p. 81, entry of April 2, 1850. For examples of farmers who paid their hands part of their wages in clothes, see *Commemorative Biographical and Historical Record of Kane County, Illinois*, pp. 605–6; Duis, *The Good Old Times in McLean County, Illinois*, pp. 739–40.

75. Tillson, *A Woman's Story of Pioneer Illinois*, p. 114.

76. Shinn Ledger, p. 73, entry of April 10, 1852.

77. Massie, *Past and Present of Pike County, Illinois*, p. 464.

78. William Henry Perrin, ed., *History of Alexander, Union and Pulaski Counties, Illinois* (Chicago, 1883), part V, p. 192. Frederick Stevens, a farm hand at Defiance County, Ohio, in the 1830's, earned $4 per month from which $1.25 per month was deducted for laundering and mending. *History of Defiance County, Ohio*, p. 212.

79. These peddlers covered a wide area and often knew every farmer along their route, according to John Andrew Russell, *The Germanic Influence in the*

show that in 1837 Joseph Beeler paid a peddler $1 for an item purchased by his hired hand, while another hand bought a $2.50 vest with his employer supplying the cash and debiting the hand's account. His son, Fielding Beeler, also financed the same type of transaction when he advanced one of his men twenty-five cents in order to purchase a book.[80]

There were few outlets for farm hands to spend their money except at the circus and fair, and, of course, for necessities at the local store in town. Most farmers were circumspect in matters of credit and cash advances. If the hired hands spent wildly or amassed too many debts at the store, there was a risk that they might disappear from the job without fulfilling their obligations. Farmers wisely limited the number of trips into town as much as possible without offending the men; this could be accomplished with judicious granting of free time to engage in fishing, hunting, or perhaps a day of relaxation during inclement weather.

Making of Michigan (Detroit, 1927), pp. 334–35. An Irishman worked for a time as a thresher in eastern Ohio, and the money earned from this employment enabled him to outfit himself as a peddler. J. A. Caldwell, *History of Belmont and Jefferson Counties, Ohio* (Wheeling, 1880), p. 478.

80. Joseph Beeler Accountbook, entries for C. Carter in 1837 and for Swain during 1838–39; Fielding Beeler Accountbook, pp. 2–3, entries for Martin Pierson. For additional mention of peddlers stopping at farms, see Frederick A. Kemper Accountbook, entry of December 26, 1836; Anson Buttles Diary, entry of July 10, 1856.

Conclusion

Many independent men everywhere in these states, a few years back in their lives, were hired laborers. The prudent, penniless beginner in the world, labors for wages awhile, saves a surplus with which to buy tools or land for himself; then labors on his own account another while, and at length hires another new beginner to help him.[1]

ABRAHAM LINCOLN'S childhood and adult life were closely intertwined with the agricultural sinews of an agrarian society; once a farm laborer himself who spent many lonely hours splitting rails, he understood the struggle of those ascending the agricultural ladder of success. Lincoln witnessed in his own lifetime certain changes in his native Midwest. The years between the War of 1812 and the Civil War reflected four and one half decades of steady growth with the establishment of over 600,000 farms. By 1860 the midwestern expanse of 322,876 square miles contained a population of over seven million, with an average of twenty-six persons per square mile.[2]

The formal enumeration of agricultural labor, as a specific occupational group, appeared for the first time in the census report of 1860. These figures are questionable because too many are listed as farmers and too few as farm laborers.[3] The occupation of farm labor was considerably more complex and multi-faceted than the standard definition of hired hand suggests. The seasonal aspect of farm employment also increased the job turnover, a trend more prevalent in the

1. T. Harry Williams, ed., *Abraham Lincoln: Selected Speeches, Messages, and Letters* (New York, 1962), p. 173. For reference to Lincoln's view of the hired laborer and the early Midwest, see J. G. Randall, *Lincoln the President* (New York, 1945), I, p. 2.
2. *Preliminary Report on the Eighth Census*, pp. 121, 131, 197; *Agriculture of the United States in 1860*, p. 222.
3. For this problem, see Gates, *Farmer's Age*, pp. 272–75; Merle Curti, *The Making of An American Community: A Case Study of Democracy in a Frontier County* (Stanford, 1959), p. 140ff.

TABLE 4. FARM LABORERS, FARMERS, AND FARMS IN THE MIDWEST, 1860

	Farm laborers	Farmers	Farms
Ohio	76,484	223,485	179,889
Indiana	40,827	158,714	131,826
Illinois	47,216	153,646	143,310
Michigan	35,884	88,657	62,422
Wisconsin	31,472	93,859	69,270
Minnesota	—	27,921	18,181

Sources: *Agriculture of the United States in 1860*, p. 222; *Population of the United States in 1860* (Washington, 1864), pp. 662–63.

North with its diversified economy. And since the Old Northwest became an economic extension of northern agriculture, especially in terms of wage labor, farm hands throughout the entire region shared certain basic traits of an earlier period.

The faithful hired hand working year 'round on the family farm evoked pleasant memories. One New Englander recalled the halcyon years after the War of 1812 when responsible young men worked on neighborhood farms:

> The sons of small farmers, wishing to raise a little money for themselves, would sometimes hire out at about three pounds a month and found. They lived with their employer, fared as he did, worked by his side; and when the hired man put on his Sunday suit, he offered his arm to the prettiest of the farmer's daughters and escorted her gallantly to meeting. The term *servant*, and the idea of service, were unknown. He was a 'hand,' or 'help.'[4]

But New England agriculture experienced the impact of changing markets, specialized production, and railroads; simultaneously the factory system enticed greater numbers of the farm labor class away from the countryside.[5] Elsewhere in the East, New York and Pennsylvania underwent change in the rural economy as the center of wheat farming advanced westward across Ohio, into Indiana and Illinois, and up into Wisconsin and Minnesota.[6] The resulting shortage of farm labor was lamented by the editor of the *New England Farmer* in 1840:

> The great variety of mechanical employments existing among us, the amount of hands occupied at high prices in our manufacturing es-

4. Thomas L. Nichols, *Forty Years of American Life* (London, 1864), I, p. 20.
5. Percy W. Bidwell, "The Agricultural Revolution in New England," *American Historical Review*, XXVI (1921), 683–702.
6. Gates, *Farmer's Age*, pp. 165–66.

tablishments, the emigration of young men into the new States, the
great numbers who go into the learned professions, the unnumbered
herds that crowd into cities . . . sweep the country almost clean of
young men, and render it next to impossible to procure the labor
necessary to manage a farm.[7]

One solution frequently mentioned in farm journals during the
1840's and 1850's was to reduce excess labor requirements through
concentrated production, particularly dairy, horticultural, and truck
farming.[8] Eastern farmers were urged not to compete against western
farmers in the large-scale production of grain, but to concentrate on
high-yield or specialized crops. Labor could be concentrated on less
acreage to produce maximum profits and thus minimize operating
costs.[9]

Another solution was to employ foreign help. Immigration was
light during the early nineteenth century but increased between 1830
and 1860. The total influx of foreign born exceeded five million during
the 1820–60 period. The census recorded their occupational backgrounds in Europe; such categories as farmer, laborer, and servant
were among the more common. Since America was mainly an agrarian
society, and because three-quarters of the populace lived on farms
or in rural areas, many in these categories probably obtained employment on farms and at road, canal, and railroad construction. According to the census report of 1860, 87 percent of the foreign born settled
in the free states, with the greatest foreign increase between 1850 and
1860 occurring in Ohio, Illinois, and Wisconsin.[10]

Decent wages and good working conditions in America, declared
James Silk Buckingham in the 1840's, awaited emigrants from the
British Isles:

If the contrast is striking between the English and American farmer,
it is still more so between the farm-labourers of the two countries. In
England it is well known what miserable wages agricultural labourers

7. *New England Farmer*, XIX (July 22, 1840), 22.
8. This type of farming was also known as "high farming," according to one
early advocate: see Morris, *Ten Acres Enough*, pp. 226–27.
9. For samples of opinion, see *New Genesee Farmer and Gardener's Journal*,
I (January, 1840), 8; *Monthly Journal of Agriculture*, I (July, 1845), 13;
American Farmer's Magazine, XII (September, 1858), 524–26; *Working Farmer*,
VII (April 1, 1855), 28; *Plough, Loom and Anvil*, IX (May, 1857), 657–59;
New England Farmer, II (June 8, 1850), 190; II (December 7, 1850), 404;
VII (March, 1855), 118–19; VIII (December, 1856), 539–41.
10. *Preliminary Report on the Eighth Census*, pp. 16–19; *Population of the
United States in 1860*, introduction, xxx–xxxi.

receive; 10 to 12 shillings, perhaps the average;—what scanty fare they are obliged to subsist upon—flesh meat once or twice a week, at the utmost; and how perpetually they stand in danger of the work-house, with all their desire to avoid it, with no education themselves, and no desire to procure any for their children. Here, there is not a labourer on the farm who receives less than a dollar a day, or 24 shillings per week; while many receive more; and those who are permanently attached to the farm have wages equal to that throughout the year. Besides that, they have as good living at the farm-house as prosperous tradesmen in the middle ranks of life enjoy in England; three substantial meals a day, and in hay and harvest time four, with abundance and variety at each.[11]

British emigration during 1815–60 has been extensively researched by Charlotte Erickson, who maintains that English agricultural laborers were more adaptable to American farming than other immigrant groups. Besides, failure in agriculture was not necessarily disastrous, since they were sufficiently skilled and educated to find employment elsewhere in the American economy.[12] Joseph Schafer suggested a similar interpretation for the Germans and Scandinavians who migrated to Wisconsin during 1845–60. Common among these groups was a dedication to hard work as a means of obtaining their own farms; agricultural employment was often the best and most practical way to achieve this goal.[13]

The initial waves of immigrants assimilated smoothly into American society with minimal problems. Englishmen, sharing a common language and Protestant background, experienced the least difficulty throughout the entire 1815–60 period. Toward the Irish migration, which was especially heavy during 1840–60, the native American welcome was shadowed with prejudice and resentment, owing mainly to strong anti-Catholic feelings. The Irish and Germans stepped into positions vacated by American farm hands who either sought employment in the factories of New England or went westward. As one observer declared, ". . . the inferior but necessary labor of a farm

11. J. S. Buckingham, *America, Historical, Statistic, Descriptive* (London, [1841]), II, pp. 412, 414–16. Henry Fearon also noted the absence of a servant class in America; *Sketches of America*, p. 80.

12. For Charlotte Erickson's articles, see "British Immigrants in the Old Northwest, 1815–1860," in David M. Ellis, ed., *The Frontier in American Development: Essays in Honor of Paul Wallace Gates* (Ithaca, 1969), pp. 323–56; and "Agrarian Myths of English Immigrants," in Ander, ed. *In the Trek of the Immigrants*, pp. 59–80.

13. Schafer, *Wisconsin Domesday Book: The Lead Region*, p. 228.

must be performed now, in the majority of cases, by the most inefficient of Americans, or by the rawest and most uncouth of Irish or Germans."[14]

Reports were common of New England farmers hiring foreigners, because American-born children no longer considered farm employment respectable. This shortage of farm help included not only able-bodied hands but also hired girls, according to the *New England Farmer*: "The younger members of the family, especially, are growing up with the idea that the washing and scouring and cooking, the harder and more unpleasant part of the labor, which is done by Irish help, is unsuitable for them, is a degradation; and they learn to despise it. . . . The pernicious effects of this change are manifest in our families and in our children."[15] Eastern farmers were not the only ones to suffer from a shortage of hired farm help, for this situation became common throughout the free states in the 1840's and 1850's.

The working conditions on farms and the status of farm hands varied little between the Midwest and the East, although a sense of egalitarianism may have been more prevalent in the developing western areas. The daily routine of farm chores was fairly standard on farms in New England, the Middle Atlantic states, and the Midwest. The average work day was determined by what could be accomplished between sunrise and sunset. "An American labourer is not regulated," declared William Cobbett, "as to time by *clocks* and *watches*. The *sun*, who seldom hides his face, tells him when to begin the morning and when to leave off at night. He has a dollar, a *whole dollar*, for his work; but then it is the work of a *whole day*. Here is no dispute about *hours*."[16]

The length of the working day approximated twelve hours or the equivalent of sixty hours per week on most northern farms, although the working day's length in New York and Illinois was thirteen to fourteen hours or the equivalent of a sixty-six hour week.[17] However, the idea of a ten-hour day gained popularity by 1840, when President Van Buren proclaimed the ten-hour day for federal employees. Several states followed the lead of New Hampshire in 1847, legal-

14. Donald G. Mitchell, *My Farm of Edgewood: A Country Book* (New York, 1912), pp. 83–85.

15. *New England Farmer*, IX (May, 1857), 247–48; see also IV (August, 1852), 377–78; VII (June, 1855), 258; VIII (November, 1856), 523; IX (August, 1857), 360–61.

16. William Cobbett, *A Year's Residence in the United States* (Carbondale, 1964), p. 180; see also Shirreff, *A Tour through North America*, p. 16; *Illinois Farmer*, IV (April 4, 1859), 243.

17. *U.S. Department of Labor Bulletin No. 499*, p. 225.

izing the ten-hour day except where negotiated contracts specified otherwise.[18]

The eastern farm press assessed the merits of a ten-hour day in agricultural occupations and considered the idea reasonable, at least in theory. Others questioned the expediency of working farm hands at a vigorous pace during ten hours rather than at a slower pace for twelve hours per day. The average farm hand knew what was a fair amount of work for a given period. If the farmer tried to demand greater speed or effort during a shorter working day, the hand trained himself to go slower simply out of necessity to conserve himself.[19] The ten-hour day was also impractical during the midsummer harvest when grain had to be cut within a limited period. Wages and working hours had to be determined instead according to the immediate operational needs of the farm.[20]

Sunday was widely acknowledged as a free day for the farm hands. Under the ten-hour-day formula, a full work week of six days, Monday through Saturday, was the norm; but if the twelve-hour workday prevailed, part of Saturday was considered free time. Most farmers released their help from work following the noon hour on Saturday, enabling the men to go into town for the afternoon or evening. The available evidence indicates that farm laborers did not work longer, either by the day or week, than other occupations. The average of sixty to sixty-six hours per week was standard in most states, except for New England, where common laborers put in a seventy to eighty-hour week. Teamsters also averaged a sixty-six to eighty-hour week.[21]

Most agricultural laborers were hired on a seasonal rather than annual basis, usually for six to eight months from March through October. The wages of men retained during the winter dropped off sharply after September and remained low until the following spring.[22] This pattern was common throughout the northern states. The winter months had a depressing effect on other occupations, including common labor and the building trades. Farm hands were thrown into un-

18. In sections of Pennsylvania and New York, a ten-hour day on farms was observed as early as 1829, according to Stuart, *Three Years in North America*, I, p. 271.

19. *New England Farmer*, XX (April 13, 1842), 326.

20. *Genesee Farmer*, XIX (July, 1858), 217.

21. *U.S. Department of Labor Bulletin No. 499*, pp. 159–60, 225, 253–54, 448.

22. T. M. Adams, "Prices Paid by Vermont Farmers for Goods and Services and Received by Them for Farm Products, 1790–1940; Wages of Vermont Farm Labor, 1780–1940," *Bulletin No. 507, Vermont Agricultural Experiment Station* (Burlington, 1944), see esp. 84–86, figure 27. Hereafter cited as Adams, "Vermont Prices and Wages."

employment at an inopportune moment and in direct competition with other seasonally distressed laborers. A common solution was to seek winter work, including logging, teamstering, driving livestock, and clearing land. Otherwise it was necessary to put up for the winter in a nearby town or city where carefully saved wages tended to dwindle away.[23] Whenever times were hard, hired hands could anticipate lower wages or even unemployment. According to a leading farm journal, farm hands were able to afford a cut in wages; such logic was based on the notion that any reduction in wage levels paralleled a proportionate reduction in the price of common goods purchased by laborers.[24]

An accurate determination of farm wages in this period leaves much to be desired, the lack of comprehensive data being the greatest problem. Information about wages usually appears in single or scattered reports, while descriptions of travelers also are helpful. Comparing the agricultural labor class of his native England to its American counterpart, James Johnston wrote in 1851:

> An interesting fact connected with the agricultural history of this country is, the change that has taken place in the relative values of human labour and of rural produce. Forty years ago the wages of a man for a year were valued at the price of one yoke of oxen, or of 50 bushels of wheat. Now they are equal to the value of two yoke of oxen, or of 100 bushels of wheat. This does not indicate a corresponding money-rise in the wages of labour. The difference is partly caused by a fall in the market-value of agricultural produce; but, as all other necessaries of life are at least as cheap as they were forty years ago, the condition of the agricultural labourer must have improved. I doubt if, in any part of our islands [United Kingdom], the same can be said in regard to the condition of our agricultural labourers.[25]

Farm wages, as this Englishman correctly observed, improved during the first half of the nineteenth century. Except for temporary declines in depression periods, this gradual upward trend prevailed

23. See Faux, *Memorable Days in America*, in Thwaites, *Early Western Travels*, XI, p. 141; Holmes, *An Account of the United States of America*, pp. 126–27; *New England Farmer*, VIII (April, 1856), 158; *Genesee Farmer*, XIII (June, 1852), 181–82.

24. *New England Farmer*, XXI (January 18, 1843), 230; see also VII (August, 1855), 361; *Daily Commercial Register*, May 4, 1858. Frederick Law Olmsted compared prices for goods and wages during 1836–43. According to his calculation, it required less labor to acquire goods whose prices fell more rapidly than wages. *A Journey in the Seaboard Slave States* (New York, 1859), p. 706. For a similar view, see Adams, "Vermont Prices and Wages," 96, figure 33.

25. Johnston, *Notes of North America Agricultural, Economical, and Social*, I, pp. 208–9.

through the late 1840's. In his history of New York agriculture, Hedrick noted fairly stable, unfluctuating wage levels with a slight downward trend in the 1840's. Lebergott reported a similar situation for the adjoining state of Pennsylvania during 1800–1835.[26] Equally informative is Adams's study of wages and farm prices for Vermont. His findings are comparable with those elsewhere, at least in the northern agricultural states. A mild wage decline occurred during 1815–21, largely a result of deflationary trends following the War of 1812 and the Panic of 1819. A gradual, long-term improvement in wages prevailed between 1821 and 1837, interrupted by the Panic of 1837. Wages did not recover until 1845, at which time they started to rise again. This last high trend continued from 1845 to approximately 1858; the Panic of 1857 was the primary factor responsible for its termination.[27]

The best single set of wage data has been compiled by Lebergott, who assembled them into approximately ten-year periods, with the

TABLE 5. MONTHLY FARM WAGES WITH BOARD, 1818–60

	1818	1826	1830	1850	1860
New England					
Maine	$12.43	$12.43	$12.43	$13.12	$14.34
New Hampshire	10.16	10.16	11.66	12.12	14.34
Vermont	10.00	10.00	10.00	13.00	14.14
Massachusetts	13.50	13.50	12.00	13.55	15.34
Rhode Island	11.93	11.93	11.93	13.52	16.04
Connecticut	13.11	11.61	11.61	12.72	15.11
Middle Atlantic					
New York	10.00	8.00	8.00	11.50	13.19
New Jersey	8.50	8.50	8.50	10.18	11.91
Pennsylvania	11.00	9.00	9.50	10.82	12.24
North Central					
Ohio	9.00	9.00	9.00	11.10	13.11
Indiana	9.00	9.00	9.00	10.50	13.71
Illinois	12.00	10.00	10.00	12.55	13.72
Michigan	—	—	—	12.00	15.27
Wisconsin	—	—	—	12.69	13.96
Minnesota	—	—	—	17.00	14.10
Iowa	—	—	—	11.80	13.18

Source: Lebergott, *Manpower in Economic Growth*, p. 539, extracted from Table A-23.

26. Ulysses P. Hedrick, *A History of Agriculture in the State of New York* (Albany, 1933), p. 352; Lebergott, *Manpower in Economic Growth*, p. 257ff.; see also Fletcher, *Pennsylvania Agriculture and Country Life*, I, p. 308.
27. Adams, "Vermont Prices and Wages," 87–91, esp. figure 28.

exception for 1840 because of a lack of reliable statistics for the years 1838–45.

These figures reflect monthly farm wages with board; but hands were also hired for shorter periods at a day rate. Short-term extra help was used for special tasks including fencing, chopping, hauling, spading, summer harvesting, and autumn corn-husking. Most farmers could not afford to hire this type of help for any considerable length of time, and usually several days or a week within a given month constituted the maximum. The price of labor hired by the day was 30 to 60 percent greater than the rates on a monthly basis.[28] If help was needed for a longer period, employers negotiated a work contract according to the monthly rate with board. Day laborers on farms could work for wages with or without board. Farmers found it advantageous to pay day laborers a slightly higher rate and let them board themselves. This arrangement was convenient for both parties, especially with young local men who still lived at home. They appreciated the extra money, while the farmer's wife reduced her burden of providing three to four meals per day for her husband's hands. A representative approximation of the differences between such wages and the weekly boarding costs for farm and non-farm laborers appeared in the census report of 1850.

If farm wages, daily, monthly, and annually, increased over the period of 1815–60, what was the relationship of higher wages to the cost of living? Did farm hands have more or less buying power with such wages? The conclusion here is that agricultural laborers in general enjoyed a good financial position; their wages remained fairly stable or increased moderately, while basic living costs such as food and rent were of no real concern to them. In fact, the cost of goods and services, as Adams shows in his study of Vermont, decreased during 1818–60, while farm wages steadily increased so as to expand the purchasing power of farm laborers.[29]

The general increase of farm wages occurred for several reasons. One factor was the growth of population, with its expansion westward into areas suitable for large-scale farming, especially the prairies of the Midwest. The combination of new farms in an undeveloped region increased the demand for hired labor of all types. Farmers

28. Lebergott, *Manpower in Economic Growth*, p. 244.
29. Adams, "Vermont Prices and Wages," 96, figure 33. Between 1800 and 1840 wages for farm hands in Pennsylvania rose faster than the prices of farm produce; it required one-third to one-half more production by 1840 to pay for labor costs. Fletcher, *Pennsylvania Agriculture and Country Life*, I, p. 308.

TABLE 6. WAGES IN 1850: DAY LABORER WITH BOARD, DAY LABORER
WITHOUT BOARD, DAY WAGES CARPENTER WITHOUT BOARD, WEEKLY
BOARD FOR LABORING MEN

	Day laborer with board	Day laborer without board	Day wages carpenter without board	Weekly board for laboring men
New England				
Maine	$ .76	$1.00	$1.40	$1.72
New Hampshire	.63	.89	1.31	1.63
Vermont	.72	.97	1.44	1.95
Massachusetts	.84	1.09	1.45	2.12
Rhode Island	.72	.95	1.23	2.06
Connecticut	.76	.98	1.30	1.95
Middle Atlantic				
New York	.67	.90	1.38	1.78
New Jersey	.65	.88	1.28	1.89
Pennsylvania	.51	.80	1.23	1.72
North Central				
Ohio	.56	.78	1.27	1.45
Indiana	.55	.78	1.30	1.43
Illinois	.62	.85	1.47	1.47
Michigan	.66	.88	1.40	1.59
Wisconsin	.71	1.00	1.54	1.88
Minnesota	.86	1.37	2.25	3.50
Iowa	.61	.83	1.50	1.58

Source: *Statistical View of the United States*, p. 164.

competed, and not very successfully, for increasingly scarce manpower. Another factor was the monotony of farm labor; responsible,
diligent hands who were ambitious ultimately sought farms of their
own. Again, the result was higher wages for those available or willing
to work as hired hands. Seasonal irregularity in many occupations,
including farm labor, also contributed to the demand for higher
wages, which laborers regarded as partial compensation in the event
of unemployment.[30]

Urban living, the lure of California gold fields, and better-paying
positions as artisans and tradesmen drained away part of the labor
supply from the countryside. This exodus of able-bodied laborers improved the bargaining position of those remaining and provided
openings for thousands of newly arrived immigrants.[31] The impact of
foreign labor on wage levels produced mixed results; for example in

30. Lebergott, *Manpower in Economic Growth*, p. 242.
31. *Valley Farmer*, II (September, 1850), 274–75; *New England Farmer*, I
(February 17, 1849), 71; *Michigan Farmer*, VII (April 1, 1849), 97–98.

the South, immigrant laborers' demands for better wages contributed to a general increase of wage levels throughout the region. On the other hand, the foreign influx may well have depressed wage levels in other sections of the nation. The percentage of wage increase for American labor as a whole was greatest when immigration was low or moderate prior to 1850. Real wages dropped in terms of growth percentage during 1850–60, when immigration became heavy.[32]

Yet it is debatable if such immigration created extensive unemployment in agriculture for native Americans. Seasonal unemployment and occasional hard times might bring temporary hardship, but there is no evidence to show that immigrants displaced native Americans at farm labor, except as native American hands went into better-paying occupations.[33] American-born farm hands usually received higher wages than the newly arrived Europeans. But the overall wage level in America for native-born and foreign laborers alike exceeded the level in Europe; according to the Patent Office, in 1845 the average American laborer earned six times as much as the European laborer.[34]

Most farm hands worked toward the goal of farm ownership, or advancement via the agricultural ladder. But the problem for the historian is not unlike that of assembling a jigsaw puzzle with some of the parts missing. In his study of Vermont agriculture, T. M. Adams noted that farms were small and fairly easy to acquire, while employment was available for those desiring to get ahead: "As to what you call day-labourers the number is few, and if industrious they can soon emerge from that situation, the farmer does not look down on them with an eye of severity or contempt, on the contrary he holds out his hand to them, and assists to raise them on a level with himself."[35]

The practical aspects of working for a farm were outlined in an early Vermont history: ". . . the labourer can procure seventy dollars a year for his work. . . . Of these wages it will take twenty dollars, to procure comfortable clothing; the remainder the labourer is able to reserve for other purposes. Thus by labouring for another two or three years, the labourer becomes independent, and works afterwards upon

32. Lebergott, *Manpower in Economic Growth*, pp. 161–62, 250–51.

33. Prior to 1860, unemployment did not exceed 8 percent of the labor force, even in depressions. *Ibid.*, pp. 187–89.

34. *Annual Report of Commissioner of Patents for the Year 1845*, 1149–54.

35. Adams, "Vermont Prices and Wages," 90, quotation from Ira Allen, *The Natural and Political History of the State of Vermont* (1798).

his own land or stock."[36] Before the Civil War such advice remained seemingly valid, and as late as 1862 an observer remarked in the *Country Gentleman*:

> The most usual course taken by farmers' sons to get this start, is working out by the month for farmers; and perhaps it is the best course open to thousands of young men in our country. But a large portion of these young men are only able to get work for seven or eight months of the busy season, leaving them idle during the winter and a part of the spring and fall. The wages they will earn in this way, will not enable them to lay up money very fast. Hence the enterprising young man that is determined to succeed, will either be sure to hire out . . . or find some kind of job-work, by which he will be able to make good wages all of the time. . . . By taking this course, a young man ought to lay up $100 a year, and many will lay up more. We will suppose he commences when he is 21, and when he is 25 has saved $500.[37]

A successful beginning at farming required practical skill in agricultural techniques as well as capital. For those raised on a farm, a few years of employment as farm help did not pose a hardship and instead broadened their experience. Those of a nonagricultural background were urged to test their ability at farming on a trial basis as farm hands. Sound advice along these lines came from a Massachusetts farmer in the 1850's: "When merchants, mechanics or professional men, or their sons, conclude to turn farmers, I advise them to try the business at first, as apprentices or 'hired men;' if they find they have stamina enough to work out the whole season, and shrewdness enough to lay up a hundred dollars a year from their wages, then they may reasonably think of setting up for themselves. . . ."[38]

The choice of location was also an important consideration. Did the agricultural ladder operate more successfully in the West than in established areas of the East? Of course, there were advantages and disadvantages to be carefully weighed. According to William Blane's assessment in 1822, "A poor man would, I think, if willing to work, live more comfortably in the State of New York, or in Pennsylvania, than in the Illinois [area]; but then he could not so easily become an

36. *Ibid.*, 90–91, quotation from Samuel Williams, *The Natural and Civil History of Vermont* (1794).
37. As cited in Morris, *How to Get a Farm*, pp. 56–57.
38. *New England Farmer*, VI (July, 1854), 302–3.

independent landholder."[39] Others pointed out the availability of
good land in the East without the necessity of going as far as Illinois.
Traveling through Pennsylvania in 1819, Dr. Richard Lee Mason
remarked that the average laborer, if prudent, could save sufficient
money to purchase a quarter section of land.[40] The letters of an Illinois pioneer wisely suggested that only single men should trek to
the West, where wages were high and laborers scarce, while established farmers were well advised to remain in the East.[41]

But the western land lured farmers and hired hands alike toward
the Midwest. Michigan became the El Dorado for ambitious New
York farm hands, who reportedly saved enough money within two
years for the purchase of eighty acres. Similarly, Pennsylvania farmers and their hired help departed for new farms in Illinois.[42] Frederick
Jackson Turner's concept of the frontier was echoed by William
Pooley's description of those migrating into Illinois: "The farm laborers who, dissatisfied with the existing scale of wages in the
older communities and understanding the science of agriculture well
enough to manage and work farms of their own, moved to the frontier,
took up government lands and laid the foundations of new settlements beyond the limits of civilization. These became the small farmers who moved along in the wake of the hunter-pioneers."[43]

Every situation was different, and the successful acquisition of a
farm depended ultimately on the individual and his goals. According
to Clarence Danhof's findings, a fifty-acre farm in the forested area
of New York could be established with a minimum of $500 in the
early 1820's.[44] A small eastern farm of good soil with some improvements might easily cost more per acre than a large, unimproved farm
in the midwestern prairies. A knowledgeable authority advised, as a
rule of thumb, that two or three years of additional labor were needed
to raise money for the purchase of an eastern farm, in contrast to one
in the West.[45]

39. Blane, *An Excursion through the United States and Canada during the
Years 1822–23*, p. 169.
40. Richard Lee Mason, *Narrative of Richard Lee Mason in the Pioneer
West, 1819* (New York, 1915), p. 15.
41. Buck, "Pioneer Letters of Gershom Flagg," 145, 162–63, 165.
42. Abdy, *Journal of a Residence and Tour*, I, p. 279; II, p. 98.
43. William V. Pooley, *The Settlement of Illinois from 1830 to 1850* (Madison,
1908), p. 331. Critical of this interpretation are Goodrich and Davison, "The
Wage-Earner in the Westward Movement," 61–116; and Danhof, "Farm-
Making Costs and the 'Safety-Valve': 1850–1860," 317–59.
44. Danhof, *Change in Agriculture*, pp. 114–15.
45. Morris, *How to Get a Farm*, p. 59. With reference to an eastern farm

Individuals with experience and stamina could acquire the cheaper large farm with the intention of improving it through their own labor. A good example was the young, unmarried Vermonter, Gershom Flagg, whose pioneer letters describe the acquisition and establishment of a midwestern farm. Trekking out to Illinois, he entered land claims for a 160-acre tract near Edwardsville in Madison County in 1817. A portion of his farm was improved by his own labor, while the other part was rented out. During the next several years he worked at sodbusting; he had expanded his holdings to 270 acres by 1821. Unfortunately, Flagg's letters were vague as to his capital resources, but it is clear that he possessed some money which enabled him to acquire land cheaply and sell it within several years at a profit. In 1818, for example, one of his letters mentioned that he sold some of his land claims and doubled his money from the transactions.[46]

Investment in a midwestern timber or prairie farm was expensive and required considerable effort to prepare it for the production of crops. Several popular guidebooks for the Midwest in the 1830's advised Easterners to select prairie rather than timber lands. According to Mitchell, a forty-acre tract of unimproved land, at the rate of $1.25 per acre, cost $50. But an additional sum of $200 was required for prairie breaking, fencing, and the construction of a cabin. A "second-hand" farm with some improvements could be acquired at a higher cost of $2.50 to $3.50 per acre. Ellsworth similarly stressed that prairie land was cheaper and easier to work than timber land. The cost of preparing prairie land for cultivation could be as low as $3.75 per acre, in contrast to $12 per acre for clearing timber land.[47]

An Illinois settler estimated the following costs for a combination prairie and timber farm of 160 acres in 1832:

The 160 acres would cost $200.00

Half the land can be broken up at $1.50 per acre which
makes 120.00

To fence this 80 acres takes 9000 rails; these cost for splitting and carrying to place $1.25 per 100 . . . . . 112.50

To set up the fence may cost 10.00

Now we say that the farm is to be divided into 60 acres for
wheat and the rest for corn and other crops, and if the

---

of $800 to $1,000 in value, Morris noted instances where seven or more years were required for an individual to work out.

46. Buck, "Pioneer Letters of Gershom Flagg," 153–54, 161, 167, 171.

47. Mitchell, *Illinois in 1837*, pp. 14, 140–41; Ellsworth, *Valley of the Upper Wabash, Indiana*, pp. 34–35, 164.

land is broken in the spring at the right time, so that the
grass roots are killed through lying fallow, and it can be
harrowed twice in order to be able to plant the seed. 60
acres harrowed twice 45.00
A man plows about 1 to 1½ acres a day and this may cost
at the most 20.00
One usually sows 1 bushel of wheat to the acre; this may
cost ½ dollar (now 75 cents), thus 60 bushels . . .   30.00
The harvesting of the wheat costs for 60 acres about . .   15.00
The gathering and bringing in, I don't know exactly, may
cost about half the cutting 7.50
To make this small farm complete about 3000 rails are
needed to separate the buildings from the cattle, etc. .   37.50
Now add a small garden and house 200.00
I suggest the following arrangement for the rest of the land
to be tilled. For corn 15 acres; this may cost for harrowing
and planting next spring, including seed 16.00
The remaining 5 acres will be used for potatoes, flax, etc.,
and also some 100 fruit trees. These cost $10 and the
planting about $2.50 . . . .   12.50
Now the live stock is to be chosen in proper proportions but
I will speak of that later, so I end this estimate with the
addition of 1 wagon, 2 plows, 1 harrow and some other
tools for general use 150.00
The total of all outlay for such a small estate adds up to . .$976.00[48]

Land values rose over the years with the influx of population. William
Oliver's reliable guidebook by the early 1840's suggested a sum of
nearly $1,300 for buying, fencing, and improving an eighty-acre Illi-
nois prairie farm, including cultivation and harvesting costs during
the first year.[49] By the following decade, a midwestern farm of 160
acres easily necessitated an outlay of $1,000 for the land itself.[50]

Capital of such proportion was admittedly desirable at the onset,
but how many new farmers possessed such amounts, even after several years of employment? The advance of the frontier usually pre-
ceded the westward flow of capital resources, and most settlers during
1815–60 operated with a minimum rather than maximum amount of
capital. As Allan Bogue shows in *From Prairie to Corn Belt*, insuf-

48. "Letters from New Switzerland, 1831–1832," 441.
49. Oliver, *Eight Months in Illinois*, pp. 134–35.
50. Danhof, *Change in Agriculture*, p. 125.

ficient capital forced many early midwesterners to concentrate on a single crop instead of diversifying their operations.[51]

Is it possible that smaller farms were acquired with considerably less money at the onset and gradually improved over a longer period of time? Biographical sketches used in this study are lacking in data on specific capital accumulation, but they give the impression that these individuals started out with very little. While farmers might naturally desire rapid improvement of their land with the latest farm implements, many developed their farms gradually over a longer period without extensive capital. As one agricultural historian observed recently, the U.S. Commissioner of Agriculture in 1862 recommended close to $1,000 for farm machinery for a successful farm operation; yet the census information for Illinois indicates the value of farm implements at $84 per farm in 1850 and $120 per farm in 1860.[52]

The conclusion here is that many started farming with much less than $1,000 or even $500, whatever the sacrifice and hardship of such an undertaking. Indeed, the increasing cost of establishing a farm, as one observer noted, placed the patient farm laborer in a better position than his employer: "It is frequently the case that the hired man, though in one sense a farm-servant, works no harder than his employer; he does not have the care and perplexity on his mind that the owner does; fares equally with the family, and at the expiration of the year has more surplus cash to put at interest than the man who has employed him."[53]

Whether the hired hand worked in the East and went westward to farm, or proceeded immediately westward and worked as a farm hand in the intended area of settlement, it was necessary to work out for an average of two to five years and sometimes longer. The time required working as a hired hand depended on how much he earned per month or year, and if he was employed seasonally or annually. Year 'round employment provided greater security and made easier the accumulation of savings over several years' time. Danhof cites a representative example in the 1850's: a New Englander worked as a farm hand for three years for $125 to $150 per year, saved $300, and applied $200 of these savings toward the purchase of 160 acres of land in Michigan.[54] The size of the intended farm also determined

51. Bogue, *From Prairie to Corn Belt*, p. 145.
52. Robert Ankli, "Problems in Aggregate Agricultural History," *Agricultural History*, XLVI (1972), 69.
53. Morris, *How to Get a Farm*, pp. 72–73.
54. Danhof, *Change in Agriculture*, p. 78.

the length of time required for raising capital. It was not necessary to work as long and raise as much money for a smaller farm of forty acres. Merle Curti calculated that an immigrant on the Wisconsin frontier in the 1850's could obtain work at 75 cents per day for 200 days of the year and easily acquire a farm of forty acres at $1.25 per acre.[55]

For those pursuing such a course of action, employment as a farm hand for several years was a valuable method of gaining experience, learning lessons from the mistakes of others, and having the opportunity to scout around before settling on a particular piece of land. Yet it was a fact that the increasing value of land and rising farm-making costs were prolonging the period required for young men working as farm hands to get ahead in life:

> . . . a young man will have to work out a great deal more than seven years, in most cases from twice to three times that length of time, before he can even pay half down for a good farm, to say nothing of the money that will be needed to begin farming with. . . . He will probably say that he has not so much objection to working out a few years in order to get a few hundred dollars to start with. But as to working out that length of time, it is useless to talk about it; he is not going to do it.[56]

This was probably the attitude of the average farm hand, and it was unreasonable to expect him to feel otherwise.

An alternative was to rent or lease a farm for several years in order to get a start. This approach was both desirable and practical for the hired hand who married and acquired the responsibility of a family. In fact, renting or working a farm on shares was considered more respectable by society than working for wages.[57] The amount of capital determined whether an individual leased land for a fixed cash fee and received all the profits from his labor, or if he tenant-farmed and shared the profits with the landowner. The terms of contract for both renting and share-cropping were determined by the rental fee per acre, the amount (or lack) of cash possessed by the renter, and the type of crops to be raised. Another major consideration, particularly with share-cropping, was who supplied the seed for planting and the

55. Curti, *Making of an American Community*, p. 149.
56. Morris, *How to Get a Farm*, pp. 59–60.
57. *Ibid.*, pp. 63, 80; Danhof, *Change in Agriculture*, pp. 91–92. For mid-western farm tenancy, see Gates, *Farmer's Age*; Bogue, *From Prairie to Corn Belt*; and Margaret Bogue, *Patterns from the Sod: Land Use and Tenure in the Grand Prairie, 1850–1900*, Collections of the Illinois State Historical Library, XXXIV (Springfield, 1959).

necessary machinery for harvesting the crop. Unlike the direct cash rental system, the tenant farmer or share-cropper split the profits of the crop with the owner of the land according to a predetermined ratio.

Ellsworth offered the following optimistic advice for the Wabash Valley during the 1830's: "I would advise to employ smart, enterprising young men, from the New England States, to take the farm on shares. If the landlord should find a house, a team, cart, and plough, and add some stock, he might then require one-half the profits of the same."[58] Similarly, two decades later, James Caird blithely remarked that a laboring man could come west, rent land in Illinois, and "in a few years realise enough to start himself in a farm of his own."[59] The system of tenant farming was obviously advantageous to the landowner, whose property was worked with the minimum of labor costs. Farm rental and share-cropping combined the best and worst aspects of farming. New farms were developed to make employment available to thousands of individuals lacking funds to acquire their own farms; but misuse and exploitation inevitably resulted with land that was worked merely for immediate profits with no regard for its long-term value.

Advancement via the agricultural ladder was accomplished through a variety of methods. Some worked as farm hands and made enough to purchase a farm outright. Others made less money or lacked the requisite sum, but they advanced themselves a rung or two by farming on rented land, acquiring their own farm after a time. Biographical and reminiscent sources used for this study clearly show that a number of men started their careers at the bottom and gradually advanced themselves by farm labor and tenant farming. Caution must be exercised not to draw a generalized conclusion that the agricultural ladder necessarily enabled everyone to acquire a farm. Indeed, contradictory evidence suggests a rather pessimistic view for the occupation of farm labor and leads to speculation that few farm hands were in the financial position to move upward.

Table 7 contains pertinent statistics extracted from the 1860 manuscript census for six midwestern townships.[60] The number of farm laborers for each township included those aged fifteen and over. No attempt was made to separate teenagers or sons in the family from

58. Ellsworth, *Valley of the Upper Wabash, Indiana*, p. 166.
59. Caird, *Prairie Farming in America*, p. 93.
60. A useful introduction to manuscript census reports is found in Curti, *The Making of An American Community*, pp. 449–58, Appendix I.

older men in the listing of farm hands, because we have no way of determining if they worked on the family farm or were employed for wages on neighboring farms. In terms of statistics they were counted, like the others, according to their enumerated identification. The total number of farm laborers in each township was broken down into categories of nativity, age, marital status, and combined value of personal assets and real estate.

Comparisons between the 1850 and 1860 census reports are not especially helpful because the 1850 report sheets did not differentiate between the types of labor; workers in predominantly rural areas were not all necessarily farm hands but may have been employed, for example, at other occupations in nearby towns. Another problem is that the 1850 census reported only real estate as a tangible asset, in contrast to the 1860 census, which included both personal assets and real estate. The fact is that while some farm hands might possess pecuniary assets, those owning real estate were few. The census was taken once every ten years; since farm hands were seasonal workers, many names did not appear in the lists in the following decade. They engaged in other employment, moved to another county, or perhaps left the region entirely. The 1860 census report, as tabulated here, provides a quantitative profile for six townships during the period of June–August, the prime months when the greatest number of men found employment on farms.

Goshen Township in Champaign County was located in an established area of west-central Ohio. The township had a rural orientation despite proximity to the town of Mechanicsburg. Farm laborers made up 9.6 percent of its population, and most of them claimed American birth; only 1.8 percent were immigrants. The figures for age groupings tell us that almost half of the farm labor force in the township was twenty years old or younger, and most were teenage sons of farmers working as hands on family farms or for neighbors. Approximately 40 percent of the labor force consisted of men in their twenties, while few, 11.1 percent, were thirty-one or older. An indicator of the community's stability was the number of married men, comprising 18.5 percent of the overall farm labor force. But most revealing are the figures which place 75 percent of the farm laborers in the category without assets; in other words, three-quarters of the farm laborers in an established farming area lacked the means to move rapidly, if at all, up the agricultural ladder.

Centre Township was located in Vanderburgh County in extreme southern Indiana. This agricultural township lay on the outskirts of

TABLE 7. FARM LABORERS IN SIX MIDWESTERN TOWNSHIPS, 1860

Farm laborers	Native born	Foreign born	Age			Married Men	Assets/Real estate	
			15–20	21–30	31 over		With	Without
Goshen Township,* Champaign County, Ohio (Population: 1,121)								
108(9.6%)	106(98.2%)	2(1.8%)	53(49.1%)	43(39.8%)	12(11.1%)	20(18.5%)	27(25.0%)	81(75.0%)
Centre Township, Vanderburgh County, Indiana (Population: 1,359)								
142(10.4%)	87(61.3%)	55(38.7%)	78(54.9%)	50(35.2%)	14(9.9%)	7(4.9%)	10(7.0%)	132(93.0%)
Millbrook Township, Peoria County, Illinois (Population: 1,024)								
79(7.7%)	61(77.2%)	18(22.8%)	49(62.0%)	26(32.9%)	4(5.1%)	3(3.8%)	2(2.5%)	77(97.5%)
Summit Township, Jackson County, Michigan (Population: 890)								
167(18.8%)	141(84.4%)	26(15.6%)	60(35.9%)	79(47.3%)	28(16.8%)	37(22.2%)	37(22.2%)	130(77.8%)
Paris Township, Kenosha County, Wisconsin (Population: 1,374)								
121(8.8%)	17(14.0%)	104(86.0%)	40(33.1%)	54(44.6%)	27(22.3%)	9(7.4%)	12(9.9%)	109(90.1%)
Rose Township, Ramsey County, Minnesota (Population: 499)								
71(14.2%)	19(26.8%)	52(73.2%)	17(23.9%)	41(57.8%)	13(18.3%)	7(9.9%)	7(9.9%)	64(90.1%)

*excluding Mechanicsburg

Source: Federal Manuscript Population Census of 1860: Ohio, Indiana, Illinois, Michigan, Wisconsin, and Minnesota (microfilm).

Evansville, a major commercial center and a steamboat port on the Ohio River. Farm hands constituted 10.4 percent of the population in this Indiana township, but significant was the number of foreign born (38.7 percent). These immigrants who came westward on steamboats readily secured employment at farm labor and in horticultural establishments in areas facing southward along the river. German, Irish, and French names often appeared in the lists. It is reasonable to assume that many were transient laborers, given the proximity of Evansville and the Ohio River. A mere 4.9 percent settled down to marry, and only 7 percent could claim any assets.

An interesting profile appeared in the census for Millbrook Township in Peoria County on the central Illinois prairie. This exclusively rural township was located in the extreme northwestern corner of the county away from the city of Peoria and the Illinois River. Although active settlement commenced during the 1830's, new farms were established as late as the 1850's. Evidence of this fact came from the census marshall's notations, which identified several persons employed at prairie breaking and ditching. Farm hands constituted 7.7 percent of the township's population, and slightly over three-quarters of them (77.2 percent) were of American birth. The township's labor force was comparatively youthful with 62 percent of the enumerated farm laborers between fifteen and twenty years of age, while the two older age brackets comprised the remaining 38 percent. Only a few of the township's farm hands assumed the responsibility of marriage (3.8 percent) or accumulated financial resources and property (2.5 percent). Unless they inherited family farms, most hired hands in this township faced years of continued employment before ascending the agricultural ladder.

Summit Township in Jackson County was situated in lower central Michigan. The frontier line advanced westward through this area in the 1820's and 1830's, drawing many settlers from the farming regions of New England and New York. Here farmers seemed to have an adequate source of laborers, who constituted 18.8 percent of the township's population. Over one-third (35.9 percent) were teenagers, mainly local boys working out at wages in the neighborhood. This assumption is reinforced by the high percentage (84.4) of native-born laborers, naturally including the sons of local farmers. These township figures parallel in certain respects those for Goshen Township in Champaign County, Ohio: the foreign born were comparatively few, a sizable minority had married, and over 20 percent possessed some assets.

A different picture of farm hands was obtained from the census for Paris Township at Kenosha County in extreme southeastern Wisconsin. This agricultural community was heavily settled by German immigrants streaming into the port of Kenosha, as well as into nearby Milwaukee and Chicago. These farm laborers were overwhelmingly of foreign origin, making up about 86 percent of the agricultural labor force. They tended to be an older group, with a high percentage (22.3) in the category of thirty-one and over. Many were newcomers who had not settled down, as the small 7.4 percent marriage rate indicates. Only 9.9 percent claimed any assets, while the remaining 90.1 percent were men without means to establish themselves at farming. This township offers rather striking proof of the financial problems confronting immigrant farm laborers.

The situation for farm hands in the upper midwestern frontier is reflected in Rose Township, Ramsey County, Minnesota. Located north of St. Paul, this small township of slightly under 500 persons was oriented toward farming and included several horticultural nurseries. The latter explain the high percentage (73.2) of foreign born who were attracted to this remote area in pursuit of employment for which they had training and experience. Where foreigners were numerous, similar to the above Wisconsin township, the age levels were higher: over three-fourths of the farm labor force in Rose Township consisted of men twenty-one or older. But accumulation of capital remained a problem, since 90.1 percent had no identifiable assets. Yet 9.9 percent of these men were married—which is surprising, given the shortage of women on the Minnesota frontier.

These profiles reinforce previous generalizations about the farm labor class—an employment best suited for young single men. The figures also confirm for farm labor what the investigations of Paul Gates, Allan Bogue, Margaret Bogue, and Clarence Danhof reveal for farm tenancy: the increasing difficulty of attaining full farm ownership. The situation was the same, or perhaps worse, for the farm laborer, because he was starting out a rung or two below the tenant farmer on the agricultural ladder. Despite high wages, the vast majority of farm hands lacked the means to buy a farm. Few made the successful jump directly from hired farm work to outright farm ownership.

The Civil War marked the end of an era; the social and economic lines of American agriculture were permanently altered after 1860. In later years men looked back on their accomplishments with a sense of pride but nostalgia, especially those who started out lowly in life and advanced upward. Farm labor offered an opportunity to achieve certain goals, but it did not guarantee automatic success. It was a mediocre occupation that could be a stepping stone for the ambitious-minded or a perpetual treadmill for the indolent. Farm labor was a distinctive aspect of American life which was never quite the same following Fort Sumter.

Bibliography

MANUSCRIPT COLLECTIONS
AND ACCOUNT RECORDS

Farmers' diaries and accountbooks constitute the most important manuscript source for this study. They are a chronicle of daily happenings on the farm, along with brief comments about crops, prices, wages, contracts, weather, illness, and occasional trips into town. Records of special value include the William Holgate Accountbook, Lewis Lesher Farm Accounts, Anthony Stranahan Farm Accounts, Johnston Thurston Farm Accounts, Elijah Wadsworth Farm Accounts, and John H. Young Daybook for Ohio; the Beeler Papers and John R. Goodwin Diary for Indiana; the Charles Bartlett Diary and Matthew T. Scott Papers for Illinois; the Warner Wright Goodale Personal Accountbook, Nathan Pierce Papers, and Henry Parker Smith Diary for Michigan; the Lathrop Burgess Papers, Spencer and Emily Carrier Diaries, and George Ogden Diary for Wisconsin; and the Francis Larpenteur Diary for Minnesota. Rarely did farmers make value judgments or discuss the personalities of their hired help in these records; but exceptions are the letters of Matthias Dunlap, who operated a farm-nursery in Illinois, and the diary of Calvin Fletcher, who owned a large farm on the outskirts of Indianapolis.

Most farm hands kept little in the way of records, which is hardly surprising. Few felt inclined to write letters or maintain diaries following a grueling day's work in the fields, and for many a lack of education was certainly an inhibiting factor. Consequently, existing manuscripts are quite unusual, such as the letters of Myron Wright in the Allen G. Wright Papers. He described employment on farms in Michigan and Illinois, with reference to wages, working conditions, and, most important, his impressions of employers. Candid views appear similarly in the diary of Daniel Thomas, a Wisconsin farm hand, while the letters of Horatio Houlton and John Shumway reveal the efforts of Minnesota farm laborers to earn money for their own farms.

American Home Missionary Letters (photostat and microfilm). Illinois Historical Survey.
Aiton Family Papers. Minnesota Historical Society.
Charles Bartlett Diary. Chicago Historical Society.
Joseph and Fielding Beeler Papers. Indiana State Library.
John Benjamin Papers. Minnesota Historical Society.
Ephraim Brown Ledger-Daybook. Western Reserve Historical Society.
Jabez Brown Diary. State Historical Society of Wisconsin.
William Brown Farm Journal. Minnesota Historical Society.
Barber G. Buell Papers. Michigan Historical Collections.
Lathrop Burgess Papers. State Historical Society of Wisconsin.
Anson Buttles Diary. State Historical Society of Wisconsin.
Orin Shepard Campbell Accountbooks. Illinois Historical Survey.
Spencer and Emily Carrier Diaries. State Historical Society of Wisconsin.
Asahel Clapp Diary (photostat). Indiana State Library.
Thomas J. Clapp Farm Accountbook. Western Reserve Historical Society.
Benjamin Coale Daybook, Accountbook, and Diary. Illinois Historical Survey.
Jeremiah Cooper Accounts of Produce, Daybook. Ohio Historical Society.
Levi Countryman Diary. Minnesota Historical Society.
Abijah Crosby Accountbook. Western Reserve Historical Society.
Philip Cumings Diary. Michigan Historical Collections.
John R. Cummins Farm Diary. Minnesota Historical Society.
E. Currier Letter Collection. Illinois State Historical Library.
Benjamin Densmore Papers. Minnesota Historical Society.
C. R. Doringh Accountbook. Illinois State Historical Library.
George Dow Papers. State Historical Society of Wisconsin.
Matthias Dunlap Papers. University of Illinois Archives (Urbana).
John B. Duret, Jr., Diary (microfilm). Indiana Historical Society Library.
Asel G. Dye Diary (microfilm). State Historical Society of Wisconsin.
Samuel and William Henry Egbert Accountbook. Western Reserve Historical Society.
Merrick Ely Accountbook. Western Reserve Historical Society.
Elisha Embree Business Papers. Indiana State Library.
Farmer's Memorandum Book, Stark County, Ohio. Ohio Historical Society.
Federal Manuscript Population Census of 1860 (microfilm). Center for Research Libraries.
John Fenton Accountbook. Western Reserve Historical Society.
Samuel Fisk Diary. Illinois State Historical Library.
Calvin Fletcher Diary. Indiana Historical Society Library.
Henry C. Friedley Diary. Minnesota Historical Society.
William Gardner Farm Accounts. Ohio Historical Society.

Warner Wright Goodale Personal Accountbook. Michigan Historical Collections.

John R. Goodwin Diary (microfilm). Indiana State Library.

Jonathan Gordon Daybook. Western Reserve Historical Society.

Martin E. Grey Farm Record. Western Reserve Historical Society.

William D. Gribbens Shoemaker Accountbook. Michigan Historical Collections.

Lovira Hart Correspondence. Michigan Historical Collections.

Thomas J. Y. Hart Store and Farm Records. Ohio Historical Society.

John Henry Notebook. Indiana Historical Society Library.

William Holgate Accountbook. Ohio Historical Society.

Cortez Perry Hooker Diary. Michigan Historical Collections.

Horatio Houlton Papers. Minnesota Historical Society.

Rufus W. Howe Ledger. Ohio Historical Society.

Charles Hubbard Farm Diary. Illinois State Historical Library.

Enoch Huggins Letter Collection. Illinois State Historical Library.

William Hunt Accountbook. Western Reserve Historical Society.

Luther Huston Account Ledger. Illinois Historical Survey.

Innkeeper-Tanner Accountbook. Indiana State Library.

George Jenkins Diary. State Historical Society of Wisconsin.

Enoch Jones Farm Accounts. Ohio Historical Society.

Elnathan Kemper Daybook. Ohio Historical Society.

Frederick Augustus Kemper Accountbook. Cincinnati Historical Society.

Hugh Fulton Kemper Accountbook. Cincinnati Historical Society.

Kennicott Papers. Minnesota Historical Society.

King Family Papers. Illinois State Historical Library.

S. Larkin Store and Farm Accounts. Western Reserve Historical Society.

Francis Larpenteur Diary. Minnesota Historical Society.

Lewis Lesher Farm Accounts. Ohio Historical Society.

Darius Lyman Accountbook. Western Reserve Historical Society.

Lucius Lyon Papers. William L. Clements Library.

Nicholas McCarty Records. Indiana State Library.

Samuel Chew Madden Papers. Indiana State Library.

Manchester Blacksmith Shop Ledger. Michigan Historical Collections.

Samuel Miller Accountbook. Indiana State Library.

Virgil D. Moore Ledger. Ohio Historical Society.

C. F. Morley Accountbook. Michigan Historical Collections.

Elhannah Morris Accountbook. Western Reserve Historical Society.

Lewis Morrison Business Papers Collection (microfilm). Illinois Historical Survey.

Hiram Moulton Ledgerbook. Ohio Historical Society.

Nessly-deSellem Papers. Ohio Historical Society.

Hiram Nourse Papers. State Historcial Society of Wisconsin.

George Ogden Diary. State Historical Society of Wisconsin.

David Palmer Diary. Michigan Historical Collections.

Phelps Family Papers. Michigan Historical Collections.
Darius Pierce Papers. Michigan Historical Collections.
Nathan Pierce Papers. Michigan Historical Collections.
Sarah Pratt Diary (typescript). State Historical Society of Wisconsin.
Asa Rice Accountbook. Michigan Historical Collections.
Edward Robbins Diary. State Historical Society of Wisconsin.
Irvin Rollin Papers. Minnesota Historical Society.
Matthew T. Scott Papers (microfilm). Illinois Historical Survey.
Joshua Shinn Ledger. Western Reserve Historical Society.
John Shumway Letters. Minnesota Historical Society.
Samuel Skewes Diaries. State Historical Society of Wisconsin.
William C. Slayton Diary. Michigan Historical Collections.
Henry Parker Smith Diary. Michigan Historical Collections.
Newton Southworth Papers. Minnesota Historical Society.
Anthony Stranahan Farm Accounts. Ohio Historical Society.
Henry F. Strong Papers. Indiana Historical Society Library.
Samuel Strong Ledger. Indiana Historical Society Library.
George Taggert Papers. State Historical Society of Wisconsin.
Templeton Letters (photocopy). Illinois Historical Survey.
Daniel Thomas Diary. State Historical Society of Wisconsin.
Nathan Thomas Ledger. Michigan Historical Collections.
Benjamin Thurston Letters. Ohio Historical Society.
Johnston Thurston Farm Accounts. Ohio Historical Society.
Elijah Wadsworth Farm Accounts. Ohio Historical Society.
Caleb Walters Farm Accounts. Ohio Historical Society.
Andrew Whiteacre Records. Ohio Historical Society.
George M. Wilkie Papers. State Historical Society of Wisconsin.
John Williams Business Papers. Illinois State Historical Library.
Augustin Williamson Tanner's Accountbook. Indiana State Library.
Jacob Wilson Accountbook. Michigan Historical Collections.
Conrad Winter Farm Accounts. Ohio Historical Society.
Wisconsin Territorial Letter Collection (photostat). State Historical So-
     ciety of Wisconsin.
Allen G. Wright Papers. Michigan Historical Collections.
William Wallace Wright Memoirs: Diary (typescript). State Historical
     Society of Wisconsin.
John Young Diary. Illinois State Historical Library.
John H. Young Daybook of Farm and General Store Accounts. Ohio His-
     torical Society.

INDIVIDUAL MANUSCRIPT LETTERS

Sarah Aiken to Julia Keese (Peoria County, Illinois, January 24, 1834).
     Illinois State Historical Library.

Joel P. Barlow to Elijah P. Barlow (Van Buren County, Michigan, May 27, 1844). Michigan Historical Collections.

H. W. Bereman to Sally Ann Bereman (Madison County, Indiana, April 8, 1837). Indiana State Library.

Asher Edgerton to Elisha Edgerton (Quincy, Illinois, May 28, 1832). Illinois State Historical Library.

W. Forbes to James Forbes (Plainville, Allegan County, Michigan Territory, April 10, 1835). Michigan Historical Collections.

Elisha Huntington to William R. Huntington (Delta, Fulton County, Ohio, March 26, 1854). Ohio Historical Society.

John L. Ketcham to Hazen Merrill (Indianapolis, December 9, 1847). Indiana Historical Society Library.

Samuel McCutchan to William McCutchan (Floyd County, Indiana, July 19, 1832). Indiana State Library.

Charles Rose to John Rose (Scotch Settlement, Columbiana County, Ohio, February 2, 1830). Ohio Historical Society.

Aaron Russell to John Wheelwright (Peoria, Illinois, April 11, 1837). Illinois State Historical Library.

John Staley to Jonathan Tutewiler (Chillicothe, Ohio, February 22, 1842). Ohio Historical Society.

Charles H. Thompson to relatives (Kewaskum, Washington County, Wisconsin, August 31, 1856). State Historical Society of Wisconsin.

MANUSCRIPT REMINISCENCES

Beebe, Mrs. W. H. "Historical Manuscript, 1896. Incidents of the Early Settlement of the northeastern portions of Howland Township, Trumbull County, Ohio." Ohio Historical Society.

Brown, Harvey. "Recollections of Harvey Brown, Elkhorn, Wisconsin." State Historical Society of Wisconsin.

Cobb, Dyar. "Incidents of Early Pioneer Life of Dyar Cobb" (typescript). Indiana State Library.

Hart, Alexis Crane. "An Autobiography of Alexis Crane Hart covering the period of his childhood spent in Jefferson and Trempealeau counties up to the year 1863" (typescript). State Historical Society of Wisconsin.

Mater, Ira. "Early Reminiscences of Parke County [Indiana] by Ira Mater." Indiana Historical Society Library.

Morris, John S. "Ancestor statement filed with Society of Indiana Pioneers." Indiana Historical Society Library.

"Reminiscences of a 92 Year Old Woman." LaSalle County Pioneer File, Illinois State Historical Library.

Scofield, John Darius. "The Biography of John Darius Scofield, By Himself" (typescript). Minnesota Historical Society.

Sherman, William. "William Sherman Reminiscences of His Journey and

Move to Wisconsin in 1836 and Farming in Waukesha County" (type-script). State Historical Society of Wisconsin.

NEWSPAPERS AND PERIODICALS

Alton Commercial Gazette (Illinois) 1839.
Alton Telegraph and Democratic Review (Illinois) 1845, 1847–49.
American Agriculturist (New York) 1847, 1849, 1858–59.
American Farmer's Magazine (New York) 1858.
Annals of Cleveland, 1818–1935: A Digest and Index of the Newspaper Record of Events and Opinions (WPA Project in Ohio. Cleveland, 1937–38. Distributed by the Cleveland Public Library), Volumes 1–43 (1818–60).
Boston Cultivator 1841.
Chicago Democrat: weekly and daily 1834, 1842, 1845, 1847–52, 1857–60.
Cincinnati Daily Gazette 1844–48.
Cincinnati Miscellaney 1844–46.
Cincinnatus (Cincinnati) 1857.
Cist's Weekly Advertiser (Cincinnati) 1847–50, 1852.
Cultivator (Albany, N.Y.) 1848–49.
Daily Commercial Register. See Daily Sanduskian.
Daily Sanduskian (Sandusky, Ohio) 1848–56, 1858.
DeBow's Review (New Orleans and Washington) 1848, 1850, 1852–53, 1855.
Edwardsville Spectator (Illinois) 1820.
Farmer and Artizan (Portland, Me.) 1852.
Farmer's Companion and Horticultural Gazette (Detroit) 1853–54.
Firelands Pioneer (Norwalk and Sandusky, Ohio) 1863, 1882, 1888, 1909.
Freeport Journal (Illinois) 1848–49, 1851.
Genesee Farmer. See New Genesee Farmer and Gardener's Journal.
Hazard's United States Commercial and Statistical Register (Philadelphia) 1841.
Hunt's Merchant Magazine and Commercial Review (New York) 1841, 1845, 1847, 1853–54, 1858–60.
Illinois Daily Journal (Springfield) 1853, 1855.
Illinois Farmer (Springfield) 1856–60.
Indiana Farmer (Indianapolis and Richmond) 1853–54, 1858.
Indiana Farmer and Gardener (Indianapolis) 1845–47.
Indiana Journal (Indianapolis) 1831.
Liberty Hall and Cincinnati Gazette 1818, 1820–21.
Michigan Farmer (Detroit) 1843, 1849–51, 1853–54, 1856–58.
"Minnesota Agriculture File" (typescripts of articles from newspapers and periodicals). Minnesota Historical Society.
Monthly Journal of Agriculture (New York) 1845, 1847.

Moore's Rural New Yorker. See *Rural New Yorker.*

New England Farmer (Boston) 1840–43, 1849–50, 1852, 1854–57.

New Genesee Farmer. See *New Genesee Farmer and Gardener's Journal.*

New Genesee Farmer and Gardener's Journal (Rochester, N.Y.) 1840–41, 1849, 1852, 1856, 1858.

Niles' Weekly Register (Baltimore) 1815–16, 1818, 1825–27, 1831, 1834–35, 1837–38, 1840–41, 1844–46.

Ohio Cultivator (Columbus) 1845, 1847–55, 1857, 1859.

Ohio State Journal and Columbus Gazette 1825.

Ohio Valley Farmer (Cincinnati) 1856–58, 1860.

Peoria Register and North-Western Gazetteer (Illinois) 1842.

"Pioneer Sketches" (manuscript clippings book of early Ohio newspapers). Cincinnati Historical Society.

Plough, Loom and Anvil (Philadelphia) 1857.

Plow (New York) 1852.

Prairie Farmer (Chicago) 1843, 1846, 1848–52.

Rural New Yorker (Rochester) 1850–51, 1854.

Southern Cultivator (Augusta, Ga.) 1843.

Southern Planter (Richmond, Va.) 1852.

Valley Farmer (St. Louis) 1850.

Watchman of the Prairies (Chicago) 1848, 1852.

Western Citizen (Chicago) 1850.

Western Cultivator (Indianapolis) 1844.

Western Farmer and Gardener (Cincinnati) 1839, 1844.

Western Farmer and Gardener (Indianapolis). See *Indiana Farmer and Gardener.*

Western Horticultural Review (Cincinnati) 1852–54.

Western Sun and General Advertiser (Vincennes, Ind.) 1819.

Western Tiller (Cincinnati) 1829.

Wisconsin Farmer (Madison and other locations; title varies) 1851, 1854, 1856.

Working Farmer (New York) 1855.

DOCUMENTS

Adams, T. M. "Prices Paid by Vermont Farmers for Goods and Services and Received by Them for Farm Products, 1790–1940; Wages of Vermont Farm Labor, 1780–1940," *Bulletin No. 507, Vermont Agricultural Experiment Station.* Burlington, 1944.

Agriculture of the United States in 1860; Compiled from the Original Returns of the Eighth Census. Washington, 1864.

Annual Report of Commissioner of Patents for the Year 1845. In *29th Congress, 1st Session, H.R. Doc. 140.* Washington, 1846.

Annual Report of Commissioner of Patents for the Year 1848. In *30th Con-*

gress, 2nd Session, H.R. Ex. Doc. 59. Washington 1849. (This report
continues as a separate volume: see *Report of the Commissioner of
Patents. Part II. Agriculture.*)

*Annual Report of the Commissioner of Statistics to the General Assembly
of Ohio.* Columbus, 1858, 1860.

*Fourteenth Annual Report of the Ohio State Board of Agriculture . . . to
the General Assembly of Ohio, For the Year 1859.* Columbus, 1860.

"History of Wages in the United States from Colonial Times to 1928,"
*United States Department of Labor, Bureau of Labor Statistics: Bulle-
tin No. 499.* Washington, 1929.

*Population of the United States in 1860; Compiled from the Original Re-
turns of the Eighth Census, Under the Direction of the Secretary of the
Interior.* Washington, 1864.

Preliminary Report on the Eighth Census. 1860. Washington, 1862.

Report of the Commissioner of Agriculture for the Year 1866. Washington,
1867.

Report of the Commissioner of Patents. Part II. Agriculture. Washington,
1850, 1852–55.

*Second Annual Report of the Indiana State Board of Agriculture for the
Year 1852.* Indianapolis, 1853.

*Statistical View of the United States . . . Being a Compendium of the Sev-
enth Census.* Washington, 1854.

Transactions of the Illinois State Agricultural Society. . . . Springfield, 1861.

Transactions of the State Agricultural Society of Michigan. . . . Lansing,
1851, 1855.

Transactions of the Wisconsin State Agricultural Society. Madison, 1852–
54.

PRINTED MATERIALS, BIOGRAPHICAL
HISTORIES, AND GENERAL STUDIES

It is impossible to cover new ground without due credit to previous
authorities whose research opened the first furrows. These include
the early work of Percy Bidwell and John Falconer, *History of Agriculture in the Northern States, 1620–1860,* and Paul Gates's comprehensive *Farmer's Age, 1815–1860.* Travelers' accounts, guide books,
and gazetteers of the period contain frequent references to agriculture, prices, and wages, but such material must be used with caution.
Similar advice applies to the numerous biographical and county histories published between the 1870's and World War I. "Biographical
sketches" portray those who successfully ascended the agricultural
ladder, but with little or no mention of those who did not. Despite
obvious commercial overtones of these publications, they contain
useful reminiscent data not found elsewhere.

Abdy, E. S. *Journal of a Residence and Tour in the United States of North America, from April, 1833, to October, 1834.* 3 vols. New York: Negro Universities Press, 1969.

Abel, Henry I. *Geographical, Geological and Statistical Chart of Wisconsin & Iowa.* Philadelphia: By the Author, 1838.

Anderson, Rasmus. *The First Chapter of Norwegian Immigration, (1821–1840) Its Causes and Results.* 4th ed. Madison: By the Author, 1906.

Andreas, A. T. *History of Cook County, Illinois. From the Earliest Period to the Present Time.* Chicago: By the Author, 1884.

Andrews, C[hristopher] C[olumbus]. *Minnesota and Decotah: in Letters Descriptive of a Tour through the North-West, in the Autumn of 1856.* 2nd ed. Washington: Robert Farnham, 1857.

Antrim, Joshua. *The History of Champaign and Logan Counties, [Ohio] from Their First Settlement.* Bellefontaine, 1872.

Arfwedson, C[arl] D[avid]. *The United States and Canada, in 1832, 1833, and 1834.* 2 vols. London: Richard Bentley, 1834.

Asbury, Henry. *Illinois Form-Book; or, Advice Concerning the Duties of Justices of the Peace and Constables. . . .* St. Louis: L. Bushnell, 1858.

Atwater, Caleb. *A History of the State of Ohio, Natural and Civil.* 1st ed. Cincinnati: Glezen & Shepard, 1838.

Bache, Soren. *A Chronicle of Old Muskego: The Diary of Soren Bache, 1839–1847.* Trans. and ed. Clarence A. Clausen and Andreas Elviken. Northfield: Norwegian-American Historical Association, 1951.

Banta, D. D. *A Historical Sketch of Johnson County, Indiana.* Chicago: J. H. Beers & Company, 1881.

Barnum, H. L. *Family Receipts; or Practical Guide for Husbandman and Housewife. . . .* Cincinnati: A. B. Roff, 1831.

Bateman, Newton, and Paul Selby, eds. *Historical Encyclopedia of Illinois and History of Carroll County. Edited by Charles L. Hostetter. Illustrated.* 2 vols. Chicago: Munsell Publishing Company, 1913.

———. *Historical Encyclopedia of Illinois and History of Champaign County. Edited by Joseph O. Cunningham. Illustrated.* 2 vols. Chicago: Munsell Publishing Company, 1905.

———. *Historical Encyclopedia of Illinois and History of Du Page County (Historical and Biographical) by Special Authors and Contributors. Illustrated.* 2 vols. Chicago: Munsell Publishing Company, 1913.

———. *Historical Encyclopedia of Illinois and History of Fulton County. Edited by Jesse Heylin. Illustrated.* Chicago: Munsell Publishing Company, 1908.

———. *Historical Encyclopedia of Illinois and History of Grundy County (Historical and Biographical) by Special Authors and Contributors. Illustrated.* 2 vols. Chicago: Munsell Publishing Company, 1914.

———. *Historical Encyclopedia of Illinois and History of Henderson County. Edited by James W. Gordon. Illustrated.* 2 vols. Chicago: Munsell Publishing Company, 1911.

————. *Historical Encyclopedia of Illinois and History of Kane County.* Edited by Gen. John S. Wilcox. Illustrated. Chicago: Munsell Publishing Company, 1904.

————. *Historical Encyclopedia of Illinois and History of Kendall County (Historical and Biographical) by Special Authors and Contributors.* Illustrated. 2 vols. Chicago: Munsell Publishing Company, 1914.

————. *Historical Encyclopedia of Illinois and History of McDonough County.* Edited by Alexander McLean. Illustrated. Chicago: Munsell Publishing Company, 1907.

————. *Historical Encyclopedia of Illinois and History of McLean County.* Edited by Ezra M. Prince, John H. Burnham. Illustrated. 2 vols. Chicago: Munsell Publishing Company, 1908.

————. *Historical Encyclopedia of Illinois and History of Ogle County.* Edited by Horace G. Kauffman, Rebecca H. Kauffman. Illustrated. 2 vols. Chicago: Munsell Publishing Company, 1909.

————. *Historical Encyclopedia of Illinois and History of Peoria County.* Edited by David McCulloch. Illustrated. 2 vols. Chicago and Peoria: Munsell Publishing Company, 1902.

————. *Historical Encyclopedia of Illinois and History of Tazewell County.* Edited by Ben C. Allensworth. Illustrated. 2 vols. Chicago: Munsell Publishing Company, 1905.

————. *Historical Encyclopedia of Illinois and Knox County.* Edited by W. Selden Gale, Geo. Candee Gale. Illustrated. Chicago and New York: Munsell Publishing Company, 1899.

————. *Historical Encyclopedia of Illinois Including Genealogy, Family Records and Biography of McHenry County Citizens.* Edited by A. L. Wing Coburn. Illustrated. 2 vols. Chicago: Munsell Publishing Company, 1903.

————. *Illinois Historical. Crawford County Biographical. Contributors: William C. Jones, Ethelbert Callahan and others.* Illustrated. Chicago: Munsell Publishing Company, 1909.

————. *Illinois Historical. Effingham County Biographical by Special Authors and Contributors.* Illustrated. Chicago: Munsell Publishing Company, 1910.

————. *Illinois Historical. Lawrence County Biographical. Editor John William McCleave.* Illustrated. Chicago: Munsell Publishing Company, 1910.

Baughman, A. J. *History of Ashland County, Ohio. With Biographical Sketches of Prominent Citizens of the County.* Illustrated. Chicago: S. J. Clarke Publishing Company, 1909.

Baxter, William. *America and the Americans.* London: Routledge & Company, 1855.

Beakes, Samuel W. *Past and Present of Washtenaw County, Michigan. . . .* Chicago: S. J. Clarke Publishing Company, 1906.

Beckwith, H. W. *History of Fountain County, Together with Historic Notes* on the Wabash Valley. . . . Chicago: H. H. Hill and N. Iddings, 1881.

————. History of Montgomery County, Together with Historic Notes on the Wabash Valley. . . . Chicago: H. H. Hill and N. Iddings, 1881.

————. History of Vermilion County, Together with Historic Notes on the Northwest. . . . Chicago: H. H. Hill and Company, 1879.

Benezet, Anthony. The Family Physician; Comprising Rules for the Prevention and Cure of Diseases; Calculated Particularly for the Inhabitants of the Western Country. . . . Cincinnati: W. Hill Woodward, 1826.

Benton, Elbert Jay. The Wabash Trade Route in the Development of the Old Northwest. Johns Hopkins University Studies in Historical and Political Science Series, XXI. Baltimore, 1903.

Berry, Thomas S. Western Prices before 1861: A Study of the Cincinnati Market. Cambridge: Harvard University Press, 1943.

Berwanger, Eugene H. The Frontier against Slavery: Western Anti-Negro Prejudice and the Slavery Extension Controversy. Urbana: University Illinois Press, 1967.

Beste, J. Richard. The Wabash: or Adventures of an English Gentleman's Family in the Interior of America. 2 vols. London: Hurst and Blackett, 1855.

Bidwell, Percy, and John I. Falconer. History of Agriculture in the Northern United States, 1620–1860. New York: Peter Smith, 1941.

Biographical and Genealogical Record of La Salle and Grundy Counties, Illinois. Illustrated. 2 vols. Chicago: Lewis Publishing Company, 1900.

Biographical and Genealogical Record of La Salle County, Illinois. Illustrated. 2 vols. Chicago: Lewis Publishing Company, 1900.

Biographical and Historical Record of Jay and Blackford Counties, Indiana. . . . Chicago: Lewis Publishing Company, 1887.

Biographical and Historical Record of Kosciusko County, Indiana. . . . Chicago: Lewis Publishing Company, 1887.

Biographical History of La Crosse, Monroe and Juneau Counties, Wisconsin. . . . Chicago: Lewis Publishing Company, 1892.

Biographical Record of Bartholomew County, Indiana. . . . [Indianapolis?]: B. F. Bowen Company, 1904.

Biographical Record of Bureau, Marshall and Putnam Counties, Illinois. Illustrated. Chicago: S. J. Clarke Publishing Company, 1896.

Biographical Record of Henry County, Illinois. Illustrated. Chicago: S. J. Clarke Publishing Company, 1901.

Biographical Record of Kane County, Illinois. Illustrated. Chicago: S. J. Clarke Publishing Company, 1898.

Biographical Record of Logan County, Illinois. Illustrated. Chicago: S. J. Clarke Publishing Company, 1901.

Biographical Record of Ogle County, Illinois. Illustrated. Chicago: S. J. Clarke Publishing Company, 1899.

Biographical Review of Hancock County, Illinois. . . . Chicago: Hobart Publishing Company, 1907.

Bishop, Isabella Lucy Bird. *The Englishwoman in America*. London: John Murray, 1856.

Blackman, W. S. *The Boy of Battle Ford and the Man*. Marion, Ill., 1906.

Blair, Walter A. *A Raft Pilot's Log: A History of the Great Rafting Industry on the Mississippi, 1840–1915*. Cleveland: Arthur Clark Company, 1930.

Blake, John L. *The Farmer's Every-Day Book; or, Sketches of Social Life in the Country*. . . . New York and Auburn: Miller, Orton & Mulligan, 1855.

———. *Lessons in Modern Farming; or, Agriculture for Schools*. . . . New York: Newman and Ivison, 1852.

Blanchard, Charles, ed. *Counties of Clay and Owen, Indiana. Historical and Biographical. Illustrated*. Chicago: F. A. Battey and Company, 1884.

———. *Counties of Howard and Tipton, Indiana. Historical and Biographical. Illustrated*. Chicago: F. A. Battey and Company, 1883.

———. *Counties of Morgan, Monroe and Brown. Indiana. Historical and Biographical*. Chicago: F. A. Battey and Company, 1884.

Blane, William. *An Excursion through the United States and Canada during the Years 1822–23 by an English Gentleman*. London: Baldwin, Cradock and Joy, 1824.

Blois, John T. *Gazetteer of the State of Michigan, in Three Parts, Containing a General View of the State . . . and a Directory for Emigrants, &c.* Detroit: Sydney L. Rood, 1838.

Bodurtha, Arthur L., ed. *History of Miami County, Indiana*. . . . 2 vols. Chicago and New York: Lewis Publishing Company, 1914.

Bogue, Allan G. *From Prairie to Corn Belt: Farming on the Illinois and Iowa Prairies in the Nineteenth Century*. Chicago: University of Chicago Press, 1963.

Bogue, Margaret B. *Patterns from the Sod: Land Use and Tenure in the Grand Prairie, 1850–1900*. Collections of the Illinois State Historical Library, XXXIV. Springfield, 1959.

Bonner, Richard Illenden, ed. *Memoirs of Lenawee County, Michigan, from the Earliest Historical Times down to the Present*. . . . 2 vols. Madison: Western Historical Association, 1909.

Bottomley, Edwin. *An English Settler in Pioneer Wisconsin: The Letters of Edwin Bottomley 1842–1850*. Ed. Milo Milton Quaife. Collections, Publications of the State Historical Society of Wisconsin, XXV. Madison, 1918.

Bradbury, John. *Travels in the Interior of America in the Years 1809, 1810, and 1811; including a Description of Upper Louisiana, Together with the States of Ohio, Kentucky, Indiana, and Tennessee, with the Illinois and Western Territories, and containing Remarks and Observations useful to Persons emigrating to those Countries*. Liverpool: By the Author, 1817.

Bradford, William J. A. *Notes on the Northwest, or Valley of the Upper Mississippi. Comprising the Country between the Lakes Superior and*

Michigan, East; The Illinois and Missouri Rivers, and the Northern Boundary of the United States;—Including Iowa and Wisconsin, part of Michigan Northwest of the Straits of Mackinaw, and Northern Illinois and Missouri. New York: Wiley and Putnam, 1846.

Brainerd, Alvah. *A Pioneer History of the Township of Grand Blanc, Genesee County, Michigan.* Flint, 1878.

Brown, Harriet Connor. *Grandmother Brown's Hundred Years 1827–1927.* Boston: Little, Brown, 1929.

Brown, William. *America: A Four Years' Residence in the United States and Canada; Giving a Full and Fair Description of the Country, as it really is.* . . . Leeds: By the Author, 1849.

Brown, William Fiske, ed. *Rock County, Wisconsin. A New History of its Cities, Villages, Towns, Citizens and Varied Interests, from the Earliest Times, Up to Date. Illustrated.* 2 vols. Chicago: C. F. Cooper, 1908.

Brownson, Howard G. *History of the Illinois Central Railroad to 1870.* Urbana: University of Illinois, 1915.

Brunson, Alfred. *A Western Pioneer: Or, Incidents of the Life and Times of Rev. Alfred Brunson, A.M., D.D., Embracing a Period of over Seventy Years. Written By Himself.* 2 vols. Cincinnati: Walden & Stowe, 1880.

Brush, Daniel Harmon. *Growing Up with Southern Illinois 1820 to 1861 from the Memoirs of Daniel Harmon Brush.* Ed. Milo Milton Quaife. Chicago: Lakeside, 1944.

Buchanan, Robert. *A Treatise on Grape Culture in Vineyards in the Vicinity of Cincinnati. By a Member of the Cincinnati Horticultural Society.* Cincinnati, 1850.

Buck, James S. *Pioneer History of Milwaukee, from 1840 to 1846, Inclusive.* Vol. 2. Milwaukee: Symes, Swain and Company, 1881.

Buckingham, J[ames] S[ilk]. *America, Historical, Statistic, Descriptive.* 3 vols. London: Fisher, [1841].

———. *The Eastern and Western States of America.* London: Fisher, [1842].

———. *The Slave States of America.* 2 vols. London: Fisher, [1842].

Buley, R. C. *The Old Northwest: Pioneer Period, 1815–1840.* 2 vols. Indianapolis: Indiana Historical Society, 1950.

Burkett, Charles W. *History of Ohio Agriculture: A Treatise on the Development of the Various Lines and Phases of Farm Life in Ohio.* Concord, N.H., 1900.

Burnham, J. H., comp. *History of Bloomington and Normal, in McLean County, Illinois.* Bloomington: By the Author, 1879.

Busch, Moritz. *Travels between the Hudson & the Mississippi 1851–1852.* Trans. and ed. Norman H. Binger. Lexington: University of Kentucky Press, 1971.

Caird, James. *Prairie Farming in America, with Notes by the Way on Canada and the United States.* London: D. Appleton, 1859.

Caldwell, J. A. *History of Belmont and Jefferson Counties, Ohio, and . . .*

the Early Settlement of the adjacent Portion of the Ohio Valley. Wheeling: Historical Publishing Company, 1880.

Calkins, Earnest Elmo, ed. *Log City Days: Two Narratives on the Settlement of Galesburg, Illinois. The Diary of Jerusha Loomis Farnham.
Sketch of Log City by Samuel Holyoke.* Galesburg: Knox College Cen-
tenary Publications, 1937.

Canfield, William H. *Outline Sketches of Sauk County; Including Its History, From the First Marks of Man's Hand to 1861, and its Topography,
Both Written and Illustrated.* Baraboo, 1861 [1890].

Cawley, Elizabeth, ed. *The American Diaries of Richard Cobden.* Princeton: Princeton University Press, 1952.

Chamberlain, E. *The Indiana Gazetteer, or Topographical Dictionary of
the State of Indiana.* 3rd ed. Indianapolis: By the Author, 1849.

Chase, Philander. *Bishop Chase's Reminiscences: An Autobiography. Second Edition. Comprising a History of the Principal Events in the Author's
Life to A. D. 1847.* 2 vols. Boston: James B. Dow, 1848.

Cist, Charles. *Sketches and Statistics of Cincinnati in 1851.* Cincinnati:
William H. Moore and Company, 1851.

Clark, John G. *The Grain Trade in the Old Northwest.* Urbana: University
of Illinois Press, 1966.

Cobbett, William. *A Year's Residence in the United States of America.* . . .
Carbondale: Southern Illinois University Press, 1964.

————. *The Emigrant's Guide; in Ten Letters, addressed to the Tax-Payers
of England; containing information of every kind, necessary to persons
who are about to emigrate; including Several authentic and most interesting Letters from English Emigrants, now in America, to their Relations
in England.* London: By the Author, 1829.

Cockrum, William. *Pioneer History of Indiana Including Stories, Incidents
and Customs of the Early Settlers.* Oakland City, Ind., 1907.

Coke, E. T. *A Subaltern's Furlough: Descriptive of Scenes in Various Parts
of the United States . . . During the Summer and Autumn of 1832.* 2
vols. New York: J. & J. Harper, 1833.

Collins, S. H. *The Emigrant's Guide to and Description of the United States
of America; including Several authentic and highly important Letters
from English Emigrants Now in America, to their Friends in England.*
4th ed. Hull: Joseph Noble, 1830.

Combined History of Edwards, Lawrence and Wabash Counties, Illinois.
. . . Philadelphia: J. L. McDonough and Company, 1883.

*Commemorative Biographical and Historical Record of Kane County, Illi-
nois. . . . From Its Earliest Settlement up to the Present Time.* Chicago:
Beers, Leggett and Company, 1888.

*Commemorative Biographical Record of the Counties of Harrison and
Carroll, Ohio . . . and of Many of the Early Settled Families.* Chicago:
J. H. Beers and Company, 1891.

Condensed History of Jefferson, Ashtabula County, Ohio. Compiled from

Early Records and verbal accounts of old residents of the town. Jefferson: J. A. Howells and Company, 1878.

Conner, John B. *Indiana Agriculture: Agricultural Resources and Development of the State. The Struggles of Pioneer Life Compared with Present Conditions.* Indianapolis, 1893.

Conway, Alan, ed. *The Welsh in America: Letters from the Immigrants.* Minneapolis: University of Minnesota Press, 1961.

Counties of La Grange and Noble, Indiana. Historical and Biographical. Illustrated. Chicago: F. A. Battey and Company, 1882.

Counties of Warren, Benton, Jasper and Newton, Indiana. Historical and Biographical. Illustrated. Chicago: F. A. Battey and Company, 1883.

Counties of White and Pulaski, Indiana. Historical and Biographical. Illustrated. Chicago: F. A. Battey and Company, 1883.

County of Douglas, Illinois. Historical and Biographical. . . . Chicago: F. A. Battey and Company, 1884.

Curti, Merle. *The Making of An American Community: A Case Study of Democracy in a Frontier County.* Stanford: Stanford University Press, 1959.

Danhof, Clarence H. *Change in Agriculture: The Northern United States, 1820–1870.* Cambridge: Harvard University Press, 1969.

Davenport, Eugene. *Timberland Times.* Urbana: University of Illinois Press, 1950.

Dickore, Marie. *General Joseph Kerr of Chillicothe, Ohio, "Ohio's Lost Senator" from the Carrell Manuscript Collection.* Oxford, Ohio: Oxford Press, 1941.

Douglass, Ben. *History of Wayne County, Ohio, From the Days of the Pioneers and First Settlers to the Present Time.* Indianapolis: Robert Douglass, 1878.

Downing, Andrew Jackson. *Rural Essays. By A. J. Downing. Edited, with a Memoir of the Author, by George William Curtis, and a Letter to His Friends, by Frederika Bremer.* New York: Leavitt & Allen, 1860.

Drake, Daniel. *Malaria in the Interior Valley of North America. A Selection by Norman D. Levine from A Systematic Treatise, Historical, Etiological, and Practical, on the Principal Diseases of the Interior Valley of North America . . . by Daniel Drake. Cincinnati, Ohio, 1850.* Urbana: University of Illinois Press, 1964.

———. *Natural and Statistical View, or Picture of Cincinnati and the Miami Country.* . . . Cincinnati: Looker and Wallace, 1815.

Duis, E. *The Good Old Times in McLean County, Illinois, containing Two Hundred and Sixty-one Sketches of Old Settlers.* . . . Bloomington: Leader Publishing and Printing House, 1874.

Durant, Samuel W. *History of Ingham and Eaton Counties, Michigan, with Illustrations and Biographical Sketches of Their Prominent Men and Pioneers.* Philadelphia: D. W. Ensign and Company, 1880.

Duus, Olaus Frederik. *Frontier Parsonage: The Letters of Olaus Frederik*

Duus, Norwegian Pastor in Wisconsin, 1855–1858. Trans. Verdandi Study Club of Minneapolis and ed. Theodore C. Blegen. Northfield: Norwegian-American Historical Association, 1947.

Eames, Charles, comp. *Historic Morgan and Classic Jacksonville, Compiled in 1884-'85 by Charles M. Eames, (Editor and Proprietor of the Daily and Weekly Journal,) With Introduction by Prof. Harvey W. Milligan, A.M., M.D., of Illinois College.* Jacksonville, Ill.: By the Author, 1885.

Eggleston, Edward. *The Hoosier Schoolmaster: A Story of Backwoods Life in Indiana. Revised with an Introduction and Notes on the District by the Author, with Character Sketches by F. Opper and other Illustrations by W. E. B. Starkweather.* Chicago: Thompson and Thomas, 1899.

Ellet, Elizabeth F. *Pioneer Women of the West.* New York: Charles Scribner, 1852.

———. *Summer Rambles in the West.* New York: J. C. Riker, 1853.

Ellsworth, Henry William. *Valley of the Upper Wabash, Indiana, with Hints on its Agricultural Advantages. . . .* New York: Pratt, Robinson, 1838.

Ellsworth, Spencer, ed. *Records of the Olden Time; or, Fifty Years on the Prairies. . . .* Lacon, Ill., 1880.

Evans, Lyles S., ed. *A Standard History of Ross County, Ohio. . . .* 2 vols. Chicago and New York: Lewis Publishing Company, 1917.

Evans, Nelson W. *A History of Scioto County, Ohio, Together with a Pioneer Record of Southern Ohio.* Portsmouth: By the Author, 1903.

Everett, Franklin. *Memorials of the Grand River Valley.* Chicago: Chicago Legal News Company, 1878.

The Farmer's Guide and Western Agriculturist. By Several Eminent Practical Farmers of the West, and Published under the Patronage of the Hamilton County Agricultural Society. Cincinnati: Buckley, DeForest and Company, 1832.

Farnham, Eliza. *Life in the Prairie Land.* New York: Harper and Brothers, 1846.

Faux, W. *Memorable Days in America, Being a Journal of a Tour to the United States, principally undertaken to ascertain, by positive evidence, the condition and probable prospects of British Emigrants; including Accounts of Mr. Birkbeck's Settlement in the Illinois* (London, 1823). In Reuben Gold Thwaites, *Early Western Travels 1748–1846. . . ,* XI–XII. Cleveland: Arthur H. Clark, 1905.

Fearon, Henry Bradshaw. *Sketches of America. A Narrative of a Journey of Five Thousand Miles through the Eastern and Western States of America. . . .* London: Strahan and Spottiswoode, 1819.

Featherstonhaugh, George W. *A Canoe Voyage Up the Minnay Sotor with an Account of the Lead and Copper Deposits in Wisconsin; of the Gold Region in the Cherokee County; and Sketches of Popular Manners.* Intro.

William E. Lass. 2 vols. Reprint ed. St. Paul: Minnesota Historical Society, 1970.

Fehrenbacher, Don E. *Chicago Giant: A Biography of "Long John" Wentworth.* Madison: American History Research Center, 1957.

Ferguson, William. *America by River and Rail; or, Notes by the Way on the New World and Its People.* London: J. Nisbet, 1856.

Ferris, Jacob. *The States and Territories of the Great West; including Ohio, Indiana, Illinois, Missouri, Michigan, Wisconsin, Iowa, Minnesota. . . .* New York: Miller, Orton & Mulligan, 1856.

Finley, Isaac J., and Rufus Putnam. *Pioneer Record and Reminiscences of the Early Settlers and Settlement of Ross County, Ohio.* Cincinnati: By the Authors, 1871.

Finley, James B. *History of the Wyandott Mission, at Upper Sandusky, Ohio, under the direction of the Methodist Episcopal Church.* Cincinnati: J. F. Wright and L. Swormstedt, 1840.

Fleischmann, Charles Lewis. *Erwerbszweige, Fabrikwesen und Handel der Vereinigten Staaten von Nordamerika. Mit besondere Rucksicht auf Deutsche Auswanderer bearbeitet von C. L. Fleischmann, Consul der Vereinigten Staaten Nordamerika's.* Stuttgart: Verlag von Franz Kohler, 1850.

Fletcher, Stevenson W. *Pennsylvania Agriculture and Country Life, 1640–1940.* 2 vols. Harrisburg: Pennsylvania Historical and Museum Commission, 1950–55.

Flint, James. *Letters from America, Containing Observations on the Climate and Agriculture of the Western States, the Manners of the People, the Prospects of Emigrants, &c. &c.* (Edinburgh, 1822). In Reuben Gold Thwaites, *Early Western Travels 1748–1846. . . ,* IX. Cleveland: Arthur H. Clark, 1905.

Flower, George. *The Errors of Emigrants: Pointing out many Popular Errors Hitherto Unnoticed . . . and a Description of the Progress and Present Aspect of the English Settlement in Illinois. . . .* London: Cleave, 1841.

————. *History of the English Settlement in Edwards County, Illinois, founded in 1817 and 1818, by Morris Birkbeck and George Flower.* Chicago Historical Society's Collections, I. 2nd ed. Chicago: Chicago Historical Society, 1909.

Ford, Henry A., and Kate B. Ford, comps. *History of Hamilton County, Ohio, With Illustrations and Biographical Sketches.* Cleveland: L. A. Williams and Company, 1881.

Ford, Ira, ed. *History of Northeast Indiana: La Grange, Steuben, Noble and De Kalb Counties.* 2 vols. Chicago and New York: Lewis Publishing Company, 1920.

Frank, Louis. *Pionierjahre der Deutsch-Amerikanischen Familien Frank-Kerler in Wisconsin und Michigan 1849–1864. Geschildert aus Briefen*

Gesammelt und heraus gegeben von Dr. Louis F. Frank. Milwaukee: By the Author, 1911.

French, Henry F. *Farm Drainage. The Principles, Processes, and Effects of Draining Land with Stones, Wood, Plows, and Open Ditches and Especially with Tiles.* . . . New York: A. O. Moore and Company, 1859.

Fries, Robert F. *Empire in Pine: The Story of Lumbering in Wisconsin, 1830–1900.* Madison: State Historical Society of Wisconsin, 1951.

Fuller, S. M. *Summer on the Lakes, in 1843.* Boston: Charles C. Little and James Brown. New York: Charles S. Francis and Company, 1844.

Gates, Paul W. *Farmer's Age: Agriculture, 1815–1860.* New York: Holt, Rinehart and Winston, 1960.

———. *The Illinois Central Railroad and Its Colonization Work.* Cambridge: Harvard University Press, 1934.

Gerhard, Fred. *Illinois as It is.* . . . Chicago: Keen and Lee. Philadelphia: Charles Desilver, 1857.

Gerke, Heinrich Christian. *Der Nordamerikanische Rathgeber, nebst den, in den Jahren 1831 und 1832 in der Union gemachten Reisebeobachtungen, ein Taschenbuch für Deutsche Auswanderer jeder Art.* Hamburg: Perthes & Besser, 1833.

Goodspeed, Weston A., and Charles Blanchard, eds. *Counties of Porter and Lake, Indiana. Historical and Biographical. Illustrated.* Chicago: F. A. Battey and Company, 1882.

Greenberg, David, ed. *Land That Our Fathers Plowed: The Settlement of Our Country as Told by the Pioneers Themselves and Their Contemporaries.* Norman: University of Oklahoma Press, 1969.

Greene, Lorenzo J., and Carter G. Woodson. *The Negro Wage Earner.* Washington: Association for the Study of Negro Life and History, 1930.

Gregg, Thomas. *History of Hancock County, Illinois.* . . . Chicago: Charles C. Chapman and Company, 1880.

Gridley, J. N. *Historical Sketches*, I. Virginia, Ill., 1907.

Griffiths, D., Jr. *Two Years' Residence in the New Settlements of Ohio: with directions to emigrants.* London: Westley and Davis, 1835.

Gross, Lewis M. *Past and Present of De Kalb County, Illinois.* . . . 2 vols. Chicago: Pioneer Publishing Company, 1907.

de Haas, Carl. *Nordamerika. Wisconsin von Dr. Carl de Haas in Calumet. Zweite Abtheilung: Beschreibung von Wisconsin.* 2 vols. Elberfeld u. Iserlohn: Badeker, 1849.

Haines, Elijah M. *Historical and Statistical Sketches of Lake County, State of Illinois.* . . . Waukegan: E. G. Howe, 1852.

Hall, A. Oakley. *The Manhattaner in New Orleans; or, Phases of "Crescent City" Life.* New York: J. S. Redfield, 1851.

Hall, Basil. *Travels in North America, in the Years 1827 and 1828.* 3 vols. Edinburgh: Cadell and Co., 1829.

Hall, James. *The West: Its Commerce and Navigation.* Cincinnati: H. W. Derby & Co., 1848.

Hamelle, W. W. *A Standard History of White County, Indiana.* . . . 2 vols. Chicago and New York: Lewis Publishing Company, 1915.

Hamilton, Thomas. *Men and Manners in America.* 2 vols. Edinburgh: William Blackwood, 1833.

Hanna, Charles A. *Historical Collections of Harrison County, in the State of Ohio.* . . . New York: By the Author, 1900.

Harden, Samuel. *Early Life and Times of Boone County, Indiana.* . . . Lebanon: Harden and Spahr, 1887.

Hazzard, George. *Hazzard's History of Henry County, Indiana 1822–1906. Military Edition.* 2 vols. New Castle: By the Author, 1906.

Hedrick, Ulysses Prentiss. *A History of Agriculture in the State of New York.* Albany: New York State Agricultural Society, 1933.

———. *A History of Horticulture in America to 1860.* New York: Oxford University Press, 1950.

Helm, Thomas B., ed. *History of Cass County, Indiana. From the Earliest Time to the Present.* . . . Chicago: Brant and Fuller, 1886.

Hesse, Nicholas. *Das Westliche Nordamerika, in besonderer Beziehung und die deutschen Einwanderer in ihren landwirthschaftlichen, Handels- und Gewerbverhältnissen.* Paderborn: Joseph Wesener, 1838.

Hibbard, Benjamin H. *The History of Agriculture in Dane County, Wisconsin.* Published dissertation in *Bulletin of the University of Wisconsin, Economics and Political Science Series* (1904). Reprint. Madison, 1905.

Hickman, Nollie. *Mississippi Harvest: Lumbering in the Longleaf Pine Belt, 1840–1915.* University: University of Mississippi, 1962.

Hicks, E. W. *History of Kendall County, Illinois, from the Earliest Discoveries to the Present Time.* Aurora: Knickerbocker and Hodder, 1877.

Hill, George William. *History of Ashland County, Ohio, with Illustrations and Biographical Sketches.* N.p.: Williams Brothers, 1880.

Historical Collections: Collections and Researches Made by the Michigan Pioneer and Historical Society. 40 vols. Lansing: Michigan Pioneer and Historical Society, and later Michigan Historical Commission, 1877–1929. Titles of individual volumes in the series vary.

History of Allen County, Ohio. . . . Chicago: Warner, Beers and Company, 1885.

History of Ashtabula County, Ohio. . . . Philadelphia: Williams Brothers, 1878.

History of Berrien and Van Buren Counties, Michigan. . . . Philadelphia: D. W. Ensign and Company, 1880.

History of Brown County, Ohio. . . . Chicago. W. H. Beers and Company, 1883.

History of Calhoun County, Michigan. . . . Philadelphia: L. H. Everts and Company, 1877.

History of Champaign County, Ohio. . . . Chicago: W. H. Beers and Company, 1881.

History of Cincinnati and Hamilton County, Ohio. . . . Cincinnati: S. B. Nelson and Company, 1894.

History of Clark County, Ohio. . . . Chicago: W. H. Beers and Company, 1881.

History of Clinton County, Ohio. . . . Chicago: W. H. Beers and Company, 1882.

History of Coles County, Illinois. . . . Chicago: William LeBaron, Jr., and Company, 1879.

History of Crawford and Richland Counties, Wisconsin. . . . Springfield: Union Publishing Company, 1884.

History of Crawford County and Ohio. . . . Chicago: Baskin and Battey, 1881.

History of Dearborn and Ohio Counties, Indiana. . . . Chicago: F. E. Weakley, 1885.

History of Defiance County, Ohio. . . . Chicago: Warner, Beers and Company, 1883.

History of De Kalb County, Indiana. . . . Chicago: Inter-State Publishing Company, 1885.

History of Delaware County and Ohio. . . . Chicago: O. L. Baskin and Company, 1880.

History of Delaware County, Indiana. . . . Chicago: Kingman Brothers, 1881.

History of Edgar County, Illinois. . . . Chicago: William LeBaron, Jr., and Company, 1879.

History of Geauga and Lake Counties, Ohio. . . . Philadelphia: Williams Brothers, 1878.

History of Genesee County, Michigan. . . . Philadelphia: Everts & Abbott, 1879.

History of Green County, Wisconsin. . . . Springfield: Union Publishing Company, 1884.

History of Greene and Jersey Counties, Illinois. . . . Springfield Continental Historical Company, 1885.

History of Greene County, Illinois. . . . Chicago: Donnelley, Gassette and Lloyd, 1879.

History of Grundy County, Illinois. . . . Chicago: O. L. Baskin and Company, 1882.

History of Hardin County, Ohio. . . . Chicago: Warner, Beers and Company, 1883.

History of Henry County, Indiana. . . . Chicago: Inter-State Publishing Company, 1884.

History of Hillsdale County, Michigan. . . . Philadelphia: Everts and Abbott, 1879.

History of Hocking Valley, Ohio. . . . Chicago: Inter-State Publishing Company, 1883.

History of Jackson County, Illinois. . . . Philadelphia: Brink, McDonough and Company, 1878.

History of Jackson County, Michigan. . . . Chicago: Inter-State Publishing Company, 1881.

History of Jo Daviess County, Illinois. . . . Chicago: H. F. Kett and Company, 1878.

History of Kalamazoo County, Michigan. . . . Philadelphia: Everts and Abbott, 1880.

History of Kent County, Michigan. . . . Chicago: Charles Chapman and Company, 1881.

History of Knox and Daviess Counties, Indiana. . . . Chicago: Goodspeed Publishing Company, 1886.

History of Knox County, Illinois. . . . Chicago: Charles C. Chapman and Company, 1878.

History of Knox County, Illinois. . . . 2 vols. Chicago: S. J. Clarke Publishing Company, 1912.

History of Lapeer County, Michigan. . . . Chicago: H. R. Page and Company, 1884.

History of La Salle County, Illinois. . . . 2 vols. Chicago: Inter-State Publishing Company, 1886.

History of Lee County [Illinois]. . . . Chicago: H. H. Hill and Company, 1881.

History of Livingston County, Michigan. . . . Philadelphia: Everts and Abbott, 1880.

History of Logan County and Ohio. . . . Chicago: O. L. Baskin and Company, 1880.

History of McDonough County, Illinois. . . . Springfield: Continental Historical Company, 1885.

History of McHenry County, Illinois. . . . Chicago: Inter-State Publishing Company, 1885.

History of McLean County, Illinois. . . . Chicago: William LeBaron, Jr., and Company, 1879.

History of Macomb County, Michigan. . . . Chicago: M. A. Leeson and Company, 1882.

History of Macoupin County, Illinois. . . . Philadelphia: Brink, McDonough and Company, 1879.

History of Menard and Mason Counties, Illinois. . . . Chicago: O. L. Baskin and Company, 1879.

History of Mercer and Henderson Counties [Illinois]. . . . Chicago: H. H. Hill and Company, 1882.

History of Oakland County, Michigan. . . . Philadelphia: L. H. Everts and Company, 1877.

History of Peoria County, Illinois. . . . Chicago: Johnson and Company, 1880.

History of Rush County, Indiana. . . . Chicago: Brant and Fuller, 1888.

History of St. Clair County, Illinois. . . . Philadelphia: Brink, McDonough and Company, 1881.

History of St. Clair County, Michigan. . . . Chicago: A. T. Andreas and Company, 1883.

History of Sangamon County, Illinois. . . . Chicago: Inter-State Publishing Company, 1881.

History of Seneca County, Ohio. . . . Chicago: Warner, Beers and Company, 1886.

History of Shiawassee and Clinton Counties, Michigan. . . . Philadelphia: D. W. Ensign and Company, 1880.

History of Stephenson County, Illinois. . . . Chicago: Western Historical Company, 1880.

History of the Early Life and Business Interests of the Village and Township of Leslie, Ingham County, Michigan. N.p.: Published under the Auspices of the Elijah Grout Chapter, Daughters of the American Revolution, 1914.

History of the Upper Ohio Valley with Historical Account of Columbiana County, Ohio. . . . 2 vols. Madison: Brant and Fuller, 1891.

History of Tuscola and Bay Counties, Mich. . . . . Chicago: H. R. Page and Company, 1883.

History of Union County, Ohio. . . . Chicago: W. H. Beers and Company, 1883.

History of Vanderburgh County, Indiana. . . . Madison: Brant and Fuller, 1889.

History of Van Wert and Mercer Counties, Ohio. . . . Wapakoneta: R. Sutton and Company, 1882.

History of Washington County, Ohio. . . . Cleveland: Williams Brothers, 1881.

History of Washtenaw County, Michigan. . . . Chicago: Charles C. Chapman and Company, 1881.

History of Wayne County, Indiana. . . . 2 vols. Chicago: Inter-State Publishing Company, 1884.

Hoffman, Charles Fenno. *A Winter in the West. By a New-Yorker.* 2 vols. New York: Harper and Brothers, 1835.

Hoffman, U. J. *History of La Salle County, Illinois.* . . . Chicago: S. J. Clarke Publishing Company, 1906.

Holmes, Francis S. *The Southern Farmer and Market Gardener.* . . . Charleston: Burges & James, 1842.

Holmes, Isaac. *An Account of the United States of America, derived from actual observation, during a residence of four years.* . . . London: Henry Fisher, [1823].

Howells, William Cooper. *Recollections of Life in Ohio from 1813 to 1840 with an introduction by his son William Dean Howells.* Cincinnati: Robert Clarke Company, 1895.

Hubbell, Homer Bishop. *Dodge County, Wisconsin. Past and Present.* 2 vols. Chicago: S. J. Clarke Publishing Company, 1913.

Huffman, A. O., and H. H. Hyer, eds. *Biographical Sketches of Old Settlers and Prominent People of Wisconsin.* Waterloo: By the Authors, 1899.

Hutchinson, William T. *Cyrus Hall McCormick: Seed-Time, 1809–1856.* 2 vols. New York: Century Company, 1930.

The Immigrants' Guide to Minnesota in 1856. By an Old Resident. St. Anthony: W. W. Wales, 1856.

Johnston, James F. W. *Notes on North America Agricultural, Economical, and Social.* 2 vols. Boston: Charles C. Little and James Brown, 1851.

Jones, A. D. *Illinois and the West. With a Township Map, containing the latest Surveys and Improvements.* Boston: Weeks, Jordan and Company, 1838.

Jones, C. E. *Madison, Dane County and Surrounding Towns; Being a History and Guide. . . .* Madison: William J. Park and Company, 1877.

Joslyn, R. Waite, and Frank W. Joslyn. *History of Kane County, Ill.* 2 vols. Chicago: Pioneer Publishing Company, 1908.

Kable Brothers. *Mount Morris: Past and Present. An Illustrated History of the Township and the Village of Mount Morris, Ogle County, Illinois. . . .* Mt. Morris: By the Authors, 1900.

Kable, H. G. *Mount Morris: Past and Present. Revised Edition. An Illustrated History of the Village of Mount Morris, Ogle County, Illinois. . . .* 2nd ed. Mt. Morris: By the Author, 1938.

Kiner, Henry L. ed. *History of Henry County, Illinois. . . .* 2 vols. Chicago: Pioneer Publishing Company, 1910.

Kingdom, William. *America and the British Colonies. An Abstract of all the most useful information relative to the United States of America. . . .* London: G. and W. B. Whittaker, 1820.

Kingsford, W[illiam]. *History, Structure, and Statistics of Plank Roads, in the United States and Canada. . . .* Philadelphia: A. Hart, 1851.

Klippart, John H. *The Principles and Practice of Land Drainage. . . .* Cincinnati: R. Clarke & Company, 1888.

Knapp, H. S. *A History of the Pioneer and Modern Times of Ashland County [Ohio], from the Earliest to the Present Date.* Philadelphia: J. B. Lippincott and Company, 1863.

Kohl, J. G. *Reisen im Nordwesten der Vereinigten Staaten.* Zweite Auflage. New York: D. Appleton and Company, 1857.

Larkin, Stillman Carter. *The Pioneer History of Meigs County [Ohio].* Columbus, 1908.

Larson, Agnes M. *History of the White Pine Industry in Minnesota.* Minneapolis: University of Minnesota Press, 1949.

Larson, Henrietta M. *The Wheat Market and the Farmer in Minnesota, 1858–1900.* Columbia University Studies in History, Economics and Public Law, CXXII. New York, 1926.

Lebergott, Stanley. *Manpower in Economic Growth: The American Record since 1800.* New York: McGraw-Hill, 1964.

Lewis, Henry. *The Valley of the Mississippi Illustrated.* Trans. A. Hermina Poatgieter, and ed. Bertha L. Heilbron. St. Paul: Minnesota Historical Society, 1967.

Lindsey, Charles. *The Prairies of the Western States: Their Advantages and Their Drawbacks.* Toronto, 1860.

Lippincott, Isaac. *A History of Manufactures in the Ohio Valley to the Year 1860.* (Published dissertation, University of Chicago.) New York, 1914.

Litwack, Leon F. *North of Slavery: The Negro in the Free States, 1790–1860.* Chicago: University of Chicago Press, 1961.

Loehr, Rodney C. *Minnesota Farmers' Diaries: William R. Brown, 1845–46. Mitchell Y. Jackson, 1852–63.* Vol. 3. St. Paul: Minnesota Historical Society, 1939.

Logan, James. *Notes of a Journey through Canada, the United States of America, and the West Indies.* Edinburgh: Fraser and Company, 1838.

Longworth, Nicholas. *The Cultivation of the Grape, and Manufacture of Wine. Also, Character and Habits of the Strawberry Plant.* Cincinnati: L'Hommedieu and Company, 1846.

Lorain, John. *Hints to Emigrants, or a Comparative Estimate of the Advantages of Pennsylvania, and of the Western Territory, &c.* Philadelphia: Littel and Henry, 1819.

———. *Nature and Reason Harmonized in the Practice of Husbandry.* Philadelphia: H. C. Carey & I. Lea, 1825.

McDermott, John F. *George Caleb Bingham: River Portraitist.* Norman: University of Oklahoma Press, 1959.

MacGill, Caroline E. *History of Transportation in the United States before 1860.* New York: Peter Smith, 1948.

MacKay, Alexander. *The Western World; or, Travels in the United States in 1846–47. . . .* 3 vols. London: Richard Bentley, 1849.

MacKay, Charles. *Life and Liberty in America: or, Sketches of a Tour in the United States and Canada, in 1857–8.* 2 vols. London: Smith, Elder and Company, 1859.

MacKinnon, Lauchlan Bollingham. *Atlantic and Transatlantic: Sketches Afloat and Ashore.* New York: Harper, 1852.

McManis, Douglas R. *The Initial Evaluation and Utilization of the Illinois Prairies, 1815–1840.* Chicago: University of Chicago Press, 1964.

Marshall, Josiah T. *The Farmer's and Emigrant's Handbook: Being a Full and Complete Guide for the Farmer and the Emigrant. . . .* Boston: H. Wentworth, 1852.

Marshall, Roujet D. *Autobiography of Roujet D. Marshall. Justice of the Supreme Court of the State of Wisconsin 1895–1918.* Ed. Gilson B. Glasier. 2 vols. Madison, 1923.

Martineau, Harriet. *Retrospect of Western Travel*. 3 vols. London: Saunders and Otley, 1838.

——. *Society in America*. 3 vols. London: Saunders and Otley, 1837.

Massie, M. D. *Past and Present of Pike County, Illinois*. . . . Chicago: S. J. Clarke Publishing Company, 1906.

Mason, Richard Lee. *Narrative of Richard Lee Mason in the Pioneer West, 1819*. Heartman Historical Series No. 6. New York: Charles Frederick Heartman, 1915.

Mattson, Hans. *Reminiscences, The Story of an Emigrant*. St. Paul: D. D. Merrill Company, 1892.

Maury, Sarah M. *An Englishwoman in America*. . . . London: Thomas Richardson and Son, 1848.

Melish, John. *Travels through the United States of America, in the Years 1806 & 1807, and 1809, 1810, & 1811*. . . . Belfast: J. Smyth, 1818.

Mills, James Cooke. *Our Inland Seas. Their Shipping & Commerce for Three Centuries*. Chicago: A. C. McClurg and Company, 1910.

Mitchell, Donald G. *My Farm of Edgewood: A Country Book*. . . . New York: Charles Scribner, 1912.

Mitchell, S. Augustus. *Illinois in 1837: A Sketch Descriptive of the Situation*. . . . Philadelphia: By the Author, and Grigg and Elliot, 1837.

Moore, John H. *Andrew Brown and Cypress Lumbering in the Old Southwest*. Baton Rouge: Louisiana State University Press, 1967.

Moore, Nathaniel Fish. *A Trip from New York to the Falls of St. Anthony in 1845*. Ed. Stanley Pargellis and Ruth Lapham Butler. Chicago: University of Chicago Press, 1946.

Morris, Edmund. *How to Get a Farm, and Where to Find One*. . . . New York: James Miller, 1864.

——. *Ten Acres Enough. A Practical Experience showing How a very small Farm may be made to keep a very large Family*. Intro. Isaac Phillips Roberts. New York: Orange Judd, 1916.

Moses, John. *Illinois Historical and Statistical Comprising the Essential Facts of Its Planning and Growth as a Province, County, Territory, and State*. . . . 2nd ed., rev. Vol. 2. Chicago: Fergus Printing Company, 1895.

Muir, John. *The Story of My Boyhood and Youth*. New York and Boston: Houghton, Mifflin, 1925.

Murray, Henry A. *Lands of the Slave and the Free: or, Cuba, the United States, and Canada*. 2 vols. London: John W. Parker, 1855.

Nichols, Thomas L. *Forty Years of American Life*. 2 vols. London: John Maxwell and Company, 1864.

Norelius, Eric. *Early Life of Eric Norelius (1833–1862). Journal of a Swedish Immigrant in the Middle West*. Rendered into English by Emeroy Johnson. Rock Island: Augustana Historical Society Publications, 1934.

Nowland, John H. B. *Early Reminiscences of Indianapolis*. . . . Indianapolis, 1870.

Nowlin, William. *The Bark Covered House, or Back in the Woods Again.*
    . . . Detroit: By the Author, 1876.
O'Brien, Frank G. *Minnesota Pioneer Sketches from the Personal Recol-
    lections and Observations of a Pioneer Resident.* Minneapolis: H. H. S.
    Rowell, 1904.
O'Hanlon, John. *The Irish Emigrant's Guide for the United States.* Boston:
    Patrick Donahoe, 1851.
Oliver, William. *Eight Months in Illinois: with Information to Emigrants.*
    Newcastle upon Tyne: William Andrew Mitchell, 1843.
Olmsted, Frederick Law. *A Journey into the Seaboard Slave States, with
    Remarks on Their Economy.* New York: Mason Brothers, 1859.
Owen, Robert Dale. *A Brief Practical Treatise on the Construction and
    Management of Plank Roads.* . . . New Albany: Kent & Norman, 1850.
Packard, Jasper. *History of LaPorte County, Indiana, and Its Townships,
    Towns and Cities.* LaPorte: S. E. Taylor and Company, 1876.
Page, O. J. *History of Massac County, Illinois.* . . . Metropolis, 1900.
Parker, A[mos] A[ndrew]. *Trip to the West and Texas. Comprising a
    Journey of Eight Thousand Miles.* . . . Concord: William White, Boston:
    Benjamin B. Mussey, 1836.
The Past and Present of Kane County, Illinois. . . . Chicago: William Le-
    Baron, Jr., and Company, 1878.
Patten, Jennie, in collaboration with Andrew Graham. *History of the So-
    monauk United Presbyterian Church near Sandwich, De Kalb County,
    Illinois.* . . . Chicago: James A. and Henry F. Patten, 1928.
Paulding, J[ames] K[irke]. *The Backwoodsman. A Poem.* Philadelphia:
    M. Thomas, 1818.
Pearse, James. *A Narrative of the Life of James Pearse.* . . . Reprint of
    1825 edition. Chicago: Quadrangle Books, 1962.
Peck, John Mason. *A New Guide for Emigrants to the West, Containing
    Sketches of Ohio, Indiana, Illinois, Missouri, Michigan, with the Terri-
    tories of Wisconsin and Arkansas, and the Adjacent Parts.* Boston: Gould,
    Kendall and Lincoln, 1836.
Perrin, William Henry, ed. *History of Alexander, Union and Pulaski Coun-
    ties, Illinois.* Chicago: O. L. Baskin and Company, 1883.
————. *History of Bond and Montgomery Counties, Illinois.* Chicago:
    O. L. Baskin, 1882.
————. *History of Cass County, Illinois.* Chicago: O. L. Baskin, 1882.
————. *History of Effingham County, Illinois.* Chicago: O. L. Baskin,
    1883.
————. *History of Stark County, with an Outline Sketch of Ohio.* Chicago:
    Baskin and Battey, 1881.
*Pictorial and Biographical Memoirs of Elkhart and St. Joseph Counties,
    Indiana.* . . . Chicago: Goodspeed Brothers, 1893.
*Pictorial and Biographical Memoirs of Indianapolis and Marion County,
    Indiana.* . . . Chicago: Goodspeed Brothers, 1893.

Plumbe, John. *Sketches of Iowa and Wisconsin.* Reprint of 1839 ed. Iowa City: State Historical Society of Iowa, 1948.

Pooley, William V. *The Settlement of Illinois from 1830 to 1850.* (Published dissertation of the University of Wisconsin.) Madison, 1908.

Portrait and Biographical Album of Champaign County, Ill. . . . . Chicago: Chapman Brothers, 1887.

Portrait and Biographical Album of Coles County, Ill. . . . . Chicago: Chapman Brothers, 1887.

Portrait and Biographical Album of De Kalb County, Illinois. . . . Chicago: Chapman Brothers, 1883.

Portrait and Biographical Album of Fulton County, Illinois. . . . Chicago: Biographical Publishing Company, 1890.

Portrait and Biographical Album of Greene and Clark Counties, Ohio. . . . Chicago: Chapman Brothers, 1890.

Portrait and Biographical Album of Henry County, Illinois. . . . Chicago: Biographical Publishing Company, 1885.

Portrait and Biographical Album of Jo Daviess and Carroll Counties, Illinois. . . . Chicago: Chapman Brothers, 1889.

Portrait and Biographical Album of Lenawee County, Mich. . . . . Chicago: Chapman Brothers, 1888.

Portrait and Biographical Album of McLean County, Ill. . . . . Chicago: Chapman Brothers, 1887.

Portrait and Biographical Album of Oakland County, Michigan. . . . Chicago: Chapman Brothers, 1891.

Portrait and Biographical Album of Peoria County, Illinois. . . . Chicago: Biographical Publishing Company, 1890.

Portrait and Biographical Album of Rock Island County, Illinois. . . . Chicago: Biographical Publishing Company, 1885.

Portrait and Biographical Album of Stephenson County, Ill. . . . . Chicago: Chapman Brothers, 1888.

Portrait and Biographical Album of Vermilion and Edgar Counties, Illinois. . . . Chicago: Chapman Brothers, 1889.

Portrait and Biographical Album of Vermilion County, Illinois. . . . Chicago: Chapman Brothers, 1889.

Portrait and Biographical Album of Warren County, Illinois. . . . Chicago: Chapman Brothers, 1886.

Portrait and Biographical Album of Woodford County, Illinois. . . . Chicago: Chapman Brothers, 1889.

Portrait and Biographical Record of Adams County, Illinois. . . . Chicago: Chapman Brothers, 1892.

Portrait and Biographical Record of Christian County, Illinois. . . . Chicago: Lake City Publishing Company, 1893.

Portrait and Biographical Record of Delaware and Randolph Counties, Ind. . . . . Chicago: A. W. Bowen and Company, 1894

Portrait and Biographical Record of Effingham, Jasper and Richland Counties, Illinois. . . . Chicago: Lake City Publishing Company, 1893.

Portrait and Biographical Record of Ford County, Illinois. . . . Chicago: Lake City Publishing Company, 1892.

Portrait and Biographical Record of Hancock, McDonough, and Henderson Counties, Illinois. . . . Chicago: Lake City Publishing Company, 1894.

Portrait and Biographical Record of Lee County, Illinois. . . . Chicago: Biographical Publishing Company, 1892.

Portrait and Biographical Record of St. Clair County, Illinois. . . . Chicago: Chapman Brothers, 1892.

Portrait and Biographical Record of Winnebago and Boone Counties, Illinois. . . . Chicago: Biographical Publishing Company, 1892.

Power, John Carroll. *History of the Early Settlers of Sangamon County, Illinois.* . . . Springfield: Edwin A. Wilson and Company, 1876.

Power, Tyrone. *Impressions of America, During the Years 1833, 1834, 1835.* 2 vols. London: Richard Bentley, 1836.

Proceedings of the Home-Coming Festival Held July 4–7, 1907 on the Seventieth Anniversary of the Founding of Whitewater, Wisconsin. N.p., 1907.

Qualey, Carlton C. *Norwegian Settlement in the United States.* Northfield: Norwegian-American Historical Association, 1938.

Randall, J. G. *Lincoln the President.* 2 vols. New York: Dodd, Mead & Company, 1945.

Regan, John. *The Western Wilds of America, or Backwoods and Prairies; and Scenes in the Valley of the Mississippi.* 2nd ed. Edinburgh: J. Menzies, 1859.

Renick, William. *Memoirs, Correspondence and Reminiscences of William Renick.* Circleville, Ohio, 1880.

Richmond, Mabel E., comp. *Centennial History of Decatur and Macon County.* Decatur: Decatur Review in Co-operation with the Decatur and Macon County Centennial Association, 1930.

Ritchie, James S. *Wisconsin and Its Resources.* . . . Philadelphia: Charles Desilver, 1857.

Robinson, Solon. *Facts for Farmers.* . . . New York: A. J. Johnson, 1866.

Rogers, Howard S. *History of Cass County, From 1825 to 1875.* Cassopolis, Mich.: W. H. Mansfield, 1875.

Rogin, Leo. *The Introduction of Farm Machinery in Its Relation to the Productivity of Labor in the Agriculture of the United States during the Nineteenth Century.* Berkeley: University of California, 1931.

Ross, Harvey Lee. *The Early Pioneers and Pioneer Events of the State of Illinois.* . . . Chicago: Eastman Brothers, 1899.

Russell, Charles Edward. *A-Rafting on the Mississip'.* New York: Century Company, 1928.

Russell, John Andrew. *The Germanic Influence in the Making of Michigan.* Detroit: University of Detroit, 1927.

Russell, Robert. *North America, Its Agriculture and Climate.* . . . Edinburgh: Adam & Charles Black, 1857.

Satterthwaite, Myrtillus N., and Martha C. Bishop. *Hoosier Courtships in the Horse and Buggy Days.* Greenfield: William Mitchel Company, 1943.

Schafer, Joseph. *Wisconsin Domesday Book: General Studies: Volume III: The Wisconsin Lead Region.* Madison: State Historical Society of Wisconsin, 1932.

————. *Wisconsin Domesday Book: General Studies: Volume IV: The Winnebago-Horicon Basin, A Type Study in Western History.* Madison: State Historical Society of Wisconsin, 1937.

Schenck, John S. *History of Ionia and Montcalm Counties, Michigan.* . . . Philadelphia: D. W. Ensign and Company, 1881.

Schmidt, Carl. *Dies Buch Gehört dem Deutschen Auswanderer. Eine geographisch-statistische und geschichtliche Beschreibung der Vereinigten Staaten von Nord-Amerika.* . . . Leipzig: Verlag von Otto Wigand, 1855.

Schmidt, Louis B., and Earle D. Ross. *Readings in the Economic History of American Agriculture.* New York: MacMillan Company, 1925.

Scott, Hervey. *A Complete History of Fairfield County, Ohio. 1795–1876.* Columbus, 1877.

Sewall, William. *Diary of William Sewall, 1797–1846: Formerly of Augusta, Maine, Maryland, Virginia and Pioneer in Illinois.* Ed. John Goodell. Lincoln, Ill., 1930.

Shirreff, Patrick. *A Tour through North America; Together with a Comprehensive View of the Canadas and United States, as adapted for Agricultural Emigration.* Edinburgh: Oliver and Boyd, 1835.

Smith, Seraphina Gardner. *Recollections of the Pioneers of Lee County.* Dixon, Ill.: Lee County Columbian Club, 1893.

Smith, William C. *Indiana Miscellaney: Consisting of Sketches of Indian Life, the Early Settlement, Customs, and Hardships of the People.* . . . Cincinnati: Poe and Hitchcock, 1867.

Smith, William Henry. *The History of the State of Indiana from the Earliest Explorations by the French to the Present Time.* . . . 2 vols. Indianapolis: B. L. Blair, 1897.

Spence, Thomas. *The Settler's Guide in the United States and British North American Provinces.* . . . New York: Davies and Kent, 1862.

Stevens, Frank E., ed. *History of Lee County, Illinois.* 2 vols. Chicago: S. J. Clarke Publishing Company, 1914.

Stevens, W. W. *Past and Present of Will County, Illinois.* 2 vols. Chicago: S. J. Clarke Publishing Company, 1907.

Stewart, Lillian Kimball. *A Pioneer of Old Superior.* Boston: Christopher Publishing House, 1930.

Stewart, W. M. *Eleven Years' Experience in the Western States of America.* . . . London: Houlston and Sons, 1870.

Stormant, Gil R. *History of Gibson County, Indiana.* . . . Indianapolis: B. F. Bowen and Company, 1914.

Stuart, James. *Three Years in North America.* 3rd ed. 2 vols. Edinburgh: Robert Cadell, 1833.

Sweet, William Warren. *Circuit-Rider Days in Indiana.* Indianapolis: W. K. Stewart Company, 1916.

Taylor, George Rogers. *The Transportation Revolution 1815–1860.* New York: Rinehart and Company, 1951.

Thomson, Gladys S. *A Pioneer Family: The Birkbecks in Illinois, 1818–1827.* London: Jonathan Cape, 1953.

Thornbrough, Emma Lou. *The Negro in Indiana: A Study of a Minority.* Indianapolis: Indiana Historical Bureau, 1957.

Tillson, Christiana Holmes. *A Woman's Story of Pioneer Illinois.* Ed. Milo M. Quaife. Chicago: Lakeside, 1919.

de Tocqueville, Alexis. *Journey to America.* Trans. George Lawrence, ed. J. P. Mayer. New Haven: Yale University Press, 1960.

Travis, William. *A History of Clay County, Indiana.* . . . 2 vols. New York and Chicago: Lewis Publishing Company, 1909.

Tremenheere, Hugh Seymour. *Notes on Public Subjects, Made during a Tour in the United States and in Canada.* London: John Murray, 1852.

Trollope, Anthony. *North America.* New York: Harper and Brothers, 1862.

Trollope, Frances. *Domestic Manners of the Americans. Edited with a History of Mrs. Trollope's Adventures in America, by Donald Smalley.* New York: Vintage Books, 1960.

Unonius, Gustaf. *A Pioneer in Northwest America 1841–1858. The Memoirs of Gustaf Unonius.* Trans. Jonas Oscar Backlund, ed. Nils William Olsson. 2 vols. Minneapolis: Swedish Pioneer Historical Society, 1960.

Valley of the Upper Maumee River with Historical Account of Allen County and the City of Fort Wayne, Indiana. . . . 2 vols. Madison: Brant and Fuller, 1889.

Warden, D. B. *A Statistical, Political, and Historical Account of the United States of North America; from the Period of their First Colonization to the Present Day.* 3 vols. Edinburgh: Archibald Constable and Company, 1819.

Washburne, E. B. *Sketch of Edward Coles, Second Governor of Illinois, and of the Slavery Struggle of 1823–24. Prepared for the Chicago Historical Society in 1882.* Clarence W. Alvord, Collections of the Illinois State Historical Library, XVI. Springfield, 1920.

Weeks, F. E. *Pioneer History of Clarksfield.* Clarksfield, Ohio: By the Author, 1908.

Weesner, Clarkson W., ed. *History of Wabash County, Indiana.* . . . 2 vols. Chicago and New York: Lewis Publishing Company, 1914.

Weik, Jesse W. *Weik's History of Putnam County, Indiana.* Indianapolis: B. F. Bowen and Company, 1914.

Welker, Martin. *Farm Life in Central Ohio Sixty Years Ago*. Cleveland: Western Reserve Historical Society, 1895.

Williams, Amos. *Scrap Book: Amos Williams and Early Danville, Illinois*. Danville, 1935.

Williams, T. Harry, ed. *Abraham Lincoln: Selected Speeches, Messages, and Letters*. New York: Holt, Rinehart and Winston, 1962.

Wing, Talcott E., ed. *History of Monroe County, Michigan*. New York: Munsell and Company, 1890.

Witte, August. *Kurze Schilderung der Vereinigten Staaten von Nord-Amerika. . . . nebst ausführlichen Vorsichtsregeln für Auswanderer nach eigenen Beobachtungen und Erfahrungen*. Hannover: Verlage der Hahn'schen Hofbuchhandlung, 1833.

Wright, Richardson. *Hawkers and Walkers in Early America: Strolling Peddlers, Preachers, Lawyers, Doctors, Players, and Others, from the Beginning to the Civil War*. Reprint of 1927 ed. in American Classics Series. New York: Frederick Ungar, 1965.

Ylvisaker, Erling. *Eminent Pioneers: Norwegian-American Pioneer Sketches*. Minneapolis: Augsburg Publishing House, 1934.

Young, Andrew W. *History of Wayne County, Indiana. . . .* Cincinnati: Robert Clarke and Company, 1872.

PRINTED MATERIALS AND ARTICLES

Abbott, Richard H. "The Agricultural Press Views the Yeoman: 1819–1859." *Agricultural History*, XLII (1968), 35–48.

Andressohn, John C. "The Kothe Letters." *Indiana Magazine of History*, XLIII (1947), 171–80.

Angle, Paul. "Story of an Ordinary Man." *Journal of the Illinois State Historical Society*, XXXIII (1940), 212–32.

Ankli, Robert. "Problems in Aggregate Agricultural History." *Agricultural History*, XLVI (1972), 65–70.

Atherton, Lewis E. "The Services of the Frontier Merchant." *Mississippi Valley Historical Review*, XXIV (1937), 153–70.

Baker, Charles M. "Pioneer History of Walworth County." *Report and Collections of the State Historical Society of Wisconsin*, VI (1872), 441–75.

Bardolph, Richard. "Illinois Agriculture in Transition, 1820–1870." *Journal of the Illinois State Historical Society*, XLI (1948), 244–64.

Bidwell, Percy W. "The Agricultural Revolution in New England." *American Historical Review*, XXVI (1921), 683–702.

Blegen, Theodore C. "Ole Rynning's True Account of America." *Minnesota History*, II (1917), 221–69.

Bogue, Allan G. "The Iowa Claim Clubs: Symbol and Substance." *Mississippi Valley Historical Review*, XLV (1958), 231–58.

Bogue, Margaret Beattie. "The Swamp Land Act and Wet Land Utilization in Illinois, 1850–1890." *Agricultural History*, XXV (1951), 169–80.

Bradford, Mary D. "Memoirs of Mary D. Bradford: Chapter I: A Pioneer Family of Paris, Kenosha County." *Wisconsin History Magazine*, XIV (1930), 3–47.

Braun, Frank, and Robert B. Brown. "Karl Neidhard's Reise nach Michigan." *Michigan History Magazine*, XXXV (1951), 32–84.

Brown, Clarence A. "Edward Eggleston as a Social Historian." *Journal of the Illinois State Historical Society*, LIV (1961), 415–20.

Buck, Solon J. "Pioneer Letters of Gershom Flagg." *Transactions of the Illinois Historical Society for the Year 1910* (Springfield, 1910), 139–83.

Burmester, Ruth Seymour. "Silas Seymour Letters." *Wisconsin History Magazine*, XXXII (1948), 188–99.

Butler, Albert F. "Rediscovering Michigan's Prairies." *Michigan History Magazine*, XXXI (1947), 267–86; XXXII (1948), 15–36; XXXIII (1949), 117–30, 220–31.

Carmony, Donald F. "Document Letter written by Mr. Johann Wolfgang Schreyer." *Indiana Magazine of History*, XL (1944), 283–306.

―――. "From Lycoming County, Pennsylvania to Parke County, Indiana: Recollections of Andrew Tenbrook, 1786–1823." *Indiana Magazine of History*, LXI (1965), 1–30.

"Childhood Reminiscences of Princeton." *Journal of the Illinois State Historical Society*, XLIX (1956), 95–110.

Clarke, Charles R. "Sketch of Charles James Fox Clark, with Letters to His Mother." *Journal of the Illinois State Historical Society*, XXII (1930), 559–81.

Cole, Arthur H. "The Mystery of Fuel Wood Marketing in the United States." *Business History Review*, XLIV (1970), 339–59.

Coleman, Charles. "Coles County in the 1840's." *Journal of the Illinois State Historical Society*, XLV (1952), 168–72.

Croft, Josie Greening. "A Mazomanie Pioneer." *Wisconsin History Magazine*, XXVI (1942), 208–18.

Danford, Ormand S. "The Social and Economic Effects of Lumbering on Michigan, 1835–1890." *Michigan History Magazine*, XXVI (1942), 346–64.

Danhof, Clarence H. "Farm-Making Costs and the 'Safety Valve': 1850–1860." *Journal of Political Economy*, XLIX (1941), 317–59.

―――. "The Fencing Problem in the Eighteen-Fifties." *Agricultural History*, XVIII (1944), 168–86.

David, Paul A. "The Mechanization of Reaping in the Ante-Bellum Midwest." In Henry Rosovsky, ed., *Industrialization in Two Systems: Essays in Honor of Alexander Gerschenkron*. New York: John Wiley & Sons, 1966, pp. 3–39.

Detzler, Jack J. " 'I Live Here Happily': A German Immigrant in Territorial Wisconsin." *Wisconsin History Magazine*, L (1957), 254–59.

"Diaries of Donald MacDonald 1824–1826." *Indiana Historical Society Publications*, XIV (1942), 143–379.

"Documents." *Wisconsin History Magazine*, XX (1937), 323–36.

"Early Letters to Erland Carlsson from a File for the Years 1853 to 1857." *Augustana Historical Society Publications*, V (1935), 107–33.

Eisterhold, John A. "Lumber and Trade in the Lower Mississippi Valley and New Orleans, 1800–1860." *Louisiana History*, XIII (1972), 71–91.

Engberg, George B. "Who Were the Lumberjacks?" *Michigan History Magazine*, XXXII (1948), 238–46.

Erickson, Charlotte. "Agrarian Myths of English Immigrants." In O. Fritiof Ander, ed., *In the Trek of the Immigrants: Essays Presented to Carl Wittke*. Rock Island: Augustana College Library, 1964, pp. 59–80.

————. "British Immigrants in the Old Northwest, 1815–1860." In David M. Ellis, ed., *The Frontier in American Development: Essays in Honor of Paul Wallace Gates*. Ithaca: Cornell University Press, 1969, pp. 323–56.

Esarey, Logan. "The Pioneers of Morgan County: Memoirs of Noah J. Major." *Indiana Historical Society Publications*, V (1915), 231–516.

"Farming in Illinois in 1837." *Journal of the Illinois State Historical Society*, XXVII (1934), 235–37.

Farrell, Richard T. "Cincinnati, 1800–1830: Economic Development through Trade and Industry." *Ohio History*, LXXVII (1968), 111–29.

Fernstermaker, J. Van. "A Description of Sangamon County, Illinois, in 1830." *Agricultural History*, XXXIX (1965), 136–40.

Fifield, Elbridge G. "Some Pioneering Experiences in Jefferson County." *Proceedings of the State Historical Society of Wisconsin*, LII (1904), 134–44.

Gara, Larry. "A Glimpse of the Galena Lead Region in 1846." *Journal of the Illinois State Historical Society*, L (1957), 85–89.

Gates, Paul W. "Cattle Kings in the Prairies." *Mississippi Valley Historical Review*, XXXV (1948), 379–412.

————. "Charles Lewis Fleischmann: German-American Agricultural Authority." *Agricultural History*, XXXV (1961), 13–23.

————. "Large-Scale Farming in Illinois, 1850 to 1870." *Agricultural History*, VI (1932), 14–25.

————. "Problems in Agricultural History, 1790–1840." *Agricultural History*, XLVI (1972), 33–58.

Gjertset, Knut, and Ludvid Hektoen. "Health Conditions and the Early Practice of Medicine among the Early Norwegian Settlers, 1825–1865." *Norwegian-American Historical Association: Studies and Records*, I (1926), 1–59.

"'God Raised Us Up Good Friends': English Immigrants in Wisconsin." *Wisconsin History Magazine*, XLVII (1964), 224–37.

Goodrich, Carter, and Sol Davison. "The Wage Earner in the Westward Movement." *Political Science Quarterly*, LI (1936), 61–116.

Gray, Anna Brockway. "Letters from Long Ago." *Michigan History Magazine*, XX (1936), 185–212.

Gustorf, Fred. "Frontier Perils Told by an Early Illinois Visitor." *Journal of the Illinois State Historical Society*, LV (1962), 135–56, 255–70.

Hayter, Earl W. "Horticultural Humbuggery among the Western Farmers, 1850–1890." *Indiana Magazine of History*, XLIII (1947), 205–24.

Hunter, Louis C. "Studies in the Economic History of the Ohio Valley: Seasonal Aspects of Industry and Commerce before the Age of Big Business." *Smith College Studies in History*, XIX (1933–34), 1–130.

Hutslar, Donald A. "The Log Architecture of Ohio." *Ohio History*, LXXX (1971), 171–271.

Jamison, Isabel. "Independent Military Companies of Sangamon County in the 30's." *Journal of the Illinois State Historical Society*, III (1911), 22–48.

Jones, Burr W. "Reminiscences of Nine Decades." *Wisconsin History Magazine*, XX (1936), 10–33.

Jones, Robert L. "Introduction of Farm Machinery into Ohio prior to 1865." *Ohio History*, LVIII (1949), 1–20. (Published under original title of *Ohio Archaeological and Historical Society Quarterly*.)

Jordan, Terry G. "Between the Forest and the Prairie." *Agricultural History*, XXXVIII (1964), 205–16.

"Journal of William Rudolph Smith." *Wisconsin History Magazine*, XII (1928), 192–220, 300–321.

Kellar, Herbert A. "Diaries of James D. Davidson (1836) and Greenlee Davidson (1857) during Visits to Indiana." *Indiana Magazine of History*, XXIV (1928), 130–36.

Kellogg, Amherst Willoughby. "Recollections of Life in Early Wisconsin." *Wisconsin History Magazine*, VII (1924), 473–98.

"Knure Steernson's Recollections: The Story of a Pioneer." *Minnesota History*, IV (1921), 130–51.

Krueger, Lillian. "Motherhood on the Wisconsin Frontier." *Wisconsin History Magazine*, XXIX (1945), 157–83.

Leavitt, Charles T. "Some Economic Aspects of the Western Meat-Packing Industry, 1830–60." *Journal of Business of the University of Chicago*, IV (1931), 68–90.

"Letters from New Switzerland, 1831–1832." *Journal of the Illinois State Historical Society*, XLIX (1956), 431–44.

Lightner, David L. "Construction Labor on the Illinois Central Railroad." *Journal of the Illinois State Historical Society*, LXVI (1973), 285–301.

Lucas, Henry S. "Reminiscences of Arend Jan Brusse on the Early Dutch Settlement in Milwaukee." *Wisconsin History Magazine*, XXX (1946), 85–90.

McCarty, F. A. "Memoir of James Knowles Kellogg." *Journal of the Illinois State Historical Society*, XII (1920), 503–14.

Main, Angie Kumlien. "Thures Kumlien, Koshkonong Naturalist." *Wisconsin History Magazine*, XXVII (1943), 194–220.

"Memoirs, Record of Events in the Life and Times of Edward William West, Belleville, Illinois, A.D. 1895." *Journal of the Illinois State Historical Society*, XXII (1929), 215–98.

New, Harry S. "The Importance of a Single Vote." *Indiana Magazine of History*, XXXI (1935), 104–8.

Nichols, Roger L. "Soldiers as Farmers: Army Agriculture in the Missouri Valley, 1818–1827." *Agricultural History*, XLIV (1970), 213–22.

Olin, Nelson. "Reminiscences of Milwaukee in 1835–36." *Wisconsin History Magazine*, XIII (1930), 201–23.

Power, Richard L. "Planting Corn Belt Culture: The Impress of the Upland Southerner and Yankee in the Old Northwest." *Indiana Historical Society Publications*, XVII (1953), 1–196.

Primack, Martin L. "Farm Construction as a Use of Farm Labor in the United States, 1850–1910." *Journal of Economic History*, XXV (1965), 114–25.

Ragatz, Lowell Joseph. "Memoirs of a Sauk Swiss by Rev. Oswald Ragatz." *Wisconsin History Magazine*, XIX (1935), 182–241.

"Reminiscences of William Austin Burt, Inventor of the Solar Compass." *Michigan History Magazine*, VII (1923), 34–41.

Reynolds, A. R. "Rafting Down the Chippewa and the Mississippi: Daniel Shaw Lumber Company, A Type Study." *Wisconsin History Magazine*, XXXII (1948), 143–52.

Robbins, Frank. "The Personal Reminiscences of General Chauncey Eggleston." *Ohio History*, XLI (1932), 284–320. (Published under *Ohio Archaeological and Historical Quarterly*.)

Rodabaugh, James H. "The Negro in the Old Northwest." In O. Fritiof Ander, ed., *In the Trek of the Immigrants: Essays Presented to Carl Wittke*. Rock Island: Augustana College Library, 1964, pp. 219–39.

Sayre, David F. "Early Life in Southern Wisconsin." *Wisconsin History Magazine*, III (1920), 420–27.

Silliman, Sue I. "Overland to Michigan in 1846." *Michigan History Magazine*, V (1921), 424–34.

Still, Bayrd. "Milwaukee in 1833 and 1849: A Contemporary Description." *Wisconsin History Magazine*, LIII (1970), 294–97.

Stout, Reed A. "Autobiography of Hosea Stout, 1810 to 1835." *Utah Historical Quarterly*, XXX (1962), 149–74.

Temple, Wayne. "The Pike's Peak Gold Rush." *Journal of the Illinois State Historical Society*, XLIV (1951), 147–59.

Townsend, Georgia Dow. "Letters of James Stark, 1841–42, Friend and 'Most Ob. Servant.'" *Wisconsin History Magazine*, XXXIII (1949), 197–215.

Transeau, Edgar N. "The Prairie Peninsula." *Ecology*, XVI (1935), 423–37.

Tucker, Louis L. "The Correspondence of John Fisher." *Michigan History Magazine*, XLV (1961), 219–36.
———. "Old Nick Longworth, the Paradoxical Maecenas of Cincinnati." *Cincinnati Historical Society Bulletin*, XXV (1967), 246–59.
Turner, J. M. "Rafting on the Mississippi." *Wisconsin History Magazine*, XXIV (1940), 56–65.
Vogel, William. "Home Life in Early Indiana." *Indiana Magazine of History*, X (1914), 1–29, 284–320.
Weaver, George H. "Autobiography of Dr. Ephraim Ingals." *Journal of the Illinois State Historical Society*, XXVIII (1936), 279–308.
Wichers, Wynard. "Autobiography of Jacob Van Zolenburg." *Michigan History Magazine*, XLVI (1962), 311–29.
Widney, S. W. "Pioneer Sketches of De Kalb County." *Indiana Magazine of History*, XXV (1929), 104–66.
Woodburn, James A. "James Woodburn: Hoosier Schoolmaster." *Indiana Magazine of History*, XXXII (1936), 231–47.

UNPUBLISHED MATERIALS

Harris, Mary Vose. "The Autobiography of Benjamin Franklin Harris. Edited with Introduction and Notes." M.A. thesis, University of Illinois, 1923.
Lybarger, Ocie. "Every Day Life on the Southern Illinois Frontier." M.A. thesis, Southern Illinois University, 1951.
Poinsatte, Charles R. "Fort Wayne, Indiana during the Canal Era, 1828–1855: A Study of a Western Community during the Middle Period of American History." Ph.D. dissertation, University of Notre Dame, 1964.

Index

described, 68; rate of cutting with, 68–69; substitutes for hand implements, 68–69, 72; use of prior to 1860, 68, 69. *See also* Mechanization

Hat, 247

Hatch, Isaac, 92

Hatfield, Cynthia, 247

Hawley, Joseph, 115

Hay: importance, 3; cutting, 67–69, 71, 74, 75, 76, 77, 78, 84, 88, 92, 94–95, 96n, 198–99; cutting compared to grain, 74, 75; cutting by contract per acre, 74, 75, 85; mentioned, 118

Hecker, John, 246

Hedalen, Anna, 198

Hedpeth, Robert, 244

Hedrick, Ulysses P., 257

Heiny, Eli, 168

Hennepin County, Minn., 189

Henry County, Ill., 50, 66, 165, 166

Henry, John, 225

Hermann, ———, 74

High farming, 252n

Hillsdale County, Mich., 16

Hillsdale, Mich., 51

Hiram, Philips, 18

Hired boys: reasons for employment, 4, 173–74; clearing land, 16, 183, 185; prairie breaking, 31, 32–33, 174n; at corn planting and picking, 40, 102–3; on dairy farms, 138; at gardening, 142; negotiating terms of employment, 174–75; working to pay family debts, 173, 179; time obligation, 175–76; abuse and poor treatment, 176, 177, 185–86, 187–88; monotony of work, 176, 188; recruitment, 178; dealing with merchants, 179; average working season, 180; schooling, 180, 188; attitude toward employers, 184–85; unreliability, 184; length of working day, 188, 189; work duties, 188–90; housing, 189

Hired girls: importance, 4, 191–95; needed in harvest season, 86, 196–

97, 206; Negroes, 86; duties, 136, 191, 194, 198–205; employed on nursery farms, 136; accompany employers to new farm sites, 191; recreation, 192n, 202–5; recruitment, 192–93, 194–95, 207, 254; terms of employment, 192–94, 196–98; 203, 205, 206; abuse and poor treatment, 194–95, 209; early marriages, 197, 202, 207–8; reliability, 197–98; 202–5; Scandinavian, 198, 199; milking cows, 199–200, 205; supervision, 201, 202; illness, 203; protecting reputations, 203–5; clothes, 204–6; schooling, 205; store goods purchased, 205–6. *See also* Domestic help

Hired hands: accompany employers to new farm sites, 7–9, 46, 162; character and good traits, 8, 137n, 210–11, 213–14, 216–21, 244n; recruitment, 11, 161–62, 216; treatment by employers, 12, 93, 135n, 209–12, 214–15, 216–17, 219n, 222, 227, 231, 233; negative aspects and problems with their employers, 20, 75, 95, 100, 168, 199, 215–21, 222, 224n, 234, 236; housing, 84, 209, 221, 228, 229, 230; supervision, 135, 149, 217–19; farm ownership, 210, 213, 260–61, 265, 268–71; length of working day, 211–12, 254–55; attitude toward employers, 212, 214–15, 242; in legal proceedings, 222n; at poor houses, 231; interest in opposite sex, 236, 238; religion, 241–44; items purchased at merchants, 244–47; possessions, 244–49; in early New England, 251; in America compared to British Isles, 252–53; in Midwest compared to East, 254. *See also* Agricultural ladder; Farm acquisition

Hirt, Alfred, 231

Hitch, Edward, 160

Hitt, Samuel, 37

Hock, James, 62